# The Bard in the Borderlands

## An Anthology of Shakespeare Appropriations en La Frontera

*Volume 1*

# The Bard in the Borderlands

## An Anthology of Shakespeare Appropriations en La Frontera

*Volume 1*

*Edited by*
Katherine Gillen
Adrianna M. Santos
Kathryn Vomero Santos

**ACMRS PRESS**
Arizona State University
Tempe, Arizona
2023

# ACMRS PRESS

*The Bard in the Borderlands: An Anthology of Shakespeare Appropriations en La Frontera* was published in 2023 by ACMRS Press at Arizona State University in Tempe, Arizona.

This book is available online at
https://asu.pressbooks.pub/bard-in-the-borderlands-volume-1/

Library of Congress Cataloging-in-Publication Data

This book has been cataloged by the Library of Congress. LC record available at https://lccn.loc.gov/2023009260

ISBN: 978-0-86698-838-4 (hardcover)
ISBN: 978-0-86698-839-1 (paperback)
eISBN: 978-0-86698-840-7 (ebook)

**Cover Illustration:**
Celeste De Luna, *Healing Borderland Hand*, 2022 (linocut print)

*Hardcover and paperback editions are printed in the United States of America.*

# Contents

# Acknowledgments

The seeds of this anthology were planted at "Latinx Shakespeare: A Borderlands Drama Symposium," which Katherine Gillen and Adrianna M. Santos hosted at Texas A&M University–San Antonio in 2018. Kathryn Vomero Santos, who was then teaching at Texas A&M University–Corpus Christi, presented at the event. The symposium brought together scholars, teachers, and theater practitioners to discuss how Latinx artists engage with Shakespeare and how to teach and perform Shakespeare in culturally relevant ways. The situatedness of the symposium in San Antonio, with its rich traditions of art and political activism, called attention to the need to study the specifics of making and remaking Shakespeare in the Borderlands. Audiences were particularly inspired by Josh Inocéncio's play *Ofélio*, which was performed at the conference by A&M–SA students and which deals powerfully with sexual and racial violence. Teachers and theater practitioners wondered how to find the play and if others like it existed. *The Bard in the Borderlands* offers a robust response to such queries.

Many people made this anthology possible, most importantly the playwrights whose brilliant work is collected here. We are grateful to them for trusting us with their plays and for sharing archival materials with us. We would also like to thank artist Celeste De Luna, who created a linocut print titled *Healing Borderland Hand* for our cover. Using the Catholic symbol of La Mano Poderosa, she has placed images drawn from the plays above each finger, decentering Shakespeare but alluding to *Hamlet*'s famous image of a hand holding a skull, an image that also resonates with the iconography of Día de los Muertos, a ritual featured in many of the plays in *The Bard in the Borderlands*. De Luna's Mano Poderosa is also situated in the landscape of the Borderlands, as it is surrounded by nopales and nochebuenas and has a river running through its palm. As she notes, this aspect of the image evokes the notion of "blood on the hands" that is so prominent in Shakespeare's *Macbeth* but transforms histories of harm "into a healing river that unites people, animals, land." The barbed wire between the fingers, moreover, symbolizes the disruption of artificial and often harmful boundaries in the region.

The Arizona Center for Medieval and Renaissance Studies (ACMRS) has played a crucial role in the development of this project. When an in-person public event that Kathryn planned for March 2020 had to be canceled due to the COVID-19 pandemic, ACMRS offered to host it as a virtual event the following year. The resulting roundtable, "The Bard in the Borderlands: Race, Language, and Coloniality," in which Kathryn, Katherine, and Adrianna were joined by Ruben Espinosa and Jesus Montaño for a vibrant discussion, demonstrated that interest in Borderlands Shakespeare is wide ranging and far reaching. We are deeply indebted to Geoffrey Way, Manager of Publishing Futures at ACMRS Press, who championed this project and guided us through every step of the publishing process. We thank the rest of the editorial and marketing team at ACMRS Press, especially Roy Rukkila, Todd Halvorsen, Leah Newsom, and Andrea Zamora Chavez, for helping us to realize our vision for an anthology that would make Borderlands Shakespeare truly accessible. Espinosa's scholarship on Shakespeare in the Borderlands has in many ways inspired this anthology, and this project has benefited from his incisive feedback and unfailing encouragement. Many thanks as well to Ayanna Thompson for her enthusiastic support of the project and her work to build a press with an open-access publishing model that amplifies projects invested in social justice.

This anthology is deeply rooted in our teaching, and it has been influenced by the many students in our classes who have engaged with these plays. A&M–SA students Yvette Chairez, Marissa Galvin, Kelly Kearns, John Milam, Alex Post, and Christen Rendon produced compelling performances that have shaped our interpretations. This project has also benefited from the contributions of four Trinity University students who participated in the Mellon Initiative's Summer Undergraduate Research Fellowship program: Kaylee Avila, Eva Buergler, Paloma Díaz-Minshew, and Sarah Pita. We thank them for their careful transcriptions, well-researched annotations, and sharp questions.

This work has also been made possible by funding from several institutions, including the Folger Shakespeare Library, the Renaissance Society of America, the Mellon Foundation, the Trinity University Humanities Collective, the Trinity University Mellon Initiative, the Trinity University Center for Innovation and Entrepreneurship, and the Department of Language, Literature, and Arts at Texas A&M University–San Antonio. Liza Posas, Christina Lehua Hummel-Colla, and Alejandra Gaeta generously facilitated Kathryn's visit to the Autry Museum of the American West to study archival materials related to James Lujan's *Kino and Teresa*.

We would also like to thank a long list of colleagues who have supported this project in various ways throughout its development: Norma Elia Cantú,

Rubén Dupertuis, Heather Eichling, Debra Feakes, Elena Foulis, James Finley, Italia Garduño, Catherine Kenyon, Justin Korver, Luis Martinez, Cynthia Teniente Matson, Jesus Montaño, Tim O'Sullivan, Elizabeth Poff, Armando Saliba, Martha Saywell, Claudia Stokes, Betsy Tontiplaphol, Laura Turchi, Lauren Turek, Rita Urquijo-Ruiz, and Patricia Zibluk. We extend our deep gratitude to the many friends and family members who have supported us during the multiple phases of this project, and to the pets and kids who made appearances during our many collaborative Zoom sessions.

Pieces of our introductions are drawn from previously published material including: Katherine Gillen and Adrianna M. Santos's "Borderlands Shakespeare: The Decolonial Visions of James Lujan's *Kino and Teresa* and Seres Jaime Magaña's *The Tragic Corrido of Romeo and Lupe*," *Shakespeare Bulletin* 38, no. 4 (2021): 549–71; their essay "Seres Jaime Magaña's *The Tragic Corrido of Romeo and Lupe* and the Power of Borderlands Community Theater," in *Shakespeare and Latinidad*, ed. Trevor Boffone and Carla Della Gatta (Edinburgh: Edinburgh University Press, 2021), 57–74; and Katherine Gillen's "Shakespearean Appropriation and Queer Latinx Empowerment in Josh Inocéncio's *Ofélio*," in *The Routledge Handbook of Shakespeare and Global Appropriation*, ed. Christy Desmet, Sujata Iyengar, and Miriam Jacobson (London: Routledge, 2019), 90–101. We thank *Shakespeare Bulletin*, Edinburgh University Press, and Routledge for the permission to use these essays here.

# Editor and Contributor Biographies

**Katherine Gillen** is Associate Professor of English at Texas A&M University–San Antonio. She is the author of *Chaste Value: Economic Crisis, Female Chastity, and the Production of Social Difference on Shakespeare's Stage* (Edinburgh University Press, 2017) and several essays on race, gender, and economics in early modern drama and Shakespeare appropriation. She is currently working on a monograph called *Shakespeare's Racial Classicism: Whiteness, Slavery, and Humanism*, which examines Shakespeare's use of classical sources within the context of emerging racial capitalism. With Kathryn Vomero Santos and Adrianna M. Santos, she co-founded the Borderlands Shakespeare Colectiva, which has received funding from the Mellon Foundation and the National Endowment for the Humanities.

**Josh Inocéncio** is a Houston-based writer and theatre artist. After finishing his Master's degree at Florida State University, he returned to Houston to tour his solo play *Purple Eyes* across Texas, which culminated in the world premiere at Stages Repertory Theatre. Two of his other plays — *The Little Edelweiss; or, An Immigrant's Fairytale* and *Chocolate Gravy & White Jesus* — were semifinalists for the Eugene O'Neill National Playwright's Conference. His work has been featured at Stages, the Museum of Fine Arts, Houston, the Greenhouse Theatre in Chicago, and Teatro Milagro in Portland, among others. He has also trained under Migdalia Cruz at the Maria Irene Fornés Playwriting Workshop. His short play *Ofélio* has been taught at several universities around the nation, including Amherst College, Texas A&M University–San Antonio, and Florida International University. Currently, Josh is completing his first novel.

**James Lujan** is a filmmaker, playwright, and educator from Taos Pueblo. Since 2012, he has served as the Department Chair of the Cinematic Arts & Technology program at the Institute of American Indian Arts in Santa Fe. In 2022, he was appointed to the New Mexico Governor's Council on Film and Media Industries.

**Seres Jaime Magaña** is a community theater director and author of the bilingual play *The Tragic Corrido of Romeo and Lupe*, performed at the Pharr Community Theater in 2018. His poems and short stories have been published across several anthologies. He has an English degree from the University of Texas Rio Grande Valley. Seres teaches acting and creative writing classes online. In addition, Seres has also hosted several poetry and music events around the Rio Grande Valley, and he served as host for Saturday Open Mic Nights at Luna Coffee House for three years. He lives in McAllen, Texas, with his wife and children.

**Tara Moses** is an award-winning playwright, director, artistic director, and a citizen of the Seminole Nation of Oklahoma, Mvskoke. Her plays have been produced and developed with companies in New York, Connecticut, California, Oklahoma, Nevada, New Jersey, Massachusetts, and Washington, D.C. As a playwright, her completed works include *Sections, He'eo'o* (Winner of the 2019 Native Storytellers Contest), *Quantum* (2020 and 2021 Finalist for the National Playwrights Conference), *Bound* (2019 Native American New Play Festival Winner), *Don Juan, Arbeka, Patchwork, Oñgwehoñwe, Snag, Sugar, OklaHOME, Billie, Poyvfekcv*, and *Hamlet, El Príncipe de Denmark*. She is Artistic Director of Red Eagle Soaring, and she co-founded Groundwater Arts and #Binge, where she also serves as Executive Producer. In addition, she serves on the Advisory Board of Broadway for Racial Justice and participated in New York Stage and Film's inaugural NYSAF NEXUS project in 2021. She was Playwright-in-Residence at AlterTheatre Ensemble, a Cultural Capital Fellow with First Peoples Fund, and an Invited Playwright with HBMG Foundation's National Winter Playwrights Retreat (2020). She is the 2019 Native Storytellers winner with the Yale Indigenous Performing Arts Program. She is currently pursuing her MFA in Directing at Brown University/Trinity Rep.

**Olga Sanchez Saltveit** is Assistant Professor of Theatre for Middlebury College and Artistic Director Emerita of Milagro; her play *¡O Romeo!* was created and performed during her service as its Artistic Director from 2003 until 2015. Her work as an actor/director/devisor has been seen throughout the US and in Peru, Venezuela, and Honduras. Olga served as co-artistic director of the People's Playhouse in New York City, artistic director of Seattle Teatro Latino, and co-founder of La Casa de Artes, a Seattle-based non-profit dedicated to celebrating the beauty of Latiné arts and culture. Olga serves on the Advisory Committee for the Latinx Theatre Commons as a member of the Fornés Institute, an initiative that aims to amplify the legacy of artist and teacher María Irene Fornés. Her research centers Latiné theatre and decolonization and is published in several journals and collections, including "¡O Romeo! Shakespeare on the Altar of Día de los Muertos" found in *Shakespeare and Latinidad* (Edinburgh University Press, 2021). With Noe Montez, she is co-editor of *The Routledge Companion to Latinx Theatre and Performance*.

**Adrianna M. Santos** is Associate Professor of English at Texas A&M University–San Antonio. Santos has built her career on publications that center Chicana/x cultural production, and her work is deeply rooted in and accountable to Chicanx communities. Her forthcoming book *Cicatrix Poetics, Trauma and Healing in the Literary Borderlands: Beyond Survival* (Palgrave, 2023) addresses often-eclipsed legacies of colonial violence and examines Chicana survival narratives as a critical facet of social justice work. With Norma E. Cantú and Rita Urquijo-Ruiz, she is co-editor of *Interplanetary Nepantla: El Mundo Zurdo 8: Selected Works from the Meeting of the Society for the Study of Gloria Anzaldúa, 2019* (Aunt Lute, 2022). She has written several articles on Chicanx literature and performance, including Borderlands Shakespeare. With Katherine Gillen and Kathryn Vomero Santos, she co-founded the Borderlands Shakespeare Colectiva, which has received funding from the Mellon Foundation and the National Endowment for the Humanities.

**Kathryn Vomero Santos** is Assistant Professor of English and co-director of the Humanities Collective at Trinity University. Her cross-historical research explores the intersections of performance with the politics of language, empire, and racial formation in the early modern period and in our contemporary moment. She is currently completing a book entitled *Shakespeare in Tongues* (Routledge, 2024), which situates Shakespeare and his legacy within conversations about imperialism, multilingualism, and assimilation in the United States. She is also co-editing a collection of essays entitled *Ethical Appropriation in Shakespearean Performance* with Louise Geddes and Geoffrey Way (Edinburgh University Press, 2024). Her most recent articles examine how Borderlands artists use Shakespeare to disrupt colonial ideologies and narratives. With Katherine Gillen and Adrianna M. Santos, she co-founded the Borderlands Shakespeare Colectiva, which has received funding from the Mellon Foundation and the National Endowment for the Humanities.

**Edit Villarreal** is a playwright and professor whose plays have been produced by professional and university theaters across the country and in numerous community teatros, colleges, and high schools. Born in Texas, her plays include *My Visits with MGM* (*My Grandmother Marta*), a memory play inspired by her migrant grandmother; *Chicago Milagro, A Small Miracle in a Big City*, about a Mexican exile turned curandero in 1895 Back of the Yards; *Ice*, a sci-fi melodrama featuring a Chicano family hiding their son from a totalitarian world; and *The Language of Flowers*, among others. Her essay "Behind Closed Doors: Sex, Lies and Servants" is published in *Playing Shakespeare's Villains, Vol. 2* and *The Play's the Thing: Selections from Shakespeare's Characters*, Vol. 1–4. Villarreal co-wrote three scripts for the award-winning series *Foto-Novelas*, produced by Carlos Avila and PBS. Other PBS credits include *La Carpa,* co-written with Avila, which aired on *American Playhouse.* A graduate of the Yale School of Drama, she studied with legendary Cuban playwright Maria Irene Fornés at the Hispanic Playwrights Laboratory at INTAR Theatre in NYC. She is currently a faculty member at the UCLA School of Theater, Film and Television in the Theater Department where she serves as Vice Chair, Graduate Programs.

# General Introduction
## *Tracing the Traditions of Borderlands Shakespeare*

Katherine Gillen, Adrianna M. Santos,
and Kathryn Vomero Santos

For several decades, Chicanx and Indigenous theatermakers have been repurposing Shakespeare's plays to reflect the histories and lived realities of the U.S.–Mexico Borderlands, creating space to tell stories of and for La Frontera. *The Bard in the Borderlands: An Anthology of Shakespeare Appropriations en La Frontera* seeks to call attention to this wide-ranging artistic practice, which we term Borderlands Shakespeare, and to make the playtexts available to broad audiences. By bringing these previously unpublished plays together in an open-access scholarly edition, this anthology celebrates dynamic, multilingual reworkings of canon and place, and it offers a critical framework for understanding the techniques and traditions that inform creative engagements with Shakespeare in this complex region. An expansive area encompassing Northern Mexico and parts of Texas, New Mexico, Arizona, and California, the Borderlands have produced vibrant hybrid cultures, languages, and art forms. The Borderlands are also a site of ongoing humanitarian crises caused by the interplay of colonization, labor exploitation, anti-immigrant policies, militarization, environmental injustice, and socioeconomic inequity. The plays collected here dramatize the linguistic, cultural, and political complexities that have shaped this region and Shakespeare's reception in it.

The Shakespeare appropriations in this anthology draw on Borderlands performance traditions to center historical and contemporary forms of resistance and resilience in the region. Shakespeare proves to be a site of contestation in this context, functioning as a representative of the English literary canon but also as a malleable set of texts, ideas, and characters that can be reimagined to serve community needs and interests. While the plays gathered here use Shakespeare to expose the material violence of ongoing colonization, they also emphasize the value, beauty, and restorative power of Indigenous and Mexican languages, mythologies, and rituals. Readers will recognize common Shakespearean themes in these multilingual plays, but the romantic relationships, family dynamics, and political conflicts they depict are decidedly shaped by the realities of La Frontera. The playwrights featured here draw on Borderlands arts and ideas, incorporating, for example, the Mexican ballad form known as the corrido, the folktale of La Llorona, the celebration of Día de los Muertos, and the political construct of Aztlán. Borderlands Shakespeare plays, therefore, do not simply reproduce Shakespeare in new contexts but rather use his work in innovative ways to negotiate colonial power, to reframe Borderlands histories, and to envision socially just futures.

In what follows, we situate Borderlands Shakespeare within the history of the region and its artistic, spiritual, and political lineages, and we contextualize these plays within conversations about Shakespeare appropriation in global, postcolonial, and decolonial contexts. As we outline our editorial approach to these texts, we also point to potential pedagogical and community-based collaborations that *The Bard in the Borderlands* may generate. Our aim is to make these texts accessible and begin building a robust archive of Shakespeare en La Frontera.

## Resistance and Resilience in Borderlands Shakespeare

First colonized by the Spanish and then incorporated into the United States following the 1848 Treaty of Guadalupe Hidalgo that ended the U.S. war against Mexico, the Borderlands have been shaped by centuries of conquest, enslavement, and exploitation. Throughout successive waves of colonization, the lands of Indigenous Peoples and their descendants have been expropriated, and their sovereignty has been eroded. As Gloria E. Anzaldúa writes of the Texas–Mexico border in particular, "This land has survived possession and ill-use by five countries: Spain, Mexico, the Republic of Texas, the U.S., the Confederacy, and the U.S. again."[1] Because of this violence, which persists in many forms today, Anzaldúa describes the border as "*una herida abierta*, where the third world grates against the first and bleeds. And before a scab forms it hemorrhages again, the lifeblood of two worlds merging to form a third country — a border culture."[2] The resulting hybridity — often termed mestizaje — reflects colonial violence as well as the persistence of Indigenous practices, languages, and artforms. Border

---

1    Gloria E. Anzaldúa, *Borderlands/La Frontera: The New Mestiza*. 5th ed. (San Francisco: Aunt Lute Press, 2022), 94.
2    Anzaldúa, *Borderlands/La Frontera*, 17.

culture, furthermore, reflects the influences of the African diaspora as well as the often obscured histories of Black communities in the region, including those of enslaved people brought to Texas following the abolition of slavery in Mexico, those who sought freedom south of the U.S. border, and the many subsequent waves of migration to and through the region.

Borderlands Shakespeare is firmly rooted within the vibrant cultures and complex histories of La Frontera. By resituating Shakespeare's sixteenth- and early seventeenth-century plays in varied contexts and temporalities, Borderlands playwrights critique the colonial legacies of the early modern period and tell stories from Borderlands perspectives in ways that disrupt dominant and often whitewashed narratives. With his play *Kino and Teresa*, for example, Taos Pueblo playwright James Lujan asks readers and audiences to consider events contemporaneous with the publication and performance of Shakespeare's *Romeo and Juliet* by transporting the play to Santa Fe, a colonial province established by Juan de Oñate in 1598, just one year after *Romeo and Juliet* first appeared in print. Set in the aftermath of the 1680 Pueblo Revolt and the 1692 Spanish Reconquista, the feud that animates the action of *Kino and Teresa* is no longer an unexplained "ancient grudge" between two families. Lujan's version of *Romeo and Juliet* depicts a conflict that is clearly created by Spanish exploitation, and his play centers Indigenous resistance.

Other Borderlands Shakespeare plays engage with later histories of oppression and activism. The Chicano civil rights movement of the 1960s and 70s, often called El Movimiento, figures prominently in this body of work. El Movimiento encompassed the labor struggles of the United Farm Workers Union led by César Chávez and Dolores Huerta in addition to voting rights initiatives, antiwar protests, and walkouts in schools across the nation that called attention to educational inequity and discrimination. Set in the agricultural fields of the Rio Grande Valley, Seres Jaime Magaña's *The Tragic Corrido of Romeo and Lupe* reflects the continued legacies of El Movimiento. In this appropriation of *Romeo and Juliet*, the lovers meet when a protest against unjust labor and environmental practices interrupts a party intended to celebrate the profitability of the "Magic Valley" for white agribusinesses. Many of the plays collected in this anthology, moreover, critique the imperialist policies that have criminalized immigration while also creating the conditions in Mexico and Central America that have forced people to seek asylum in the U.S.[3] Edit Villarreal's *The Language of Flowers*, Herbert Siguenza's *El Henry*, and Stephen Richter and Mónica Andrade's

---

3   For more on Latinx theatrical engagement with neoliberal policies and their consequences, see Patricia A. Ybarra, *Latinx Theater in the Times of Neoliberalism* (Evanston, IL: Northwestern University Press, 2017).

*Marqués: A Narco Macbeth* draw particular attention to the U.S. economic and military policies that have made migration necessary for many and that have given rise to illicit economies.

As they transpose Shakespeare into Borderlands settings, many of the plays in this anthology inhabit several temporalities at once, reflecting the palimpsestic histories of the region and exploring what Ruben Espinosa describes as the "temporal borderlands of Shakespeare."[4] In *Invierno*, for instance, José Cruz González embraces *The Winter's Tale*'s famous "gap of time" as an opportunity to blur the boundary between present-day and pre-statehood California. *The Tragic Corrido* similarly activates the multilayered history of the Rio Grande Valley by allowing multiple periods in Texas history to co-exist. Reimagining a history play as a future play, Siguenza's *El Henry* transposes the political tensions and intergenerational conflicts in *Henry IV, Part 1* to the streets of a post-apocalyptic and post-revolutionary Aztlán, the mythical home of the Mexica people that became a symbol of liberation during the Chicano Movement. As it moves across histories and futures, Borderlands Shakespeare disrupts colonial timelines and reminds audiences of the enduring presence of Indigenous Peoples in the region. In this way, these plays contribute to the political work of Borderlands cultural production, which often crafts what historian and theorist Emma Pérez calls the "decolonial imaginary," a "rupturing space, the alternative to that which is written in history."[5] By rupturing both colonial histories and canonical works, Borderlands Shakespeare facilitates healing and amplifies Borderlands stories.

## Borderlands Shakespeare and the Teatro Tradition

The tradition of Borderlands Shakespeare has given rise to collaborations among diverse artists with personal connections to the region. Many, but not all, of the playwrights collected in this anthology are border residents or have Chicanx or Indigenous heritage themselves. While they often have classical theater training, these playwrights are also rooted in Latinx and Indigenous performance traditions and practices.[6] In particular, Borderlands Shakespeare is influenced by El Teatro Campesino. Founded by Luis Valdez in 1965 on the picket lines of

4   Ruben Espinosa, "Traversing the Temporal Borderlands of Shakespeare," *New Literary History* 52, nos. 3/4 (2021): 606, https://doi.org/10.1353/nlh.2021.0028.

5   Emma Pérez, *The Decolonial Imaginary: Writing Chicanas into History* (Bloomington: Indiana University Press, 1999), 6.

6   For an overview of Chicanx theater, see Jorge Huerta, *Chicano Drama: Performance, Society and Myth* (Cambridge: Cambridge University Press, 2000). For an introduction to Native American and First Nations theater, see Jaye T. Darby, Courtney Elkin Mohler, and Christy Stanlake, eds.,

the Delano Grape Strike in Delano, CA, this theatrical wing of the United Farm Workers Union made specific use of "actos," short scenes performed on flat-bed trucks and in union halls. The actos were often performed by farmworkers, and they caricatured foremen, landowners, and corrupt politicians in an effort to bring attention to injustices in the fields. As David Román argues, El Teatro Campesino became central to the political work of El Movimiento, as Chicanxs "reformulated their sense of identity from one of oppression and victimization to one of resistance and survival."[7] As other teatros have developed in the spirit of El Teatro Campesino, Borderlands Shakespeare appropriations have become part of this radical activist tradition.

Many of the playwrights in this anthology ground their work in the teatro tradition and some even gesture to it in their plays. The protesters in Magaña's *The Tragic Corrido*, for instance, put on a disruptive performance that is reminiscent of an acto in which models dressed as fruit expose the harm caused by exploitative agricultural practices in the Rio Grande Valley. Siguenza's *El Henry* provides another salient example of Borderlands Shakespeare's indebtedness to teatro, as it was influenced by the vision of Culture Clash, a theater troupe that Siguenza co-founded to adapt teatro to urban settings. As Matthieu Chapman observes, moreover, *El Henry* explicitly reflects the lineage of teatro in its casting of Luis Valdez's sons Kinan and Lakin in the key roles of El Henry of Barrio East-cheap and El Bravo of Barrio Hotspur.[8] Part of La Jolla Playhouse's Without Walls series and performed in San Diego's gentrified but still largely Mexican American East Village, *El Henry* embraces the spirit of teatro by incorporating Shakespeare into Chicanx space and into Chicanx political, linguistic, and theatrical genealogies. Additionally, Josh Inocéncio's *Ofélio*, which premiered in Houston as part of the T.R.U.T.H. Project's campaign to raise awareness about sexual violence in LGBTQIA2+ communities, channels the activist ethos of teatro to address the specific concerns of queer communities of color. Though very different from one another, Magaña's, Siguenza's, and Inocéncio's plays reflect the diverse ways in which Borderlands artists have adapted teatro to serve community needs.

The legacy of teatro has also influenced the development of other community-based theater initiatives throughout the Borderlands. *The Merchant of Santa Fe*, for example, was produced by La Compañía de Teatro de Alburquerque, "a bilingual community theater comprised of a core of professional actors working

*Critical Companion to Native American and First Nations Theatre and Performance: Indigenous Spaces* (London: Bloomsbury, 2020).

7  David Román, "Latino Performance and Identity," *Aztlán: A Journal of Chicano Studies* 22, no. 2 (1997): 153.

8  Matthieu Chapman, "Chicano Signifyin': Appropriating Space and Culture in *El Henry*," *Theatre Topics* 27, no. 1 (2017): 61, https://doi.org/10.1353/tt.2017.0003.

with community actors from all walks of life and of all ages," and it was developed through a series of "tertulias," or open meetings with the public to discuss the script-in-progress and related issues.[9] James Lujan, author of *Kino and Teresa*, was an actor in this production and collaborated with playwright and executive director Ramón Flores on a play about the Pueblo Revolt titled *Casi Hermanos* in the following years. Drawing on the power of community-based theatrical performance to retell New Mexican history, Lujan later developed *Kino and Teresa* — his own appropriation of a Shakespeare play — with Native Voices at the Autry, a Los Angeles-based company designed to center Native American stories and actors. Telatúlsa, the company that produced Tara Moses's *Hamlet, El Príncipe de Denmark*, and Teatro Milagro, which produced Olga Sanchez Saltveit's *¡O Romeo!*, are similarly committed to community education and empowerment through theater.

The plays featured in this anthology arise from a desire to tell culturally relevant stories and to create opportunities for Latinx and Indigenous playwrights, actors, and directors within a largely white classical theater repertoire. As José Cruz González asserts, community theater is valuable for both artists and audiences: "To have these communities come to a theatre space that oftentimes they have felt excluded from for many reasons and then all of a sudden see themselves reflected onstage and in the language is a really powerful thing."[10] This inclusion is important in educational spaces, too, and many Borderlands Shakespeare plays were created in colleges and universities in collaboration with students who wanted to engage with Shakespeare on their own terms. Borderlands Shakespeare productions thus serve communities in a range of ways as sites of activism, education, and professional development.

---

9   Mary Montaño, *Tradiciones Nuevomexicanas: Hispano Arts and Culture of New Mexico* (Albuquerque: University of New Mexico Press, 2001), 345. For more details on the tertulias for *The Merchant of Santa Fe*, see Elizabeth Klein and Michael Shapiro, "Shylock as Crypto-Jew: A New Mexican Adaptation of *The Merchant of Venice*," in *World-Wide Shakespeares: Local Appropriations in Film and Performance*, ed. Sonia Massai (New York: Routledge, 2005), 34–35, https://doi.org/10.4324/9780203356944.

10  José Cruz González and David Lozano, "Diálogo: On Making Shakespeare Relevant to Latinx Communities," in *Shakespeare and Latinidad*, eds. Trevor Boffone and Carla Della Gatta (Edinburgh: Edinburgh University Press, 2021), 159, https://doi.org/10.3366/edinburgh/9781474488488.003.0014.

## Shakespearean Afterlives and Appropriations in the Americas

Although many Borderlands Shakespeare plays could be described as adaptations, we emphasize the term "appropriation" in *The Bard in the Borderlands* because the playwrights radically reimagine Shakespeare and redirect his cultural capital to advance their political and social aims. As Julie Sanders suggests in her delineation of adaptation and appropriation, "appropriation effects a more decisive journey away from the informing text into a wholly new cultural product and domain."[11] Sujata Iyengar and Christy Desmet remind us, however, that there is no absolute line between adaptation and appropriation and that they instead operate on a continuum.[12] The full range of this continuum is represented in this anthology, with some plays diverging quite far from Shakespeare's plays and others sticking more closely to Shakespeare's plots but making them multilingual or setting them in border spaces. Further, many of the plays included here can be classified as "tradaptations," a term developed by Québécois poet, playwright, and actor Michel Garneau to capture the interplay and overlap between translation and adaptation. As Alfredo Michel Modenessi argues, translations that emerge from colonized spaces call attention to power asymmetries, even among colonial languages, and they generate new and creative linguistic forms.[13] For Garneau, translating Shakespeare into Québécois French, which is often compared negatively to European French, necessarily involved a form of adaptation that was attuned to the political dimensions of language. A similar dynamic adheres in the Borderlands, where Spanish first functioned as a colonial language and was later subordinated to English, coming to be associated with racialized Mexican American identity.[14] In this context, language carries fraught class-based and racial valences, and border Spanish and Spanglish are often disparaged as improper or impure.

As they engage with the entangled colonial histories that shape La Frontera, Borderlands Shakespeare appropriations contribute to a dynamic body of global, postcolonial, and anticolonial responses to Shakespeare and his legacy. With

---

11  Julie Sanders, *Adaptation and Appropriation*, 2nd ed. (New York: Routledge, 2016), 35.

12  Christy Desmet and Sujata Iyengar, "Adaptation, Appropriation, or What You Will," *Shakespeare* 11, no. 1 (2015): 16, https://doi.org/10.1080/17450918.2015.1012550.

13  Alfredo Michel Modenessi, "'A double tongue within your mask': Translating Shakespeare in/to Spanish-Speaking Latin America," in *Shakespeare and the Language of Translation*, ed. Ton Hoenselaars (London: Arden Shakespeare, 2004), 242–43, http://dx.doi.org/10.5040/9781408 179734.ch-013.

14  For more on the relationship between language and race in the construction of Latinx identity, see Jonathan Rosa, *Looking Like a Language, Sounding Like a Race: Raciolinguistic Ideologies and the Learning of Latinidad* (Oxford: Oxford University Press, 2019).

the expansion of the British Empire, Shakespeare's works became instruments of imperial power, as they were frequently taught in colonial education systems and used to promote English cultural supremacy. Moreover, Shakespeare's dates align loosely with those of the Spanish conquests in the Americas in the sixteenth century, and his plays were written at a time when England was embarking on its own imperial ventures and beginning to enslave and traffic African people. Scholars such as Miles P. Grier, Laura Lehua Yim, and Jace Weaver examine the colonial dynamics surrounding Shakespeare as they played out in the territories now known as the United States, where English and U.S. authorities used Shakespeare as means of mediating encounters with Indigenous Peoples.[15] As Weaver writes, Europeans often used theater — most prominently Shakespeare — "to define themselves by comparison with, and in opposition to, the Indigenous Other."[16] Scott Manning Stevens and Madeline Sayet have demonstrated that the imperial weaponization of Shakespeare continued with the formation of the Indian boarding school system, where Shakespeare's plays were taught as part of a federally funded assimilationist program designed to eradicate Native languages, beliefs, and cultures.[17] Such practices intersect with a history traced by scholars such as Ayanna Thompson, Brigitte Fielder, and James Shapiro in which Shakespeare productions, some of which employed blackface minstrelsy, promoted anti-Black racism.[18] These interrelated histories gave rise to the notion that Shakespeare is what Arthur Little describes as "white property."[19] Appropriation, therefore, has become a powerful means through which artists throughout the Americas have claimed Shakespeare for their own communities and disrupted ideologies of white supremacy and coloniality.

---

15  See Miles P. Grier, "Staging the Cherokee *Othello*: An Imperial Economy of Indian Watching," *The William and Mary Quarterly* 73, no. 1 (2016): 73–106; Laura Lehua Yim, "Reading Hawaiian Shakespeare: Indigenous Residue Haunting Settler Colonialism," *Journal of American Studies* 54, no. 1 (2020): 36–41, https://doi.org/10.1017/S0021875819001993; and Jace Weaver, "Shakespeare Among the 'Salvages': The Bard in Red Atlantic Performance," *Theater Journal* 67, no. 3 (2015): 433–43.

16  Weaver, "Shakespeare Among the 'Salvages,'" 433.

17  Scott Manning Stevens, "Shakespeare and the Indigenous Turn," in *Histories of the Future: On Shakespeare and Thinking Ahead*, ed. Carla Mazzio (Philadelphia: University of Pennsylvania Press, forthcoming); and Madeline Sayet, "Interrogating the Shakespeare System," *HowlRound*, August 31, 2020, https://howlround.com/interrogating-shakespeare-system.

18  See Ayanna Thompson, *Passing Strange: Shakespeare, Race, and Contemporary America* (Oxford: Oxford University Press, 2011); Brigitte Fielder, "Blackface Desdemona: Theorizing Race on the Nineteenth-Century American Stage," *Theatre Annual* 70 (2017): 39–59, http://dx.doi.org/10.17613/M6K284; and James Shapiro, *Shakespeare in America: An Anthology from the Revolution to Now* (New York: The Library of America, 2014) and *Shakespeare in a Divided America: What His Plays Tell Us About Our Past and Future* (New York: Penguin Press, 2020).

19  Arthur L. Little, Jr., "Re-Historicizing Race, White Melancholia, and the Shakespearean Property," *Shakespeare Quarterly* 67, no. 1 (2016): 88, https://doi.org/10.1353/shq.2016.0018.

Caribbean invocations of Shakespeare, and of *The Tempest* in particular, are central to this literary and political resistance. In *Une Tempête,* composed by the Martinican writer and politician Aimé Césaire, Caliban explicitly calls out Prospero's colonial domination and aligns himself with a Black radical tradition when he rejects Prospero's attempts to name him:

> Appelle-moi X. Ça vaudra mieux. Comme qui dirait l'homme sans nom. Plus exactement, l'homme dont on a *volé* le nom. Tu parles d'histoire. Eh bien ça, c'est de l'histoire, et fameuse! Chaque fois que tu m'appelleras, ça me rappellera le fait fondamental, que tu m'as tout volé et jusqu'à mon identité! Uhuru!

> [Call me X. That's best. Like a man without a name. Or, more precisely, a man whose name was stolen. You speak of history. Well that's history, known far and wide! Every time you'll call me that will remind me of the fundamental truth, that you stole everything from me, even my identity! Uhuru!][20]

Césaire's Caliban connects the theft of land, language, and labor to the violence of colonial naming practices that impose European identities and worldviews on Indigenous American and African peoples. Césaire's play magnifies Caliban's resistant energy in order to speak back to these colonial and canonical forces. Cuban author Roberto Fernández Retamar also invokes the figure of Caliban in his writing to meditate on the fact that colonized subjects are often forced to resort to colonial languages and canonical European authors to speak truth to power: "¿qué otra cosa puede hacer Calibán sino utilizar ese mismo idioma — hoy no tiene otro — para maldecirlo . . . ?" ["What else can Caliban do but use that same language — today he has no other — to curse him . . . ?"].[21] Shakespeare's plays thus present a paradox: on the one hand, they can be useful for thinking through questions of power and anticolonial resistance, while on the other, they are a reminder of the colonial imposition of European languages, literatures, and cultures.

For these reasons, Shakespeare appropriations in the Americas make important contributions to global conversations about colonialism — contributions

---

20  Aimé Césaire, *Une Tempête* (Paris: Éditions du Seuil, 1969), 28; Aimé Césaire, *A Tempest*, trans. Philip Crispin (London: Oberon Books, 2015), 25.

21  Roberto Fernández Retamar, *Calibán. Apuntes sobre la cultura en nuestra América* (México: Diogenes, 1971), 30. The English translation is drawn from Roberto Fernández Retamar, "Caliban: Notes Toward a Discussion of Culture in Our America," trans. Lynn Garafola, David Arthur McMurray, and Roberto Márquez, *The Massachusetts Review* 15, nos. 1/2 (1974): 24.

that, as Walter Mignolo argues, are often obscured by the Anglocentric misconception that "postcolonial theories could only emerge from the legacies of the British Empire."[22] In their essay collection *Latin American Shakespeares*, Bernice W. Kliman and Rick J. Santos highlight the diversity of Latin American responses to Shakespeare, observing that "Shakespeare's work has been used equally to support and to contest the establishment."[23] As Modenessi has detailed in his scholarship, Mexico has been a particularly generative site of Shakespearean production and appropriation. Many Mexican directors and adaptors have employed Shakespeare's plays to highlight issues of local concern, often taking "what some might call radical, disruptive or dissident approaches."[24] For example, the *Macbeth* adaptation *Mendoza* (2016, dir. Juan Carrillo) dramatizes the effects of the Mexican Revolution, and *Hamlet P'urhépecha* (1990, dir. Juan Carlos Arvide) attests to the persistence of Indigenous communities and languages in Mexico. As Trevor Boffone and Carla Della Gatta's essay collection *Shakespeare and Latinidad* demonstrates, furthermore, U.S.-based Latinx playwrights and directors have also adapted Shakespeare in innovative ways that speak to the colonial histories of the Americas and the forms of migration and cultural hybridity that have arisen from them.[25]

Borderlands Shakespeare is part of these broader genealogies, but it also constitutes its own artistic and political project, born of a region shaped by Indigenous, Spanish, Mexican, Black, and European American influences. By focusing specifically on the U.S.–Mexico Borderlands, we use what Marissa Greenberg calls a "critically regional approach" that "enhances our ability to more accurately describe the interactions of Shakespeare's local and global functionality by discovering regions as loci of international and intercultural relations."[26] By definition, the Borderlands cross national boundaries and disrupt other demarcations imposed by the state. As Espinosa has powerfully demonstrated, residents of the Borderlands bring vital perspectives to Shakespeare, treating his works as "an element to which [they], on the temporal and physical borderlands, can add

---

22 Walter Mignolo, *The Darker Side of the Renaissance: Literacy, Territoriality, and Colonization* (1995, repr., Ann Arbor: University of Michigan Press, 2003), ix.

23 Bernice W. Kliman and Rick J. Santos, "*Mestizo* Shakespeares: A Study of Cultural Exchange," in *Latin American Shakespeares*, eds. Bernice W. Kliman and Rick J. Santos (Madison, NJ: Fairleigh Dickinson University Press, 2005), 14.

24 Alfredo Michel Modenessi, "'Meaning by Shakespeare' South of the Border," in *World-Wide Shakespeares: Local Appropriations in Film and Performance*, ed. Sonia Massai (New York: Routledge), 107.

25 Trevor Boffone and Carla Della Gatta, eds., *Shakespeare and Latinidad* (Edinburgh: Edinburgh University Press, 2021).

26 Marissa Greenberg, "Critically Regional Shakespeare," *Shakespeare Bulletin* 37, no. 3 (2019): 343, https://doi.org/10.1353/shb.2019.0039.

nuance and layer with manifold meanings."[27] The plays collected in *The Bard in the Borderlands* are a testament to the ways of knowing and creating that fronterizos have developed in response to the ongoing coloniality that has shaped the region. As they bring Borderlands epistemologies, languages, and creative practices to bear on Shakespeare, the playwrights in this anthology incorporate his plays into the hybridity and decolonial imagination of Borderlands arts.

## Hybridity and Decoloniality in Borderlands Shakespeare

Language is a primary site of decolonial work in Borderlands Shakespeare. The plays featured in *The Bard in the Borderlands* employ a range of languages, including English, Spanish, Indigenous languages, and the hybrid languages spoken throughout the region today. By refusing to observe any hard linguistic boundaries, Borderlands playwrights resist what Anzaldúa has described as institutional and social acts of "linguistic terrorism" that insist upon keeping English and Spanish separate and "pure."[28] As Anzaldúa writes of the relationship between linguistic and ethnic identity,

> Ethnic identity is twin skin to linguistic identity — I am my language. Until I can take pride in my language, I cannot take pride in myself. Until I can accept as legitimate Chicano Texas Spanish, Tex-Mex, and all the other languages I speak, I cannot accept the legitimacy of myself.[29]

In the process of translating and adapting Shakespeare to reflect the realities of the region, Borderlands playwrights affirm the identities and everyday language practices of border residents. In *Hamlet, El Príncipe de Denmark*, for example, Tara Moses (Seminole Nation of Oklahoma, Mvskoke) makes specific use of translanguaging to call attention to the linguistic politics of the Borderlands. Hamlet's oscillation between Spanish and English not only reflects his internal struggles as a colonized subject but also serves as an act of rebellion against the forces of colonial power with which Claudius is aligned. Set in present-day San Diego, Bernardo Mazón Daher's *Measure for Measure | Medida por medida* uses the political and moral conflicts that animate *Measure for Measure* to emphasize the ways in which linguistic injustice often enables abuses of power in border communities.

---

27 Espinosa, "Traversing the Temporal Borderlands of Shakespeare," 606.
28 Anzaldúa, *Borderlands/La Frontera*, 61–67.
29 Anzaldúa, *Borderlands/La Frontera*, 66.

By remaking Shakespeare within the traditions of Borderlands arts and culture, Borderlands playwrights create dramatic works that are perhaps best understood through their deep intertextual relationships to a range of Indigenous and
Chicanx stories, songs, and plays. Borderlands Shakespeare is fundamentally a
hybrid project, with its blending of English texts with Chicanx and Indigenous
art forms, genres, and myths. Several plays in this anthology, for example, fea-
ture corridistas who assume the role of the Shakespearean Chorus and narrate
dramatic events in the form of a corrido, a hybrid Mexican song form adapted
from European ballads and commonly featured in teatro. Other plays include
raps, Indigenous music, songs from Broadway musicals, dances, face painting,
protest art, and arborglyphs. Many of the playwrights in *The Bard and the Borderlands* adopt the Chicanx spirit of rasquachismo, defined by Tomás Ybarra-
Frausto as an "underdog perspective" of "making do" that "engenders hybridiza-
tion, juxtaposition, and integration" and favors "communion over purity."[30] The
ethos of rasquachismo is prevalent in Borderlands cultural production, including
in teatro, where performers built sets and costumes from available materials. A
rasquache approach, therefore, takes from Shakespeare what it needs and irrev-
erently incorporates pieces of his plays into new, hybrid worlds that challenge
visions of white, canonical purity.

Much as Shakespeare's own plays do, Borderlands Shakespeare appropriations draw from a range of sources and mix comic modes with serious critique, a
practice also common to teatro and to Chicanx art more broadly. Plays such as *El
Henry*, *La Comedia of Errors*, and *¡O Romeo!*, for example, engage in witty banter,
word play, and physical humor while also addressing in earnest issues of white
supremacy, family separation, and Indigenous erasure. Carl Gutiérrez-Jones
explains that Chicanx artists have used "engaged humor" in order "to rethink
both literacy and victimization," noting that they have "built on the traditions
of political humor derived from Mexico."[31] Teatro, in particular, was influenced
by the Mexican tradition of carpas, traveling theatrical performances that often
included political satire as well as physical comedy. Traces of this influence arise
in several Borderlands Shakespeare plays. *¡O Romeo!*, for instance, draws on the
practice of satirizing authority figures by parodying Shakespeare himself, pre-
senting him as fallible and naive. Fausto, the Falstaff character in Siguenza's *El
Henry*, embodies another resonant use of humor, as his raucous joy for life sig-

---

30  Tomás Ybarra-Frausto, "Rasquachismo: A Chicano Sensibility," in *Chicano Art: Resistance and
    Affirmation, 1965–1985*, eds. Richard Griswold del Castillo, Teresa McKenna, and Yvonne Yar-
    bro-Bejarano (Los Angeles: Wright Art Gallery, University of California, 1991), 156.
31  Carl Gutiérrez-Jones, "Humor, Literacy and Trauma in Chicano Culture," *Comparative Litera-
    ture Studies* 40, no. 2 (2003): 112–26, esp. 113, https://doi.org/10.1353/cls.2003.0014.

nals a resistance to the oppressive structures that seek to discipline him and his community.

As they employ a range of techniques to repair the harm caused by colonization, Borderlands Shakespeare plays center Indigenous and Mexican perspectives, offering counterpoints to the Western epistemologies conveyed in their source texts. Some plays, such as Lujan's *Kino and Teresa* and González's *Invierno*, depict specific Native American communities and address the need for Indigenous sovereignty. Others work to reclaim spirituality, knowledges, languages, and practices for those who lack a direct link to their Indigenous ancestries. As Jorge Huerta writes, Chicanx drama often "shows a fascination with and respect for the Chicanos' Indigenous roots" and "affirm[s] the Chicano as Native American."[32] Some of the plays in the anthology draw upon the mixing of Catholic and Indigenous belief systems in the Borderlands, reflecting what Teresa Delgadillo examines as "spiritual mestizaje."[33] The veneration of La Virgen de Guadalupe in *The Tragic Corrido* and the many references to Indigenous gods and goddesses in *The Language of Flowers* and *¡O Romeo!* speak to the healing power of Borderlands spirituality. Several playwrights in this anthology draw on the ritual of Día de los Muertos to explore points of convergence and conflict between Christian and Indigenous notions of the afterlife. The cyclical worldview that infuses this ritual both disrupts the linearity of myths of Western progress and points to the persistence and resilience of Indigenous lifeways.

Storytelling is an integral part of the decolonial imaginary, which, as Pérez theorizes, often necessitates rereading and retelling Western narratives "to retool, to shift meanings and read against the grain, to negotiate Eurocentricity."[34] Embodied performance, Chela Sandoval, Arturo J. Aldama, and Peter J. García argue, is a key vehicle for such decolonial storytelling, as it ruptures present realities to envision new ones, thus "generat[ing] a pause in the activity of coloniality" and becoming "an effective means to individual and collective liberation."[35] Borderlands Shakespeare participates in this project of disrupting colonial narratives and performance traditions, reworking central texts of the Western canon to imagine decolonial futures. The potential of such cross-temporal engage-

---

32 Jorge Huerta, "Feathers, Flutes, and Drums: Images of the Indigenous Americans in Chicano Drama," in *Native American Performance and Representation*, ed. S. E. Wilmer (Tucson: University of Arizona Press, 2009), 182.

33 Theresa Delgadillo, *Spiritual Mestizaje: Religion, Gender, Race, and Nation in Contemporary Chicana Narrative* (Durham, NC: Duke University Press, 2011).

34 Pérez, *The Decolonial Imaginary*, xvii.

35 Chela Sandoval, Arturo J. Aldama, and Peter J. García, "Toward a De-Colonial Performatics of the US Latina and Latino Borderlands," in *Performing the US Latina and Latino Borderlands*, eds. Arturo J. Aldama, Chela Sandoval, and Peter J. García (Bloomington: Indiana University Press, 2012), 2–3.

ment to destabilize Euro-American colonial histories is perhaps best articulated by Paulina, a Chumash healer woman and the storyteller figure in González's *Invierno*, when she says, "Sometimes there are tiny cracks, small openings, allowing the past to live differently in the present and the present to become truthful because of the past, joining us together in ways we never thought possible."[36] The plays in *The Bard in the Borderlands* use Shakespeare to pry open generative spaces within colonial forms and narratives. They thus create what Cathryn Josefina Merla-Watson calls "altermundos," alternate worlds that, even if dystopian, rewrite the past, present, and future to remind us that an "otro mundo es posible."[37]

## Editorial Praxis and Terminology

Our intention in editing this anthology is to amplify the vital work of Borderlands playwrights and to generate paratextual materials that call attention to the critical insights and aesthetic sophistication of their plays. Fundamentally, we believe that it is important not to circumscribe knowledge within the academy. We therefore strive to align our editorial praxis with what Alexis Pauline Gumbs calls "community accountable scholarship," ensuring that the anthology honors and benefits the communities in which the plays were created.[38] In preparing these playtexts for publication, we have employed antiracist and decolonial editorial practices. We have worked closely with the playwrights and have made editorial decisions collaboratively and transparently. We have decided not to include translations of Spanish dialogue into English, opting instead to preserve the plays' linguistic specificity and to honor the dynamic language practices of the Borderlands. Similarly, we have chosen not to italicize words in Spanish or Indigenous languages because they are not considered foreign in this context. We have included a glossary that is intended to serve not as a comprehensive dictionary but rather as a guide for understanding some culturally and regionally specific terms. We have retained the playwrights' formatting where possible but have made some changes in the interest of consistency and to adhere to the house

---

36  José Cruz Gonzalez, *Invierno*, Prelude.
37  Cathryn Josefina Merla-Watson, "(Trans)Mission Possible: The Coloniality of Gender, Speculative Rasquachismo and Altermundos in Luis Valderas's Chican@futurist Visual Art," in *Altermundos: Latin@ Speculative Literature, Film, and Popular Culture*, eds. Cathryn Josefina Merla-Watson and B. V. Olguín (Los Angeles: UCLA Chicano Studies Research Center, 2017), 355.
38  Alexis Pauline Gumbs, "Daily Bread: Nourishing Sustainable Practices for Community Accountable Scholars," *Brilliance Remastered*, July 31, 2012.

style of ACMRS Press. Our quotations of Shakespeare's texts come from the third edition of *The Norton Shakespeare*.

The plays collected in this anthology reflect the diversity of identities that overlap and bleed into one another in the Borderlands. We maintain the terminology that the authors use to self-identify and to describe their characters, and we aim to use the most specific, current, and inclusive terms possible in our introductions and other paratextual materials. Many people in the Borderlands trace their ancestry to the original inhabitants of the land. We use the word "Indigenous" to reflect this situatedness, and we capitalize it when referring to people and their cultural practices. When available, we use specific tribal designations and self-identifiers to refer to people and traditions, and we are mindful of the dangers of homogenizing Indigenous experiences.[39] The term "Chicana/o/x" signals both the Indigenous ancestry of Mexican Americans and a political commitment to working class power, immigration rights, and educational opportunity. Many Mexican Americans began to identify as Chicano during the Movimiento of the 1960s and 1970s. The term is thought to have originated from the word "Mexica," which evolved to "Mexicanos," "Xicanos," and then "Chicanos." What was, and sometimes still is, used as a derogatory term to refer to Indigenous ancestry was reclaimed by activists to emphasize and celebrate this heritage. The term "Chicana/o/x" is frequently used in relation to the intellectual, political, and artistic traditions of the Borderlands, and we adhere to this practice.

Several other identity markers are prominent in the Borderlands and in this anthology. Some people emphasize national origin, or use the qualifier "American," as in terms such as "Mexican American" or "Salvadoran American," reflecting the ongoing effort to name and embrace compound identities. Other people use the more general terms "Hispanic" and "Latina/o/x/e." The term "Hispanic" was created by the U.S. government for the 1970 census and is generally used to refer to people whose heritage derives from Spanish-speaking countries. "Latino" became popular in the 1980s and emphasizes Latin American heritage. Both "Hispanic" and "Latino" have been critiqued for eliding the Indigenous and African roots of many people throughout the Americas.

Since at least the 1990s, activists and scholars have been moving towards identifications that are more inclusive of sexual and gender diversity. Terms such as "Latinx" and "Chicanx" emphasize the limitations of the gender binary upheld by masculine and feminine word endings in Spanish, in which the masculine is

---

39  For a guide to best practices that inform these linguistic choices, see Gregory Younging, *Elements of Indigenous Style: A Guide for Writing by and about Indigenous Peoples* (Edmonton: Brush Education, 2018).

the default for referring to mixed-gender groups.[40] Chicana feminist resistance to being subsumed into masculine or androcentric language led to the creation of terms such as "Latina/o" or "Latin@." The conversation has since expanded to explicitly include non-binary gender identification. To reflect these conversations, we use the gender neutral "Latinx" and "Chicanx" as general terms, though we acknowledge the increasing use of the -e ending as a gender neutral alternative. We use "LGBTQIA2+ ," standing for Lesbian, Gay, Bisexual, Trans*, Queer, Intersex, Asexual, Two Spirit, and more, to talk about specific communities as a whole, and we also use "queer" and "queer of color" when referring to particular intellectual, artistic, and political traditions. As language and understandings of social difference continue to evolve, more terms will likely emerge to refer to the multitudes of identities of people who inhabit border spaces.

## Pedagogy, Politics, and Possibilities

Our writing of this introduction coincided with the tenth anniversary of the founding of the "librotraficantes," a group of educators, activists, and scholars whose mission was to "smuggle" banned books to students in the wake of Arizona State House Bill 2281. Permanently blocked in 2017 after a seven-year court battle, this law attempted to stifle the success of the Mexican American Studies program in the Tucson Unified School District by banning ethnic studies curricula. As Houston-based scholar, cultural critic, and leader of the librotraficantes Tony Diaz notes, this legislation represented a backlash against educational approaches designed to affirm Mexican Americans and Latinxs more broadly: "It's clear to me that our intellectual advancement is a threat to some people, because they tried to make it illegal."[41] Such efforts to deny students opportunities to learn about their cultures and identities are neither new nor a relic of the past. They are part of a long legacy of anti-immigrant and white supremacist racism which has escalated once again in recent decades. In Texas, for example, backlash to recently approved ethnic studies curricula has led to censorship and laws prohibiting educators in public schools from teaching the full history of systemic racism and its social impacts. Efforts to whitewash history and marginalize non-white stories are a very real and present threat.

---

40 For a discussion of these terms, see Catalina (Kathleen) M. de Onís, "What's in an 'x'?: An Exchange about the Politics of 'Latinx,'" *Chiricú Journal: Latina/o Literatures, Arts, and Cultures* 1, no. 2 (2017): 78–91.

41 J. Weston Phippen and National Journal, "How One Law Banning Ethnic Studies Led to Its Rise," *The Atlantic*, July 19, 2015, https://www.theatlantic.com/education/archive/2015/07/how-one-law-banning-ethnic-studies-led-to-rise/398885/.

As several news outlets covering the fallout of HB 2281 emphasized in their headlines, Shakespeare's *The Tempest* was among the texts removed from the curriculum in Tucson.[42] "Shakespeare loomed large throughout this episode," writes Espinosa, "as critics of the law clung to the Bard's iconic status to criticize the misguided nature of the legislation."[43] As Espinosa has argued, the outsized emphasis on the apparent absurdity of banning Shakespeare — the canonical Anglophone author *par excellence* — detracted attention from the educational experiences of Mexican American students and the value of Mexican American literature. It assumed that Shakespeare was somehow an outlier in the list of books removed from Tucson classrooms. This response is indicative of the whiteness that often surrounds Shakespeare and the reception of his works. Indeed, because Shakespeare's work has been used as a tool of assimilation and gatekeeping in education for centuries, it often carries fraught associations for Latinx students. Both material and perceived, these tensions inform what Espinosa theorizes as a "Shakespeare-Latinx divide," wherein Shakespeare is positioned as a representative of white, Anglocentric culture, and Latinxs are imagined as its antithesis — if they are imagined at all.[44] In this context, Latinxs are perceived to have difficulty reading and comprehending Shakespeare, and, as Espinosa writes, "attitudes about Shakespeare's place in the establishment of English linguistic and cultural identity certainly drive these views."[45]

The presence of *The Tempest* in the Tucson Mexican American studies curriculum, however, does less to reinscribe Shakespeare's canonical status and association with whiteness than it does to reflect a long tradition of engagement with Shakespeare by residents of the U.S.–Mexico Borderlands. The forms of colonialism, enslavement, and linguistic domination dramatized in *The Tempest* resonate with many of the concerns addressed in other texts taught in ethnic studies courses. But, as Espinosa argues and as the plays in *The Bard in the Borderlands* attest, Borderlands engagements with Shakespeare also transcend *The Tempest* to consider a range of Shakespeare's works in relation to

---

42 See, for example, Jeff Biggers, "Who's afraid of 'The Tempest'?" *Salon*, January 13, 2012, https://www.salon.com/2012/01/13/whos_afraid_of_the_tempest/. See also Sam Favate, "Shakespeare's 'The Tempest' Barred from Arizona Public Schools," *The Wall Street Journal*, January 17, 2012, https://www.wsj.com/articles/BL-LB-41723.

43 Ruben Espinosa, "Beyond *The Tempest*: Language, Legitimacy, and *La Frontera*," in *The Shakespeare User: Critical and Creative Appropriations in a Networked Culture*, eds. Valerie M. Fazel and Louise Geddes (New York: Palgrave, 2017), 42, https://doi.org/10.1007/978-3-319-61015-3_3.

44 Ruben Espinosa, "'Don't it Make My Brown Eyes Blue': Uneasy Assimilation and the Shakespeare-Latinx Divide," in *The Routledge Handbook of Shakespeare and Global Appropriation*, eds. Christy Desmet, Sujata Iyengar, and Miriam Jacobson (New York: Routledge, 2019), 48–58, https://doi.org/10.4324/9781315168968.

45 Espinosa, "Beyond *The Tempest*," 45.

Borderlands stories, songs, and other art forms. We see this anthology as part of the longstanding effort to affirm such responses and to teach Borderlands literature, histories, and cultural traditions.

Indeed, *The Bard in Borderlands* arises from our own teaching of Shakespeare and Mexican American literature in the Borderlands. Through conversations with students and fellow teachers in the region and beyond, we recognized the need not only to make Borderlands Shakespeare plays available in print and digital formats but also to offer an accessible critical framework through which to understand the complex work that they do. As Borderlands playwrights reimagine Shakespeare to reflect their identities and concerns, their plays give students the tools to interrogate Shakespeare's cultural place; to interpret his works in conversation with their lived experiences; and to create their own artistic responses to canonical works of literature. Teaching Borderlands Shakespeare opens space for thinking critically with students about how we can best serve our communities when we teach, produce, or adapt Shakespeare and how we can do so in ways that avoid replicating colonialist and white supremacist ideologies. To invoke the work of the librotraficantes, Borderlands Shakespeare provides a means of smuggling Chicanx and Indigenous literature and history into increasingly surveilled educational spaces.

This edition honors and endeavors to extend the community-based efforts from which Borderlands Shakespeare has arisen. We therefore see this open-access anthology as an invitation, and we hope that it will encourage robust engagement among readers, teachers, students, scholars, activists, artists, and theater practitioners as we continue to explore intersections of Shakespeare and Borderlands arts. We hope that it fosters future collaborations that destabilize the artificial boundaries often separating universities, community colleges, high schools, and community arts organizations, opening space for dialogue and shared learning. We look forward to continuing the work of building the field of Borderlands Shakespeare studies and sustaining art, theater, and storytelling in the region and beyond. Adelante.

# Introduction to Volume 1

KATHERINE GILLEN, ADRIANNA M. SANTOS,
AND KATHRYN VOMERO SANTOS

This volume of *The Bard in the Borderlands* focuses on appropriations of two of the most ubiquitous and frequently taught Shakespeare plays: *Romeo and Juliet* and *Hamlet*. Theater artists of La Frontera frequently use these canonical plays to center the voices, histories, and ways of knowing of Borderlands residents, highlighting the regional resonance of questions about life, death, love, and power raised by these two tragedies. As they transform Shakespearean plots, characters, and poetry, Borderlands playwrights emphasize linguistic and cultural hybridity, political struggle, connection to the land, and Indigenous spirituality. By incorporating Shakespeare into Borderlands theater traditions and reworking scenes using Borderlands languages and settings, these playwrights challenge the ways that Shakespeare's works have been used in service of white hegemony. They also claim agency within Shakespeare's worlds, suggesting that the plays belong in the Borderlands and can be transformed — sometimes broken open and subverted — by fronterizos. The plays collected in this volume are therefore particularly powerful entry points to Borderlands Shakespeare. These appropriations show that Shakespeare's most famous stories resonate powerfully when they are merged with Borderlands traditions.

This volume contains three appropriations of *Romeo and Juliet*: Edit Villarreal's *The Language of Flowers*, James Lujan's *Kino and Teresa*, and Seres Jaime Magaña's *The Tragic Corrido of Romeo and Lupe*. In some ways, these productions employ what Carla Della Gatta calls the *"West Side Story* Effect," in which the interfamilial feud at the heart of *Romeo and Juliet* is recast in cultural terms.[1] Like the 1957 Broadway musical *West Side Story*, these Borderlands *Romeo and Juliet* appropriations reimagine the conflict between the Capulets and the Montagues through socioeconomic and racial difference. The drama unfolds between

---

1   Carla Della Gatta, "From *West Side Story* to *Hamlet, Prince of Cuba*: Shakespeare and Latinidad in the United States," *Shakespeare Studies* 44 (2016): 152.

upwardly mobile Mexican Americans and recent immigrants in *The Language of Flowers*; between the Pueblo Peoples and the Spanish colonizers in *Kino and Teresa*; and between agribusiness bosses and farmworkers in *The Tragic Corrido*. Because they emerge from within the communities they depict, however, these productions diverge in several respects from *West Side Story,* which has been critiqued both for its use of brownface and for representing Puerto Rican culture in stereotypical ways. Villarreal has noted, for example, that she chose not to depict gangs in *The Language of Flowers* because she "really wanted to avoid *West Side Story*" and did not want to replicate media stereotypes about urban violence in Latinx communities.[2] Further, in their focus on colonial and racial inequities, these Borderlands plays avoid the sense, present in many *Romeo and Juliet* adaptations, that the feuds are senseless or that they can be solved by Romeo and Juliet's love and or by their deaths. Instead, Villarreal, Lujan, and Magaña appropriate *Romeo and Juliet*'s love story to highlight the trauma of colonial and racist violence and to explore potential modes of resilience, resistance, and restitution.

Restitution, the plays indicate, cannot be realized fully within the trajectory of Shakespeare's plot, as it does not address systemic inequities. Reconciliation between the feuding parties is punctured in Lujan's *Kino and Teresa* by the dissenting voice of Kino's mother Anieri, who calls for the surrounding Pueblos, Navajos, and Apaches to join in an attack on Santa Fe, in which they will "kill the Spaniards and finally take back [their] land." As such, the détente brought about by Kino and Teresa's deaths constitutes only a "glooming peace," as the "woe" of the characters extends beyond themselves to encapsulate the colonial trauma inflicted on Pueblo Peoples (2.13). As in Shakespeare's play, the union between the Romeo and Juliet figures in these appropriations cannot transcend the violence that shapes their social worlds. In Magaña's *The Tragic Corrido*, Romeo and Lupe come to understand that, while their love is born of La Frontera, it can be sustained only in the afterlife, which Lupe imagines as a "world where our love can be free" (1.1). Similarly, Villarreal's *The Language of Flowers*, which is set during Día de los Muertos, ends with Romeo and Juliet entering the thirteen heavens of the Mexica afterlife. Shakespeare's tragic ending is thus reinterpreted through Indigenous cosmologies. The central characters cannot resolve deep structural conflicts in these plays, but Borderlands belief systems offer an alternate framework through which to interpret their deaths.

Indeed, Borderlands cultural practices are frequently used to reframe the elements of tragedy in several of the plays in this anthology. Tara Moses's *Ham-*

---

2   Mark Pinsky, "Una Noche to Remember: Hispanic Playwrights Project Takes Center Stage at SCR Beginning Tonight," *The Los Angeles Times,* August 8, 1991, https://www.latimes.com/archives/la-xpm-1991-08-08-ol-268-story.html.

*let, El Príncipe de Denmark* and Olga Sanchez Saltveit's *¡O Romeo!*, for instance, were created as part of community-based Día de los Muertos celebrations. In this context, Indigenous belief systems create space for healing that Shakespeare's tragic endings foreclose: the border between life and death is permeable, as spirits return to their altars and engage with the living. In *Hamlet, El Príncipe de Denmark*, Indigenous spirituality reshapes Hamlet's famous existential quandary. Hamlet struggles to communicate with the spirit of his father, and his bilingual "To be or not to be" soliloquy reflects his oscillation between Christian and Mexica spiritual beliefs. Hamlet exists in a state of nepantla, a Nahuatl word that Gloria E. Anzaldúa defines variously as "torn between ways" and "tierra entre medio."[3] Indigenous beliefs also permeate Josh Inocéncio's *Ofélio*, which subverts the sexual and racial politics of *Hamlet* by transforming Ophelia into a queer Latino who has suffered from sexual assault. In his lyrical monologues, Ofélio reimagines Ophelia's "muddy death" and floral imagery to envision himself being healed and renewed by natural elements (5.1.182).

Shakespeare himself benefits from the healing power of Indigenous beliefs in *¡O Romeo!*, a play in which his life, death, and corpus are reimagined through Borderlands perspectives. While attempting to complete a play about colonial Mexico on his deathbed, Shakespeare is visited by the spirit of his deceased son Hamnet as well as the spirits of several of his characters. This reunion allows Shakespeare to reflect upon the choices he made during his lifetime and to reconcile with his son, whom he neglected in favor of his work. Although its title gestures to *Romeo and Juliet*, and *Hamlet* figures prominently throughout, Sanchez Saltveit's play draws on several Shakespearean texts and engages with their many global afterlives. Through its references to popular adaptations and the inclusion of Shakespearean lines in multiple languages, *¡O Romeo!* celebrates global efforts to imagine a life after death for Shakespeare that affirms diverse perspectives and reflects audiences beyond those for whom he wrote. As the plays collected in this volume attest, Borderlands perspectives are vital to this ongoing tradition.

---

3    Gloria E. Anzaldúa, *Borderlands/La Frontera: The New Mestiza*. 5th ed. (San Francisco: Aunt Lute Press, 2022), 84, and "Preface: (Un)natural bridges, (Un)safe spaces," in *This Bridge We Call Home: Radical Visions for Transformation*, eds. Gloria E. Anzaldúa and AnaLouise Keating (New York: Routledge, 2002), 1.

# Introduction to Edit Villarreal's
## *The Language of Flowers*

Edit Villarreal's *The Language of Flowers*, which first premiered at California State University, Los Angeles (Cal State LA) in 1991 under the title *R and J*, is set in a Mexican American community during Día de los Muertos, a ritual commemoration with deep roots in Mexica spiritual practices. The tragic arc of *The Language of Flowers*, in which the protagonists die on the cusp of adulthood, is shaped by the sequence of Día de los Muertos celebrations, from Día de los Chicos, which is reserved for honoring the lives of children who have died, to Día de los Difuntos, "the day of the dearly departed adults" (2.6). Reflecting these traditions, calaveras, or skeletons, appear throughout the play — although the living characters usually do not notice them — and their presence destabilizes the stark line between life and death that characterizes the tragic ending of Shakespeare's *Romeo and Juliet*.

The play's central conflict is between Mexican Americans who feel pressure to assimilate into white capitalist structures of power and those who embrace their Indigenous roots and imagine a future in which freedom is possible. Juliet's father, Julian, embodies the former, as he wishes to deport undocumented Mexicans and hopes to marry his daughter to a young lawyer with "the right credentials" and "[t]he right friends" (2.8) — a stark contrast to Romeo, an undocumented immigrant from Michoacán. In Villarreal's appropriation, Romeo and Juliet's love is doomed not by a feud between their families but by endemic colonial violence and its aftershocks, as Romeo is killed at the border while attempting to return to Juliet at the end of play.

The colonial dynamics of the Borderlands informed the creation of *The Language of Flowers* from the outset. The development process began in 1990 at the Borderlands Theater in Tucson, Arizona, where José Cruz González was directing Villarreal's best-known play, *My Visits with MGM (My Grandmother Marta)*, which depicts her grandmother's life as a Mexican refugee in Brownsville, Texas. As theater professors based in Los Angeles, Villarreal and González were both frustrated with the lack of roles for their Latinx students and wanted to produce versions of the classics that resonated with audiences in LA.[1] Appropriating *Romeo and Juliet* for their contemporary context, then, expanded not just who could perform in the play but also which audiences might see themselves represented on stage. Indeed, as Villarreal explains in her essay, "Catching the Next Play: The Joys and Perils of Playwriting," writing a play can be an opportunity to create from and for the margins:

> Plays are also about marginal people, that is, people on the edges of society, either entering it, or being exiled from it. I too have always felt marginal. As a Latina growing up in the United States, as a woman playwright in professional theater, as a woman professor working in academia, it is impossible to feel otherwise.[2]

Villarreal and González continued to work on the play together over the next few years, staging it under González's direction at Cal State LA; at the South Coast Repertory in Costa Mesa, California, as part of the Hispanic Playwrights Project; and during the multi-venue "Shakespeare in the Non-English Speaking World" conference held in Los Angeles in 1991. The version of the play that appears in this anthology is based on Villarreal's 1995 revision. Germaine Franco, who is now well known for her work on the films *Coco* and *Encanto*, composed the music. *The Language of Flowers* had its Equity premiere at A Contemporary Theatre in Seattle under the direction of Norma Saldívar that same year and has been performed in universities, community colleges, high schools, and community and professional theaters.

The innovation of *The Language of Flowers* lies in its merging of *Romeo and Juliet* with the tradition of Chicanx theater, or teatro. In keeping with the convention of teatro, Villarreal replaces Shakespeare's Chorus with a corridista, a performer of corridos or narrative ballads popular in Mexico and the Borderlands, who intermittently sings throughout the play. The corridista highlights the connections between several Latin American migration patterns resulting from poverty, violence, and war, often due to U.S. intervention. The lyrics of one corrido state that the city is filled with

> Nicaragüenses y salvadoreños,
> Guatemaltecos all fleeing from war,

---

1   Susan Mason, "Romeo and Juliet in East L.A.," *Theater* 23, no. 2 (1992): 88–92, https://doi.org/10.1215/01610775-23-2-88.

2   Edit Villarreal, "Catching the Next Play: The Joys and Perils of Playwriting," in *Puro Teatro: A Latina Anthology*, eds. Alberto Sandoval-Sánchez and Nancy Saporta Sternbach (Tucson: University of Arizona Press, 2000), 331.

Pobres cubanos, también mexicanos,
Searching for work for themselves,
Bringing their families here to stay. (1.2)

*The Language of Flowers* dramatizes the impacts of U.S. economic and military policies in the 1990s, which made living conditions difficult in Mexico and Latin America. At the same time, immigration was criminalized and migrants were often met with violence, both at the militarized border and once they settled in cities such as Los Angeles. Villarreal's use of the corrido in *The Language of Flowers* highlights Mexican appropriations of European forms and signals that she is performing similar work with Shakespeare's *Romeo and Juliet*.

In keeping with teatro's emphasis on the Indigenous ancestry of Chicanxs and their long struggle against colonial power, *The Language of Flowers* brings Mesoamerican mythology into conversation both with Shakespeare's *Romeo and Juliet* and with the technologies of the colonial surveillance state that has imposed militarized borders on Indigenous land.[3] In the play's opening scene, Romeo's friend Benny, a combination of Shakespeare's Benvolio and Mercutio, responds to the accusation that he is a "wetback" saying,

We're all wetbacks from somewhere. Some of us walked over here. Like the Indians. Across Alaska, mano. In winter. Red-brown indio mules, they walked all the way to Patagonia. Later, some of these same indios changed their minds and came back. They flew out of the valles of Mexico, the barrios of Central America, the favelas and barrancas of South America like hungry birds. "We're back," they said. "Buenos días." (1.1)

This opening situates Los Angeles within a Pan-American Indigenous history, calling attention to the original inhabitants of the Americas and to broader patterns of voluntary and involuntary migration. Benny critiques the settler colonial idea of national borders, which deems some people citizens and others "illegal." Whereas this earlier migration of Indigenous people is depicted as relatively peaceful, the play exposes the colonial dynamics of poverty and war that influence modern migrations. Benny closes his monologue by recalling that, "Eventually somebody said, 'Why can't we all get along?' But nobody listened," referencing the question posed by Rodney King, whose beating by white police officers in 1991 sparked a series of uprisings in the following years when they were acquitted

---

3   For the role of Indigeneity in Chicanx drama, see Jorge Huerta, "Feathers, Flutes, and Drums: Images of the Indigenous Americans in Chicano Drama," in *Native American Performance and Representation*, ed. S. E. Wilmer (Tucson: University of Arizona Press, 2009), 182–92.

(1.1). In this act of quotation, Benny calls attention to the experience of Black residents of LA, whose migration was shaped by histories of enslavement and who experience anti-Black state violence.

These racial and colonial dynamics are reflected in the play's treatment of language. Juliet's father and his associates reject Spanish, seeking to speak without a Mexican accent and objecting when their names are given Spanish pronunciations. Even as Juliet begins to learn Spanish, however, Romeo and Juliet find a more fundamental connection in "the language of flowers," a phrase that encapsulates a Mexica linguistic genealogy that transcends English and Spanish and signifies a more embodied and land-based language of love. Romeo and Juliet meet near a magnolia tree, which prompts Romeo to note, "In México, we call magnolias 'yoloxochitl.' Flowers of the heart" (1.9), and he later refers to Juliet herself as a yoloxochitl, explaining that "It's Nahuatl, the language they spoke in Mexico before it was Mexico" (1.13). Romeo's use of Nahuatl aligns with Villarreal's emphasis on the Indigenous roots of Día de los Muertos, and the play's imagery of flowers includes the marigolds, or cempasúchitl, which were sacred to the Mexica and are traditionally placed on graves during Día de los Muertos to entice souls to return from the dead.

Romeo also frequently thinks about his experiences in relation to Mexica mythology. He feels especially connected to Tezcatlipoca, the god of the Great Bear constellation whose name translates as Smoking Mirror and whose worship was central to sacrificial traditions, in which a young prisoner of war lived in luxury for a year, impersonating the god, before he was sacrificed. Romeo invokes Tezcatlipoca's smoke as a sign of the death that surrounds Los Angeles but also as part of a broader, rejuvenating spiritual cycle. Los Angeles, he says, is full of "[n]othing but hate. You can smell it. The barrio on fire with uzis light as feathers. Tezcatlipoca's dark smoke burning bright. Brighter than the sun. And nobody sleeps. Even at night" (1.4). This darkness ultimately prevails. Romeo also notes, however, that "Tezcatlipoca's smoke . . . burns in the eyes of those in love" (1.4), and he imagines his reunion with Juliet as occurring in the presence of his "favorite Mexican god, somewhere in his palacio, his house of love" (2.18). Read in relation to the Tezcatlipoca myth, Romeo and Juliet function as sacrifices, but they also live on in the afterlife, in the thirteen heavens of Mexica belief systems.

Indigenous healing practices promise to facilitate Romeo and Juliet's reunion after Romeo is deported to Mexico, but this happy ending is thwarted by state repression. María, the housekeeper employed by Juliet's father, recognizes the plants Father Lawrence cares for as indigenous to her own country, where they are "[u]sed by curanderos . . . [t]o cleanse the body and calm the mind" (2.13), and it is she, not Father Lawrence, who uses the plants to facilitate Juliet's false death. Upon hearing that Juliet has died, Romeo finds a coyote, or trafficker, to take him across the border, but they are ambushed by a huge figure of Uncle Sam who shoots at them. Romeo explains that he is an American who speaks English and is married to an American, but Uncle Sam rejects him, shouting, "COWARD! BEGGAR! YOU THINK AMERICA WANTS YOUR KIND?" (2.22). Although Romeo has purchased fatal poison from a curandero, he doesn't need to use it, as he is killed by the violence of the militarized border and of the streets of Los Angeles, violence that is conflated in the rapid succession of images at the end of Villarreal's play. Bloodshed in Los Angeles, Villarreal suggests, results from colonial state repression and cannot be disconnected from the racist violence that Romeo and his fellow migrants face at the border.

Although Romeo cannot reunite with Juliet in life, death brings them peace within the play's Indigenous worldview. The spirits of the dead, manifesting as calaveras, help to facilitate this passage. When Juliet sees Benny Calavera holding Romeo in the form of a "Mesoamerican pietà," she runs to him and stabs herself with a knife given to her by another calavera (2.26). Revising the Christian ethos of Shakespeare's play, Villarreal's ending charts Romeo and Juliet's physical reintegration with the earth and spiritual integration into a Mexica afterlife. Benny Calavera prays, "*Romeo* and Julieta, may your souls fly to the thirteenth heaven. And with the bodies of hummingbirds, may they fly free forever," while the other calaveras chant:

> Your body a flower
> Your heart a flower
> Give them to earth
> And return! (2.26)

Romeo and Juliet, "children of Mexico," are ready to begin their next journey and to "become what [they've] always been. Flowers and song" (2.26). Amidst Texcatlipoca's rising smoke, Romeo and Juliet pledge not to be separated, with Romeo using the Spanish "juntos" and Juliet saying "together" (2.26). Beyond merging Spanish and English, though, Romeo and Juliet end the play speaking the language of flowers, the language of the heart and of their Indigenous ancestry.

— Katherine Gillen, Adrianna M. Santos,
and Kathryn Vomero Santos

# The Language of Flowers

## Edit Villarreal

A free adaptation of William Shakespeare's *Romeo and Juliet*
Music by Germaine Franco

SETTING: 1990s Los Angeles. The play takes place on October 31st, November 1st, and November 2nd, combining the American holiday of Halloween and the two Mexican holidays referred to as Day of the Dead, or Days of the Dead. It's commonly believed that during Día de los Muertos the dead return in the form of calaveras to commune with family and friends.

## CHARACTERS

| | |
|---|---|
| **JULIAN BOSQUET** | Banker, second generation Mexican American. |
| **JULIET BOSQUET** | His daughter. |
| **CANDELARIA MARTINEZ** | Romeo's mother. In the U.S. illegally. |
| **ROMEO MARTINEZ** | Her son. Also undocumented. |
| **BENNY MARTINEZ** | Romeo's cousin. American born. Combines the qualities of Shakespeare's Benvolio and Mercutio. |
| **TOMMY BOSQUET** | Juliet's cousin. Julian's nephew. |
| **RUBEN GUTIERREZ** | Law school student. In love with Juliet. |
| **SGT. LOPEZ** | With the LAPD. Distantly related to the Bosquet family. Though of the same generation as Julian, considers himself Chicano. |
| **FATHER LAWRENCE** | Hispanophile priest. Avid researcher of rainforest plants. |
| **MARIA** | Maid in Bosquet home. Unwilling mistress of Julian. |
| **MANUEL** | Servant in Bosquet home. A calavera. |

| | |
|---|---|
| **CURANDERA/O** | Herbalist. |
| **CORRIDISTA** | Mexican balladeer. |
| **CALAVERAS** | Día de los Muertos skull figures. |
| **COYOTE CALAVERA** | Trafficker. |
| **DRAG TRICK-OR-TREATER** | |
| **UNCLE SAM** | |
| **HOMEBOY** | |
| **COP** | |
| **WAITER** | |
| **PARTY GUESTS** | |

**PLAYWRIGHT'S NOTE:** Romeo Martinez, Julian Bosquet, and Ruben Gutierrez have first names that are sometimes pronounced in English and sometimes in Spanish. When the Spanish pronunciation is emphasized in the dialogue, the names are italicized. More generally, when characters are speaking in Spanish or using Spanish pronunciation, names are accented where appropriate.

# ACT 1
## Scene 1

*October 31st, morning. Indeterminate street sounds, a little Spanish, lots of English. Lights rise in two areas. From the shadows of one area, BENNY speaks.*

**BENNY**

This morning it hit me. Laying in my bed, the sheets around my neck. I'm tired. My back. Heavy. My legs. Like two trucks.

*A cigarette is lit in the other area, an incendiary moment. TOMMY speaks from the shadows.*

**TOMMY**

Jerk.

**BENNY**

Payaso.

*Both step into full light.*

**TOMMY**

You're the clown, Benny. (*pause*) Wetback.

**BENNY** (*with a shrug, holding a can of Olde English 800*)

¡Híjole! Wetback. Salud, I was born here. But it don't matter, Tommy. We're all wetbacks from somewhere. Some of us walked over here. Like the Indians. Across Alaska, mano. In winter. Red-brown indio mules, they walked all the way to Patagonia. Later, some of these same indios changed their minds and came back. They flew out of the valles of Mexico, the barrios of Central America, the favelas and barrancas of South America like hungry birds. "We're back," they said. "Buenos días." At the same time, other people started floating in on boats. From both sides. The east side and the west side. When they saw the land, the boat people poured out of their dirty little boats like hungry tuna, shrimp, and albacore. "The ocean is no place to live," they said. "It moves around too much. The sky turns so black at night, you can't even see it." So they ditched their boats. Right out there on the beach. And then they started looking around. For land. This land. And that's how it happened. Everybody in the whole world found themselves right here in the middle of pinche L.A. Hungry. Tired. Sweaty. And pissed off at everybody. Eventually somebody said, "Why can't we all get along?" But nobody listened.

*CANDELARIA MARTINEZ runs across the stage.*

**CANDELARIA**
¡Malditos! My purse! You took my purse! ¡Policía! ¡Policía!

*She exits. A police siren rises.*

**TOMMY**
Wetbacks. Working for nothing in basements. Give 'em anything, they burn it. Trash it. Loot it. Kill each other on the streets like flies. Because of them there's a war going on.

**BENNY**
Why should you live, Tommy? And they die? Why should you eat? And they die?

**TOMMY**
It's war. They steal from me. I get it back.

**BENNY**
War. Big word. You win. They fight. You take. They take back. Even in the movies, Tommy, the good guys don't get everything.

**TOMMY**
You don't like it? So leave.

**BENNY**
Maldito.

**TOMMY**
You want to stay and fight, Benny? Come on. Come on.

*A fight seems about to break out. Suddenly, the stage explodes into full light, and the streets of L.A. come alive. TOMMY pulls out a .44 Magnum.*

**BENNY**
You think I'm afraid of your gun, Tommy? I'm from Mexico, mano.

*Police sirens rise again.*

**TOMMY**
Cops. Better run.

**BENNY** (*referring to the gun*)
Keep it out, payaso.

# Scene 2

*SGT. LOPEZ and CANDELARIA MARTINEZ enter.*

**SGT. LOPEZ** (*giving her the purse*)
Óyeme, Señora Martínez. The streets are no place for you.

> *JULIAN BOSQUET enters impeccably dressed in Ivy League khaki pants and a blue blazer.*

**CANDELARIA**
Buenos días, Señor Bosquet.

**JULIAN**
Lock 'em up, Tony. Throw away the key.

**SGT. LOPEZ**
Yeah, Julian?

**JULIAN**
Tax payers need a break. Get 'em out of town. On the first plane.

**SGT. LOPEZ**
Yeah, Julian?

**TOMMY**
Don't even feed 'em.

**SGT. LOPEZ**
You think so, Tommy?

**TOMMY**
Gotta break even somewhere.

> *He puts the gun behind his back.*

JULIAN
Hey, Tony, haven't seen you around. Come over sometime. Have a few beers.
I'm serious.

SGT. LOPEZ
It's Antonio, to you, *Julián*. Antonio.

JULIAN (*acknowledging the put down*)
Yeah. Well. Come over anyway, Tony. We'll catch up on old times.

SGT. LOPEZ
You got something new to say about turning Republican? *Julián*?

JULIAN
Tony, Tony, wake up. The movimiento is over.

SGT. LOPEZ
That's not what the streets tell me.

JULIAN
So get out of 'em. (*beat*) Come by the bank. I'll work up a portfolio for you. So
you can get a decent job. And relax for a change.

SGT. LOPEZ
I like my job, *Julián*. I like being a cop. Tommy, give me the gun.

TOMMY
I got a permit.

SGT. LOPEZ
And I got a right to take it in and check the papers. Tommy? You have trouble
understanding cops for some reason? (*pause*) I could take both of you in.

> Another COP comes out of the shadows, gun drawn.

I could also make sure you were both forgotten for a while. In the holding
tank. (*pause*) For a couple of days. A week or two.

JULIAN
All right, Sgt. Lopez. Have it your way.

(*to TOMMY*) Give him the gun.

**TOMMY**
Hell no!

**JULIAN**
TOMMY!

**SGT. LOPEZ** (*to TOMMY*)
Slowly. Slowly.

**TOMMY**
Julian!

**JULIAN**
Tommy. Give him the gun. Now.

> *TOMMY hands the gun to SGT. LOPEZ.*

**JULIAN** (*to TOMMY*)
And now I want to talk to you.

**TOMMY**
All right.

**JULIAN**
Just what the hell —

**TOMMY**
All right!

**BENNY** (*to TOMMY*)
Cabrón.

> *TOMMY stops and turns around.*

Congratulations. You understand Spanish.

**TOMMY**
I'll get you, man.

> *JULIAN and TOMMY exit.*

**SGT. LOPEZ** (*to BENNY*)
And you, wise guy. Get outta here. NOW!

> *A CORRIDISTA enters and sings "Corrido El Lay."*

**CORRIDISTA**

Nuestro corrido begins in this city.
Los Ángeles, also known as El Lay.
Una ciudad, a very big city,
With mucha gente de muchos lugares
Arriving here each day
To live in El Lay.
Nicaragüenses y salvadoreños,
Guatemaltecos all fleeing from war,
Pobres cubanos, también mexicanos,
Searching for work for themselves,
Bringing their families here to stay
Right here in El Lay.
But nuestro corrido is not about war,
Nuestro corrido is all about love.
Juliet, an American, met *Romeo*, a poor Mexican.
Their love started boiling,
They were meant for each other,
It was written that way.
But El Lay is not for loving,
El Lay is not for love,
El Lay is not for dreaming,
And El Lay is not for luck.
Now I've started this corrido,
But now I'll end my song.
*Romeo* and Julieta
Should tell their story
On their own.

# Scene 3

**CANDELARIA**

¿Qué pasó, sobrino? Dime. What happened?

**BENNY**

Just Tommy. Up to his old tricks.

**CANDELARIA**

¿El loco Tomás?

**BENNY**
No better than his coconut uncle.

**CANDELARIA**
And *Romeo*? Have you seen him?

**BENNY**
Yeah. This morning. Walking. Muy agüitado —

**CANDELARIA**
¿De veras?

**BENNY**
He thinks he's in love. I went to him, but he didn't see me. And me, pos, I wasn't feeling so good. La cruda y todo —

**CANDELARIA** (*taking beer can away from him*)
Ay, Benito, you drink too much!

**BENNY** (*taking beer can back*)
¡Ni modo! (*beat*) So I left. And he kept on walking.

**CANDELARIA**
¡Ay, Benito! I don't know what to do! When the moon comes out, *Romeo* wakes up. And then, when the sun rises, he sleeps. Benito, men should sleep when the sun sleeps, pero *Romeo* —

**BENNY**
¡Caramba, tía! What am I supposed to do?

**CANDELARIA**
Talk to him. In this country, sons don't talk to their mothers.

**BENNY**
In this country, tía, no one talks to anyone.

**CANDELARIA**
But Benito, *Romeo* is like a flower. With a worm inside. And every morning when the sun comes out to give us life and strength, the worm gets hungry. And eats. Chewing on my son's corazón. In México, Benito, I would take the flower to a curandero. But here —

**BENNY** (*seeing ROMEO*)
Ay, viene. He's coming.

**CANDELARIA**
Talk to him, Benito. Tell him how things are in this country —

**BENNY**
In this country, we have nothing, tía. Unless we fight for it every minute of every day.

**CANDELARIA**
Bueno.

**BENNY** (*seeing ROMEO approaching*)
Ay viene. I'll talk to him, all right?

> *ROMEO enters wearing a white house painter's outfit.*

**CANDELARIA**
Gracias, Benito, gracias.

> *She exits.*

**BENNY**
De nada. De nada.

(*to ROMEO*) ¿Y tú? What's happening, bro?

# Scene 4

**ROMEO**
Lots of noise, Benito.

**BENNY** (*with a shrug*)
Cops. You know . . .

**ROMEO**
Nothing but hate. You can smell it. The barrio on fire with uzis light as feathers. Tezcatlipoca's dark smoke burning bright. Brighter than the sun. And nobody sleeps. Even at night.

**BENNY**
Chingao.

**ROMEO**
You think it's funny?

**BENNY**
Simón, it makes me want to cry.

**ROMEO**
¿Por qué, primo?

**BENNY**
Because you're messed up, man.

**ROMEO**
No Benny! I'm in love. Con Carolyn. But she's so heavy.

**BENNY**
I thought you were the one on top.

**ROMEO**
She's messing me up, primo!

**BENNY**
Like I said! (*beat*) And guess what?

**ROMEO**
What?

**BENNY**
I got more news on your Carolyn.

**ROMEO**
She's doing something.

**BENNY**
How old is she? Eighteen?

**ROMEO**
Who is it?

**BENNY**
Your Carolyn, *Romeo*, is about to expand her horizons. See, girls like Carolyn mess around with guys like us —

**ROMEO**
Because we're suave, que no?

**BENNY**
But they don't marry us. You understand, baboso?

**ROMEO**
So what?

**BENNY**
You listening to me?

**ROMEO**
Yeah. I'm listening.

**BENNY**
We're suave, all right.

**ROMEO**
Yeah. Smooth. Like midnight.

**BENNY**
But that don't write no checks. ¿M'entiendes, Mendes? ¿M'entiendes?

**ROMEO** (*hurt*)
All right! So what?

**BENNY**
So pop out of it. This is El Lay, mano. The whole city is full of beautiful brown-eyed rucas. From everywhere! Half of Central America is already here. And the other half is praying and packing. Don't get strung out on one girl. Leave that to the pinche americanos.

**ROMEO**
Okay. Okay . . . pero . . .

**BENNY**
Pero, nothing! ¡Ya estuvo! Right?

**ROMEO**

Right. Okay.

**BENNY**

Bueno.

**ROMEO**

Bueno. (*pause*) But Tezcatlipoca's smoke, Benny —

**BENNY**

¡Chingao!

**ROMEO**

— burns in the eyes of those in love. When you're in love you can't forget.

**BENNY**

Survival, *Romeo*. Survival is the only thing you need to remember.

**ROMEO**

It's not for me to fall out of love.

**BENNY**

Then it's up to me to make you fall.

>	*They exit.*

# Scene 5

>	*October 31st, noon. Lights rise on JULIAN BOSQUET and RUBEN GUTIERREZ, both dressed in Ivy League khaki pants and blue blazers.*

**RUBEN**

Well, Mr. Bosquet? My heart is on my sleeve.

**JULIAN**

She's young, Ruben.

**RUBEN**

And beautiful.

**JULIAN**
But still a baby. Just eighteen.

**RUBEN**
A lot of Hispanic girls get married at eighteen, sir.

**JULIAN**
My wife didn't wait even that long.

**RUBEN**
The beautiful ones should get married right away, don't you think?

**JULIAN**
Best place for them. They do say beauty is a weapon. Especially in the form of an attractive woman.

**RUBEN**
Mr. Bosquet, I meant no disrespect —

**JULIAN**
*Rubén*, I never thought for a second —

**RUBEN**
My name is Ruben, sir.

**JULIAN**
I'm sorry, in Spanish, Ruben is pronounced *Rubén*.

**RUBEN**
Yeah, but that's not what anybody calls me. See, my name is Ruben.

**JULIAN**
Yeah. Ruben. (*beat*) Hey, it's my problem. The old neighborhood comes out sometimes. You know, the old crowd —

**RUBEN** (*a world apart*)
What crowd, Mr. Bosquet?

**JULIAN**
Just . . . nothing. Forget it. It doesn't matter. Tonight is going to be special. Because tonight — with my blessing — you and Juliet will start being a couple. In public, I mean.

**RUBEN**

Thank you, Mr. Bosquet. Juliet said you were old fashioned —

**JULIAN**

Old fashioned? Just because I want the very best for my daughter?

**RUBEN**

What I mean is . . . don't get me wrong, sir. I love Juliet. Actually, I'm kind of wild about her. But not in a bad way —

**JULIAN**

Of course! Of course! Manuel?

> *MANUEL, a servant of the household, enters. He is a calavera,*
> *though JULIAN does not see him as such.*

**MANUEL**

¿Sí, señor?

**JULIAN** (*giving him a stack of small envelopes*)
Take these and deliver them by hand.

(*to RUBEN*) Some people won't bother to come without a personal gesture.

**RUBEN**

People are busy . . .

**JULIAN**

And Halloween parties have to be fun. Or else . . .

(*to MANUEL*) Deliver them all by 2 o'clock. You understand?

**MANUEL**

Sí, señor.

**RUBEN**

Could I interest you in some lunch, Mr. Bosquet?

**JULIAN**

Call me Julian. And, yeah, lunch would be great. You can bring me up to date on law school.

**RUBEN**

I'm already boning up for Moot Court.

**JULIAN**
Ruben, that's months away!

**RUBEN**
You can never be too ready!

*JULIAN and RUBEN exit.*

**MANUEL**
Chingao. I can't read these.

# Scene 6

*Lights rise on BENNY and ROMEO.*

**BENNY**
You put out one fire with another fire. Play the field. Check things out, hombre! ¡Asi hacen los americanos! It's the American way. Kill one poison, love, with another poison, partying. Get loose, you're too uptight.

**ROMEO**
Cállate, okay?

**BENNY**
Are you pissed off again?

*MANUEL enters.*

**ROMEO**
You don't understand, primo. To me Carolyn is like food. Like water.

**MANUEL**
¿Señores? Con permiso.

**ROMEO**
I need her. I can't stop!

**MANUEL**
We all stop. Sooner or later.

**ROMEO**
What?

**MANUEL**

Forget it. I know you will.

> *For a brief moment, ROMEO sees MANUEL as he really is,*
> *a calavera.*

**ROMEO**

Old man, what are you?

**MANUEL**

I'm just passing through, señor.

**ROMEO**

Leave me alone.

**BENNY**

¡Flaco! ¿Qué quieres, viejo?

**MANUEL**

Hágame el favor, señor, de leer estas cartitas —

**BENNY** (*ripping open one envelope*)

Hey. Check this out, mano. Coconut Bosquet is throwing his "annual Halloween party." And look at these names: Anglos, Arabs, Jews, not one Latino name. He's inviting the entire United Nations but nobody south of the border. And check this out: "Southwestern cuisine will be served."

**ROMEO**

Southwestern? What is that?

**BENNY**

No beans. And watery salsa.

**MANUEL**

Come to the party, anyway, señores. Don Bosquet wants a full house. And drink his beer. If you can't be happy when you're young, estás bien chingado, que no?

**BENNY**

Come on, primo. Your Carolyn will probably be at this fancy "Southwestern" party. Let's go. And check her out.

**ROMEO**
If Carolyn is there, I have to see what she's up to —

**BENNY**
Okay, but no crying if you see her with another guy —

**MANUEL** (*grabbing envelopes from BENNY's hands*)
Señores, por favor —

**BENNY**
¡Ay, que chivo!

> *He takes an invitation.*

See this guy? He's going to be out of town. Okay?

> *He slips MANUEL some money.*

Okay?

**MANUEL** (*taking the money*)
¡Seguro que sí! Come to the party. Señor Bosquet never runs out of beer —

**BENNY**
Yeah. But it's Coors.

# Scene 7

> *October 31st, late afternoon. Lights rise on JULIAN and MARIA.*

**JULIAN**
¡Ay, María!

**MARIA**
¿Sí, señor?

**JULIAN**
Raising a daughter would be so much easier if I had a wife.

**MARIA**
I agree, señor. But you divorced her.

**JULIAN**
Where is Juliet?

**MARIA**

In the house, Don Julián.

**JULIAN**

I told you to always keep track of her. Juliet!

*JULIET enters, carrying several shopping bags.*

**JULIET**

I'm right here, Dad.

**JULIAN**

Shopping? Again?

**JULIET**

For the party! I hardly spent anything. Except for one thing, but it's —

**JULIAN**

Hey! It's all right. Anything that makes you beautiful is money well spent.

**JULIET**

Dad!

**JULIAN**

Because eventually, I'll get my return. As soon as you're engaged to Ruben —

**JULIET**

Ruben? Ruben who?

**JULIAN**

Ruben Gutierrez.

**JULIET**

Dad, I hardly know him!

**JULIAN**

He's almost out of law school, and he's crazy about you. Successful men like Ruben need good looking women. Jules, I want you to look perfect tonight.

**JULIET**

Dad, it's just a party —

**JULIAN**
It's never "just a party." As the wife of an up-and-coming lawyer, you're going to learn that.

**JULIET**
Dad, I think we should sit down and —

**JULIAN**
Later. Tonight, I want everything perfect. Your hair. Your face. When you're young, Jules, there's not a moment to waste. Maria?

**MARIA**
¿Sí, señor?

**JULIAN**
Make sure she's beautiful —

**MARIA**
I will, señor.

>    *MANUEL enters.*

**MANUEL**
Don Bosquet, todo está listo, the food is here —

**JULIAN**
Why don't you speak English? Just English?

**MANUEL**
— the yard is clean, ya llegaron las flores —

**JULIAN**
Go back to the kitchen and make sure the caterers have everything they need.

**MANUEL**
Sí, señor

>    *He exits.*

**JULIAN**
And you, young lady, go get ready.

**JULIET**
All right. Sure.

**JULIAN**
Juliet?

**JULIET**
Yes?

**JULIAN**
Yes, what?

**JULIET**
Yes. (*pause*) Sir.

**JULIAN**
You'll be beautiful, Jules. I know it.

*He exits.*

**JULIET**
Why should I be beautiful? Just to please him?

**MARIA**
Men like to have their way, mija.

**JULIET**
Around you, maybe.

**MARIA** (*understanding the insult*)
¡Sinvergüenza! To you life is a joke.

**JULIET**
Living with Dad, what else can it be?

*They exit.*

# Scene 8

*October 31st, evening. Lights rise on BENNY and ROMEO on their way to the party. ROMEO, still in his painter's whites, is now wearing a Halloween mask. BENNY is decked out as Zorro.*

**ROMEO**
Benny, maybe we shouldn't go to this pinche party. I don't even have a costume —

**BENNY**

Tell 'em you're a house painter.

**ROMEO**

I *am* a house painter!

**BENNY**

Yeah, but tonight you're a *pretend* house painter. *Romeo*, get with the program. They'll laugh at us. We'll hit the beers. And then we'll leave. You ready? (*beat*) Silence on the set! Action!

> *Lights rise on the Halloween party. BENNY makes a flamboyant entrance.*

**PARTY PERSON**

Oh, wow! Zorro just walked in!

**ROMEO** (*to BENNY*)

This is really stupid, man.

**BENNY**

Chill. I like my costume.

**ROMEO**

If you don't think this is stupid —

**BENNY**

Keep your mask on. That way you can eyeball the rucas up and down, and they won't even know you're looking. Come on, *Romeo*, have fun! Eat them up!

**ROMEO**

No. I'm going to be a flower on the wall.

**BENNY**

Baboso, se dice "wallflower."

**ROMEO**

Okay! Like that!

**BENNY**

Sometimes, you know, I don't know where you learned English. You can't be a wallflower. You'll stick out! You gotta dance.

**ROMEO**

I don't want to dance. Tezcatlipoca's smoke sits like smog in front of my eyes. I'll just watch. Okay?

**BENNY**

Okay. But at least drink. Coconut Bosquet ain't gonna run out of nothing. *Romeo*, I gotta tell you something. I'm your cousin, right? Your primo and your best friend. Your ONLY friend. Since you crossed over, illegally —

**ROMEO**

Shut up! ¡Cállate! (*beat*) You know, you drink too much.

**BENNY**

You just figured that out?! I think you got Old Timer's Disease —

**ROMEO**

And cut the stupid jokes.

**BENNY**

We're at a party! The perfect place for stupid jokes! But seriously, I have three things to tell you. Yeah, I drink too much. Women are nothing but trouble. And number three? In this country, the americanos don't know how to have any fun. But me, primo? Tonight I'm Zorro. I'm gonna mess around real good mano, because nobody knows who the hell I am.

**ROMEO**

I don't think we should be here.

**BENNY**

So leave.

**ROMEO**

I had a dream last night.

**BENNY**

I did too. Mine was wet.

**ROMEO**

That's all? That's all you remember?

**BENNY**

Let me think. Oh yeah. It was a lie. This (*clutching his crotch*) was the only real part.

**ROMEO**

¡Ay, Benito! Dreams always come true. You know that.

**BENNY**

¡Chingao, hombre! When the hell are you gonna grow up?

**ROMEO**

And be like you? Too American?

**BENNY**

And you're the Mexican, huh? The REAL Mexican? *Romeo*, listen to me. The Tooth Fairy and the Fairy Godmother and all the other pinche American lies you think are so real, they don't belong to you. And Carolyn, with her little fanny hiding under a short skirt, you think she's real? In Mexico, they know what women are really like. La Llorona.

**ROMEO**

You know, you're full of —

**BENNY**

The first time you see her, she's young and beautiful. Like your Carolyn. And you give it to her, ¿que no? Because she wants it too. But then, *Romeo*, women turn on you. They wrinkle and get fat. They lose their hair. And their teeth. Even their voice.

**ROMEO**

¡Caramba, mano!

**BENNY**

And then, they begin to smell. Like old wallpaper and soap. And then they kill your children and take your money. And babosos like you let them.

**ROMEO**

You're crazy, you know that?

**BENNY**

Because you're in love. Forever in love. Only to the grave, mano. And even then, you'll look up and see an old woman, La Llorona, planting flowers on your chest. Check it out, man. Women get old quick. And they're old much longer than they're young.

**ROMEO**

That's nothing but babosadas.

**BENNY**

You don't like La Llorona? Chill. She's just a fairy tale. A Mexican fairy tale.

**ROMEO**

Benito, listen to me. Just for a moment.

**BENNY**

I'll listen . . . But you remember this: aunque te cases, even though you get married, mira lo que haces, watch your back. Now let's eat.

**ROMEO**

Benito, I don't like it here. This house. These people. They don't want us. When my mother and me came to this country, we were crawling, primo. Full of guilt and shame. Why is it a sin to try and make your life better, Benito?

**BENNY**

You're here. You want a medal?

**ROMEO**

I'm going to pay for it. I know it. I know it.

**BENNY**

Snap out of it! You're not the first one to crawl over. And you sure as hell ain't gonna be the last. And I'm here for you, primo. I'm here for you!

**ROMEO**

Chale.

**BENNY**

No matter what.

**ROMEO**

Bueno. Dios me va a cuidar. God brought me here. And whatever He wants, what He wants, will happen, ¿que no? (*beat*) Where's the beers?

**BENNY**

¡Ándale!

> *BENNY and ROMEO mingle.*

# Scene 9

*JULIAN, JULIET, RUBEN, and MARIA enter. JULIAN is dressed as an Argentine "gaucho" or cowboy. MARIA is dressed like a French maid. JULIET is dressed like a fairytale princess. RUBEN is dressed like a pirate.*

**JULIAN**
Ruben?

**RUBEN**
Yes, sir?

**JULIAN**
Look at the two of you. The American Dream! Keep her in line. If you know what I mean.

**RUBEN**
Yes, sir.

**JULIET**
Don't mind Dad. He's into fantasy.

**RUBEN**
Actually, I like fantasy too, Jules. I'm proud of you. You look beautiful.

**JULIET**
Is that all you can say?

**RUBEN**
You want more? You want me to say all the other women here are dogs compared to you?

**JULIET**
Ruben, that's not —

**JULIAN**
Everybody! Eat! Drink! Dance! Anybody who doesn't dance has flat feet. Or, as we say in Spanish, they have corns.

*Music plays. Everyone dances to soft rock.*

**JULIET** (*to a passing WAITER*)
White wine? Thanks.

**JULIAN**
Manuel? Bring more ice. Maria? Open the window. Everybody dance!

*BENNY, swashbuckling like Zorro, backs into JULIET, causing her to spill wine on her dress.*

**JULIET**
Oh, God! Look what you've done!

**BENNY**
It's white wine. Who's gonna notice?!

**JULIET**
I have to do something. Maria?!

*ROMEO stops a WAITER as he rushes past him.*

**ROMEO**
Oye —

**WAITER**
Yes, sir?

**ROMEO**
Digame —

**WAITER**
You speak Spanish?

**ROMEO**
Soy de Michoacán, hombre.

**WAITER**
¡Ay, Michoacán, que lindo!

*TOMMY enters.*

**ROMEO** (*referring to JULIET*)
Who is that chamaca over there? The one in white?

**WAITER**
¿Quién sabe? I was jobbed in for the night.

**ROMEO**
She's beautiful, ¿que no? Like a saint. Surrounded by fools and freaks.

**WAITER**
If you say so. Want another drink?

**ROMEO**
God never showed me beauty. Not until tonight.

**TOMMY** (*to ROMEO*)
Is that a fact, wetback?

**ROMEO**
What?

**TOMMY**
Who let you into my uncle's house?

**ROMEO**
Tommy. Chill. I'm not going to do anything.

**JULIAN**
Tommy? What's wrong? Why are you so upset?

**TOMMY**
Did you invite this wetback here tonight?

**JULIAN**
What wetback?

**TOMMY**
This one. Standing right in front of you!

**JULIAN**
Oh, come on, Tommy, you're the one causing all the trouble.

**TOMMY**
But, Julian —

**JULIAN**
Settle down, Tommy. I don't want a scene.

**TOMMY**
But, Julian, you can't let vagrants —

**JULIAN**
Are you high? I told you never to come to my house stoked —

**TOMMY**
"Stoked"?! I'm not "stoked"!

**JULIAN**
A lot of this stuff is cut bad. You know that! (*beat*) Manuel! More food!

**TOMMY**
I don't have to take this.

**JULIAN**
You're in my house. Act like family.

**TOMMY**
Family? We ain't got no family!

**JULIAN**
Tommy, get a grip. Or take it outside. Okay?

**TOMMY**
No prob, Julian. If total strangers . . . wetbacks . . . are more important to you, then you can take your yuppie stuff and shove it.

**JULIAN**
This is my house, Tommy. STOP THIS. RIGHT NOW.

**TOMMY**
Hey. I'm outta here.

(*to ROMEO*) I'll get you, man.

  *TOMMY exits.*

**BENNY** (*to JULIET*)
You know, if you just dance, your dress would dry up.

**JULIET** (*disgusted*)
What!?

**BENNY**
You know, drip dry?

**JULIET**
Excuse me.

**ROMEO**
Señorita, don't mind my, uh, my friend here, he's just a firecracker —

**BENNY**
I'm a wisecracker, vato, not a firecracker.

(*to JULIET*) And this guy here ain't my friend. He's my primo. Cheerio, sweetheart.

**ROMEO** (*taking her hand*)
¿Señorita? Con su permiso.

**JULIET** (*removing her hand*)
I'm sorry. I don't speak Spanish.

**ROMEO**
It's simply a courtesy.

      *He takes JULIET's hand again.*

Encantado de conocerle.

      *He tries to kiss her hand.*

**JULIET** (*removing her hand again*)
You shouldn't speak like that. I mean, in Spanish.

**ROMEO**
Then I'll be quiet.

**JULIET**
Yes?

**ROMEO**
And with only this — one finger barely resting on yours, I'll introduce my humble self —

**JULIET** (*getting into it*)
With no words. Remember?

**ROMEO**

Of course. Listen. (*pause*) The room is quiet. (*pause*) And this (*taking her hand firmly*) needs absolutely no translation.

**JULIET**

But if we continue touching hands —

**ROMEO**

Not anymore. We'll switch.

**JULIET**

Yes?

**ROMEO**

And kiss.

> *He kisses her on the cheek.*

Your cheek is softer than your hand. Gracias, señorita, for this most silent introduction.

**JULIET**

Now mine.

**ROMEO**

Yes?

> *JULIET tries to kiss ROMEO on the cheek, but at the last minute he turns his face towards her.*

**JULIET**

Oh.

**ROMEO**

Yes?

**JULIET**

Hello.

> *She kisses him lightly on the mouth.*

**ROMEO**

¡A sus órdenes!

> *He kisses her back fully.*

I only go where my heart tells me.

**JULIET**
Usually a faux pas, don't you think?

**ROMEO**
A fo what?

**JULIET**
A thing. A beautiful . . . quick . . . impromptu . . . kind of thing.

*ROMEO and JULIET kiss, this time both participating fully.*

**MARIA**
¡NIÑA!

**JULIET**
Oh God. It's Maria.

**ROMEO**
I want to talk to you.

**MARIA**
¡Niña!

**ROMEO**
Where?

**JULIET**
I don't know. Outside.

**ROMEO**
Where outside?

**JULIET**
In the backyard. Later. Near the magnolia.

**ROMEO**
In México, we call magnolias "yoloxochitl." Flowers of the heart.

**JULIET**
That's nice.

**MARIA**
¡NIÑA!

**ROMEO**
When?

**JULIET**
What?

**ROMEO**
What time? What time will I see you?

**JULIET**
I don't know.

**ROMEO**
Tell me.

**JULIET**
Later. Later.

**ROMEO**
Ok! Later.

**JULIET** (*to MARIA*)
¿Sí?

**MARIA**
Your father wants you.

**ROMEO**
You *do* speak Spanish.

**JULIET**
A little. Sometimes Maria talks to me in Spanish. Ciao.

**ROMEO**
What!?

**JULIET**
Just kidding. Adiós.

**ROMEO** (*to MARIA*)
Who is that girl?

**MARIA**
She lives here, manito. And you are a guest in her father's home.

**ROMEO**
She lives in *this* house?

**MARIA**
I have taken care of her since she was born.

**ROMEO**
She's rich. That's not good.

**MARIA**
The guapo who gets her, manito, is going to get a lot of money. But also a lot of love. She's a flower.

**ROMEO**
Yoloxochitl.

**MARIA**
A beautiful flower on this earth.

**ROMEO**
And her name?

**BENNY**
Hey, primo!

**MARIA**
Juliet. Juliet Bosquet. To you.

**BENNY** (*pulling out a flask*)
Look what I found.

**ROMEO**
¡Ay Benito!

**BENNY**
What's wrong?

**ROMEO**
I've sinned.

**BENNY**

Again?

**ROMEO**

Let's get out of here.

**BENNY**

Right now?

**ROMEO**

Right now. (*pause*) Something bad is going to happen. I know it.

*They exit.*

# Scene 10

*Moments later.*

**JULIET**

Maria? That good looking guy who just left? He kissed me.

**MARIA**

¿De veras?

**JULIET**

And I don't even know who he is.

**MARIA**

Your cousin Tommy knows him. He's illegal.

**JULIET**

But he speaks English.

**MARIA**

He's still illegal.

**JULIET**

And a gentleman. The only one at this party, really. To me anyway. (*beat*) Illegal. That ruins everything.

**MARIA**

I saw him kissing you. Puro mexicano.

**JULIET**

He told me the name for magnolias. In Spanish, I think.

**MARIA**

You better forget him fast, mija.

**JULIET**

But it's too late. I told him —

**MARIA**

Told him what?

**JULIET**

Nothing.

**MARIA**

If your father heard any of this, who knows what he would do?

*JULIAN and RUBEN are off to the side, toasting.*

**JULIAN**

To law school!

**RUBEN**

To life AFTER law school!

**JULIET**

Happy Halloween! Look at them. Two cowboys. From different continents. Giving orders. Always right.

**MARIA**

Men are like that, mija.

**JULIET**

They don't have to be. Do they, Maria? (*pause*) Do they?

**MARIA**

In this world, mija, some things never change.

**RUBEN**

Good night, Jules. Call me?

**JULIET**

Good night, Ruben. (*pause*) Thanks for coming.

> *RUBEN exits.*

I hate Dad's parties! Especially this one!

**MARIA**
Well, mija, in a few minutes, it will be midnight. Halloween will be over and Día de los Muertos —

**JULIET**
Day of the Dead.

**MARIA**
Will begin again. Tomorrow morning we'll celebrate with pan de muerto for breakfast —

**JULIET**
And then we'll eat candy skulls all day!

**MARIA**
Asina.

**MANUEL** (*entering and addressing MARIA*)
Pssst!

**MARIA**
But now, corazón, it's late. You should go to bed.

**JULIET**
Yeah. And dream of flowers. Flowers of the heart. Good night, Maria.

> *She exits.*

**MARIA**
Buenas noches, mija.

# Scene 11

**JULIAN** (*singing, drunk*)
"THE PARTY'S OVER. IT'S TIME TO CALL IT A DAY."

> *He clutches at MARIA.*

How about a tequila in my room?

**MARIA**
¡No, Julián!

**JULIAN**
Manuel, good night.

**MANUEL**
Sí.

> *He doesn't leave.*

**JULIAN**
Manuel, now. Good night now. NOW.

**MANUEL**
¡Ay! ¡Sí, señor!

> *He doesn't leave.*

**JULIAN**
"THE PARTY'S OVER. IT'S TIME TO CALL IT A DAY." Maria, come with me.

**MARIA**
But, Julián. I have to lock the house.

**JULIAN**
Later. You'll do that later. Later.

**MARIA** (*reluctantly*)
Bueno, Julián.

**JULIAN**
Now. Which way?

**MARIA**
This way, Julián, this way

> *JULIAN and MARIA exit. A CALAVERA carrying marigolds appears from the direction in which they exited.*

**MANUEL**
Buenas noches.

**CALAVERA #1**
Buenas.

*He drops a flower. Voices are heard offstage.*

**VOICES**
Trick or treat! Trick or treat!

*Another CALAVERA, also carrying marigolds, appears.*

**CALAVERA #2**
Saludos.

**MANUEL**
Welcome — both of you — to the house of Don Bosquet.

**CALAVERA #1**
Welcome to Day of the Dead.

*As MANUEL exits, another CALAVERA appears, also carrying marigolds.*

**CALAVERA #3**
Bienvenidos a todos.

**OFFSTAGE VOICES**
Trick or treat! Trick or treat!

**ALL CALAVERAS**
¡Bienvenidos!

*As the CALAVERAS follow MANUEL, they drop marigolds behind them.*

**CALAVERA #1**
Bienvenidos a Los Ángeles.

**CALAVERA #2**
A la casa Bosquet.

**CALAVERA #3**
¡A Día de los Muertos!

**ALL CALAVERAS**
¡Salud!

*They exit.*

# Scene 12

*November 1st, 12:30 a.m. The CORRIDISTA enters.*

**CORRIDISTA**

Ahora viene el amor
Y yo no sé qué hacer
Yo ya no quiero pelear
Pero a ella no la debo tener . . .

*Lights rise on JULIET, pacing back and forth.*

**JULIET**

I don't know what to do.

**CORRIDISTA**

Ahora viene el amor
Castigo de mi corazón
Soy de abajo
Pero ella es mi liberación . . .

*Lights rise on ROMEO and BENNY, roughhousing.*

**ROMEO**

She'll be there! She told me.

**BENNY**

You're crazy, man!

**JULIET**

I'll do it! I have to.

**CORRIDISTA**

Ahora viene el amor
Pa' uno que no debo tocar . . .
Pero yo no me muevo de aquí
Porque tengo derecho a vivir!
¡Ahora sí!

**ROMEO** (*seeing JULIET*)

She looks like a saint, Benny.

**BENNY**

¡Caramba, *Romeo*! For someone who says he's blind, you sure got your sights fixed now, mano.

**JULIET**

Where is he?

**BENNY**

Later, primo. I ain't gonna sleep in no bushes while you get laid.

(*to the CORRIDISTA*) Órale. Good costume.

> *BENNY exits.*

# Scene 13

**ROMEO**

Julieta.

**JULIET**

You're here.

**ROMEO**

Under the moon, you're more beautiful than the moon herself. I never told you my name. It's *Romeo*.

**JULIET**

*Romeo*. Spanish.

**ROMEO**

Or Romeo.

> *ROMEO and JULIET kiss.*

**MARIA** (*offstage*)

¡Ay no, Julián!

**JULIET** (*breaking away*)

You shouldn't have come.

**ROMEO**
Tonight, Julieta, I would find you, even if all the lights in your house were dark. Even if all the lights in the neighborhood were dark. Even if all the lights in the whole city were dark.

**JULIAN** (*offstage*)
One more tequila. Just one!

**JULIET**
I'm sorry, it's not a good time. (*beat*) Do you know my cousin Tommy?

**ROMEO**
El loco Tommy? Everybody knows him.

**JULIET**
What do you call him?

**ROMEO**
El loco Tommy. Crazy Tommy.

**JULIET**
Sorry. I don't speak Spanish.

**ROMEO**
That's funny. You look —

**JULIET**
Spanish?

**ROMEO**
Mexican. You look Mexican.

**JULIET**
Maybe. But I still don't speak it.

**ROMEO**
Tommy doesn't scare me.

**JULIET**
He's wild. He does things without thinking. And he doesn't care —

**ROMEO**
Cálmate, preciosa. Don't let all the hate in Tommy's sad life scare you.

**JULIET**
But you don't know —

**ROMEO**
Forget Tommy. And think of us. The night is giving us shelter and La Luna, Our Lady the Moon, has stopped for us, see?

*He tries to kiss her.*

¡Ay, Julieta, debemos de gozar —

**JULIET** (*pushing him away gently*)
What did Tommy call you? A wetback?

**ROMEO**
Yeah, that's what he called me.

**JULIET**
And are you?

**ROMEO** (*beat*)
Yeah. I am.

**JULIET**
You're a Mexican, but you speak English.

**ROMEO**
And you're American, but you look Mexican.

**JULIET**
Touché.

**ROMEO**
Asina.

**JULIET**
My father never wanted me to learn Spanish.

**ROMEO**
Why not? It's beautiful.

**MARIA** (*offstage*)
One minute, Julián!

**JULIET**
That's not my mother. It's Maria. Our maid.

**ROMEO** (*caressing her hair*)
I talked to her. She loves you like a mother.

**JULIET**
I know. But she's not my real mother.

**ROMEO**
And where is she? Your real mother?

**JULIET**
Somewhere. Not here.

**ROMEO**
A mother and a daughter should —

**JULIET**
What did you call the magnolias? In Spanish, I mean.

**ROMEO**
Yoloxochitl. But it's not Spanish. It's Nahuatl, the language they spoke in Mexico before it was Mexico.

**JULIET**
You know a lot about it then, don't you? About Mexico.

**ROMEO**
Julieta, I was born there.

**JULIET**
A wetback. Really?

**ROMEO**
Yes. But this is where I live. But I will always carry México with me, Julieta. Because she's beautiful. More beautiful than you are.

**JULIET** (*pleased with his passion and charm*)
Oh yeah? How often do you go there?

**ROMEO**
My mother and I visit sometimes, but it's dangerous —

**JULIET**
Because you might not be able to come back?

**ROMEO**
Not me. I can fake being American. You believed me.

**JULIET**
Yes. I did.

**ROMEO**
But my mother can't.

**JULIET**
She's illegal?

**ROMEO**
As illegal as me.

**JULIAN** (*offstage*)
¡María, ven aquí! María, don't leave!

**ROMEO**
And your mother, Julieta? Where is she?

> *MARIA enters, watching ROMEO and JULIET from the shadows.*

**JULIET**
She wasn't like my father. She was younger. She never got the education he did.

**ROMEO**
Julieta —

**JULIET**
She had an accent, I think. And she was pretty but not light enough. She was too dark, I think, not right for Dad's bank career. So he divorced her.

**ROMEO**
Julieta . . .

> *They kiss.*

. . . mi amor y mi corazón.

> *They kiss again.*

I'm alive, Julieta! For the first time in this country, I'm alive!

*MARIA steps out of the shadows, wearing a faded house robe and frayed slippers.*

**MARIA**
Julieta. Come inside.

**JULIET**
Oh God, she's here.

**ROMEO**
I adore you, worship you —

**MARIA**
If your father —

**JULIET** (*to ROMEO*)
Don't go. I'll be right back.

**ROMEO**
¡Dios mío! My mother says that things arranged at night always go bad. But if this is wrong, may God strike me dead!

**MARIA**
This is dangerous, mija.

**JULIET**
But Maria —

**MARIA**
No, Julieta. No.

**JULIET**
One minute. Just one more minute.

**MARIA**
Bueno, corazón. Just one.

**JULIET**
Romeo, you're wonderful. I think I could love you.

**ROMEO** (*taking her in his arms*)
Not as much as I could love you.

**MARIA**
Julieta.

**JULIET**
I should go.

**ROMEO**
Julieta, I promise. By Doña Luna, Our Lady the Moon, and all the moonlight you see around us —

**JULIET**
You're amazing!

**ROMEO**
— to love you.

**JULIET**
Totally amazing.

**ROMEO**
So let's get married.

> *Beat.*

**JULIET**
When?

**ROMEO**
¡Dios mío!

> *Beat.*

**JULIET**
Say something!

> *Beat.*

**ROMEO**
Tomorrow.

**JULIET**
When?! When tomorrow?!

**ROMEO**
I'll tell you tomorrow.

**MARIA**

¡CARAMBA, NIÑA! Your father!

**JULIET**

Good night, Romeo. Until tomorrow.

**ROMEO**

Hasta mañana. (*pause*) ¿Julieta?

**JULIET**

Yes?

**ROMEO**

May Doña Luna —

**JULIET**

The moon.

**ROMEO**

— fall on your eyes.

**JULIET**

And help us both rest. (*pause*) You're wonderful.

*She exits.*

**ROMEO**

Marriage?! ¡Dios mío! I have to see the priest.

*Beat.*

Gracias, Señor. I am blessed.

*He exits.*

# Scene 14

*November 1st, dawn. FATHER LAWRENCE's garden. It's a hydroponic garden with water tubes and neon lights shining on grids of leafy plants. A CALAVERA watches nearby.*

**FATHER LAWRENCE**
My little rainforest, look at you, raising your heads to the light. Every one of you messengers of God. Even though we may not know yet what your message could be. But, with God's mercy and the help of science, we will find your powers. And turn you into medicine. To cure the sick, the wounded, and the dying. Quiet and patient as you are, your power is still a force unknown. Some of you can make us well, but others can make us sick. And some of you can even kill. The Earth is frightening and vicious. Like Kali. But also sweet. Like the Virgin herself. And it is up to us, men and women, to choose which is which. Without study, we are merely animals, unable to exercise the free will given to us by God.

**ROMEO** (*entering*)
Buenas noches, padre.

*The CALAVERA exits.*

**FATHER LAWRENCE**
*Romeo,* it's not even dawn. Where have you been?

**ROMEO**
Padrecito, I have trespassed. I went where I wasn't wanted.

**FATHER LAWRENCE**
Did you?

**ROMEO**
And I met someone I never should have met. But still, padrecito, we met, and now only you can cure us. We're sick, padre, sick with love.

**FATHER LAWRENCE**
And Carolyn?

**ROMEO**
Carolyn?

**FATHER LAWRENCE**
How does she feel about all this?

**ROMEO**
I forgot about her already. But this one. ¡Ay, padre!

**FATHER LAWRENCE**
¡Ay, *Romeo*!

**ROMEO**
You could cure us in ten minutes.

**FATHER LAWRENCE**
What the hell are you talking about?

**ROMEO**
I want to get married.

**FATHER LAWRENCE**
To who?!

**ROMEO**
Juliet. Juliet Bosquet.

**FATHER LAWRENCE**
The banker's daughter? ¡Ay, no, *Romeo*! She's not the girl for you!

**ROMEO**
But I love her. And she loves me. And all we need is the blessed sacrament of marriage.

**FATHER LAWRENCE**
But *Romeo* —

**ROMEO**
Father, we kissed.

**FATHER LAWRENCE**
Yes, yes, of course.

**ROMEO**
When she was in my arms, Father, I could feel her breathing. Between my hands.

**FATHER LAWRENCE**
My God.

**ROMEO**
And afterwards —

**FATHER LAWRENCE**
Afterwards? After what?

**ROMEO**
When she looked up at me.

**FATHER LAWRENCE**
Up?

**ROMEO**
I had the strength —

**FATHER LAWRENCE**
Stop! That's enough. I don't want to hear another word.

**ROMEO**
Father, we didn't do that!

**FATHER LAWRENCE**
Not yet! But, but I can tell . . . you're more than ready . . . to run down the wrong path . . . oh yes!

**ROMEO**
Yes!

**FATHER LAWRENCE**
No!

**ROMEO**
To marriage. How can that be wrong? I want to get married, Father. Today. This morning.

**FATHER LAWRENCE**
You can't get married today. And you know why. Better than I do. It's the Day of the Dead. Not the time to begin new things.

**ROMEO**

But padrecito, God brought us together. And now we want to be married in His eyes. And follow His will.

**FATHER LAWRENCE**

Well . . . maybe . . . but . . .

**ROMEO**

Julieta and me, I swear to you, padre, we will love each other forever. May God strike me dead if I ever stop loving her.

**FATHER LAWRENCE**

Holy Mary Mother and Joseph, you're in a bad way!

**ROMEO**

Father, I am so full of love.

**FATHER LAWRENCE**

You don't have to convince me. I see it.

**ROMEO**

I think God brought Juliet into my life for a purpose.

**FATHER LAWRENCE**

And what might that purpose be?

**ROMEO**

As a test. Father, she is the only good thing that has ever happened to me in this hard country.

**FATHER LAWRENCE**

¡Ay, *Romeo*! It hurts me to hear you say that. America wasn't always like this. So full of hate. There was a time, long before you were born, when love filled us all. We marched. We felt strong. United. "¡El pueblo! ¡Unido! ¡Jamás será vencido!" Yes, I chanted in Spanish! So many of us were happy then. And confident. And proud. We were very proud.

**ROMEO**

Yes, Father?

**FATHER LAWRENCE**

But today everyone has forgotten how to be patient. Everybody is against everything: taxes, regulations, law, and order. There are many — too many

— who think the only time the government hears them is when they bomb and kill. It's senseless! Senseless! Look at these plants, *Romeo*. From the rainforest. One of the most delicate habitats on earth. We're killing them daily. Why? How can we kill something given us to us by God, before we even know why he gave it to us? Before we find out what goodness might be inside of them?

**ROMEO**
So you'll do it, Father?

**FATHER LAWRENCE**
Everything is growing beyond us now. Ozone layers, shrinking rainforests, nuclear wastes that we don't know what the hell to do with. All of our precious God given potential is slipping. Because we no longer love. We no longer respect.

**ROMEO**
So you'll do it? This morning?

**FATHER LAWRENCE**
This morning?

**ROMEO**
The marriage!

**FATHER LAWRENCE**
Oh yes, the marriage. God listens. I know he does. But even so, sometimes we need to push Him a little. You're both from good Mexican families . . . even if Julian —

**ROMEO**
Father, you said it yourself, how can love be bad?

**FATHER LAWRENCE**
Your mind is set?

**ROMEO**
I will never love anyone else the way I love her. Father, she is beautiful.

**FATHER LAWRENCE**
Love. It always begins in young men's eyes. But then it moves quickly to other places.

**ROMEO**
So you'll do it? This morning?

**FATHER LAWRENCE**
This business of Chicano fighting Chicano has to end. Yes.

**ROMEO**
You'll do it? Yes? Yes?

**FATHER LAWRENCE**
Yes. Yes, yes. This morning I'll do it. But now you should go. It's dawn. I have mass in fifteen minutes.

**ROMEO**
Thank you, padrecito, thank you.

**FATHER LAWRENCE**
*¿Romeo?*

**ROMEO**
Yes, Father?

**FATHER LAWRENCE**
Go straight home. The streets are not safe. For you. Or anybody.

*He exits.*

**ROMEO**
Sure, Father.

# Scene 15

*November 1st, 6 a.m. Loud street sounds rise. MANUEL enters.*

**MANUEL**
Dime, joven, por favor —

**ROMEO**
You again? What are you doing out here?

**MANUEL**
I'm working, mijo. What do you think?

*A trick or treater, in drag, steps out of the shadows.*

**DRAG TRICK-OR-TREATER**
Compañero, trick or treat!

**ROMEO**
¡Caramba! You're old enough to be my sister.

**DRAG TRICK-OR-TREATER**
¡Caramba! I AM your sister.

*The DRAG TRICK-OR-TREATER exits.*

**BENNY** (*stepping out of the shadows*)
What's the matter, *Romeo*?

**ROMEO**
Benny! You scared me!

**BENNY**
I scared you? Haven't you ever seen a boy toy before?

**ROMEO**
Chale. Sure. The streets, mano, are full of everything.

**BENNY**
You're awfully relaxed, chulito.

**ROMEO**
I'm just tired, primo.

**BENNY**
Why are you tired? Come on, you can tell me. I keep chismes to myself.

**ROMEO**
Like hell you do.

**BENNY**
So, how's it hanging? Loose? Real loose? How loose?

**ROMEO**
What are you talking about, Benny?

**BENNY**

Did you give it to her?

**ROMEO**

No! I didn't touch her. She deserves something good. Not a roll in her back-yard.

**BENNY**

I called you last night. Your mother said you didn't come in.

**ROMEO**

I was busy.

**BENNY**

El loco Tommy called too.

**ROMEO**

What does he want?

**BENNY**

He wants to mess with you.

**ROMEO**

Yeah, right.

**BENNY**

Yeah. For sure. But don't worry. I told him you don't need any help when it comes to messing yourself over.

**ROMEO**

¿Qué te pica, hombre? I went to the pinche party like you wanted.

**BENNY**

He wants to kill you, man.

**ROMEO**

I don't think so. Because looking for me would take too much time away from his "extracurricular drug activities."

**BENNY**

I'm telling you, he has it out for us, primo.

**ROMEO**

So what? Lots of people don't like us.

**BENNY**

Yeah. (*beat*) But someday, someday, I'm gonna set him straight.

**ROMEO**

Hey, primo, the Bosquets, are they Mexican?

**BENNY**

Yeah. I mean, I THINK they are.

**ROMEO**

Old man Bosquet doesn't live with his wife.

**BENNY**

Yeah. Instead he's got a maid. Whoo! We all need maids sometimes.

**ROMEO**

And Tommy is completely loco. And none of them, even the old man, talks with an accent. And they don't live in the barrio. So I'm wondering, are they Mexican? Really Mexican?

**BENNY**

To the bone, mano. To the bone.

  *MARIA enters.*

**MARIA**

*Romeo*, al fin.

**BENNY**

Another trick or treater.

**ROMEO**

Buenas noches, María.

**MARIA**

I need to speak with you. In private.

**BENNY**

No treat, I guess. Just a trick. Hey, primo, don't give her what nobody else got tonight.

(*to MARIA*) Buenas noches, señora. Ten cuidado que no te lo comas entero.

**MARIA**

¡Sangrón! ¡Malcriado! ¡Y cabrón!

**BENNY**

Hey, *Romeo*. She's a Mexican. A REAL Mexican.

(*to MARIA*) Mucho gusto.

 *He exits.*

# Scene 16

**MARIA**

Juliet wanted me to find you. Pero, I want to tell you something. Yo te conozco, mosco. La niña tiene honra, m'entiendes?

**ROMEO**

Everybody's out to get me!

**MARIA**

All I'm saying is, she's a good girl. Treat her with respect.

**ROMEO**

I want to marry her, señora.

**MARIA**

¡Híjole! Marry! That's a very nice word.

**ROMEO**

I saw the priest last night. Tell Julieta to come this morning for confession, and afterwards he said he'd marry us.

**MARIA**

This morning? You gotta be kidding. It's Día de los Muertos.

**ROMEO**

¿Y qué? They say the dead do everything the living do. They even fall in love and marry.

**MARIA**

Yeah. Love never dies.

**ROMEO**

And tonight, María, you'll help us? It's our wedding night, tú sabes?

**MARIA**

You're broke.

**ROMEO**

Sí. No tengo dinero.

**MARIA**

For the poor, the only wealth is love.

# Scene 17

*November 1st, 8 a.m. Lights rise on JULIET in her bathrobe.*

**JULIET**

Maria promised to return in half an hour. Maybe she couldn't find him.

*MARIA enters.*

What's wrong? You look sad.

**MARIA**

I stopped to eat.

**JULIET**

Good.

**MARIA**

And then I saw *Romeo.*

**JULIET**

And? (*pause*) Maria?

**MARIA**

And now, I have to rest.

**JULIET**

But what did he say?!

**MARIA**

It's a jungle out there. Even in the morning.

**JULIET**

Maria! What did he say!!!?

**MARIA**

Can you go to confession with Father Lawrence in one hour?

**JULIET**

Yes . . . but . . . Maria, does he still want to, you know, get married?

**MARIA**

Well, after confession, mija —

**JULIET**

Maria!!!!

**MARIA**

After confession, he said the priest would marry you.

**JULIET**

Yes!

>   *She throws off her robe, revealing a white outfit underneath.*

I knew it!

**MARIA**

Look at you! All ready and excited! You better get to the church, honey!

**JULIET**

And then Romeo will come. Maria? And spend the night?

**MARIA**

Of course.

**JULIET**

Without Dad knowing? Maria, please, you have to help us.

**MARIA**

Of course, I will help you. Both of you.

(*embracing JULIET*) Julieta. Mija. I have always loved you like my own daughter. I know you even better than my own daughter.

**JULIET**

Thank you, Maria. Thank you.

**MARIA**

And I want you to have everything, mija. Everything.

# Scene 18

*November 1st, 9 a.m. Lights rise on FATHER LAWRENCE's garden. ROMEO, still in his painter's whites, has a red sash around his waist. FATHER LAWRENCE has on formal vestments.*

**FATHER LAWRENCE**

This morning, thanks to God, we are filled with happiness. No matter what the future brings.

*JULIET and MARIA enter. JULIET runs into ROMEO's arms.*

An angel has arrived. Her feet hardly touching the ground.

**JULIET**

Father Lawrence. Good morning. And Romeo. Buenos días.

**FATHER LAWRENCE**

Ah! You speak Spanish now?

**JULIET**

I will.

**ROMEO** (*placing a rebozo around JULIET's shoulders*)

Mi paloma, mi sol, y mi alma. Bless us with your holy ceremony, Father, and then death itself can do anything it wants.

**FATHER LAWRENCE**

Thinking of death, *Romeo*? At such a happy moment?

**ROMEO**

Why not? In México we have a saying: "Death is always around the corner." But soon, padrecito, with your help, I can die. And in dying say that she was mine.

**FATHER LAWRENCE**
You Mexicans, please forgive me, always get so emotional.

*ROMEO and JULIET kiss, as if forever.*

In the United States, you should learn to be more moderate . . . your love will last longer if you take it a little bit slower . . .

*ROMEO and JULIET are now locked into a firm embrace.*

. . . we're young for such a short period of time . . . I think we should begin. In the name of the Father, Son, and Holy Ghost . . .

*MANUEL enters.*

**MARIA** (*to MANUEL*)
Ay, Manuel, look at her, the beautiful bride! She's a wildflower searching for love.

**MANUEL**
Yes, and marrying on the day we honor dead children.

**JULIET**
Yes. I will. I mean, I do.

**MANUEL** (*beckoning offstage*)
¡Compadres! ¡Vengan! Come to the wedding!

*CALAVERAS begin to appear.*

(*to CALAVERAS*) Compadres, a wedding on Día de los Chicos! With this wedding, they celebrate our deaths.

**ROMEO** (*affectionately imitating JULIET*)
I will. I mean, I do.

**MANUEL**
These two children are making vows that will last forever. And we, compadres, have two days to celebrate with them. Two days before we must die. Again.

*The CALAVERAS stand around FATHER LAWRENCE, ROMEO, and JULIET, who do not notice them. Lights dim on the stage tableaux. Halloween is over, and El Día de los Chicos, the first Day of the Dead, set aside to honor dead children, has begun in Los Angeles once again.*

# Scene 19

*November 1st, noon. Lights rise on MANUEL on yet another errand. A police siren rises. MANUEL stops briefly, then keeps walking. BENNY steps out from the shadows.*

**BENNY**
Is that you, *Romeo*?

**MANUEL**
Benny. Go home.

**BENNY**
What home? These days all everybody wants to do is fight, man.

**MANUEL**
Not me.

**BENNY**
Oh, yeah?

**MANUEL**
I used to be like that once. But not anymore.

**BENNY**
The whole barrio's going at it. In the morning two guys. In the night, one. People get shot because their hair is too long. Other people get shot because they got the wrong color eyes. People are crazy.

*From the shadows, a cigarette is lit, another incendiary moment.*

**TOMMY** (*stepping out from the shadows*)
Hey, Benny? Let's talk. Huh? A few words.

**BENNY**
A few words? Why not more? How about a couple of words, Tommy, and a couple of chingazos?

**TOMMY**
I could do that, Benny.

**BENNY**
Well, what are you waiting for? An invitation?

**TOMMY**

You know, Benny, lots of people are wondering. You're "friends" with Romeo, right? Real close?

**BENNY**

What do you mean "friends"? He's my primo, you maricón —

**TOMMY**

Hey, man, take it easy. Everybody's looking at us.

**BENNY**

Nobody sees nothing in the street.

> *ROMEO enters.*

**TOMMY**

Hey Romeo, you know what I think?

**BENNY**

Forget him, man. You started messing with me.

**TOMMY** (*to ROMEO*)

Romeo, I think you're a crook and a thief.

**ROMEO**

Tommy, I'm not a thief, man.

**TOMMY**

You break into people's houses.

**ROMEO**

No! ¿Cómo se dice? I'm a "changed man." Asina. You don't know me.

**TOMMY**

Don't try and make excuses, wetback. You broke into my uncle's house and now you have to pay for it.

**ROMEO**

I've never hurt you, Tommy. And now we're close. I can't tell you why right now. But, believe me, I respect your name. As if it was mine.

**BENNY**

Primo, what the hell —

> *A CALAVERA slides a switchblade towards BENNY.*

**CALAVERA**
Ándale.

**BENNY**
Hey Tommy, vendido?

> *He picks up switchblade.*

Let's take it outside. You still owe me from yesterday, ¿recuerdas?

> *The CALAVERA slides another switchblade towards TOMMY.*

**CALAVERA**
Ándale.

**ROMEO**
Benito —

**TOMMY**
I'm ready.

**BENNY**
Show me what you have, cabrón.

**ROMEO**
¡Benito! Don't do this!

> *BENNY and TOMMY fight.*

**ROMEO**
¡Benito! Stop! Tommy, Benito, the sergeant said he didn't want no more fights. Tommy! ¡Benito! ¡Párense, pendejos!

> *TOMMY, under ROMEO's arm, stabs BENNY.*

**BENNY**
¡Ay! He got me! Why the hell did you get in the way?!

**ROMEO**
¡Ay, Benito! Don't be angry.

**BENNY**
Look at this!

**ROMEO**
You're not that hurt.

**BENNY**
You're wrong, primo. This is not a scratch.

**TOMMY**
Wetbacks. Scum. Bloodsuckers all of you.

>    *TOMMY exits.*

**BENNY**
Get me outta here.

**ROMEO**
Benito, you're gonna be alright.

**BENNY**
Why the hell do you always screw me over? GET ME OUTTA HERE!

**ROMEO** (*struggling with him*)
Okay, primo. Okay.

**BENNY**
Put me down. ¡Ay! Put me down.

**ROMEO**
Okay, primo, Benito, okay.

**BENNY** (*looking at the wound in his chest*)
It's not too big. Smaller than a gunshot. But just as deadly. ¿*Romeo*?

>    *He tries to laugh.*

*Romeo*, you know what? Tomorrow I'm gonna be a dead man.

**ROMEO**
Benito, don't say that.

**BENNY**
Yeah! I'm gonna celebrate this Day of the Dead right! ¡Ay! Why did you get in the way?! I had him!

**ROMEO**
I was trying to help you. I wanted to stop it.

**BENNY**

I had him! You're always at the wrong place at the wrong time.

**ROMEO**

¡Ay, Benito, por favor! I'm sorry!

> *A CALAVERA appears in front of BENNY, unseen by ROMEO who has his back to it.*

**BENNY** (*to CALAVERA*)

You?

(*to ROMEO*) It's time for you to leave, primo.

**ROMEO**

No! Benny!

**BENNY**

It'll be alright ¡Ándale! The last thing you need, you crazy wetback, is the cops finding you with a dead body. Go. GO! ¡¡¡VETE!!!

**ROMEO**

¡Ay, Dios mío! ¿Por qué me viene este mal?

**BENNY** (*staring at CALAVERA*)

Is this it?

> *He dies.*

**ROMEO**

Benny? ¿Benito? ¿Primo? Benito, you were hurt because of me.

> *The knife drops out of BENNY's hand. ROMEO picks it up.*

**ROMEO**

Tommy! Tommy! ¡Asesino! You killed my primo!

> *The knife falls out of ROMEO's hand.*

**ROMEO**

¡Ay, Julieta! Loving you has made me soft.

**MANUEL**

*Romeo*, run! Benny ran out of time, and now he's looking for the thirteen heavens.

*ROMEO sees MANUEL as a calavera for the first time.*

**ROMEO**

You're Death, aren't you? Coming for Benny. I feel it. Tezcatlipoca's smoke is rising, covering us with the smell of death.

**MANUEL**

¡Pélate! Get out of here!

**ROMEO** (*picking up the knife*)

No. Not until Tommy sees the other side. Tommy! TOMMY!!!!

# Scene 20

*TOMMY enters.*

**ROMEO**

You killed Benny. But his soul, man, his soul is flying, all around us. See it? It's right over there.

**TOMMY**

Go back to the jungle, you stupid Indian.

**ROMEO**

Nobody goes to the thirteen heavens alone. One of us has to go with him.

**TOMMY**

You liked him so much, you go with him —

**ROMEO**

Or maybe you.

> *They fight. ROMEO stabs TOMMY. TOMMY falls into the arms of the CALAVERA, who places him on the ground.*

**CALAVERA**

¡Romeo! ¡Vete! He's dead.

**ROMEO**

Dios mío.

**CALAVERA**

And López is going to blame it on you. Run. ¡Ándale! Con prisa!

**ROMEO**

The padre. I'll go see the padrecito.

*He exits.*

# Scene 21

*A police siren rises, then fades. The CORRIDISTA enters, stands by the dead BENNY, and sings "Ranchera Sin Razón."*

**CORRIDISTA** (*singing*)

> Mal destino en la vida es la cosa más terrible.
> Es la cosa que nos hace siempre llorar.
> ¡Nacer pobre sin remedio!
> ¡Vivir solo sin cariño!
> ¡Aguantarse por toda la vida!
> ¡Es destino sin sentido¡
> ¡Es pecado sin razón!

*CANDELARIA and SGT. LOPEZ enter.*

**CANDELARIA**

¡Ay, Sargento López! Pobre Benito!

**CORRIDISTA** (*singing*)

> ¡Ay ya ya yay!
> La vida es castigo.
> ¡Ay ya ya yay!
> Pecado sin razón.

*JULIAN enters.*

**JULIAN**

Tony?

**SGT. LOPEZ**

What, Julian?

**JULIAN**
I want an eye for an eye.

**CANDELARIA**
Sargento López, I'm sure it was self-defense.

**JULIAN**
It's in the Bible, Tony.

**CANDELARIA**
But *Romeo* was defending the honor of his primo and his familia.

**JULIAN**
Tommy's blood is ours, Tony. You go after him with everything you've got. Or else you're gonna hear from me. Tony? TONY?

**SGT. LOPEZ**
All right!

(*to the COP*) Put out an all-points bulletin.

**JULIAN**
I want him out of the country —

**SGT. LOPEZ**
— where he belongs. I know, Julian. I know.

**CANDELARIA**
¡Ay, Sargento López! ¡Pobre Benito!

**SGT. LOPEZ**
Señora Martínez, let me help you.

**CANDELARIA**
In México, men kill for honor!

**SGT. LOPEZ**
Yes, Señora Martínez. But this is not México. It's the United States.

    *CANDELARIA exits.*

**CORRIDISTA** (*singing*)
    To be born without a future is the worst thing
    Life can offer.

It's the only thing that tears can never erase.
To be poor and have no options!
To live lonely with no kindness!
To accept injustice daily!
To live life without redemption!
Greater curse no man can claim!
¡Ay ya ya yay!
To live is to suffer!
¡Ay ya ya yay!
A curse no prayer can cure.

**COP**
Sgt. Lopez?

**SGT. LOPEZ**
Yeah?

**COP**
Should I call the wagon? Sir?

**SGT. LOPEZ**
Yeah. Call the wagon.

*SGT. LOPEZ and the COP exit.*

**CORRIDISTA** (*singing*)
¡Ay ya ya yay!
La vida es castigo.
¡Ay ya ya yay!
Pecado sin razón.

*The stage is bare, except for the two dead bodies of TOMMY and BENNY. After a beat, TOMMY CALAVERA sits up and sees BENNY lying on the ground nearby.*

**TOMMY CALAVERA**
Hey, Benny?

*After a pause, BENNY CALAVERA answers.*

**BENNY CALAVERA** (*quietly*)
What?

**TOMMY CALAVERA**
I ain't through with you yet. Get up.

**BENNY CALAVERA** (*resigned*)
Maldito.

> *He rises.*

I'm ready.

> *The two men square off yet again, this time as calaveras. The CORRIDISTA strums the guitar once.*

# ACT 2
## Scene 1

*November 1st, 6 p.m. Lights rise on JULIET.*

**JULIET**
It's dark. Six o'clock. Tonight the moon, what did he call it? Doña Luna. Our Lady the Moon can't rise soon enough. Oh, Romeo. *Romeo.* Come. I'm married, but not yet a woman. Married but still so unmarried.

**MARIA** (*entering, with flowers*)
Julieta. These are for you.

**JULIET**
From Romeo? No, Ruben. Maria. What's wrong?

**MARIA**
He's dead.

**JULIET**
Romeo?

**MARIA**
Your father saw it too. Right on the street.

**JULIET**
Romeo?

**MARIA**
Tommy. And *Romeo*, el pelón, is hiding.

**JULIET**
Romeo killed Tommy?

**MARIA**
With a knife.

**JULIET**
Romeo?

**MARIA**
He's no better than a dog, this secret husband of yours.

**JULIET**

Maria, no! You're wrong. Tommy's always been crazy, but Romeo, Romeo has sense. Maria, he's smart, he tells me things —

**MARIA**

Men lie, Julieta. They say things just for show. Even your Romeo.

**JULIET**

No. Not Romeo. He's young, but not a murderer.

**MARIA**

Yes, he is. And hiding. Like a crook, a pelón.

**JULIET**

What is that word you're using, "pelón"?

**MARIA**

A troublemaker, fast talker, lowlifer. A loser, Julieta. A loser.

**JULIET**

No! Not Romeo! Maria, I know him. I have to speak with him.

**MARIA**

He killed your cousin.

**JULIET**

He's my husband! Maria, Romeo is hiding? Because of murder? With a knife?

**MARIA**

This house, Julieta, is cursed. This morning, we ran to the church. Like school girls. And now . . .

**JULIET**

I want you to go find him —

**MARIA**

I can't.

**JULIET**

Maria! Do it! Do you hear me? DO IT.

**MARIA** (*shocked*)

¡Julieta!

**JULIET**

Bring me my husband. Give him back this ring. I won't wear it again until I speak with him. Now. Do it now.

**MARIA** (*taking the ring*)

A wife . . . and a señora. It happens so quickly.

**JULIET**

Go.

**MARIA**

Sí, señora. (*pause*) Sí, señora.

> *MARIA exits.*

# Scene 2

> *Lights rise on FATHER LAWRENCE's garden.*

**FATHER LAWRENCE**

¿*Romeo*? Bad luck seems to follow you like a dog, chamaco. (*beat*) I have a message. From Sgt. Lopez.

**ROMEO**

He's related to Tommy. He wants to kill me.

**FATHER LAWRENCE**

Lopez doesn't want to kill you. But he does want you out of the country. Back in Mexico.

**ROMEO**

But, Father, I've lived here since I was ten! This is my country. Not Mexico.

**FATHER LAWRENCE**

But, *Romeo*, you and your mother came over —

**ROMEO**

Eight years ago! When I was a child!

**FATHER LAWRENCE**

You have to go back to Mexico. So what? It's a big world out there.

**ROMEO**

No, I have a life here now.

**FATHER LAWRENCE**

*Romeo*, you're a murderer here. But if you leave, mijo, you'll be able to have a better life.

**ROMEO**

But I want a better life here. Padrecito, people fly here from all over the world. And they're not sent back. Political asylum — that's what they get. There's nothing for me in Mexico. What do you think I am? A pendejo who just crossed over?

**FATHER LAWRENCE**

*Romeo*, listen to me. I know you're scared, and your heart is here in L.A. But right now, you're out of balance.

**ROMEO**

Father, please.

**FATHER LAWRENCE**

But philosophy can change that. *Romeo*, hear me out. With philosophy will come peace. "Philo," love, and "sofia," wisdom, together make "philosofia," wisdom with love, or love and wisdom. Either way —

**ROMEO**

Father!

**FATHER LAWRENCE**

Hear me out, mijo, hear me out! With philosophy you will be able to transform this adversity —

**ROMEO**

You know, sometimes you are so full of it.

**FATHER LAWRENCE**

Great! Close your ears.

**ROMEO**

What good are ears if "wise men" don't know what the hell they're talking about!

**FATHER LAWRENCE**

You know what they're saying on the streets about you? You're an illegal two-bit punk, who killed another two-bit punk in broad daylight. And you did it with a knife. And then you ran. *Romeo*, you ran.

**ROMEO**

Father, you don't know what happened out there. I saw death, Father. I saw it on the street. Right after Benny died.

**FATHER LAWRENCE**

You saw your future, mijo. Because right now, in this city, you're free game. Dead meat.

**ROMEO**

Father, you don't know how I'm suffering! Just married to Juliet. And even before embracing her for the first time, this? I killed him, Father. Tommy! I want to throw myself on the ground, Father. I want to beg God to kill me. I want to die. I want to die.

*A loud knock is heard.*

The cops!

*Another loud knock is heard.*

**FATHER LAWRENCE**

This house is God's sanctuary. If it's the police, I'll talk to them. But be ready to run, mijo —

*MARIA enters.*

Maria, how can I help you?

**MARIA**

Where's Romeo? ¡ROMEO!

**FATHER LAWRENCE**

Quiet! With that voice, you'll wake the dead.

**ROMEO**

¿María? ¿Cómo está Julieta?

**MARIA**

¡Pelón! How do you think? You've broken her heart and scared her to death with this killing.

**ROMEO**

Julieta thinks I'm a pelón? María, I wanted to make her my queen!

**MARIA**

And now she's crying like a widow.

**ROMEO**

¡Julieta!

**MARIA**

She thinks the cops are going to cut you down on the street before she has a chance to see you one more time.

**ROMEO**

María, I defended Benito and his honor. But at the same time, I killed Julieta's love?

**MARIA**

¡Pelón! You've brought her nothing but hate, when all she wanted was love.

**ROMEO**

Father, beg God to come and take me! I don't want to live like this! I don't want to live!

**FATHER LAWRENCE**

Hombre, listen to me! You just told us you defended Benito's honor. Like a man. And before that, you were married. Like a man. So now act like a man.

*MARIA notices FATHER LAWRENCE's garden. She picks at some plants and smells them.*

**ROMEO**

You're right, Father. I'll go. I'll go. And disappear.

**FATHER LAWRENCE**

*¡Romeo!* Listen to me. Tommy wanted to kill you, and you killed him. God chose you to survive. And now Sgt. Lopez, who could arrest you, wants to deport you instead. *Romeo,* there is good in bad and bad in good. Go to your Julieta and comfort her. And then leave. Go to Tijuana. But do it tonight.

**MARIA**

One more day is all López will need to track you down.

**FATHER LAWRENCE**

Romeo, go to Mexico. Tonight, mijo.

**ROMEO**

In México we say the only thing that is forever is death. I can come back. Eventually.

**FATHER LAWRENCE**

Of course you can.

**ROMEO**

I'll go see Julieta. And then I'll leave.

**FATHER LAWRENCE**

Tonight. Not tomorrow morning. Tonight, mijo.

**ROMEO**

Gracias, padrecito. Gracias.

*FATHER LAWRENCE and ROMEO embrace. ROMEO exits.*

**FATHER LAWRENCE**

Maria, what are you doing?

**MARIA**

I didn't know you grew yerbas, Father. What do you do with them?

**FATHER LAWRENCE**

Keep them alive. It's a hobby.

**MARIA**

Some of these plants grow in my country. Not here.

**FATHER LAWRENCE**

No. You're mistaken. These are very rare plants. From endangered areas in the rainforest.

**MARIA**

You import them?

**FATHER LAWRENCE**

Of course not. People bring them in. For me.

**MARIA** (*chuckling*)
Contrabando. Across international borders! And a priest!

**FATHER LAWRENCE**
Don't laugh. I'm protecting them. These frail plants are the work of God.

*Lights rise on ROMEO approaching JULIET's house.*

**ROMEO**
¿Julieta?

**FATHER LAWRENCE**
How can we kill something created by God? There may be a purpose, there MUST be a purpose for these frail plants that we don't yet understand.

*Lights rise on JULIET.*

**JULIET**
You came.

**ROMEO**
Yoloxochitl. My flower. My love.

**MARIA**
Of course, Father. We have no right to destroy anything which God creates.

*ROMEO and JULIET embrace.*

# Scene 3

*ROMEO and JULIET exit, arm in arm. MANUEL strolls by, keeping guard.*

# Scene 4

*Lights rise on JULIAN and RUBEN having drinks.*

**JULIAN**
Sorry, but Juliet isn't feeling well tonight. Tommy's death was a big shock to her.

**RUBEN**

I'm sure. You've kept her well protected.

**JULIAN**

Tommy always ran with the wrong crowd. But what could I do? His father's gone — and it fell to me to keep track of him. I hope you don't think, Ruben —

**RUBEN**

Can't you contact him? Tommy's father, I mean —

**JULIAN**

He's in prison.

**RUBEN**

Oh.

**JULIAN**

For a felony.

**RUBEN**

I see.

**JULIAN**

He's not coming out, Ruben. You understand?

**RUBEN**

Hey! Things happen! I understand.

**JULIAN**

You grow up around here, especially in the time when my brother and I were coming up —

**RUBEN**

Julian, it's okay. Situations get out of control.

**JULIAN**

They keep him alive, but he might as well be dead.

**RUBEN**

All right. Okay. It's okay.

**JULIAN**

I did everything I could to keep Juliet away from the street. Gangs. Guns.

**RUBEN**
Julian, I still want to marry her.

**JULIAN**
But now I want to finish off that old life. I want it to die with Tommy. Every single remnant of it.

**RUBEN**
Okay, Julian. Okay.

**JULIAN**
What Juliet needs, Ruben, is what I've always given her — stability.

**RUBEN**
And so will I, Julian. So will I.

**JULIAN**
I did everything I could.

**RUBEN**
I should go, Julian.

**JULIAN**
Wait.

**RUBEN**
Yeah, Julian?

**JULIAN**
There'll never be another embarrassment like this in our family again. I promise.

**RUBEN**
Of course.

    *They exit.*

# Scene 5

*November 2nd, 3 a.m. Lights rise on ROMEO and JULIET. The*
*CORRIDISTA plays the guitar nearby.*

**JULIET**

Don't go!

**ROMEO**

I have to. The moon is setting.

**JULIET**

But it's practically the middle of the night.

**ROMEO**

The moon is almost gone, Julieta. I have to go.

**JULIET**

No. Stay. You can stay.

**ROMEO**

Okay. I'll stay. God, Julieta, with you I have lived!

(*embracing her*) Mi alma, talk to me. Tell me things.

**JULIET**

Are we going to see each other again?

**ROMEO**

Of course, paloma. Someday, we're going to be viejitos, little old people, sitting
in our chairs, with dry food on our chests. And we're going to laugh, Julieta,
about how we started. You and me. We're going to laugh.

**JULIET**

We're never going to be old. You look sad.

**ROMEO**

We're both sad. Sadness makes the blood sink into the body. Un beso, y me
voy. I have to go.

*They kiss.*

**JULIET**
Romeo? No, *Romeo*. Your name is really *Romeo*.

**ROMEO**
Or Romeo.

> *They kiss again.*

I'll be back, Julieta. And when I return, I'll never leave.

> *He kisses her.*

Hasta luego, mi reina. My queen.

**JULIET**
Goodbye.

**ROMEO**
No. See you later. Hasta luego.

**JULIET**
Hasta luego.

**ROMEO** (*pleased at her attempt at Spanish*)
Ándale, reina.

> *He exits.*

# Scene 6

> *MARIA enters.*

**JULIET**
He left.

**MARIA**
Good. It's still dark. He'll cross the border before day.

**JULIET**
Maria, what is it like to wake up with someone in the morning? After the sun is up?

**MARIA**

Sometimes, niña, it's like paradise. But now you should sleep. You've had a very long day.

**JULIET**

It's still my wedding night. Maria, stay with me. Okay?

**MARIA**

Bueno, mija. Bueno.

**JULIET**

It's like this with Dad, isn't it?

**MARIA**

Go to sleep, mija.

**JULIET**

He comes and goes.

**MARIA**

Men are like that.

**JULIET**

I'm sorry, Maria. I'm sorry I said those terrible things that hurt you.

**MARIA** (*embracing JULIET*)

It's all right, mija. It's all right.

# Scene 7

*Moments later. Lights rise on ROMEO. At the same time, nearby
in the shadows, a cigarette is lit, another incendiary moment.*

**ROMEO**

Benny?

*A CALAVERA steps out of the shadows, nearly colliding with ROMEO.*

**CALAVERA**

Sorry to scare you, chamaco. It's just that I'm in a little bit of a hurry. It's the second Day of the Dead.

**ROMEO**

So what?

**CALAVERA**

El Día de los Difuntos, the Day of the Dearly Departed Adults. Yesterday we honored dead children. Today we honor adults. Which one are you?

**ROMEO**

Get away from me.

*They exit.*

# Scene 8

*November 2nd, 7 a.m. JULIAN is fixing his tie, ready to go to work. JULIET enters.*

**JULIAN**

Good morning. Still not feeling well?

**JULIET**

No.

**JULIAN**

Carrying on won't bring Tommy back, you know. If you act too emotional, people will think you're putting on a show.

**JULIET**

I'm not faking it.

**JULIAN**

I'm not saying you shouldn't be upset. This punk who murdered Tommy, probably a gang member, is running around loose and fancy free.

**JULIET**

Who is that, Dad?

**JULIAN**

Romeo Martinez. That wetback who entered my house under false pretenses.

**JULIET**

It was Halloween. Your big night to impress everyone. Everything was fine. Until Tommy showed up.

**JULIAN**

By the way, Tony thinks this Romeo went to TJ. He is a Mexican, after all. But TJ's not a problem. A couple of guys in the neighborhood still owe me a favor.

**JULIET**

You're going after him? It's against the law.

**JULIAN**

Honey, sometimes, things are resolved better man to man. But don't you worry about things like that. We should talk about other things. Like Ruben.

**JULIET**

What about Ruben?

**JULIAN**

He's proposed, hasn't he? And you've accepted, haven't you?

**JULIET**

No, he hasn't. And I wouldn't accept right after Tommy was killed.

**JULIAN**

Tommy is never going to interfere in our family again.

**JULIET**

Dad, you're planning a wake for him. Right here, in the house. A wake, followed by an engagement?

**JULIAN**

I have worked very hard, young lady, to find someone for you. And frankly, your behavior tells me that Ruben is better than you deserve.

**JULIET**

Dad!

**JULIAN**

You told me he was a good match!

**JULIET**

I didn't say that.

**JULIAN**
You did.

**JULIET**
I didn't.

**JULIAN**
I heard you. I HEARD YOU SAY IT!

**JULIET**
No, Dad. No. You heard yourself say it.

**JULIAN**
Juliet, you're not going to do better than Ruben —

**JULIET**
What?

**JULIAN**
He's perfect. And he's like us.

**JULIET**
Us?

**JULIAN**
Yes. Like us. But connected. With the right credentials, Juliet. The right friends. And he happens to love you.

**JULIET**
Dad, give me some time.

**JULIAN**
You think it has been easy being a mother and a father to you?

**JULIET**
You think it's been easy for me? But that's how you wanted it.

**JULIAN**
You think I've enjoyed thinking of a husband for you all the time?

**JULIET**
Why, Dad? Why? Why do you have to think of a husband for me?

**JULIAN**
For the family.

**JULIET**
What family?

**JULIAN**
This family. We deserve a lot more, Juliet, than we've ever gotten.

**JULIET**
Dad, we've never been a family.

**MARIA** (*entering with JULIAN's briefcase*)
Don Julián —

**JULIAN**
I'm not going to let you ruin this. You're beautiful and young. And people like us —

**JULIET**
Us?

**JULIAN**
Us! You and me. When something good comes along we have to grab it fast and hold on. Because in one instant, it can all be taken away from us. Over anything. We're too dark, too light, too short, too tall, too loud. It can be anything!

**JULIET**
Dad, do you really think —

**JULIAN**
Juliet, how many banks have I been at? Do you know?

**JULIET**
Dad —

**JULIAN**
I'm not even fifty yet. And it's over. They've let me go as high as they'll let me. No V.P. No more fancy titles. But Ruben is different.

**JULIET**
Dad —

**JULIAN**

With Ruben as your husband, nobody, nobody will ever slam the door on your face.

**JULIET**

Like you did with Mom?

**JULIAN**

You *are* my daughter, and I *do* know what to do.

**JULIET**

Like you did with Mom?

**JULIAN**

You wanna go out on the street like Tommy? Go do it! I'll disown you.

**JULIET**

Like Mom?

**JULIAN**

Your mother has nothing to do with this. I will disown you!

**JULIET**

Dad! Please! Ruben isn't right for me.

**JULIAN**

He's perfect!

**JULIET**

He's still not right. For me.

**JULIAN**

I'm still your father. And I'm still responsible for this family.

**JULIET**

Dad, without Mom —

**JULIAN**

Juliet, don't —

**JULIET**

Don't what? Don't say it? Again?

**MARIA**

¿Don Julián? Your briefcase.

**JULIET**

Dad, without Mom, we've never been a family.

**JULIAN** (*taking briefcase*)

Day in. Day out. Smile when they promote everyone around me. Why do I do this? For you? (*pause*) Maria?

**MARIA**

Go to work, Julián. I'll watch her. I'll watch her.

> *JULIAN exits.*

# Scene 9

**JULIET**

Maria, I was married in church. I have a husband. I can't marry twice.

**MARIA**

Julieta. Mija. *Romeo* is gone. And we both know he's never going to get his papers. Maybe you should marry Ruben.

**JULIET**

Maria, I'm already married.

**MARIA**

Yes. But who knows? Who was there? Nobody! Julieta, *Romeo* is not even a citizen. With Ruben you'll have a second chance, mija. Go for it!

**JULIET**

No.

**MARIA**

*Romeo* is never coming back. You know that, don't you?

**JULIET**

I can't marry twice.

**MARIA**

In church, no. But city hall?

**JULIET**
No! I'm going to see Father Lawrence.

**MARIA**
What can he do?

**JULIET**
I don't know. He's a priest. Something.

*JULIET exits.*

**MARIA**
Mija, wait! Wait!

*MARIA runs after JULIET.*

# Scene 10

*November 2nd, 10 a.m. Lights rise on FATHER LAWRENCE and RUBEN.*

**FATHER LAWRENCE**
You want to get married? To Juliet Bosquet? I think this is a bit premature.

**RUBEN**
Mr. Bosquet is worried. He thinks Juliet is dwelling on Tommy's death. A wedding will get her mind off things.

**FATHER LAWRENCE**
I wish I could agree with him —

**RUBEN**
We want a private ceremony. Just family. Because of Tommy.

**FATHER LAWRENCE**
Tommy. Yes, of course.

*JULIET enters.*

**JULIET**
Father?

**FATHER LAWRENCE**
Juliet! Speaking of —

**JULIET**
Are you free, Father? Or should I come later?

**FATHER LAWRENCE**
Oh no, I'm free.

*MARIA enters.*

Oh, Maria too! Ruben, if you don't mind . . .

**RUBEN**
Bring her up to date, Father. You know, time. Date. Place.

(*exiting*) Jules? Call me?

**JULIET**
Yes. Yes. I'll call you.

**RUBEN**
Good.

**JULIET**
Sure. I'll call you. Later. Later.

*RUBEN exits.*

# Scene 11

**FATHER LAWRENCE**
He wants to marry you!

**JULIET**
Everything is totally messed up!

**FATHER LAWRENCE**
If your father insists on this wedding —

**JULIET**
You're not going to tell 'em? About me and Romeo?

**FATHER LAWRENCE**
I don't know. I never expected —

**JULIET**
Because if you do (*picking up a spade*) I'll take this and kill myself —

**FATHER LAWRENCE** (*struggling with JULIET*)
Oh stop this! You can't kill yourself. It's against the teachings of the Church.

**JULIET**
Great! That's very comforting. Exactly what I needed to hear! But don't worry. I'll do it somewhere else.

**FATHER LAWRENCE**
Juliet, I never thought Romeo would —

**JULIET**
You married us in church. I'm not going to let anybody else touch me —

**MARIA** (*selecting plants from FATHER LAWRENCE's garden*)
It's all right, mija. We'll just go home and work things out.

**FATHER LAWRENCE**
Maria, what are you doing?

**MARIA**
Come on. Let's go.

**FATHER LAWRENCE**
Wait a minute. Not with those.

**MARIA**
Father, I know these yerbas better than you do.

**FATHER LAWRENCE**
Just because some of them grow in your country? You don't know anything about —

**MARIA**
What don't I know? That you got them illegally? That you're trading across borders? You talk about this girl's problem with anyone, and I'll talk about your problem. With the cops.

**FATHER LAWRENCE**
Maria, those plants may not be what you think they are —

**MARIA** (*picking more plants*)
She has a right to live. I need to help her. Julieta, vámonos.

**JULIET**
No. You're both crazy.

> *She runs out.*

**FATHER LAWRENCE**
Juliet! (*beat*) Now look what you've done!

**MARIA**
She needs our help, Father. You want to force her into sin? Into adultery?

**FATHER LAWRENCE**
Adultery? Dear Lord . . . has it come to this?

**MARIA**
We have to help her. She has nobody. Except us.

# Scene 12

> *Minutes later. JULIET runs into a CALAVERA.*

**CALAVERA**
Excuse me. I'm sorry.

**JULIET**
No. It was my fault. I didn't see you —

**CALAVERA**
Hey. It's all right. Mistakes happen.

> *The CALAVERA exits.*

# Scene 13

*Lights up on MARIA picking leaves off the plants she took from*
*FATHER LAWRENCE's garden. JULIET enters.*

**MARIA**
Juliet, your father is so stubborn, such a cabezón.

**JULIET**
Maria, I just saw the strangest person on the street.

**MARIA**
The only way to change him is to shock him, ¿sabes?

**JULIET**
Maria? Isn't it kind of late for trick or treaters?

**MARIA**
These leaves have special medicine. When you chew them, they'll make you
feel cold and sleepy, your breath will get very light, and your cheeks and lips
will turn white. You'll become very still. And you'll stay like that for one day.
One whole day.

**JULIET**
What are they?

**MARIA**
Medicine. Medicina.

**JULIET**
Herbal medicine? Maria, I don't believe in that stuff!

**MARIA**
This is medicine! Used by curanderos. Holy men. In my country. To cleanse
the body and calm the mind.

**JULIET**
One whole day?

**MARIA**
But then, you'll wake up. Exactly as if from a nap. But until then, mija, you'll
lie in bed and look calm, very still —

**JULIET**

I'll look dead. That's what you're saying.

**MARIA**

This way, your father won't do anything. And while you're sleeping, I'll find *Romeo*. Together, you'll go to México, where you'll live like love birds.

*Lights up on JULIAN, seen by JULIET.*

**JULIAN**

You want to go out on the street? Like Tommy? I'LL DISOWN YOU!

**JULIET**

Oh, Maria! Find Romeo. Please.

**MARIA**

Are you brave, mija? Brave enough to do this? Brave enough for love?

**JULIAN**

I'LL DISOWN YOU!

**JULIET**

But Dad will never forgive me.

**MARIA**

After the first grandchild, even the hardest father forgives everything.

**JULIET** (*taking green leaves*)

Okay then. I'll do it.

**MARIA**

The leaves are bitter. You have to chew and chew and chew. No matter what.

**JULIET**

Love will give me strength. I'll do it. I'll do it.

**MARIA**

Ándale, mija. And now, I have to go talk to someone who knows where *Romeo* is.

**JULIET**

Gracias, María.

**MARIA**
    De nada. Adiós, mija.

**JULIET**
    Adiós. I'll do it, Maria, I promise.

**MARIA**
    Que Dios te bendiga.

       *MARIA exits.*

**JULIET**
    Yeah.

# Scene 14

    *November 2nd, noon. JULIAN and MANUEL enter.*

**JULIAN**
    Go to the caterer and give him this. This is exactly what I want. No substitutions.

**MANUEL**
    ¡Chingao! I can't read this!

       *He exits.*

**JULIAN**
    And how are you?

**JULIET**
    Good.

**JULIAN**
    You went to see Father Lawrence?

**JULIET**
    Yes.

**JULIAN**
    And he helped you see things my way?

**JULIET**
    Yes.

**JULIET**

Someday, Juliet, you'll understand —

**JULIET**

Dad, it's okay. You're right. You're right!

**JULIAN**

And everything will go as planned? A brunch tomorrow. And then the following day, a small, tasteful affair.

**JULIET**

Yes. Everything will go as planned.

**JULIAN**

Good. I think Father Lawrence deserves a generous donation for this.

**JULIET**

He'll like that.

**JULIAN**

Poor Jules. You look tired. You should take a nap, sweetheart.

**JULIET**

I will. I'll try. I'm sorry you have so many things to do, Dad.

**JULIAN**

Yes. But all for you. Jules?

**JULIET**

Yes?

**JULIAN**

I know you'll be up to it.

**JULIET**

Yeah. I will. I promise, Dad.

**JULIAN**

That's a good girl.

>     *JULIAN exits.*

**JULIET**

Goodbye. God knows when we'll see each other again.

# Scene 15

*November 2nd, 12:30 p.m.*

**JULIET**

I feel cold. Like I'm going to faint. I could be dying! Maybe I should call him back! (*pause*) No. He wouldn't understand. And besides, I have to do this by myself.

*She plays with the leaves.*

They're just drugs. Everybody takes drugs. It's no big deal. Maria thinks these are even purer than regular drugs. (*beat*) But what if they don't work? What if I have to marry Ruben after all? No, that won't happen. It can't. Thanks to these.

*She begins to chew. The leaves are bitter. A CALAVERA appears.*

**CALAVERA #1**

Nice!

**JULIET**

Oh!

**CALAVERA #1**

Can you see me?

**JULIET** (*dismissing the vision*)

But what if these plants are really poisonous, and Father Lawrence is trying to kill me so that no one will know about my marriage which he, after all, performed?

*Another CALAVERA appears.*

**CALAVERA #2**

Hey! You know what? I think that's possible.

**JULIET**

I could die. Just to protect him.

**CALAVERA #2**

Do you see me?

**JULIET**
But that's crazy.

*She chews.*

Father Lawrence is a priest in the eyes of God, after all.

*Another CALAVERA appears.*

**CALAVERA #3**
But he's not very smart. Is he?

**JULIET**
And what if I wake up?

**CALAVERA #3** (*amused*)
Wake up!

**JULIET**
Before Romeo comes. Then what do I do? I can't pretend I'm dead.

**CALAVERA #1**
It's not that hard.

**JULIET**
But if I do wake up, I'll go crazy.

*She chews more.*

Alone in the house. With Tommy.

**CALAVERA #2**
It's possible.

**JULIET**
They say that spirits fly, especially if they died suddenly, like Tommy did.

*TOMMY CALAVERA appears with a switchblade.*

**TOMMY CALAVERA**
First Benny. Then Romeo. Then you.

**JULIET**
Tommy! Put down that horrible knife.

*BENNY CALAVERA appears.*

**BENNY CALAVERA**
Hey Tommy? What are you waiting for? An invitation?

*TOMMY CALAVERA and BENNY CALAVERA fight.*

**JULIET**
Benny! Tommy! Stop it! Tommy! I'm sorry I married Romeo behind your back!

*BENNY CALAVERA falls under TOMMY's knife again.*

**TOMMY CALAVERA** (*to JULIET*)
I'll get you next. And then Romeo. Do you see me?

**JULIET** (*chewing more*)
No! No! Please! I'm chewing.

*A revelation — she knows now that TOMMY CALAVERA is real.*

I *do* see you.

*JULIET faints. BENNY CALAVERA catches her in his arms. Lights rise on ROMEO seen by JULIET.*

**ROMEO**
With you, Julieta, I have lived!

**JULIET**
Romeo?

**BENNY**
Sleep, Julieta.

**JULIET**
Benny? Where am I?

*She has another revelation.*

Benny! You're here.

*She falls into a stupor.*

**BENNY CALAVERA**
Sleep, Julieta, sleep. And dream of justice.

*BENNY CALAVERA lays JULIET down, then exits.*

# Scene 16

*November 2nd, 3:30 p.m. MARIA crosses to JULIET.*

**MARIA**
Julieta? Julieta? The leaves were good.

**JULIAN** (*entering*)
Is something wrong?

**MARIA**
It's Juliet, señor. She's not moving.

**JULIAN**
Well, wake her up.

**MARIA**
She's very still.

**JULIAN**
Maria. Wake her up.

(*touching JULIET*) She's cold.

**MARIA**
The blood has gone deep inside her body.

**JULIAN**
There's no breath from her lips. (*beat*) She's dead. First Tommy, now this.

**MARIA**
Julián, I'm sorry.

**JULIAN**
I'll talk to Tony. Romeo Martinez did this.

**MARIA**
Julián, forget about —

**JULIAN**
Look at my girl! Every low-lifer on this block is going to hear about this. I'm going to put up money. Lots of money. And Romeo Martinez is going to pay. One way or another.

*JULIAN exits.*

**MARIA**
¡Julián!

# Scene 17

*FATHER LAWRENCE and MANUEL enter.*

**FATHER LAWRENCE** (*touching JULIET*)
She's very cold, Maria.

**MANUEL**
Like a flower frozen by a cold wind.

**MARIA**
And forgotten again. While Julián chases devils.

**FATHER LAWRENCE** (*giving MANUEL a piece of paper*)
Go to Tijuana. This is where I think Romeo is. Tell him her death is a lie, made up to give him time to come and get her and then return to Mexico. Tell him to get here quickly. Anything could happen.

**MANUEL**
Sí, padre.

*MANUEL exits.*

**FATHER LAWRENCE**
Maria, those plants are not supposed to be used like this.

**MARIA**
Father, can we pray?

# Scene 18

*November 2nd, 4 p.m. Lights rise on ROMEO and a CALAVERA, though he does not see the figure as such, in Tijuana.*

**ROMEO**
So this is Tijuana?

**CALAVERA**

Pos, sí.

**ROMEO**

It's not bad. Not bad.

**CALAVERA**

Chale. I don't live here. I live on the other side.

**ROMEO**

The other night I had a dream that I was dreaming. And in my dream, I got some real good news. I could see love, my favorite Mexican god, somewhere in his palacio, his house of love. And I was walking on clouds, man, como un pingo, jumping up and down, and getting in the way of everything. And then I saw Julieta.

    *Lights rise on JULIET, seen by ROMEO.*

And she told me I was dead. And then she turned to me. And kissed me.

**JULIET**

And gave you everything. I gave you everything.

**ROMEO**

And then I woke up.

    *Lights fade on JULIET.*

You know, Julieta and me have a pretty good thing going, mano, when even a dream can make me feel that good.

**CALAVERA**

Chale. Too bad she's dead.

**ROMEO**

Who's dead?

**CALAVERA**

Your girl. Her father is bribing the whole barrio. He's mortgaged his house y no sé que. To get who did it. They say he's offering money to everybody. Just like the cops!

**ROMEO**

Get me a coyote. I have to get across the border fast.

**CALAVERA**
Take it easy, mano. You look crazy. Immigration will take one look at you and lock you up for sure.

**ROMEO**
You see this? American dollars. Get me a coyote. A good coyote. And I'll give you more.

**CALAVERA**
Okay, man. I'll see what I can do. ¡Ay, te watcho!

*The CALAVERA exits.*

**ROMEO**
¡Pobre Julieta!

*A CALAVERA appears.*

Why should she die and I live?

**CALAVERA**
¿*Romeo*? ¿Recuerdas el curandero?

*The CALAVERA exits.*

**ROMEO**
I saw an old curandero near here. An old man with dirty clothes and sad eyes. Pobre flaco, he probably hasn't eaten in a week. His poor tienda is full of snake skins, deer horns, beetles, and crushed bone. Everything in little boxes. Este pobre will sell me poison. Even if it's against the law. ¡CURANDERO! ¡AYUDA!

*Lights rise on the CURANDERO.*

(*referring to the money*) Half of this is for the coyote. And the other half for the curandero. And certain death. (*beat*) Curandero. Ayuda.

# Scene 19

*November 2nd, 5 p.m.*

**CURANDERO**
¿Quién habla?

**ROMEO**

¡Venga, hombre! Tengo dinero.

**CURANDERO**

¿Y qué?

**ROMEO** (*to himself*)

I need poison strong enough to stop a man in minutes and take his breath away. As quickly as an uzi burning through his heart. ¿Curandero? ¡Necesito veneno! ¿Lo traes?

**CURANDERO**

¡No! ¡No! Eso no tengo. Sabes que no puedo vender cosas así. ¡N'ombre! Me matan. ¡Me ponen en la cárcel!

**ROMEO** (*to himself*)

Poor man. Scared to live. The world his enemy, the law his jailer. And no one cares if he lives or dies.

(*to the CURANDERO*) ¡Tengo dolares! American dollars!

> *The CURANDERO holds one hand out for money while the other hand is carrying a small vial.*

**CURANDERO**

¡Ay! Pues . . .

**ROMEO**

De los Estados Unidos. American money.

**CURANDERO**

¡No me digas!

> *He offers the vial to ROMEO.*

Ay, 'sta. Trágalo cuando quieras. Aunque tengas la fuerza de veinte hombres, caes como un ladrillo.

**ROMEO**

Gracias.

> *He offers him money.*

This is for your poverty, old man.

**CURANDERO** (*taking the money*)
Ay, gracias. (*beat*) Mi pobreza me hace hacerlo.

**ROMEO** (*taking the vial*)
I know. Your will belongs to God.

**CURANDERO** (*counting money*)
Gracias. Gracias.

**ROMEO**
I give you money — worse poison than this. It kills more people in this ugly world, more than any of your dry weeds and powders. Gracias a usted, viejo.

**CURANDERO**
De nada. No hay de que.

    *The CURANDERO exits.*

**ROMEO**
Buy food, old man. And some tequila for your soul.

(*to the vial*) And you, sweet death, I'll drink you when I find my love.

    *ROMEO exits.*

# Scene 20

    *Moments later. Lights rise on JULIET, waking up, early, from the leaves. TOMMY's body lies next to her.*

**JULIET**
Where am I? Is it time? Maria? Romeo? (*beat*) It's so quiet.

    *TOMMY CALAVERA sits up.*

**TOMMY CALAVERA**
Have you been to the morgue yet, Juliet?

**JULIET**
Tommy?!

**TOMMY CALAVERA** (*flicking open a switchblade*)
I hear they have a space there waiting for you.

**JULIET**

Romeo? Maria? No, Tommy. Please!!

**TOMMY CALAVERA**

Go out into the street, little girl. I'll still find you. You thought you could escape. Get out. No one ever escapes.

**JULIET**

I'm sorry, Tommy. For me. For Romeo.

**TOMMY CALAVERA**

Your daddy wanted to throw you out. And now I'm doing it.

(*quietly*) Boo. Boo.

**JULIET**

Tommy, it's okay. I'm going. See? I'm going.

**TOMMY CALAVERA**

Boo.

> *JULIET runs out.*

Boo.

> *He looks at himself and heaves a huge sigh.*

# Scene 21

*November 2nd, 8 p.m. Lights rise on ROMEO and COYOTE CALAVERA.*

**COYOTE CALAVERA**

Hey, Romeo? I got a ride going north. No tickets, no seats, no snacks, no water, no toilets, no cops. You want a ride?

**ROMEO**

More than my life!

**COYOTE CALAVERA**

Pues, let's go.

**ROMEO**
Is it only me tonight?

**COYOTE CALAVERA**
Are you kidding? Everybody wants to come to the United Estates of America.
¡Miralos!

> *CALAVERAS appear from every direction scurrying around, look-*
> *ing for a way to get across the border.*

**CALAVERA** (*scurrying*)
Which way, hombre? Which way?

**COYOTE CALAVERA**
Do you see all those bright lights from the bottom of the hill all the way to the
top of the hill?

**ALL CALAVERAS**
¡Un chorro de luces!

**COYOTE CALAVERA**
The United Estates of America. It's a wonderland. A big park. With lots of
room. For everybody!

> *Loud sirens rise, followed by screeching car brakes. Shots ring out.*
> *The CALAVERAS tumble and dive. A few are hit by cars. Some are*
> *hit by bullets.*

**ROMEO** (*to COYOTE CALAVERA*)
Cut the bullshit. Just get me across.

**COYOTE CALAVERA**
Okay, mano. I'll take you to my favorite spot.

> *ROMEO and COYOTE CALAVERA crawl on their hands and*
> *knees. Lights rise on a tall UNCLE SAM.*

This is it. The United Estates of America. Are you ready?

**ROMEO**
I got across before. I'll do it again.

> *As ROMEO and COYOTE CALAVERA run towards UNCLE SAM,*
> *he starts moving too, forcing a standoff.*

**COYOTE CALAVERA** (*tumbling into darkness*)
Good luck, mano. You're gonna need it!

*He exits.*

# Scene 22

**ROMEO** (*to UNCLE SAM*)
I'm an American! ¡From los Estados Unidos!

**UNCLE SAM**
Are you?

**ROMEO**
And I speak English!

**UNCLE SAM**
So what?

**ROMEO**
I have a wife there now.

**UNCLE SAM**
COWARD! BEGGAR! YOU THINK AMERICA WANTS YOUR KIND?

*ROMEO and UNCLE SAM dodge each other.*

**ROMEO**
Coward? Beggar? Sinner and thief to you. An americano to me.

*ROMEO rolls between UNCLE SAM's legs, tumbling into darkness.*

# Scene 23

*Lights rise on MANUEL and a CALAVERA in Tijuana. The CALAVERA has his back to MANUEL.*

**MANUEL**
¿Con permiso?

CALAVERA (*turning around*)
A sus órdenes.

*He has a moment of recognition.*

Compadre.

MANUEL (*recognizing him*)
¡Dios mío!

CALAVERA
Why surprise? It's still Day of the Dead, compadre. For one more hour. (*beat*)
¿Y tú? Your business?

MANUEL
I'm looking for someone —

CALAVERA
¿*Romeo*? He went back. To the other side. Running. Full of love. With a bottle
of poison in his pocket.

MANUEL
Poison? Love? And lies? May God forgive us all!

CALAVERA
Poison, love, and lies. ¡Híjole! There are times, compadre, when nothing,
nothing in this world, ever goes right.

# Scene 24

*November 2nd, 11 p.m. Lights rise on a HOMEBOY tagging the
Bosquet home.*

ROMEO
¡Muchacho travieso! ¿Qué estás haciendo? What have the dead ever done to
you, chamaco?

HOMEBOY
Who's dead?

**ROMEO**

A girl. As beautiful as a flower, soft and white like a magnolia. With a soul as delicate as silk.

**HOMEBOY**

¡Híjole, man! There ain't nobody in the whole world like that!

**ROMEO**

Ándale, chamaco. Go home! ¡Vete!

**HOMEBOY**

¡Híjole! All right.

> *He exits. Lights rise on TOMMY's body lying in wake. CALAVERAS surround him, arranging flowers. Freeze frame: ROMEO seeing the CALAVERAS and the CALAVERAS seeing ROMEO.*

**ROMEO**

¡Dios mío!

**CALAVERAS**

Ah!

**ROMEO**

¡La Muerte!

**CALAVERAS**

¡Despacio!

**ROMEO**

¡La Muerte!

**CALAVERAS**

¡Silencio!

**ROMEO**

¡Ay, que espanto!

> *He turns away, terrified. The CALAVERAS exit quickly. ROMEO looks again, furtively.*

# Scene 25

**ROMEO**

Juliet's house. Surrounded by death, hatred, and pain. Flowers. Shrouds. Candles. And cold. As cold as a morgue.

*He sees TOMMY's body.*

Tommy? Still covered with blood? The undertaker cleans, but the blood comes back. Manchas on your soul.

*TOMMY CALAVERA enters.*

**TOMMY CALAVERA**

Wetback!

**ROMEO**

Tommy!

**TOMMY CALAVERA**

You broke into my uncle's house.

**ROMEO**

Still full of hate? Why? I didn't hate you. But everybody wanted us to hate each other. Before we became cousins, Tommy, we should have been carnales. Brothers.

**TOMMY CALAVERA**

Juliet is out. Out of your life. Out of my life. Out of this house. Out.

**ROMEO**

Dead?

**TOMMY CALAVERA**

May as well be. She's on the street. At the store. Walking against a red. At the park. She could be anywhere. Anywhere she goes, she shouldn't be.

**ROMEO**

I'll find her.

**TOMMY CALAVERA**

Anywhere she is, she shouldn't be.

**ROMEO**

I'll find her. I'll find her!

*ROMEO runs out.*

**TOMMY CALAVERA**

On the street. At the store. At a red light. In the park. Go, Romeo, go. Look for your Juliet.

*ROMEO exits.*

# Scene 26

*Moments later. The stage is empty. Night sounds rise. After a beat a CALAVERA appears.*

**CALAVERA #1**

Darkness. Heat.
Dry winds. Shadows.

(*singing*)

El Lay at night. Tossing and turning.
Hour by hour. El Lay turning.

*Another CALAVERA appears.*

**CALAVERA #2**

Another day of God's creation.
Life and Death in celebration.

*Gunshot, far and distant. The CALAVERAS listen to it briefly.*

**CALAVERA #2**

Day of the Dead is almost complete.

**CALAVERA #1**

While El Lay tries to sleep.

*Another CALAVERA appears.*

**CALAVERA #3**

Shouting and crying.
Screaming sirens.
El Lay at night. Tossing and turning.

**CALAVERA #1**

Hour by hour. El Lay is burning.

*Another CALAVERA appears.*

**CALAVERA #4**

Another day of God's creation.
Life and Death in celebration.

**ROMEO** (*entering*)
Juliet! Juliet!

*Gunshot, far and distant. The CALAVERAS listen to it briefly.*

**CALAVERA #4**

Day of the Dead almost complete.

**CALAVERA #3**

While El Lay tries to sleep.

**ROMEO**
Juliet!

**CALAVERA #1**

¿*Romeo?* The streets of El Lay are no place for you.

**CALAVERA #2**
For anybody.

**ROMEO** (*seeing the CALAVERAS*)
Death? Again?

*He has a realization.*

No!

**CALAVERA #3**
¡*Romeo!* ¡*Romeo!*
El Lay is dying!

**ROMEO**
Stay away from me!

**CALAVERA #4**
Bleeding from knives, bullets, and rage!

**ROMEO**
No! Not yet! No!

**CALAVERA #1**
*¡Romeo! ¡Romeo!*

**CALAVERA #2**
El Lay is crying!

**ROMEO**
No!

**CALAVERA #4**
*¡Romeo! ¡Romeo!*

**CALAVERA #3**
Be still! Be quiet!

**CALAVERA #2**
*Romeo. Romeo.*

**CALAVERA #1**
Your time has come.

> *BENNY CALAVERA steps out of the shadows.*

**BENNY CALAVERA**
Bullets fly through the air night and day, their steel bodies crashing through us daily.

**ROMEO**
Benny?

**BENNY CALAVERA**
Steel vultures, naked and blind. Hitting us daily. Hitting us daily. With all of their might.

**ROMEO**
And nobody sleeps. Even at night.

**CALAVERAS**
*¡Romeo! ¡Romeo!*

**BENNY CALAVERA**
The bullet is flying.

**CALAVERAS**
*¡Romeo! ¡Romeo!*

**BENNY CALAVERA**
Your time has come.

> *A gunshot, this time closer and louder. As the CALAVERAS follow its imaginary path, all their eyes turn slowly towards ROMEO. A flute plays.*

**ROMEO**
Benny?

(*clutching the side of his face*) Benny!

(*looking at the blood on his hand*) I wanted. To see. Her. Touch. Her. Gone? My love. Gone?

(*staggering, losing control of his legs*) Gone. Gone.

> *As ROMEO falls, BENNY CALAVERA catches him.*

**ROMEO**
Benny. (*beat*) You're still here, man. You're still here.

**BENNY CALAVERA**
Ain't I always been here for you, primo? From the day you came across the border, I've been here. For you.

**ROMEO**
I was ready, Benny. I was ready.

> *He drops the vial of poison, and BENNY CALAVERA picks it up.*

**BENNY CALAVERA**
With this?

**ROMEO**

I was ready. But you know what? I was wrong. In this world, primo, nobody needs poison.

*ROMEO dies. Mesoamerican music rises.*

**CALAVERAS** (*singing*)

This house!
This earth!
We do not inhabit it!

**BENNY CALAVERA**

¡*Romeo*!

**CALAVERAS**

This house!
This earth!
We only borrow it.

**BENNY CALAVERA**

¡Primo!

**CALAVERAS**

We borrow it
Daily!
Briefly!
Briefly!

We borrow it
Briefly
Just once!

*Lights rise on JULIET and HOMEBOY.*

**HOMEBOY** (*entering*)

I saw it. I saw it.

**JULIET**

Where?

**HOMEBOY**

Over there. See? Over there.

*Freeze frame: JULIET sees an otherworldly sight —*
*BENNY CALAVERA holding ROMEO with other CALAVERAS*
*surrounding them, a Mesoamerican pietà.*

**JULIET**
No!

**HOMEBOY**
It ain't right, you know? It ain't right.

*He exits.*

**CALAVERAS #1 & #2**
    This house!
    This earth!
    We do not inhabit it.

**JULIET**
Romeo?

**CALAVERAS #1 & #2**
    This house.
    This earth.
    We only borrow it.

**CALAVERAS**
    Daily!
    Daily!
    Briefly!
    Briefly!

**JULIET**
Romeo? Crying? Tears on your cheek. Crying?

**BENNY CALAVERA**
It's too late, Julieta, too late.

    *JULIET kisses ROMEO.*

**JULIET**
Tears and blood on your face. Tears and blood on your sweet face. No! No!
*Romeo.* Dead. Broken and torn. My only love. Broken and torn. (*beat*) And me,
my love? What about me?

*A CALAVERA offers JULIET a knife.*

**JULIET**
With this?

*She picks up the knife.*

Romeo, *Romeo*, one last kiss. (*beat*) So much love given. (*beat*) So much . . . and more.

*JULIET stabs herself. As she falls, BENNY CALAVERA catches her.*

**BENNY CALAVERA**
*Romeo* and Julieta, may your souls fly to the thirteenth heaven. And with the bodies of hummingbirds, may they fly free forever.

*BENNY CALAVERA gently lays JULIET next to ROMEO. Suddenly, city sounds explode in a wild cacophony of noise — Los Angeles, once again, momentarily gone mad. Specials rise on MARIA and JULIAN.*

**MARIA**
It was love, Julián. Love.

**CALAVERAS #1 & #3**
 Your body a flower
 Your heart a flower
 Give them to earth
 And return!

**MARIA**
Some of us are given one chance to really love. One chance to see ourselves in others. And loving them, love ourselves.

**CALAVERAS #2 & #4**
 Give them to earth!
 Give them to earth!
 Give them to earth
 And return!

**JULIAN**
And without love?

**MARIA**

Without love?

**CALAVERAS**

> Your body a flower
> Your heart a flower

**MARIA**

Without love, there is nothing. Nothing.

**CALAVERAS**

> Given them to earth
> And return!

*Specials rise on FATHER LAWRENCE and SGT. LOPEZ.*

**FATHER LAWRENCE**

A man of the cloth, and I know so little. Almost nothing.

**CALAVERAS #2 & #4**

> Your body a flower
> Your heart a flower

**FATHER LAWRENCE**

Sometimes, as I sit in my garden and see the smog above me, yellow and thick, I get scared.

**CALAVERAS**

> Give them to earth
> And return!

**FATHER LAWRENCE**

God could forget us. Under the smog. And never think of us again.

**SGT. LOPEZ**

Well, Father, maybe. But maybe something else could happen.

**FATHER LAWRENCE**

What?

**CALAVERAS**

> Give them to earth!
> Give them to earth!

**SGT. LOPEZ**

Maybe under the smog, we're going to be the ones to forget. You know, God.

**CALAVERAS**

    Give them to earth

    And return!

    Return!

*Special rises on CANDELARIA.*

**CANDELARIA**

I had one son. And one daughter. *Romeo* and Julieta, Señor Bosquet. Now what do I do? In this cruel and heartless country, what do I do?

**SGT. LOPEZ**

The only thing I know, Father, is what we do to each other shouldn't be allowed.

*Special rises on JULIAN.*

**JULIAN**

Tony?

**SGT. LOPEZ**

Yes, Julian?

**JULIAN**

It's beyond us, isn't it? The streets. Where we are right now. It's beyond us. Don't you think?

**SGT. LOPEZ**

I hope not, *Julián*. I hope not.

**CALAVERAS**

    Your body a flower

    Your heart a flower

**SGT. LOPEZ**

Someday. Call the wagon.

*Specials fade on MARIA, JULIAN, CANDELARIA, FATHER LAWRENCE, and SGT. LOPEZ.*

**CALAVERAS**

    Give them to earth

And return!
Return!

*MANUEL appears, now dressed as a skeleton, having removed the clothes of the living that he has worn throughout the play.*

**MANUEL CALAVERA**

*Romeo* and Julieta, niños, children of Mexico, your next journey has begun. Like flowers our bodies bloom. Fed by the sun and cooled by the wind. Like flowers they wither, their flower blush gone. *Romeo* and Julieta. Flowers of earth. Arise. Arise and become what you've always been. Flowers and song.

**ROMEO** (*waking*)

Tezcatlipoca's smoke is rising . . . rising . . . ¿Julieta? Julieta.

**CALAVERAS #2 & #4**

Give them to earth

**ROMEO**

¿Julieta? Julieta.

**CALAVERAS**

Give them to earth!
Give them to earth!
And return!

*JULIET awakens.*

**ROMEO**

Julieta.

*ROMEO and JULIET embrace.*

Julieta, they say the gods like to make fun of us. Maliciosos. They give us life and then they play with us. And torment us. I'm sorry for leaving you. But never again, mi linda. Never again.

**JULIET**

Romeo? *Romeo.* Never more wanted. Never more loved. Together, my *Romeo.* Finally. Together.

**ROMEO**

Juntos.

**JULIET**
Together.

**MANUEL**
Earth flowers, spirits, niños. Come. Vengan.

**CALAVERAS** (*singing*)
>Earth flowers, spirits, niños,
>We welcome you to our home.
>Let love flower between us,
>Let love flower among us,
>Here in our house,
>The house of flowers,
>Welcome to our home.

*A bright light appears in the direction of the sun. All the CALA-VERAS, including TOMMY CALAVERA, BENNY CALAVERA, ROMEO, and JULIET, turn towards it and begin to sing.*

**CALAVERAS**
>Earth flowers, spirits, niños,
>We welcome you to our home.
>Let life flower between us,
>Let death flower between us,
>Here in our house,
>The house of flowers,
>Welcome to our home.
>Flores, santos, niños,
>Bienvenidos a nuestra casa.
>Allí celebramos la vida,
>Allí celebramos la muerte,
>Allí en nuestra casa,
>Divina casa de flores.
>¡Bienvenidos a nuestra casa!
>¡BIENVENIDOS A NUESTRA CASA!
>¡BIENVENIDOS A NUESTRA CASA!
>¡BIENVENIDAS A NUESTRA CASA!

*All the CALAVERAS walk into the light.*

**END OF PLAY**

# Introduction to James Lujan's
# *Kino and Teresa*

Through an innovative recontextualization of *Romeo and Juliet*, Taos Pueblo playwright James Lujan's *Kino and Teresa* demonstrates the power of appropriation to call attention to the racial and colonial dynamics surrounding Shakespeare's plays. In 1598, just one year after Shakespeare's *Romeo and Juliet* was first published in London, Juan de Oñate led an expedition of Spanish settlers and established the province of Santa Fe de Nuevo México. Lujan brings these two histories together in *Kino and Teresa*, which takes place after the Pueblo Revolt of 1680 and the subsequent Reconquista of 1692, when the Spanish, led by Governor Diego de Vargas, reclaimed the land amidst ongoing Pueblo resistance. Lujan's tragic love story crosses this colonial divide, as Kino is the son of the governor of Pecos Pueblo, Felipe Chistoe, and Teresa is the daughter of Lorenzo Madrid, el Maestre de Campo de Santa Fe. While some characters see their union as a pathway to peace in the wake of recent turmoil, others regard it as an acceleration of cultural genocide. Because the feud between the families is shaped by decades of colonization and anticolonial resistance, it ultimately cannot be solved by Kino and Teresa's love.

Written for Native actors, *Kino and Teresa* emerged from a multi-phase development process involving many collaborators. Lujan was first commissioned to write *Kino and Teresa* in 1999 by Marjorie Neset of the South Broadway Cultural Center in Albuquerque, New Mexico. Americans for Indian Opportunity hosted a reading shortly thereafter. In the following years, the play was further developed in collaboration with Native Voices at the Autry, the resident theater program at the Autry Museum of the American West, which "puts Native narratives at the center of the American story to facilitate a more inclusive dialogue about what it means to be 'American.'"[1] It premiered in 2005 at the Wells Fargo Theater at the Autry National Center in Los Angeles. The play was produced again the

---

1   Jean Bruce Scott and Randy Reinholz, "Native Voices at the Autry," in *Casting a Movement: The Welcome Table Initiative*, eds. Claire Syler and Daniel Banks (New York: Routledge, 2019), 147.

following year by Teatro Nuevo México at the VSA North Fourth Art Center in Albuquerque, where it was directed by Sabina Zuñiga-Varela.

In contrast to many works of Borderlands Shakespeare in which Spanish signals a resistance to Anglo hegemony, Spanish functions exclusively as a colonial language in *Kino and Teresa*, with colonial officials punctuating declarations with words such as "¡Silencio!" (1.1) and "¿Claro?" (1.2). English, then, operates as a more removed language, one that would not have been spoken in the historical setting of the play but which is widely spoken by audience members. The lack of Pueblo language in the playtext points to intersecting histories of linguistic and cultural oppression. By centering Native actors and perspectives within the framework of *Romeo and Juliet*, *Kino and Teresa* reaffirms the sense, as Laura Lehua Yim observes of Indigenous appropriations of Shakespeare, that "a seemingly vanquished Native people continue in their actions and words, even when articulated out from beneath the structures of white settler colonialism."[2]

*Kino and Teresa* addresses the devastating effects of Spanish colonial rule on the Indigenous Peoples of New Mexico. Whereas the Prince is portrayed as an arbiter of justice and the law in Shakespeare's play, Gobernador Vargas clearly represents Spanish colonial interests, and it is his son Juan who takes on the greatly expanded role of the Paris figure. Despite the Governor's calls for peace, many of the Spanish continue to regard Pueblo people as "godless heathens" in order to justify the dispossession of their land and the exploitation of their labor (1.1). Rebuking Spanish acts of genocide, a Pueblo soldier contends:

> You are the treacherous, murdering savages. You came to our land, we welcomed you with open arms. How did you return our friendship? You turned us into slaves; you tortured and killed us for speaking our language and practicing our ceremonies. (1.1)

Indeed, it is the devastating effects of the exploitative labor system known as the "repartimiento" that fuel the deep-seated anger of Kino's mother Anieri, wife of the historical don Felipe de Chistoe. Meaning "partition" or "distribution," the repartimiento was a Spanish colonial system in which Indigenous people were distributed among Spanish settlers and forced to labor on their behalf. In *Kino and Teresa*, Pueblo people toil in Spanish fields, while their own communities starve. As Kino's mother Anieri remarks, "This isn't peace. It's slavery" (1.1). Anieri's powerful resistance as a respected matriarchal figure reflects an egali-

---

2   Laura Lehua Yim, "Reading Hawaiian Shakespeare: Indigenous Residue Haunting Settler Colonialism," *Journal of American Studies* 54, no. 1 (2020): 42, https://doi.org/10.1017/S0021875819001993.

tarian Indigenous worldview that counters the oppressive patriarchal dominance of both the Spanish crown and the Catholic church.

In this colonial context, Kino and Teresa's love is viewed as miscegenation by the Spanish and as cultural capitulation by the Pecos Pueblo community. Their love story, then, is by necessity tragic, and it is characterized by racialized power dynamics. Teresa's desire for Kino to shed his identity takes on the logic of cultural erasure, as she laments in the balcony scene that "It would be so much easier if you could simply cast off your Indian skin and become Spanish and earn the acceptance of my family" (1.6). Her willful innocence reflects her privilege to ignore the effects of colonialism, including forced assimilation, as she asks, "What is an Indian, after all?" (1.6) and "Why should color matter? A red rose and white rose are still roses, no matter what the color" (1.6). In his love for Teresa, Kino is willing to comply with her colonialist fantasies, offering to abjure both his name and his people "if either [she] dislike" (1.6) and wishing for the "glorious day . . . when it matters not if one is Indian or Spanish" (1.6). Even the love of the two young protagonists cannot escape colonial tensions.

Rather than unproblematically embracing the lovers' proclamations, *Kino and Teresa* offers Anieri as a compelling voice of dissent. To her, the potential marriage constitutes an act of betrayal and erasure, a continuance of colonial efforts to destroy Pueblo culture, which include exacting "severe penance" for "practicing . . . Indian ceremonies in kivas hidden in the mountains" (1.2). For Anieri, the prospect of interracial marriage portends destruction, and she predicts that "One day, our great, great grandchildren won't be Indians anymore. They'll be Spaniards" (2.3). As such, Anieri considers killing Teresa and provides encouragement to Juan Vargas, Kino's rival for her love, in an attempt to protect the one thing she has left to ensure a future for her people: "The Spanish have taken away my land, my religion, and my language. But they will not take away my son" (2.2). Anieri's trenchant commentary problematizes Kino's willingness to forfeit his identity for the sake of love.

*Kino and Teresa*'s rejection of the facile view that interracial union will solve colonial conflicts is also evinced through the figure of the mixed-race Cristóbal, the play's Mercutio figure. Cristóbal is "at war with [him]self all the time" and "want[s] to tear [him]self apart, tear either the Spanish side or the Indian side, whichever comes out first" (1.4). His mixed-race status precipitates his tragic demise, and he dies cursing both peoples and "watch[ing] as all the Spanish and Indian blood flows out [his] veins!" (2.5). Whereas Cristóbal reports that his Spanish girlfriend left him after discovering that he "wasn't a full-blood Spaniard" (1.4), Teresa explains that she loves Kino even "after everything [she's] been taught — after everything [her] family told [her] about Indians and their godless ways" (1.6). For his part, Kino believes in the power of love to bring about not just social reconciliation but also a broader rejuvenation of the land and Indigenous communities.

Kino's faith in intercultural exchange is influenced by his close relationship with Fray Olvera. The friar expresses sympathy toward the Pueblo people, from whom he has learned the "power of plants and herbs," and he bemoans the policies that "force them to unlearn what they know" (1.7). Despite Fray Olvera's concern for Kino and his community, however, his teachings support the colonial project, as Christianization often served as a force of oppression. Ultimately, this colonial legacy hampers the friar's efforts to save Kino, who escapes to Taos after he is banished, a punishment that echoes the violent history of Native removal. When Fray Olvera's friend, Fray García, travels to Taos to tell Kino of the plan to reunite him with Teresa, he is reprimanded by the Medicine Man, who fills the roles of Chorus and Apothecary and serves as a connection to the spirit world. This connection, the Medicine Man sharply reminds Fray García, is not one that can be maintained in the language of the colonizer. "I have nothing to say to a Spanish priest. Except in my own language," he retorts, as he "spews out a Pueblo curse," according to the stage direction (2.11). A holder of Pueblo cultural, spiritual, and linguistic knowledge, the Medicine Man resists both the religious oppression of Christianity and the linguistic dominance of Spanish. In Lujan's version, it is the Medicine Man's poverty that ultimately forces him to "consent" to sell poisonous herbs to Kino, thus evoking the play's larger commentary on colonial systems of enforced agricultural labor and unequal access to food for Native people (2.11).

Kino and Teresa's love cannot survive in this violent context. Instead, as the Medicine Man says in his version of the play's famous prologue,

> The future can only be seen in the realm of the spirit world, where the souls of the departed return to where they started. In this land of Indians and Spanish, hope for the future does not bode well for these two peoples, both alike in dignity, but whose ancient feuds will mark the end for a pair of star-crossed lovers, children of old enemies, who, as in so many tragedies must pay for their fathers' sins. It is the lessons of such sacrifice that will decide the fate of fair Santa Fe, where we lay our scene. (1.1)

Crucially, Lujan's play does not end with peace after the death of its title characters, and Spanish dominance remains unsettled in the years following the Reconquista. Indeed, the "glooming peace" described in the epilogue takes on new meaning in the voice of the Medicine Man (2.13). Whereas Chistoe wishes to bury the strife between the Spanish and the Pecos People along with his son,

Anieri vows to avenge Kino's death as she proposes to band together with other Pueblos and Indigenous Peoples of the region to "kill the Spaniards and finally take back our land" (2.13). By avoiding what can be perceived as a hollow sense of reconciliation at the conclusion of *Romeo and Juliet*, this ending reminds modern readers and audiences that the subsequent centuries of colonization by Spain and the later annexation of New Mexico by the United States were not inevitable, leaving space for resistance in multiple forms.

— KATHERINE GILLEN, ADRIANNA M. SANTOS,
AND KATHRYN VOMERO SANTOS

# Kino and Teresa

James Lujan

Based on Shakespeare's *The Tragedy of Romeo and Juliet*

**SETTING:** New Mexico in the years following the Pueblo Revolt of 1680 and the Spanish Reconquest of 1692.

## CHARACTERS

| | |
|---|---|
| **KINO** (*Romeo*) | Son of Governor Chistoe of Pecos Pueblo |
| **TERESA** (*Juliet*) | Daughter of Maestre de Campo Madrid |
| **DON DIEGO DE VARGAS** (*The Prince*) | Governor of New Mexico |
| **JUAN DE VARGAS** (*Paris*) | Son of Governor Vargas |
| **LORENZO MADRID** (*Capulet*) | Maestre de Campo of Santa Fe |
| **CATALINA** (*Lady Capulet*) | Madrid's wife |
| **NURSE** | To Teresa, an Indian woman from Socorro Pueblo |
| **ELADIO** (*Tybalt*) | Nephew of Madrid |
| **FELIPE CHISTOE** (*Montague*) | Governor of Pecos Pueblo |
| **ANIERI** (*Lady Montague*) | Wife of Chistoe |
| **CRISTÓBAL** (*Mercutio*) | Friend of Kino |
| **NICOLÁS** (*Benvolio*) | Nephew of Chistoe and cousin of Kino |
| **FRAY OLVERA** (*Friar Lawrence*) | Franciscan Friar |
| **MEDICINE MAN** (*Apothecary*) | From Pecos Pueblo |
| **FRAY GARCÍA** (*Friar John*) | Friend of Fray Olvera |
| **HERNÁN** | Spanish manservant to Governor Vargas |
| **MATEO** | An Indian soldier in the Pecos Pueblo auxiliary |

**MONTOYA**                         Governor's right-hand man
**WATCHMAN**
**OLD WOMAN**
**STREET VENDOR**
**SPANISH MUSICIAN**
**INDIAN MUSICIAN**


**PLAYWRIGHT'S NOTE:** To draw a visual distinction between the two cultures, the Indian wardrobe should be confined to browns, off-whites, soft blues, and yellows, whereas the Spanish wardrobe should be striking reds, purples, black, and sharp whites.

# ACT 1
# Scene 1

*Dark stage. Spotlight fades up on HERNÁN, an exuberant Spanish man outfitted in colonial-style servant's garb, a sword strapped to his side. He speaks as if addressing the audience directly.*

**HERNÁN**
Bienvenido, O weary traveler. From where do you come? El Paso? Mexico City? Perhaps our mother country of Spain? Ah, it matters not. For this is the wondrous land to which we have ventured to begin our lives anew. Welcome to Santa Fe!

*Stage lights fade up, revealing the town plaza of Santa Fe, the year 1697. HERNÁN continues, offering his welcoming hands.*

Come with me, mi amigo. Hernán is my name. Step forth and I shall be your humble guide. Tell me what brings you to our fair town.

*From the audience emerges JUAN, a young, awkward Spanish man in his early 20s. His overdone wardrobe suggests Spanish aristocracy. He steps forth, trying to carry himself as a man of importance, but ends up clumsily tripping over himself. Amused, HERNÁN reaches to help him up. His fingers take note of JUAN's fine attire.*

Watch your step, mi señor! For shame if I were to allow such a distinguished stranger to sully attire of such obvious finery.

*JUAN pulls away and straightens himself up. He starts to say something, his mouth forming the words, but nothing will come out. HERNÁN hangs on every word, or lack thereof.*

¿Sí, señor? What is it? Please, sir, tell me.

**JUAN** (*speaking with a very severe stutter*)
I-I am l-looking f-for my f-f-f-father.

**HERNÁN** (*taken aback by the stammer, he chuckles*)
Your f-f-father? Perhaps you should t-t-tell me his name.

*Though clumsy, stuttering, and insecure, JUAN overcompensates by indignantly carrying himself with an inflated sense of entitlement.*

**JUAN**
Y-you f-f-fool! I am the s-son of D-Don D-Diego de Vargas!

**HERNÁN** (*immediately starting to behave with deferential respect*)
¿D-Don D-Diego de Vargas? ¿*Gobernador* Vargas? Perdóneme, a thousand pardons, for not recognizing you as the son of the Governor of all of Nuevo México. I shall proudly escort you to the Governor's Palace at once. My own master, Lorenzo Madrid, is his Maestre de Campo. This way, your grace.

> *HERNÁN starts to escort JUAN around the town plaza. As he does, in the background, we start to see some life in the plaza. An OLD WOMAN comes out to do business with a STREET VENDOR.*

Behold the new world your father has worked so hard to build and re-build after years of Indian uprisings and rebellions. Now, thanks to the blessings of our Lord Jesus Christ, your father has those godless heathens firmly under control.

> *At that moment, stepping onstage is a long-haired Indian, MA-TEO. He wears traditional Pueblo clothing augmented by a Spanish military sash with an accompanying sword. Upon seeing MATEO, HERNÁN nervously stops in his tracks.*

**JUAN**
L-l-look! A-a-an Indian! In th-the middle of t-town!

**HERNÁN**
Have no fear, Excelencia. This is one of our Indian allies from nearby Pecos Pueblo. Sworn they are to guard our township. Truth be told, your father has more faith in their loyalty than I.

> *He starts speaking loud enough for MATEO to hear.*

As far as I can see, they will always be treacherous, murdering savages!

> *Hearing this, MATEO immediately turns to HERNÁN.*

**MATEO**
What foul words does the wind blow my way?

**HERNÁN** (*grinning at MATEO*)
Foul words to you, the truth to me.

> *Barely controlling his hair-trigger temper, MATEO marches over to HERNÁN.*

**MATEO**

Truth, from a vile servant? The truth is this: you are the treacherous, murdering savages. You came to our land, we welcomed you with open arms. How did you return our friendship? You turned us into slaves. You tortured and killed us for speaking our language and practicing our ceremonies. Finally, one day, we struck back and banished your stinking hides from this land for twelve glorious years.

*HERNÁN turns away from MATEO, insulting him by addressing JUAN instead.*

**HERNÁN**

He and his people killed hundreds of women and children. They destroyed our towns and churches. In those "glorious" years he talks about, his people were at war with each other. His "great" Chief Popay was a tyrant — pitted tribe against tribe. His Pecos Pueblos practically begged us to come back and save them.

*At this point, a young, gentle Indian soldier, wearing an Indian military outfit similar to MATEO's, comes onstage. This is NICOLÁS.*

**MATEO**

"Begged you"? We allowed you to come back. You Spaniards number less than three hundred families. All the Pueblos combined have thousands upon thousands of warriors. With a single strike, we could slaughter you all.

*Meanwhile, the OLD WOMAN and the STREET VENDOR have started to take note of the dispute brewing between HERNÁN and MATEO. They back off.*

**HERNÁN** (*turning to MATEO*)

Oh? Look around, Indian. See who controls this township. Not you. You "brave" Indian warriors couldn't slaughter a pig.

*MATEO has had enough. He furiously unsheathes his sword.*

**MATEO**

Then come to me, pig! And be the judge of how well I slaughter!

*MATEO prepares to charge at HERNÁN, but NICOLÁS alertly places his sword between the two men.*

**NICOLÁS**

Mateo! Stop this at once!

**MATEO**
Away you, Nicolás! It's time we cleanse the land once again of this Spanish filth!

**NICOLÁS**
Violence will do us no favors, my friends.

**ELADIO**
Well, well, well. What have we here?

> *All eyes turn to see that ELADIO has entered. He is a tall, well-built Spanish man in his early 20s, wearing a military uniform with the rank of teniente. He carries himself with the arrogant swagger of a bully who knows he's feared and relishes it. He immediately draws his sword and brandishes it at the back of NICOLÁS's neck.*

Appears you unruly savages need to be taught a lesson in respect. Mind you, the punishment is death for these transgressions. Turn around, Nicolás, your punishment awaits.

**NICOLÁS**
All I do is but keep the peace. Please, Eladio, sheathe your sword, or manage it to help me part these men.

**ELADIO** (*scoffing*)
Use a sword in the name of peace? How I hate that word, as I hate hell and all you Indians. In the name of our lord and Mother Spain, I sentence you to death!

> *Whipping out his sword, HERNÁN pushes JUAN back.*

**HERNÁN**
Get behind me, my lord! As I show this Indian once and for all that God and Spain are his masters!

**ELADIO**
Have at thee, coward!

> *Swinging his sword, ELADIO attacks NICOLÁS, who immediately raises his sword to defend himself. HERNÁN attacks and clangs his sword with MATEO's. As JUAN backs away, he accidentally bumps into the OLD WOMAN, who was also trying to get away but instead is knocked down to the ground. JUAN starts to leave her, but*

*he pauses, as his conscience gets the better of him. He quickly goes to her side, helps her up, and ushers her to safety as the battle swirls around them.*

*From one side of the stage comes Maestre de Campo MADRID, a robust Spanish man in his 50s. He is followed by his attractive but stern, well-dressed wife, CATALINA, 40s.*

**MADRID**
My sword, I say! Fetch me my sword!

**CATALINA** (*trying to hold him back*)
Stir not one foot into this fray, my husband.

**MADRID**
The Indians are attacking! They must be stopped before they seize the town!

*Almost simultaneously, from the other side of the stage comes CHISTOE, the governor of Pecos Pueblo, 50ish, a somewhat meek-looking Indian man dressed in informal Pueblo clothing. He is being urged onstage by his wife, ANIERI, a fiery and forceful Indian woman in her 40s. She is trying to push a sword into the hand of her husband.*

**CHISTOE**
If I go with a sword, we'll be plunged back into war.

**ANIERI**
Open your eyes! We are already at war. If you won't fight for our people, I will!

*With sword in hand, ANIERI starts to march toward the fight, but CHISTOE grabs her arm.*

**CHISTOE**
Wait! Give it to me. I do this against my own wishes.

*CHISTOE takes the sword and looks across the stage to MADRID, who calls out to him.*

**MADRID**
Chistoe! I knew in my bones your people possessed no honor!

**CHISTOE**
This is the thanks we get for letting you back into our land!

*Meanwhile, ELADIO slashes NICOLÁS's arm, knocking the sword out of his hand. He then pushes him to the ground and is about to finish him off, but he hears HERNÁN's cry. He turns to see that MA-TEO has just stabbed HERNÁN, who collapses, dead. MATEO then launches an attack on ELADIO, but ELADIO is too skilled a swordsman. He overcomes MATEO and stabs him. He falls, dead.*

*Suddenly, we hear the sound of Spanish military trumpets. NICOLÁS gets to his feet.*

**NICOLÁS**

'Tis El Gobernador! Don Diego de Vargas is coming! Lay down your arms!

*Things start to calm down as MADRID and CHISTOE cautiously retreat. The Spaniards quickly surround the dead body of HERNÁN, while the Indians flock around the lifeless body of MATEO.*

*From the audience comes VARGAS, a tall, distinguished Spanish man, impeccably groomed, dressed in elegant attire befitting one in his position. He walks up the steps onto the stage and briefly surveys the deadly results of the brawl.*

**VARGAS**

Rebellious subjects all, enemies of peace! Throw down your mistempered weapons and hear the pronouncement of your greatly movèd governor.

*MADRID, ELADIO, and CHISTOE lay down their swords.*

**MADRID** (*standing over HERNÁN*)

¡Excelencia! Look what they've done to my faithful servant!

**ANIERI** (*standing over MATEO*)

How can we live in peace if this is the way our people are treated?

**VARGAS**

¡Silencio! Five years ago, I arrived with cross and crown to reclaim this territory for Mother Spain, and did so in a fair, just manner. But memories of the Indian rebellion of 1680 are still opening old wounds. Three civil brawls bred of an airy word have thrice disturbed our fair town. As Governor, I will not allow you to tear down the peace I've worked so hard to build! Should there be another disturbance, the first two who raise their swords shall pay with their lives the forfeit of the peace. Maestre de Campo Lorenzo Madrid and Chief

Felipe Chistoe — I will see you both in my chambers this afternoon. All the rest, depart away now!

*The crowd starts to disband, walking offstage. VARGAS starts to walk offstage but is suddenly met by JUAN, who anxiously runs up to him.*

**JUAN**
F-father?

*VARGAS pauses and looks at JUAN closely.*

**VARGAS** (*stunned*)
Juan? My eyes deceive me. Is it really you, my son, all the way from Spain?

**JUAN**
Y-yes, father. It is I. W-w-when y-you s-saw me last, I w-was a b-boy. Now, as a m-m-man, I have c-come to help you re-conquer this n-new w-world.

**VARGAS**
Juan! Long have I hoped I would one day have my only son back at my side. I will help you start your life in this new world, my boy. And you will proudly carry on the Vargas name with your own family and hope for the future.

*VARGAS puts his arm around JUAN and leads him offstage, leaving only the bodies of the dead lying onstage. Stage lights dim. A mysterious hooded figure makes its way center stage. This is an old Indian MEDICINE MAN whose ethereal presence should suggest death.*

**MEDICINE MAN** (*speaking with a Pueblo accent*)
The future can only be seen in the realm of the spirit world, where the souls of the departed return to where they started. In this land of Indians and Spanish, hope for the future does not bode well for these two peoples, both alike in dignity but whose ancient feuds will mark the end for a pair of star-crossed lovers, children of old enemies, who, as in so many tragedies, must pay for their fathers' sins. It is the lessons of such sacrifice that will decide the fate of fair Santa Fe, where we lay our scene.

*As the mysterious hooded figure begins to depart, the bodies of the dead rise and follow him offstage. As they clear the stage, ANIERI and CHISTOE enter with NICOLÁS, who wears a bandage on his wounded arm.*

**ANIERI**

Governor Vargas treats the people of Pecos Pueblo not as men, but as tools. Your nephew Nicolás is a soldier, and our son Kino toils all day in their fields. This isn't peace. It's slavery.

**CHISTOE**

Only for the time being. Things will change, my wife, I promise you.

**ANIERI**

Does it not bother you that the other Pueblos speak of us as traitors? What if they decide to attack? We'll be slain with the Spaniards.

**NICOLÁS**

Not all the Pueblos feel that way, my aunt. There are many who still believe in peace and unity with the Spaniards.

**ANIERI**

There will be no peace until the Spanish are driven out of this land — again.

*With that, ANIERI spins on her heel and marches offstage. Both CHISTOE and NICOLÁS heave sighs.*

**CHISTOE**

Right glad I am that Kino was not at this fray. Saw you him today, Nicolás?

**NICOLÁS**

This morning, as I set forth from the Pueblo, I spied your son. Standing alone at the riverbank he was. I strode toward him, but he was wary of me and stole into the covert of the woods. What could be the cause of his sadness, uncle?

**CHISTOE**

I have sought answers many times for his sorrowful mood, but he chooses to confide in no one.

*Enter KINO, a very handsome 17-year-old Pecos Indian, wearing the rugged clothing of a Pueblo farmer. He spots his father and cousin and dashes behind a wall to conceal himself, but they've already spotted him. They pretend not to see him.*

Young men cannot remain silent forever. Perhaps he'll choose this occasion to disclose his sufferings to another young man. Take care, nephew.

*CHISTOE exits. NICOLÁS playfully tiptoes up to the wall and surprises KINO.*

**NICOLÁS**
Hello, Kino! Going to start your day in the Governor's fields?

**KINO** (*sighing*)
The clock has struck nine, but it feels already a whole lamentable day has passed.

**NICOLÁS**
Tell your cousin what causes such despair that makes your hours so long?

**KINO**
Not having the very precious gem that would make those hours race away.

**NICOLÁS** (*taking a second to think*)
Only one such treasure comes to mind. Love. Are you in love, Kino?

**KINO**
I thought I was, but I've learned that love can only exist when it is two who share those precious feelings. When the ache is felt by only one, it wallows in the soul like a song no one can hear.

**NICOLÁS**
What cruel maiden could have done this to you?

**KINO**
Did it to myself by pining from afar, for Rosalita from Picuris.

**NICOLÁS**
Ah, I hear she's a beauty, but I understood she was already pledged to marry.

**KINO**
A cruel twist my heart discovered only too late. I never even had a chance to tell her how I truly feel. Probably for the best since we never actually met.

> *KINO pauses. He has finally taken notice of the bloody bandage wrapped around NICOLÁS's arm.*

Nicolás? What happened? Oh, tell me not, for I already see it in your eyes. Another quarrel, more death, and no end to the hatred. Why must it be so impossible for our peoples to simply live in peace?

**NICOLÁS**
Well said, my cousin. Peace and a respect for all things living is the Pueblo way.

**KINO**

Don't they know this war and hatred brings despair to Mother Earth? That's why the rains never come, our crops are dying, and the people are poor. Only with more love and joy will the land grow green and healthy again. But sometimes it seems like the world will never know of love again. Nor will I.

**NICOLÁS**

Fret not, Kino. The seasons will change, and love will enter your life once again.

**KINO**

I can always count on you to lift my spirits, cousin. But I fear a life without love is a life unworthy of being lived.

*They exit.*

# Scene 2

*The Governor's office. Governor VARGAS awaits as MADRID enters, accompanied by ELADIO. CHISTOE is followed by ANIERI. VARGAS is taken aback by her presence.*

**VARGAS**

I did not call for this woman's attendance.

**CHISTOE**

I apologize, Excelencia, but my wife —

**ANIERI**

Governor, my people will no longer stand for the way they are being treated.

**MADRID**

Foolish woman! You will not speak to El Gobernador in such a manner!

**ANIERI** (*to VARGAS, refusing to be deterred*)

You lied to my husband, Governor. When you first sought the protection of my tribe, you promised my husband that our people would be treated with dignity and respect. You promised the repartimiento would come to an end, but our people are still toiling in the Spanish cornfields while the farmland of our own families is drying up, untended. I demand that you share your food supplies with our sick and elderly and treat us with the simple courtesy that is our due.

**ELADIO**

Gobernador, if I may, these are devil worshippers. You must not give into them! Lest you forget what murderers they are, remember the atrocities of 1680.

**ANIERI** (*still focused on VARGAS*)

Last year, when the Cochiti and Santo Domingo Pueblos attacked, did not the Pecos people rise to help you defend your precious Spanish town? You are vulnerable, Governor. Every day, you live under threat of attack from Apache, Comanche, and Navajo raiders. What if my husband were to tell his men to stand down? You and your people would be … defenseless.

**MADRID**

This is sedition! Chistoe, I suggest you control your wife, unless these are words you are too cowardly to speak yourself!

**CHISTOE**

Hold your tongue, my wife! Gobernador, please forgive me.

> *After patiently listening to all this, VARGAS steps toward ANIERI, who defiantly stands her ground.*

**VARGAS**

Doña Anieri, you should know I've had men hanged for issuing lesser threats. You would do well not to place too many demands on a governor who has been extremely tolerant. I know for a fact that many of your people have been secretly practicing their Indian ceremonies in kivas hidden in the mountain. The previous governors would have exacted severe penance for such sacrilege.

(*looking at CHISTOE*) However, these are difficult times for all of us, and the goodwill of the Pecos people has been much appreciated. Therefore, I shall see what I can do about sharing our provisions with those of your people most in need.

**ELADIO**

Gobernador, this is an outrage!

**VARGAS** (*to MADRID*)

Maestre de Campo! You will instruct your men to treat the good people of Pecos with the courtesy and respect that is their due.

(*to CHISTOE*) Chief Chistoe, I expect the unconditional loyalty and service of your tribe.

(*to both men*) It's the only way we're going to make peace work. You are both sworn to uphold that peace. ¿Claro?

*MADRID and CHISTOE give their hesitant affirmation.*

Good. Now, I know that I cannot make disappear the bad blood of two hundred years — but perhaps I can help us take the first steps toward learning to live without drawing blood. You may have heard my son Juan is newly arrived in town. Tomorrow night, I'm throwing a welcoming celebration in his honor. I want to show him that his father has made great strides in uniting the Spanish and Indian peoples. I'll expect you all to be in attendance. ¡Hasta mañana!

*CHISTOE salutes VARGAS and exits with ANIERI. MADRID salutes and starts to go offstage with ELADIO, but VARGAS beckons.*

Don Madrid, a word, por favor.

*MADRID gives a nod for ELADIO to go without him. Still displeased with the meeting, ELADIO heaves a sigh, shakes his head, and marches out.*

That nephew of yours is a hothead.

**MADRID**
He hates all Indians because of what they did to his family. He still grieves for his mother and father who were killed in the attacks those many years ago.

**VARGAS**
Family is very important to us. It's the reason we came to this new world. I trust you'll bring the entire Madrid household to the fiesta tomorrow.

**MADRID**
Of course, Excelencia.

**VARGAS**
If memory serves, you have a daughter, no? Quite a young beauty, as I recall.

**MADRID**
Teresa. Many years ago, I lost two older sons to sickness and disease, but not my baby girl. A strong flower she is, the only light and beauty left in my heart.

**VARGAS**
And how old is she? Of marrying age yet?

**MADRID**

Oh, not at all. She's seen the sum of hardly sixteen summers. One or two more she must ripen before we consider her a proper bride.

**VARGAS**

Younger than she are happy wives made.

**MADRID**

Forgive me, Excelencia, may I ask why such inquiries of my daughter?

**VARGAS**

As I said, my son Juan has arrived. Nothing would make me happier than to find a beautiful bride for him.

**MADRID**

I have no doubt your son is a fine young man, Excelencia, but are you saying it is your wish for my daughter to be betrothed to a man we've never met?

**VARGAS**

Meet him at the fiesta you will, and I promise you will find him the most charming son-in-law.

**MADRID**

Please understand, Excelencia, that I have always been very protective of my daughter. Rarely do I permit her to leave the hacienda.

**VARGAS**

She must fly the nest someday, old friend, unless your intent is to hide her in a convent. I assure you, she'll be well taken care of. As will you. I know the drought has been hard on your crops and food supplies. I promise you, when our children are married, all your family will become mine to care for. Now, may I expect you and your lovely daughter to be in attendance tonight?

**MADRID** (*taking a moment to think about it*)

It has always been my wish that, when the time came, my Teresa would meet a fine young man with the means to provide for her. And surely no finer family exists than the Vargas family. Be there we shall.

# Scene 3

*A balcony leading off to a well-kept room in the Madrid house-hold. Lingering about the balcony is TERESA, a radiantly beauti-ful Spanish girl, not quite 16. Her wardrobe is pretty but conserva-tive. She has a natural glow of innocence that, now, is somewhat dimmed by sadness, a languid melancholy.*

**TERESA**
The hour of boredom has struck again. Every day, the same thing. My stud-ies, chores, dinner, bedtime. My father keeps me locked in the house like a prisoner, only letting me out for church, family gatherings, and shopping on occasion. He leaves me no friends to speak of or speak with.

**NURSE** (*from within*)
Teresa? Querida? Teresa!

**TERESA**
All I have is my faithful nurse, but I can't do with her the fun things I want to do in life. I want to explore the world. I read books all the time about adven-ture and love, but I fret I will never know of such joys myself. How I long to fall in love with a handsome prince. But my father won't let me even look at a young man, let alone talk to one. Sometimes I wonder if a life such as mine is worth living. What would happen if I were to hurl myself over this balcony? Would I be killed or crippled? Would my father care? At least, it would be a break in the day.

*In walks the NURSE, a jolly, middle-aged Indian woman, dressed in servant's garb.*

**NURSE**
Straighten up now, sweet girl. The mother who bore you wants to speak to you.

(*calling out*) She's here waiting for you, señora!

*At that moment, CATALINA walks in, carrying herself like the imperious lady of the house that she is. She always seems preoccupied with herself. She treats her daughter like a stranger, and TERESA acts accordingly, greeting her mother with a formal curtsey.*

**TERESA**

I am here, señora. What is your will?

**CATALINA**

A very important matter. Leave us, Nurse. My daughter and I require privacy.

> *Disappointed, the NURSE starts to head offstage. CATALINA awkwardly looks at TERESA and starts to say something, but it becomes apparent that she's uncomfortable being alone with her. She turns to the NURSE, who has just stepped out the door.*

Nurse, come back. I think it better if you hear our counsel.

> *The NURSE happily comes back and stands next to TERESA.*

Would you say my daughter is of a pretty age?

**NURSE**

A very pretty age and only to get prettier. It's been near sixteen years since I first held this beautiful baby girl in my arms. It was the summer after the Great Revolt, after I was taken as an Apache slave by the Spanish colonists when they retreated to Socorro Pueblo. I thought it would be a miserable life, more miserable than when I caught ill and spent the entire week in the outhouse.

**CATALINA**

Nurse —

**NURSE**

But when I found I would be raising such a wonderful child, my future turned bright with joy. And I said to myself, maybe the Spanish aren't so bad after all, especially if it was possible that such a beautiful thing could spring from their Christian loins.

**CATALINA**

Nurse, please!

**NURSE**

Forgive me, señora. It's been my only remaining wish that I might live to see her wedding day.

**CATALINA**

Ah, yes! Her wedding day is the very theme of which I wish to speak. Please, my daughter, sit and tell me how you stand on the subject of marriage.

**TERESA** (*taken aback*)
It is an honor I have dreamt not of.

**CATALINA**
Younger than you here in Santa Fe are ready mothers made. By my count was I your mother much upon these years that you are now a maid. Know you that no less than the son of Don Diego de Vargas himself seeks your hand in matrimony.

> *The NURSE is overjoyed. She takes a bewildered TERESA into her arms.*

**NURSE**
A husband, señorita! If he is even half as handsome as his father, then there will be no luckier young lady in all of Santa Fe!

**CATALINA**
What say you, my child? Tomorrow night shall you behold him at a fiesta at the Governor's Palace. But before, you must know something. There is more to a good husband than mere good looks. He brings with him his father's vast fortune.

**NURSE**
Your mother is wise here. My own dear husband, rest in peace, was fat and had a face that looked as though smashed by a rock, but never a sweeter man there will ever be, or a better hunter. He always provided for me. And in bed? Oh, I tell you, my child, there were nights he made me see stars.

**CATALINA**
That will be all, Nurse. Now, my child, I ask you, can you like of the young man's love?

**TERESA** (*overwhelmed*)
I know not what to say. All these years, my father denies me visitors, and now, he wishes me to marry? I'll look to like, if liking is what you think I should do. Your consent tells me I would be a fool to do otherwise.

**CATALINA**
Excellent. Nurse, take her into town, and find her the finest gown in all of Santa Fe.

**NURSE**

Tomorrow night, you'll be the most beautiful girl anyone's ever seen. It'll be the first of many happy days and happier nights.

*The excited NURSE leads TERESA offstage.*

# Scene 4

*A street in Santa Fe. Enter KINO, NICOLÁS and Kino's best friend, CRISTÓBAL, early 30s, a robust, vibrant soldier, who is half-Indian and half-Spanish, with a full uniform and rank of al-férez. NICOLÁS wears his Spanish military sash, and KINO still wears his farm clothes. NICOLÁS and CRISTÓBAL have to coax KINO forward.*

**NICOLÁS** (*holding up the parchment invitation*)

The invitation says half past the hour. Come now, Kino, we don't want to be late, lest all the best dance partners be taken.

**KINO**

You two are the ones wearing dancing shoes with nimble soles. Dance partners will not do for a soul like mine that weighs as heavy as lead. You go, have fun.

*KINO starts to walk back offstage, but CRISTÓBAL stands in his path.*

**CRISTÓBAL**

Oh, dreary, weary Kino, locked away in your room like a monk. It's time for you to come out, throw away your vow of chastity, and learn to live life again!

**KINO**

What if Rosalita is at the party? I don't know if I could bear to look upon the face of a love so tragically lost.

**CRISTÓBAL**

Good God, man, you didn't even know her! For all you know, she was as hairy and smelly as a buffalo. Believe me, you're much too young a lad to know the true meaning of "a love so tragically lost." Forget the unattainable female and come to the party where, I promise you, we'll find many more just itching to be attained.

**KINO**

Is it so easy, Cristóbal, to give up on finding your true love? Haven't you met a woman so special she consumes your every waking thought and precious dream?

**CRISTÓBAL**

I don't have time to waste my affections on one woman, especially when the world is crowded with so many.

**NICOLÁS**

His words are meant to sound carefree and fickle, but I was there when our friend Cristóbal was struck by the thunderbolt.

**CRISTÓBAL**

You keep that hole in your face shut, Nicolás!

**KINO** (*amused*)

Could this be true? Cristóbal in love?

> CRISTÓBAL *roughly but playfully pushes NICOLÁS aside for revealing this.*

**CRISTÓBAL**

I should strike you down, you traitor, just as she struck me down. She was the descendant of Spanish royalty, as she always took pleasure in reminding me. She told me over and over how much she loved me, and I made the mistake of uttering those embarrassing proclamations as well. What a simp I was. When she found out I wasn't a full-blood Spaniard, that my mother was from Taos Pueblo, she turned her nose up at me and refused ever to speak to me again. I gave her my heart and she destroyed it, crushing it in her hands until it all poured out between her fingers and soaked into the ground.

**KINO**

It seems you know better than I the tragedy of a love lost, Cristóbal. I'm sorry.

**CRISTÓBAL**

Please, pity me not. You don't offer pity to the blind man who regains his sight. 'Twas a blessing, for it taught me that love, true love, can never exist.

**KINO**

I agree that love can bring pain, but it can also bring the most joyous and wondrous of feelings. One cannot deny the existence of something so powerful.

CRISTÓBAL

True love is supposed to be that which lasts forever, an unbreakable bond that never dies. But men and women are simply incapable of pledging that kind of eternal devotion to each other. What married men and women do you see actually smiling or holding hands? Your grandparents? Your mother and father? That's why love is nothing but a fool's dream. It's as much an illusion as the reasons for this party tonight.

> *He rips the invitation out of NICOLÁS's hands and reads it sarcastically.*

"Don Diego de Vargas does hereby invite the soldiers under the command of Governor Felipe Chistoe of Pecos Pueblo to attend a special celebration honoring the friendship between the Spanish and the Pecos people."

(*scoffing*) Friendship? The Spanish and Pueblo people can scarcely get through the day without a public brawl. Just how does Governor Vargas expect them to get through a party?

KINO

If what you say is true, Cristóbal, that Spaniards and Indians are doomed to quarrel, then you with your mixed blood are fated to be at war with yourself all the time.

CRISTÓBAL

Let me ask you, my dear, deluded Kino, what man is not at war with himself? Each man, every day, must struggle with right and wrong, war and peace, good and evil, living and dying, pinching or not pinching a shy maiden's rump.

KINO

But to whom do you pledge your allegiance? Do you call yourself Spanish or Indian?

CRISTÓBAL

It depends on what time of day it is. In the morning, when I wake, it is the Indian part of me that gives thanks for the beauty of the sun, land, and sky. In the afternoon, as I walk around town and see who rules this province, it is the Spanish part of me that wants to be on the side of the winners. But when night falls and I contemplate the day, I realize I'm neither. I don't fit into either world. Everywhere I go I'm treated like an outsider. And, in those times, I want to tear myself apart, tear the Spanish side or the Indian side, whichever comes out first!

**KINO**

Peace, Cristóbal, peace. I was only teasing you. You're Indian. You're here amongst your Indian friends.

**CRISTÓBAL**

So, tell me, my Indian friend, will you come to the fiesta willingly, or shall we pick you up and carry you there?

**KINO**

Scoundrel, my better nature tells me to walk away. But I'll go, if only to keep an eye on you, my friend. I pray I don't live to regret this.

# Scene 5

*Outside the Governor's Palace. Long tables of food are arranged outside a stately hacienda. On one side of the stage, a SPANISH MUSICIAN plays a Spanish guitar. On the other side, an INDIAN MUSICIAN alternates between flute and drums. CHISTOE and ANIERI arrive, promptly greeted by VARGAS.*

**VARGAS**

Don Felipe, Doña Anieri. Bienvenidos. You honor me with your presence.

**ANIERI**

All I can say is it's about the time that Indian people are allowed to attend the same social gatherings as Spaniards.

**VARGAS**

Please, help yourselves to food and drink.

*ELADIO arrives and contemptuously regards CHISTOE and ANIERI. He then sees CATALINA, who comes out from the Governor's Palace.*

**ELADIO** (*to CATALINA*)

My uncle told me tonight was a festive occasion, yet we're forced to share the night with these savages. What next? Dining with dogs?

**CATALINA**

Patience, dear boy, give your governor some credit. The true fiesta is inside.

*CATALINA leads ELADIO past a doorway which is manned by an armed Spanish guard, MONTOYA. They proceed inside the Governor's Palace where we find MADRID having a drink.*

*Meanwhile, TERESA and the NURSE are curiously scouting the room.*

**TERESA**
Which one do you think he is? That one? What about that one?

**NURSE**
No, that's Rodrigo Anaya's son. I'm sure the son of Gobernador Vargas must carry himself with the most perfect manners and civilized grace.

*Suddenly, JUAN stumbles onto the stage, causing a commotion as he accidentally knocks over a serving tray. He tries to clean it up but just ends up making things worse by knocking over more things.*

*TERESA and the NURSE look at each other as if to say, "Could he be the one?" They then shake their heads, thinking, "no, couldn't be." The NURSE quickly ushers TERESA away to continue their search in another part of the room. Meanwhile, VARGAS enters to see his hapless son struggling to clean up the mess. VARGAS quickly directs a SERVANT toward JUAN. JUAN looks up to see the SERVANT and then his father. He climbs to his feet.*

**JUAN** (*to the SERVANT*)
C-clean this m-m-mess up at once, you f-fool!

*JUAN makes his way over to VARGAS.*

**JUAN**
F-f-father, wh-wh-where is the one you say will be my b-b-bride? Is-is she here yet? She b-b-better not be ugly.

**VARGAS**
Follow me, my son, and I will introduce you to the most beautiful angel in all of Santa Fe.

*VARGAS leads JUAN through the palace. Meanwhile, coming into the area outside the Governor's Palace are KINO, CRISTÓBAL, and NICOLÁS.*

**CRISTÓBAL**

Ah, wine, women, and song. I'll see if I can find me a Spanish wench who prefers me Spanish, or an Indian wench who prefers me Indian, or the other way around.

*He pauses, looking around.*

But by the looks of it, I see a lot of Indians and not many Spanish.

**NICOLÁS**

Could it be we've arrived too early?

*At that moment, the trio of friends takes note of ANIERI, followed by CHISTOE, who walks over to the entrance to the palace. Her passage is blocked by MONTOYA.*

**ANIERI**

Why will you not let me pass? Stand aside.

**MONTOYA**

Uh, the Governor has private business.

**ANIERI** (*looking through the doorway*)

Private business? Or a private party? I should've known.

(*to* CHISTOE) More Spanish lies. Are you going to sit still for this?

**CHISTOE**

Please, my wife, can we have one night without you causing trouble?

*CHISTOE imploringly ushers his angry wife away from the door. CRISTÓBAL, KINO, and NICOLÁS react to this.*

**CRISTÓBAL**

Ah, looks like our esteemed Governor is up to his old tricks, keeping the Indians out of the real party. What say you we see for ourselves what they try to keep hidden from our prying eyes?

**NICOLÁS**

But how do we get in if they're keeping the Indians out?

**CRISTÓBAL**

Leave that to me. Much experience I have gaining entry into parties that others have forgotten to invite me to. Come with me!

*CRISTÓBAL quickly heads offstage, followed by KINO and NICO-LÁS. Meanwhile, inside the Governor's Palace, TERESA and the NURSE are still searching the crowd for her intended suitor.*

**MADRID**
¡Teresa, mi querida!

*Coming through the crowd are MADRID and CATALINA, followed by VARGAS and JUAN. They head over to TERESA and the NURSE, who exchange glances, as if to say "no, it can't be," as soon as they see JUAN.*

I'd like you to meet Don Juan Francisco de Vargas. Don Juan, may I present my lovely daughter, Teresa.

*JUAN bows to TERESA, who, in response, politely curtsies.*

**JUAN**
'T-t-tis an honor and p-p-pleasure to m-m-meet you, T-T-Teresa.

**TERESA**
It is my privilege, señor.

*There is an awkward silence as JUAN and TERESA don't know what else to say. VARGAS decides to strike up the band.*

**VARGAS**
Why not have some dancing? Music!

*Responding, the SPANISH MUSICIAN begins playing dance music. VARGAS starts to urge everyone onto the dance floor. JUAN gestures for TERESA to accompany him to the dance floor, which she does. They begin a square-dance type of folk step, and she is taken aback by JUAN's chronic clumsiness as he misses steps and stumbles. VARGAS and MADRID watch from the sidelines.*

He merely needs a little more practice. But he will treat your daughter well. And, in turn, because you will be my family, I will treat you well.

**MADRID** (*trying to convince himself*)
They look good together, Excelencia.

*Meanwhile, CRISTÓBAL, KINO, and NICOLÁS make their way to the entrance of the Governor's Palace. Their faces are partially obscured by oversized conquistador helmets, and they wear full Spanish military uniforms. They walk up to MONTOYA, who eyes them suspiciously.*

**MONTOYA**

Who are you?

**CRISTÓBAL**

Mi amigo, Don Montoya, do you not recognize the men who saved your fat hide in battle last year?

*Silence as MONTOYA stares at him. CRISTÓBAL suddenly bursts out laughing, as do KINO and NICOLÁS, though they're not sure why. After a moment, MONTOYA shrugs and joins the laughter and lets them pass through. Once the trio of Indian friends enters the party area, they stop laughing.*

**KINO**

What, pray tell, were we laughing about?

**CRISTÓBAL**

As long as he knows, that's all that matters. Now that we've made it into the lion's den, let's see if we can bag ourselves a lioness.

*The trio starts to move around the room. Meanwhile, the song ends, and the dance partners break up and head off the floor. TERESA immediately runs to the NURSE.*

**TERESA**

Oh, Nurse, help me. Awake me from this nightmare, for this cannot truly be the one my father wants me to marry.

**NURSE**

Oh, I know, my dear. But he's rich. Keep remembering that.

*Another song begins. JUAN makes his way over to TERESA.*

**JUAN**

D-Doña T-T-Teresa, w-w-we didn't f-f-finish our dance. O-o-one more, please.

*TERESA looks to the NURSE for help. All she can do is whisper.*

**NURSE**

Remember — rich, rich, rich.

*TERESA reluctantly goes with JUAN out to the dance floor again, where they embark on another visibly awkward attempt to dance. Meanwhile, KINO and NICOLÁS are standing at the perimeter of the dance floor, surveying the crowd, but we can see that KINO's heart isn't into it.*

**NICOLÁS**

Look at all these beautiful women. What if one of them is your true love?

**KINO**

Finding my true love here would be a miracle found only in a fairy tale.

*NICOLÁS sympathetically pats KINO on the back and walks off. Suddenly, TERESA, who has been struggling to coordinate her dance movements with JUAN's, is caught off balance by more of his clumsiness. JUAN stumbles backward while TERESA falls forward next to KINO's feet. KINO immediately offers his hand to help her up.*

Señorita, are you all right?

*TERESA's hand touches KINO's. As TERESA stands, she looks up to see mostly a conquistador's helmet. KINO lifts up the helmet to reveal his face. Their eyes meet, resulting in an instantaneous moment of magic which is indescribable, but recognizable to all who have been young and in love. He smiles at her. She smiles back. She starts to say something, but —*

**JUAN**

T-Teresa, come.

*JUAN takes her arm and pulls her away from KINO, back to the dance floor. She continues to look back at him. Suddenly, ELADIO comes forward. He has apparently taken notice of this incident. KINO is about to go after TERESA, but ELADIO steps into his path.*

**ELADIO**

What manner of treachery is this, Indian boy? In disguise? Trespassing?

**KINO**

I merely came to enjoy the festivities, good Eladio. Are they not for all?

**ELADIO**

I know you. Kino, son of our enemy Chief Chistoe. And now, I witness your vile touch upon the hand of my virgin cousin. By stock and honor of my kin, I shall now strike you dead for this sin!

*ELADIO starts to draw his sword, but MADRID suddenly steps in.*

**MADRID**

Teniente, step back and dare not mar this time of celebration for my daughter.

(*to KINO*) I hear that you are a well-mannered boy, and well-mannered boys would do well to not create ill-mannered company.

**KINO**

Perdóneme, Don Madrid.

*KINO walks off, and ELADIO is ready to explode with fury.*

**ELADIO**

Did you not see the insult upon our family's honor? Are you going to stand by and let that Indian heathen desecrate your daughter's purity?

**MADRID**

I saw nothing. I will not have you ruin this night. Now, take no more note of him and cause not one ounce of trouble! For if you do, it is *I* who will bear the brunt of the Governor's wrath.

*At that moment, CATALINA walks up to them.*

**CATALINA**

What is the meaning of this conference?

**MADRID**

Nothing, my dear. The night is joyous and rosy.

*MADRID walks off as ELADIO fumes.*

**ELADIO**

My uncle expects me to stay my sword while an Indian boy makes fools of us. Patience will stay willful choler not for a beggar's pittance.

**CATALINA**

You are a princox. But you're right to be wary of the Indians. Always be mindful of them.

*Meanwhile, KINO is anxiously circling the dance floor, searching the crowd, looking out from under his helmet.*

**KINO**

Where is that radiant angel who suddenly descended from the heavens and landed at my feet? Never have I seen such beauty too rich for use, for earth too dear. Her face, it glows more radiant than all the torches in town. Perhaps I never knew the meaning of true love — until now.

*KINO continues his search, disappearing into the crowd. Meanwhile, a troubled MONTOYA finds his way over to VARGAS.*

**MONTOYA**
Gobernador, forgive me, but some angry Indian woman demands to come inside. If I don't let her in, she says she'll send Indian warriors to my house and have them feed me to the wolves.

*MONTOYA doesn't realize it, but ANIERI is right behind him, as is CHISTOE. ANIERI marches up to VARGAS.*

**ANIERI**
Is this your idea of courtesy and respect, Governor? Keeping the Indians outside, away from the real celebration?

**VARGAS** (*quickly coming up with an excuse*)
Doña Anieri, I merely thought your people would be more comfortable with your own music and food. But you are, of course, welcome to join us.

*With that, VARGAS curtly bows and walks away with MONTOYA. CHISTOE looks at the dancing, then looks at his wife.*

**CHISTOE**
What say you, my wife? Will you join me in a dance?

**ANIERI**
No. This music of the Spaniards is too strange for me. I have no like for it.

*The song comes to an end, and TERESA and JUAN walk off the dance floor.*

**TERESA**
You are a most unique dancer, señor. Dare I say, you have worn me to a frazzle. Would you mind fetching me some water while I sit here and rest?

**JUAN**
Your w-w-wishes are m-my wishes.

*As JUAN goes off to get some water, the NURSE goes over to TERESA.*

**NURSE**
How fared you, my child?

**TERESA**

At least he didn't drop me on the floor this time. Nurse, a young soldier helped me when I fell. Do you know who he was?

**NURSE**

Forgive me, dear, I did not catch sight of his face.

**TERESA**

I was pulled away before I had the chance to properly thank him.

> *TERESA sees that JUAN is coming back over. She quickly hides behind the NURSE.*

He's coming back. I pray you, tell him not where I've fled.

> *TERESA rushes off, searching the faces in the crowd. Meanwhile, KINO heads outside the walls of the palace, to a courtyard area, out of sight from everyone else. He takes off his helmet and sighs.*

**KINO**

Truly, I am cursed. For an instant, I glimpsed the face of perfection, only to have it vanish in a faceless crowd. How cruel the fates can be, revealing my first true love, then mercilessly hiding her from my sight.

> *The INDIAN MUSICIAN has made his way to the courtyard. He starts playing his flute. KINO smiles as he hears what is an Indian love song. He stands up and, as he turns around, he almost bumps into TERESA, who has just stepped outside, looking for him. Both are caught off guard for a moment, speechless, as they clearly recognize each other. KINO finally manages to compose himself.*

Señorita, you must forgive my haste. For I was in search of an angel who earlier landed at my feet. My intention was to make sure she wasn't hurt, for it would be blasphemous of me to allow one of the Lord's most sacred, beautiful works of art to be injured or damaged. Do you know where I might find her?

**TERESA**

This I can tell you — she has gone off to look for the gallant soul who came to her rescue. She is unhurt and seeks to reward him for his heroism. Might you know this kind stranger's name?

**KINO**

Kino, I've heard him called. And the name of this angel he seeks?

**TERESA**

Teresa. Not an angel, merely a damsel looking for a hero. We must make sure they find each other. What sort of reward would this Kino accept for his heroism?

**KINO**

I'll wager he would be most honored to share a dance with her.

**TERESA**

I fear Teresa cannot be seen dancing with any other man tonight, except the one to whom she's been assigned for the evening.

**KINO**

What if they were to dance out here, out of everyone's view?

**TERESA**

Perhaps, but what if we can't find this star-crossed pair?

**KINO**

Then, let us dance in their stead.

> *KINO holds out his hand. After a bit of nervous hesitation, TERESA puts her hand in his hand. To the beautiful flute music, he engages her in a two-step which shouldn't be too obviously Indian, but it's something that KINO teaches her. They move together with effortless grace. Meanwhile, ANIERI has made her way to the courtyard area. She stops in her tracks behind the wall as she lays eyes on KINO dancing with TERESA.*

**ANIERI**

The sound of an Indian flute has led me to this — to the sight of my son consorting with a Spanish girl? No, I will not stand for this.

> *She starts to step out from behind the wall, but CHISTOE takes her arm.*

**CHISTOE**

What do you hope to do by embarrassing the boy? Please, allow our unhappy son one moment of happiness. Talk to him you will when he comes home.

> *Not happy about this, ANIERI relents and follows CHISTOE offstage. The song comes to an end and KINO and TERESA look into each other's eyes and smile, their hearts ready to burst.*

**TERESA**
Thank you for the dance … Kino.

**KINO**
Thank you … Teresa.

**NURSE** (*calling from the dance floor*)
Teresa! Where are you, dear girl? It's time to go home!

**TERESA**
I must go.

**KINO**
So soon?

**TERESA**
I'd stay for hours, but I mustn't let anyone find us here. I wish to thank you again for coming to my rescue. I was very much in need of a hero to come to my rescue tonight.

**KINO**
The honor was mine, my lady. In the books I've read, whenever a hero rescues a damsel in distress, he is rewarded with a kiss. What say you we be faithful to the written word?

> *A beat. TERESA has never kissed anybody before. But she moves forward and kisses KINO. Suddenly, the NURSE steps into the courtyard.*

**NURSE**
My lady, please behave! Your mother and father are looking for you.

> *TERESA touches KINO's hand as long as she can, then quickly heads into the palace area. KINO starts to follow, but the NURSE stops him.*

**NURSE**
Count your lucky stars it was I who caught you. Had you been seen by the Governor or his son, you'd be bound for the gallows. You wear a Spanish uniform, but you look to be a Pueblo boy. What family are you?

**KINO**
My father is Chistoe. Tell me, who is that beautiful creature who has taken my heart?

**NURSE**

She is the daughter of Maestre de Campo Lorenzo Madrid. Best you stay away, young Chistoe. Stay away.

*The NURSE runs into the crowd while the realization of TERESA's identity begins to sink in with KINO.*

**KINO**

That she was a Spaniard I had already guessed, but daughter of my father's worst enemy? My mother will become my worst enemy if she ever hears of this. But I can't ignore this song in my heart, a song that fills me with such unbelievable joy. I must see her again.

*KINO quickly goes offstage. Meanwhile, in the palace, the party is ending. The NURSE heads over to TERESA, who is anxiously waiting for her.*

**TERESA**

Come hither, Nurse. Who was this Kino you found me with?

**NURSE**

Trust me, dear girl, you would do well to stay away from him. He's an Indian boy. Son of your father's enemy. Believe me, nothing good can come of this.

*The NURSE takes TERESA by the hand. She is shocked, confused, but in love.*

# Scene 6

*Outside of the Madrid hacienda, a Spanish style edifice with balcony on the second story. KINO tentatively wanders out from the orchard. He looks at the house.*

**KINO**

Many times I have passed by this dwelling, never imagining the beauty dwelling within.

**MADRID** (*offstage*)

I made your apologies to Don Juan de Vargas, my child.

*KINO quickly hides behind the orchard as the Madrid family (MADRID, CATALINA, TERESA, and the NURSE) walk onstage up to the house.*

**CATALINA**

There is much riding on this marriage, Teresa — namely, your future. So, I will expect you to conduct yourself as a proper bride to be.

*They all walk into the hacienda. KINO steps out from behind the orchard.*

**KINO**

Can this be true? My true love already promised to another? If they weren't laughing before, surely, the ancient spirits are laughing at me now.

**NICOLÁS** (*offstage*)

Kino! Kino!

*KINO again quickly hides behind the orchard as CRISTÓBAL and NICOLÁS walk onstage.*

**CRISTÓBAL**

He's gone home to bed, I tell you. No doubt he was wallowing in the dark humor at the gathering. I'll wager he left early to further pine away for Rosalita.

**NICOLÁS**

Of that I am doubtful. When last I saw my cousin, he had just been swept away by the charms of another girl he desperately sought to find.

**CRISTÓBAL**

Another one? Our dear Kino falls in love more than leaves fall in the fall. If he only knew. Whenever a heart such as his is open to all the love in the world, it's also an open wound for just as much pain. Remember that Cupid's arrows are still arrows, and arrows are fashioned to kill. Kino! Wherever you are! Spare yourself! If you ever see one of Cupid's arrows coming, jump out of the way! The pain of death itself will cause you less suffering than the pain of love.

*CRISTÓBAL and NICOLÁS walk offstage. KINO emerges from the orchard.*

**KINO**

I have no doubt that the pain of love is great, my friend, especially if not returned by the object of your affection. This is why I must learn the truth from Teresa. Does she love me, or will she marry another?

*The door to the upper balcony suddenly opens and TERESA comes strolling out, looking into the night sky.*

What is that light from yonder window? Why, it's my lady, my love! Look at her, how the brightness of her eyes puts all the twinkles in heaven to shame. How could it be that, all this time, such a beauty was hidden away in Santa Fe? Look how she leans her cheek upon her hand. If only I could be a glove upon that hand, that I might touch that cheek.

TERESA (*sighing*)

Ay me!

KINO

She speaks! Speak again, my bright angel! Let me hear the song of your voice once more.

TERESA

How can it be, after everything I've been taught — after everything my family told me about Indians and their godless ways — how can it be that I could fall in love with one? O, Kino, Kino! Why have you come into my life, Kino?

KINO

Shall I answer her now, or dare I hear more?

TERESA

It would be so much easier if you could simply cast off your Indian skin and become Spanish and earn the acceptance of my family. But you can no more do that than can I shed my Spanish skin and become Indian. Oh, but why must it matter who's Indian and who's Spanish? What is an Indian, after all? Isn't he a person, the same as the Spanish? We all walk and talk and breathe the same air. All that is different is the color of our skin and hair. Why should color matter? A red rose and white rose are still roses, no matter what the color. O, Kino, if only you could be an Indian no more, we could be together forevermore.

KINO

If I take you at your word, then consider me no longer Indian!

> *KINO suddenly climbs up the orchard walls and leaps onto the balcony, startling TERESA, who jumps back.*

TERESA

Who comes to me under the cover of night to spy my counsel?

**KINO**

I fear to say, for I would be risking your contempt for my people.

**TERESA**

My ears have not drunk a hundred words of your voice, yet already I recognize it as a voice I hold not in contempt. Are you not Kino — an Indian?

**KINO**

Neither, señorita, if either you dislike.

**TERESA**

From where did you come? The orchard walls are high and hard to climb, and this place could be certain death for you if any of my family were to find you.

**KINO**

With love's wings did I ascend these walls; for neither walls nor fear of death can stop what love does attempt. For I cannot go on until I have the answer to this: Are you to be married? Does your heart already belong to another man?

**TERESA**

It's true when the evening began, I was intended, but, at the evening's end, my intentions have changed. But before I answer where my heart belongs, you must first tell me where your heart dwells. If I ask if you love me, surely you will say you do. And even if you swear, how will I know if it's the truth you speak? At lovers' perjuries they say Jove laughs. O, gentle Kino, if you do love me, pronounce it faithfully.

**KINO**

Lady, by yonder blessèd moon I vow —

**TERESA**

Wait, swear not by the moon, the inconstant moon that changes monthly, lest your love prove likewise variable.

**KINO**

Then tell me what to swear by and I shall do it.

**TERESA**

Perhaps swear not at all tonight. Best we bid a sweet good night. Then, this bud of love, by summer's ripening breath, may reveal itself to be a beautiful flower when next we meet. Buenas noches, and may you sleep the same joyful sleep I will sleep tonight.

*TERESA starts to leave, but KINO is insistent.*

**KINO**

Teresa, will you leave me so unsatisfied?

**TERESA** (*innocent but coy*)

Kino, what satisfaction do you think you can have this night?

**KINO**

Merely an answer to my question. You still have not told me to whom your heart truly belongs. Would you abandon my love and marry another?

**TERESA**

I would think my feelings would make clear what words do not. But if you wish, I will say it. I knew not the look of love's face until I looked into yours.

**KINO**

And you will not marry this other man?

**TERESA**

In truth, the son of Gobernador Vargas means more to my parents than to me. If they could marry him, they probably would, if only to collect the dowry.

**KINO**

You will defy your family, forego the promise of wealth?

**NURSE** (*offstage*)

Teresa!

**TERESA**

Anon, good Nurse! Kino, I would trade all the riches in the world for the promise of true love. If your love is honorable and your purpose is marriage, send word tomorrow. Tell me where and what time the rite will be performed, and I will come. I'll leave my family and fortune behind and follow you to the ends of the earth. Tomorrow, I will send a friend to the town plaza to collect your message.

**NURSE** (*offstage*)

Señorita! Where are you?

**TERESA**

Till then, a thousand times a good night!

*TERESA quickly heads inside.*

**KINO**

She leaves me a thousand reasons to yearn for the light of day. What a glorious day will dawn when it matters not if one is Indian or Spanish.

*KINO starts to climb down the orchard wall. As he does, TERESA comes back on the balcony.*

**TERESA**

Kino? I cannot speak loudly lest my family hear. Are you still near?

**KINO**

My sweet! I will never be far.

**TERESA**

I forgot why I called you back.

**KINO**

I shall stay till you remember.

*TERESA giggles.*

**TERESA**

I shall forget again to have you staring at me; for I will be lost in your eyes. Ah, no I remember. What time tomorrow shall I send to you?

**KINO**

By the hour of nine. By then, all that needs to be will be taken care of.

**TERESA**

Then I will not fail. Buenas noches, Kino. What sweet sorrow does parting bring. I wish I could say goodnight over and over till morning.

*KINO leans forward to try to kiss her, but she coyly backs away.*

On our wedding day, we will seal our love with a kiss. Sleep well, my hero.

*TERESA smiles at him and goes back inside.*

**KINO**

A restful sleep will not befall me tonight, for there are many plans to be made. And tomorrow at this time, I will be Teresa's husband and she will be my wife.

*KINO ecstatically races offstage.*

# Scene 7

*The next morning, Outside the Spanish church. Dressed in mendi-
cant garb, the kindly FRAY OLVERA tends to his garden, carrying
a basket, gathering herbs.*

**FRAY OLVERA**

The gray-eyed morn smiles on the frowning night and reveals nature for all its
wondrous beauty and might. The Indian medicine men taught me the divine
power of plants and herbs. This one induces sleep. This one can cure. This
can kill. We can learn so much from the Indian people. 'Tis a pity that we
force them to unlearn what they know. Too much blood has spilled over that
already.

*KINO enters on a cloud, filled with exuberant joy.*

**KINO**

Good morning, Fray Olvera!

**FRAY OLVERA** (*recognizing the voice of one of his best pupils*)

Why, Kino, my dear boy! My best student. When all the other Indian boys
were resentful and mistrustful of the Lord's teachings, you were the one who
always believed that all knowledge is holy. This is an uncommon hour for you,
young lad. What stirs you up so early?

*FRAY OLVERA turns around to get his first look at KINO and is
taken aback to see that he's wearing a Spanish military uniform.
Amused, he continues.*

By the looks of you, I'd say that young Kino has not even been to bed. Dressed
in a Spanish uniform, are you? What hast thou done?

**KINO**

I had been feasting with my enemy, when suddenly I found myself pierced in
the heart by Cupid's arrows. My enemy was then hit by the very same arrow.
I come here, for both our remedies are to be found with your help and your
holy medicine. I bear no hatred, for, lo, my intercession likewise steads my foe.

**FRAY OLVERA**

Be plain, good son, and homely in thy shrift. Riddling confession finds but
riddling shrift.

**KINO**

Then plainly know my heart's dear love is set on the fair daughter of Maestre de Campo Lorenzo Madrid. And now we wish to combine our hearts in holy matrimony.

**FRAY OLVERA** (*shocked by what he's hearing*)
Jesu Maria! What a change! What of a girl named Rosalita whom thou lovest so dear, so soon forsaken?

**KINO**

I pray you, chide me not now. For I know that my love for Rosalita was an illusion. I have found my true love; for she loves me as much as I do her.

**FRAY OLVERA**

My son, the whims of your ever-changing heart are not my only concerns. What concerns me most is the Maestre de Campo. He will never give consent to this union. There has never been a Christian wedding for an Indian man and Spanish woman, and I can firmly say there will not be one today!

> *On that note, FRAY OLVERA rushes back into the church and puts his basket on a table filled with jars and beakers of medicines and potions. KINO follows him into the church.*

**KINO**
Father, please. Above all others, I thought you would be the one to understand. You were the one who taught me that we have to learn to see past our differences and share what we have in common. What Teresa and I have in common is our love. And isn't love what our Lord Jesus Christ wants for us anyway?

> *To emphasize the point, KINO crosses himself. FRAY OLVERA takes a moment to meditate on what KINO has said. He then turns to a porcelain statue of Christ on the cross.*

**FRAY OLVERA**

He wanted us all to live in peace and harmony. He sacrificed himself for our sins, but it seems all we do is repeat them. Perhaps you are right, young Kino. Perhaps a marriage between an Indian lad and a Spanish lady will be the first step in forging a peace between your warring families. And perhaps the Lord has chosen me to be the vessel to seal this holy union. In that respect, I'll thy assistant be. For this alliance may so prove to turn your peoples' vile rancor to pure love.

> *KINO gratefully kisses FRAY OLVERA's hand.*

**KINO**

Thank you, good father, thank you!

**FRAY OLVERA**

I'll await you this afternoon. Go now.

> *KINO happily runs offstage.*

What a glorious day this is when lovers can make enemies unite!

> *FRAY OLVERA spreads out his arms joyously. As he does, he accidentally knocks over the statue of Christ, and it falls to the floor and shatters. He stands over the broken pieces with a look of dread on his face.*

Oh, dear Lord, what I have done? Is this a sign that we move too much in haste? For it is often said that those who run too fast are bound to fall.

> *The lights fade to black and the curtain falls.*

# ACT 2
## Scene 1

*The Santa Fe town plaza. CRISTÓBAL and NICOLÁS enter,*
*looking around.*

**CRISTÓBAL**

Where the devil should this Kino be? For weeks he rarely steps out of the house. Now he rarely steps in.

**NICOLÁS**

This morning when I checked, his mother told me he had been out the whole night. She did not seem very happy.

**CRISTÓBAL**

That woman rarely is. You said you saw Kino consorting with some girl last night? Perhaps our friend has finally rid himself of Rosalita's woe and found yet another pitiless nymph to reap his agonies.

**NICOLÁS**

If he has, I fear it's not an Indian maiden he's found.

**CRISTÓBAL**

Ah, so you think Kino trots after a Spanish girl? Perhaps the young buck is more courageous than I give him credit for.

*At that moment, KINO strolls into the plaza with a bounce in his step and a smile on his face. He still wears remnants of the soldier's uniform.*

**KINO**

Good morning, my dear friends.

**CRISTÓBAL**

Ah, our man of mystery finally returning to those whom he unfairly gave the counterfeit last night.

**KINO**

What counterfeit did I give you?

CRISTÓBAL
The slip, señor, the slip. Can you not conceive? Or has your mind gone soft
with the scent of love again?

KINO
Forgive me, good Cristóbal, but last night my business was pressing.

CRISTÓBAL
Is that so? Who was she, and how hard were you pressing her?

KINO
I know you are an atheist at love's altar, my good friend, but I'll have you know
my eternal faith has been rewarded with a divine revelation.

NICOLÁS
Friends, coming this way, look.

> *The NURSE enters.*

CRISTÓBAL
I wonder what an ancient lady like that would want with us.

NURSE
Buenos días, gentlemen.

CRISTÓBAL
Buenas tardes, gentlewoman.

NURSE
Is it buenas tardes already?

CRISTÓBAL
'Tis no less, I say. For the bawdy hand of the dial is upon the prick of noon.

NURSE (*taken aback by his ribaldry*)
Out upon you! What kind of man are you?

KINO
The kind of man, good gentlewoman, that God himself regrets.

NURSE
Well said, señor. You are Kino, are you not? The one I met last night?

**CRISTÓBAL**

"Last night"? No, Kino, don't tell me. This is not the new fair maiden who has stolen your heart? Where did you come upon her? At a house of skainsmates?

**KINO**

Quiet, you scoundrel. Yes, good woman, it is I, Kino.

**NURSE**

Ah, then I do desire a private conference with you.

*CRISTÓBAL and NICOLÁS burst out laughing.*

**CRISTÓBAL**

"Desire a private conference"? Kino, if I were you, I'd take care.

*He goes up to the NURSE, taunting her.*

Sometimes these old ladies of the evening don't have the strength to make it through the evening. I'd hate to see you get your heart broken again.

**NURSE**

Away from me, you scurvy knave!

*KINO pushes CRISTÓBAL and NICOLÁS away.*

**CRISTÓBAL**

Farewell, ancient lady!

*CRISTÓBAL and NICOLÁS exit, laughing.*

**NURSE**

If this is the type of company you keep, dear boy, perhaps my mistress would be better off not knowing one such as you.

**KINO**

Nurse, I beg you, commend me to your lady and mistress.

**NURSE**

How do I know you won't lead her into a fool's paradise? My lady is young and innocent. Therefore, if you should deal double with her, it will prove that you are no better than your friends and unworthy of affection.

**KINO**

I will prove myself worthy, dear lady. And here is the proof: bid Teresa to devise some means to slip away this afternoon, and there she shall at Fray Olvera's church be married to her love Kino.

**NURSE** (*overcome with joy*)

Married? Then your intentions *are* honorable! I knew it all along! My lady will be so happy! I anger her sometimes when I tell her that Juan de Vargas is the more proper man, but, deep down in my heart, it gives me joy to know that it is one of my own kind — an Indian — who has won her heart.

**KINO**

Then you will commend me to your lady?

**NURSE**

Oh, a thousand times!

**KINO**

Thank you, beautiful lady, thank you!

> *KINO kisses the NURSE on the cheek and runs offstage.*

# Scene 2

> *Outside the Madrid hacienda, near the orchard. TERESA paces around, impatiently waiting.*

**TERESA**

What's taking my nurse so long? Hour passes upon hour. An eternity upon eternity. Love's heralds should be ten times faster than the sun's beams.

> *Peering from behind one of the orchard walls is ANIERI who spies on her.*

**ANIERI**

So, this is the one who turns my son's good sense to corn mush. Pretty, even for a Spaniard, I'll give her. But no grandchild of mine will be cursed with Spanish blood. The Spanish have taken away my land, my religion, and my language. But they will not take away my son.

> *ANIERI suddenly pulls out a weapon that resembles an ice pick.*

Shall I do it now? Better to get it over with, I think.

**JUAN** (*offstage*)

¿D-D-Doña Teresa?

*ANIERI quickly shields herself behind the wall as JUAN comes onstage, holding a bouquet of roses. TERESA smiles politely.*

**TERESA**

Don Juan. Buenas tardes, señor.

**JUAN**

B-b-buenas tardes, to you, my lady. I-I-I-I …

*(taking a deep breath)* These are for you.

*JUAN hands the bouquet of roses to her.*

**TERESA**

Thank you, Don Juan. That's very sweet of you.

**JUAN**

I-I-I w-w-want us to be m-married very soon. I w-will take g-g-good care of you. W-w-would you like to go f-for a w-walk?

**TERESA**

Forgive me, señor, I must await my nurse. She is tending to a very urgent matter for me. Perhaps another time?

**JUAN**

M-m-may I g-get a k-k-kiss?

*Suddenly, JUAN tries to force a kiss on her. Shocked, she pushes him back.*

**TERESA**

¡Señor! You dishonor me with such behavior! I think it proper you leave at once, lest I be forced to call my father and inform him of your lusty advance!

**JUAN**

I'm s-s-sorry, s-s-señorita! F-forgive me! Shame now hangs over my bead.

*JUAN runs off, almost in tears. TERESA breathes a sigh of relief. Before JUAN can run completely offstage, out of TERESA's view, he is intercepted by ANIERI who steps in his way.*

**ANIERI**

Hold, young man! Why run so fast from the one you hope to call your wife?

**JUAN**

Out of m-m-my way, Indian w-w-woman!

**ANIERI**

What, are these tears on your face? Do you call yourself a man or not?

**JUAN**

Th-this doesn't c-concern you!

**ANIERI**

It concerns me more than you know, you coward. You're the son of the Governor, are you not? Go back to her, and don't take no for an answer.

**JUAN**

I c-c-can't! Sh-she f-f-favors me not. I l-lack g-grace in s-speech and m-movement. N-never in my life has a w-w-woman g-given me a k-k-kind eye.

**ANIERI**

Why should a woman give a kind eye to a simpering twit too feckless and fearful to fight for her? You must be strong and stake your claim before a real man does it first, before your father discovers what a spineless fool you really are.

*JUAN stomps offstage. ANIERI watches him go.*

For if you can find the strength to claim her, it will stay my hand from killing her. At least for now.

*ANIERI exits. Meanwhile, TERESA continues to pace back and forth.*

**TERESA**

Where could she be? Had she affections and warm youthful blood, she would move as swift as the wind. But old folks move about as if they were almost dead — unwieldy, slow and heavy as lead.

*Enter the NURSE, looking haggard and exhausted.*

Oh, here she comes! Good Nurse, what news do you bring? Did you meet with him? Oh, God, why do you look so sad?

**NURSE**

I am aweary. What a long walk I've had. Oh, how my bones ache.

**TERESA**

I pray you, speak. Good, good Nurse, speak.

**NURSE**

All you young people are always so much in a hurry. Can you not see that I'm out of breath?

**TERESA**

How can you be out of breath when you have the breath to tell me you're out of breath? Is the news good or bad? Just answer that and for the rest I'll wait.

**NURSE**

Are you sure you've thought this through, querida? He's an Indian. You must be sure that this is not a lark, but that your heart is set firm; for once you commit to this course, there is no turning back.

**TERESA**

Nurse, I know my father will never approve, but I can't change the feeling in my heart, which is set firmer than stone. That's why I must learn the truth in Kino's heart. Did he mention marriage to you?

**NURSE**

Lord, how my back aches! Shame on your cruel heart for sending me about to catch my death.

**TERESA**

I am sorry you are not well. Sweet, sweet, sweet nurse. I will let you rest the whole day, but tell me now what says my love, or I will go mad!

*The NURSE, figuring that she's tortured TERESA enough, smiles.*

**NURSE**

Your love tells you to go hence to Fray Olvera's church. There you will find a husband to make you a wife.

*TERESA shrieks with delight. She and the NURSE embrace.*

I'll tell your parents you're deep in study. But be back before dinner. Now, get you gone before they start the ceremony without you.

**TERESA**

Thank you, dear Nurse! When next you see me, a joyous bride I shall be!

*TERESA excitedly runs offstage.*

# Scene 3

*Inside the Chistoe house. KINO happily hums a Pueblo song as he puts on his best Pueblo clothes. ANIERI quietly enters behind him.*

**ANIERI**
Going somewhere?

**KINO** (*startled*)
Mother? I didn't hear you come in. I'm going to meet Cristóbal and Nicolás.

**ANIERI**
Dressed in your best clothing?

**KINO**
Uh … one of Cristóbal's friends is having a party. I was invited.

**ANIERI**
What kind of boy have I raised? Staying out all night, coming home only to go out again, and not even stopping to greet his mother.

*ANIERI holds her arms out to KINO.*

**KINO**
Forgive me, mother.

*KINO hugs his mother. As he does, ANIERI's embrace starts to tighten around him, uncomfortably so.*

Mother?

**ANIERI** (*in an almost threatening whisper into his ear*)
I know about the girl.

*With a look of disgust, ANIERI pushes away from KINO, not looking at him.*

You lied to me. You're going off to see her. Aren't you?

*KINO's mood is too upbeat to be spoiled.*

**KINO**
Mother, please don't be angry. She's a vision of beauty like no other. She's taken away all my sadness. I never knew such happiness was possible.

**ANIERI**

Is she not promised to another?

**KINO**

She loves no one else. I'm the only one in her heart. As is she in mine.

**ANIERI** (*exploding*)

She's a Spaniard! Your love is wasted. She'll destroy you. And mixing with the likes of her will destroy us all. Don't you understand? One day, our great, great grandchildren won't be Indians anymore. They'll be Spaniards.

**KINO**

Mother, this is your fear talking, but I do not share your fears.

> *KINO starts to leave, but ANIERI embraces him again, this time tenderly.*

**ANIERI**

Please, don't go. I know I must seem harsh, but know that I love you. You hold all my hopes, fears, and dreams for the world. I couldn't bear to lose you.

**KINO**

You're not going to lose me. I'll be back.

> *KINO pulls away from his mother, smiles at her, and walks out.*

# Scene 4

> *The church. The scene is dark. A wide spotlight fades up on FRAY OLVERA, who stands center stage at the altar. KINO walks in from stage left, TERESA from stage right. TERESA wears a make-shift veil and carries flowers with her. They meet at the center of the stage, smile at each other, and turn to face FRAY OLVERA.*

**FRAY OLVERA**

Our dear heavenly father, the union that takes place here today is a small miracle. For a hundred years, the Spanish and the Indians have been at war with each other. But today, an Indian man and a Spanish woman have managed to look beyond the hate and find the love buried underneath. So, it is with great joy that I bring these young people together in holy matrimony. It is my hope that this will be the birth of a new era between the Spanish and the Indians, that their families will be inspired to forge a path that will lead to cooperation, friendship, and love.

*FRAY OLVERA proceeds to conduct the ceremony, speaking in Latin. As he does, KINO and TERESA join hands.*

# Scene 5

*The town plaza. Enter CRISTÓBAL and NICOLÁS.*

**NICOLÁS**

I pray you, good Cristóbal, let's retire early. The day is hot and so are the Spaniards. The festivities last night left many of them in a mood not so festive. If we run into them, I fear we will not escape a brawl.

**CRISTÓBAL**

Retire early? We're supposed to be loyal auxiliary troops, standing by to protect these hot-headed Spaniards from the even hotter-headed Navajo and Apache raiders. Yet it's the Spaniards who give us greater cause to fight and, for my rusty rapier, greater pleasure to do so.

**NICOLÁS**

Come, my friend, let's away to the cantina for a cold drink to cool you down.

*CRISTÓBAL and NICOLÁS start to walk off, but, as they do, they see ELADIO.*

By my head, here comes Eladio.

**CRISTÓBAL**

By my heel, I care not.

**ELADIO**

Buenas tardes, fellow soldiers. A word with one of you.

**CRISTÓBAL**

Just one word with one of us, old boy? Why not couple it with something and make it a word and a blow.

*Not in the mood for CRISTÓBAL's antics, ELADIO draws his sword.*

**ELADIO**

You shall find me apt enough for that, señor, and you will give me occasion.

**CRISTÓBAL**

Could you not take some occasion without giving?

**ELADIO**

Cristóbal, it is well known that you are in concert with Kino.

**CRISTÓBAL**

"In concert"? What do you take us for, musicians? If you seek music from us, then look to hear nothing but discords.

*He unsheathes his sword.*

Behold my fiddlestick! Perhaps you'd like to see how it shall make you dance!

**ELADIO**

Do you seek to make a quarrel with me, old boy?

**NICOLÁS**

Gentlemen, please. We talk here in the plaza, in the public haunt of men. Either reason coldly of your grievances, or else depart.

**CRISTÓBAL**

I will not budge for any man's pleasure.

**KINO** (*offstage*)

Cristóbal! I have news!

*Everyone turns to look as an excited KINO runs onstage.*

**ELADIO** (*to CRISTÓBAL*)

Well, peace be with you, señor. This is the Indian I seek.

**CRISTÓBAL**

Stay you away from my fellow musician.

*With his sword ready, ELADIO walks up to KINO.*

**ELADIO**

You seem awfully happy for someone who is about to meet their doom. You are a villain, Kino Chistoe. You have dishonored me and my family.

**KINO**

Don Eladio, I have done nothing to dishonor you. Indeed, I have nothing but the greatest admiration and respect for your family.

**ELADIO**

You touched the hand of my beloved virgin cousin. You disgraced her before her family and her betrothed. Now, turn you and draw.

**KINO**

Dear Eladio, all I did was seek to be a gentleman and help a lady in need. If I did anything to offend you, I sincerely apologize and beg your kind forgiveness.

**ELADIO**

Your feeble attempt at making amends will not undo the injuries you have done to my honor. I say again, draw if you be a man.

**CRISTÓBAL**

He's not a soldier. He carries a dagger, not a sword. He's not prepared for a duel.

**ELADIO**

Men must always be prepared to duel, just as criminals must always be prepared to pay for their crimes.

**CRISTÓBAL**

If you draw against Kino, then consider yourself drawn against me!

*CRISTÓBAL brings his sword to ELADIO's neck.*

**ELADIO**

If Kino needs someone to fight his battles for him, then so be it. I am for you.

*He uses his sword to knock CRISTÓBAL's away.*

I have always found your so-called wit very tiresome, Cristóbal. We'll now see if your sword is at least sharper than your tongue.

**KINO**

Gentlemen, please. Put up your rapiers. There is no cause for this.

**CRISTÓBAL**

Back away, Kino! This is between me and the Spaniard!

*CRISTÓBAL lashes his sword at ELADIO, who is more than capable of defending himself. During the course of their battle, it becomes clear that ELADIO is a master swordsman. Although CRISTÓBAL is quite skilled, he prefers to dance around and taunt like the clown that he is. ELADIO, who doesn't have a highly developed sense of humor and isn't playing around, eventually manages to fling the sword out of CRISTÓBAL's hand. During the course of the fight, KINO and NICOLÁS have been pleading with them to stop, but their entreaties fall on deaf ears. CRISTÓBAL runs to retrieve his sword. ELADIO charges after him. CRISTÓBAL grabs his sword, but KINO runs in front of him, trying to break up the fight.*

**KINO**

Cristóbal! You must stop! If the Governor gets wind of this, you'll be whipped!

*At that moment, ELADIO thrusts his sword under KINO's arm, sticking CRISTÓBAL in the chest.*

**CRISTÓBAL**

Good God, I've been nicked!

**ELADIO**

There! Let that be a lesson to you Indians never to dishonor your Spanish masters!

*That said, the triumphant ELADIO marches off. Meanwhile KINO and NICOLÁS help pull CRISTÓBAL to his feet. He clutches his chest.*

**NICOLÁS**

Cristóbal, are you hurt?

**CRISTÓBAL**

Ah, 'tis but a scratch, a mere scratch. All the same, perhaps you should fetch me a surgeon.

**KINO**

The hurt can't be that much, can it?

**CRISTÓBAL**

'Tis not so deep as a well, nor so wide as a church door, but it'll do. Ask for me tomorrow, and you may find me a grave man.

*CRISTÓBAL suddenly stumbles to his knees. KINO tries to help him.*

**KINO**

Give me your hand, let me help you.

**CRISTÓBAL**
You've helped me quite enough. Why the devil did you come between us, Kino? I was stabbed under your arm.

**KINO**
I'm sorry, Cristóbal, I was trying to help you.

*CRISTÓBAL pushes KINO away and tries to get to his feet.*

**CRISTÓBAL**
O, what dark humor this is! All my life, caught between the Spanish and Indian I've been, the blood of both flowing through my veins.

*CRISTÓBAL can't help but laugh and cry at the cruel irony.*

Now, here caught between them again, I watch as all the Spanish and Indian blood flows out my veins! I've never known which to truly call myself — Spaniard or Pueblo. Well, I proclaim to call myself neither! I cast you both out of my soul. And I say a *curse* on both your peoples!

*CRISTÓBAL collapses. KINO and NICOLÁS rush to his side.*
*NICOLÁS checks CRISTÓBAL, who is unmoving.*

**NICOLÁS** (*tears coming to his eyes*)
He's dead! O Kino! Brave Cristóbal is dead!

*KINO tries to awaken CRISTÓBAL, to no avail.*

**KINO**
Dead? This cannot be. Not Cristóbal! This day's black fate on more days does depend; this but begins the woe others must end. Eladio leaves in triumph? And Cristóbal slain?

*With a burst of grief-stricken rage, KINO suddenly picks up CRIS-TÓBAL's sword and starts shouting toward the offstage area.*

Eladio!

**NICOLÁS**
Kino! Please, don't do this!

**KINO**
Eladio! Come back here, or all of Santa Fe will know of your bloody cowardice!

*Suddenly, KINO quiets down as ELADIO steps back onstage.*
*ELADIO wields his sword, which is stained with blood.*

**ELADIO**

First you dishonor my family. Now, you dare slander me, wretched boy? Choose your next words carefully, for there is no one left to fight your battle this time.

**KINO**

You called me a villain, but the only villain I see is one whose sword is stained with the blood of a man he slew when his back was as good as turned. Cristóbal's soul is but a little way above our heads, and now you will join him.

*Fueled by vengeful fury, KINO wildly attacks with his sword, which ELADIO easily deflects.*

**NICOLÁS**

I beg of you, stop this at once!

*What KINO lacks in skill, he makes up for with a relentless ferocity. He attacks ELADIO with passionate rage, eventually putting him on the defensive. After a while, it becomes apparent that ELADIO wasn't such a determined opponent, but he manages to force the sword out of KINO's hands. ELADIO then lunges at KINO, swinging his sword. At the last second, KINO manages to dodge the attack. He unsheathes his dagger, which he plunges into ELADIO's chest. ELADIO falls, dead. Holding the bloody dagger, KINO stands frozen over the dead body, as if he can't believe he's just killed another human being. We hear approaching Spanish military trumpets.*

Kino, stand there not amazed, be gone! The Governor is coming. Run, Kino, run!

**KINO**

Oh, fortune! What a fool you've made of me!

*KINO turns and runs offstage. Shortly, CHISTOE and ANIERI enter. Shocked, they quickly head over to NICOLÁS and the slain CRISTÓBAL. From the opposite side of the stage, MADRID and CATALINA enter with ELADIO's men. Overcome with rage and grief, they rush over to ELADIO's fallen body.*

**CATALINA**

Look what they've done! They've spilled the blood of our dear Eladio! He was our family's protector, and now they've killed him!

**MADRID**

The Indian savages! They will pay!

*Enter TERESA and the NURSE, who survey the scene and are shocked by what they see. The NURSE crosses herself.*

**TERESA**

My cousin Eladio slain? By Indians?

*VARGAS enters and surveys the scene with disappointment and anger. He is followed by a horrified JUAN.*

**VARGAS**

You! Nicolás! You are charged to keep the peace. Tell me who started this bloody fray.

**NICOLÁS**

It was Eladio who first drew his sword. He killed Cristóbal, and Kino took it upon himself to avenge his friend. They fought fairly and Kino won.

**TERESA**

O, God, Nurse. Did he say it was my Kino who did this?

**CATALINA**

I beg for justice, Gobernador! Kino slew Eladio, so Kino must not live!

**ANIERI**

You vile shrew, don't you ever say my son's name!

*ANIERI and CATALINA charge toward each other. A commotion erupts as the women have to be pulled apart. VARGAS is at the end of his patience.*

**VARGAS**

Enough! Kino slew Eladio. Eladio slew Cristóbal. Who now should pay the price for Cristóbal's spilled blood?

**CHISTOE**

Please, Don Diego, not Kino. He was Cristóbal's friend. His fault concludes but what the law should end — the life of Eladio.

**VARGAS**

And for that offense, he is to be immediately exiled from all of Nuevo México! Let Kino now run as far and fast as he can; for when he's found, that hour shall be his last.

**ANIERI**

This is not justice!

**VARGAS**

The Governor's word is final!

> *NICOLÁS and a few other Indian soldiers carry off the body of CRIS-*
> *TÓBAL while the Madrid family carries off the body of ELADIO.*
> *Soon, everyone has left the stage, except for VARGAS and JUAN.*
> *VARGAS turns to his son.*

I'm sorry you had to see this, my son. It was always my hope to create a land where we could live in peace with the Indians.

**JUAN**

It's n-not your f-f-fault.

**VARGAS**

Juan, I'm going to move up the date of your wedding to two days hence.

> *JUAN is shocked.*

All this grief and death, it's not good for the people. They need something to give them hope for the future. And that's what your wedding will bring. The day after tomorrow will be the start of a new family in Santa Fe.

> *Satisfied, VARGAS walks offstage, leaving JUAN frustrated.*

**JUAN**

I am such a coward! When I'm alone, my thoughts are clear and concise, the words flow like a river, but around others, I'm stumbling and bumbling. Too fearful I was to tell my father that Teresa is disgusted by me. I couldn't bear to look at the disappointment in his eyes. I've been a disappointment all my life.

> *He takes a moment to think.*

Perhaps that Indian woman was right. Perhaps the time has come for me to be a man. I will take Teresa as my wife, and I will make my father proud of me.

# Scene 6

*The church. KINO paces around impatiently. Enter FRAY OLVE-RA, who looks very agitated and upset.*

**KINO**

Father, what news do you carry? What is the Governor's sentence?

**FRAY OLVERA**

The Governor was as lenient as could be called for. He called not for thy body's death, but thy body's banishment.

> *Devastated, KINO sinks to his knees and buries his face in his hands.*

**KINO**

Banishment? Be merciful, good father, say "death," for exile has more terror in its look, much more than death.

**FRAY OLVERA**

Just from New Mexico banished. Be patient, for the world is broad and wide.

**KINO**

For me, there is no world without New Mexico. The Governor condemns me to a fate worse than death!

**FRAY OLVERA**

There is no fate worse than death, for as long as you have breath in your body, there is always hope.

> *Suddenly, there is a knock on the door.*

Who calls for me?

**NURSE** (*behind the door*)
I come from Doña Teresa.

> *FRAY OLVERA quickly opens the door.*

Oh, Fray Olvera, tell me — where's my lady's lord?

**FRAY OLVERA**

There, on the floor, with his own tears made drunk.

**NURSE**

Same as my mistress. I left her in her chamber, weeping so piteously. Kino, your wife needs you.

*Hearing TERESA's name, KINO pulls himself to his feet, wiping away tears.*

**KINO**

Nurse, how is it with my lady love? Does she think of me as a murderer now that I've stained our joy with blood removed but little from her own?

**NURSE**

She only wishes to see you, my lord.

**KINO**

All I do is cause her misery and pain. We'd all be better off if I were dead!

*KINO suddenly pulls out his dagger and offers to stab himself.
FRAY OLVERA quickly snatches the dagger away.*

**FRAY OLVERA**

Stay the desperate hand! Rouse thee, man! Thy Teresa, thy love, is alive and calls out for you. There art thou blessed. Eladio would kill thee, but thou slewest Eladio. There art thou blessed. The law, that threatened death, becomes thy friend and turns it to exile. There art thou blessed. A pack of blessings is upon thee. Go get thee to thy love. But look not to stay past dawn. We must get thee to Taos where thou shalt live in secret till we find the proper time to announce your marriage, reconcile your families, beg pardon of the Governor, and call thee back with a thousand times more joy than when thou left in sadness. Go, Nurse, tell your lady Teresa that Kino is coming.

**NURSE**

Thank you, good Father, your wisdom is beyond compare.

*KINO walks up to FRAY OLVERA and embraces him.*

**KINO**

Your words give me hope, Father. Thank you.

*The NURSE and KINO exit. FRAY OLVERA prays.*

# Scene 7

*Inside Teresa's chamber. It is before dawn. KINO is putting on his shirt. TERESA, in her nightgown, sits up in bed.*

**TERESA**

Must you leave so early? It is not yet near day. It can hardly be much past the middle of the night.

**KINO**

Night's candles are burnt out, my love. I must be gone and live or stay and die.

**TERESA**

This day, the light is my enemy. If only we could stop the coming day like one reigns in an unwieldy steed, then we could live in this moment, in each other's arms forever, without fear of death or decay.

**KINO**

Time can be merciless, but memory is a great friend. I will always remember our night together for days without end.

*KINO starts for the balcony, but TERESA holds him back.*

**TERESA**

Kino, wait. The notion of parting with you is starting to tear me apart. Take me with you. I've always longed to see what the world is like beyond Santa Fe.

**KINO**

How I wish I could take you with me, but if we were to flee hand in hand, our families would lay blame and tear each other apart until all the Spanish and Indians were at war. I couldn't bear that our love would be the cause of such strife.

*Suddenly, there is a knock on the door.*

**NURSE** (*from behind the door*)

My lady! Are you awake? Your mother is coming to your chamber.

**TERESA**

I hear you, Nurse!

**KINO**

One last kiss, my love.

*KINO and TERESA kiss passionately. KINO heads for the balcony,*
*but TERESA desperately holds him back.*

**TERESA**

Kino, I fear I'll never see you again. Please tell me you'll come back to me.

**KINO**

You're the love I've looked for my whole life. I'll always come looking for you.
It'll only be a few months to let hot tempers cool down. When the time is
right, Fray Olvera will announce our marriage and make things right with
the Governor. Then, I'm as sure as the sun rises that we will be together again
and forever.

**TERESA**

I shall dream of that day every night.

**CATALINA** (*offstage*)

Teresa?

**KINO**

Farewell.

*KINO quickly kisses TERESA one last time and descends the*
*orchard wall. At that moment, CATALINA enters the chamber. She*
*finds her daughter in tears.*

**CATALINA**

You're up early, my daughter. Evermore weeping for your cousin?

**TERESA**

I am weeping for a loss most felt.

**CATALINA**

I've come to bring you joyful tidings.

**TERESA**

And the joy comes well in such a needy time. Tell me, señora.

**CATALINA**

The day of your wedding has been advanced. Tomorrow you will marry Don
Juan de Vargas.

**TERESA** (*shocked*)

Tomorrow? My tears for my cousin have yet to dry, and now I'm expected to put on a dress and a smile for my wedding tomorrow?

**CATALINA**

You knew very well that this marriage was near.

**TERESA**

You've seen what he's like, mother! You would condemn your own daughter to spend her life with such a man? I will not do it!

**MADRID** (*offstage*)

What's all this shouting I hear?

**CATALINA**

Here comes your father. Tell him so yourself.

*MADRID enters, followed by the NURSE.*

**MADRID**

Why is my girl in tears? Have you not given our daughter the joyous news, my wife?

**CATALINA**

She did not take it so joyously. She doesn't want to marry Don Juan.

**TERESA**

I beseech you, father. I am still grieving for dear Eladio. Delay this wedding a month, even a week, so that I may have time to find a happier face.

**MADRID**

You will find your happy face tomorrow, girl. I have taken great pains to find you a gentleman of noble parentage and significant means. So, I say unto you now — you shall be married tomorrow!

**TERESA**

Father, please don't make me share the name and bed of one I don't love!

**MADRID**

That's enough! You are stuck with the delusions of a romantic schoolgirl. Marriage has nothing to do with love!

(*quickly, to CATALINA*) Forgive me, Madam, what I mean to say is this — all the time men and women are married on grounds of a practical nature.

(*to TERESA*) There are very honorable reasons for you to marry this young man. His family has wealth and standing.

**TERESA**

I don't care!

**MADRID**

Well, better you start caring! After last summer's drought, we've had to ration our food. If you marry this man, you will always be provided for!

**TERESA**

I'd rather starve than marry that man!

**MADRID**

Disobedient wretch! Ungrateful child!

> *MADRID steps toward TERESA as if he means to hit her. The NURSE immediately runs between them to shield TERESA.*

**NURSE**

No!

**MADRID**

Out of my way, you fool!

**NURSE**

I pray thee, sir, you are too angry.

**MADRID**

Yes, by God's grace, I am mad! I seek to send my only child out into the world with safety and security, and she spits it back in my face! Hang, beg, starve, die in the streets for all I care!

> *MADRID turns and marches out of the room. CATALINA follows him. TERESA, in tears, turns to the NURSE for comfort.*

**TERESA**

O God, Nurse, what should I do? I can't marry another man, for I am already married to my heart's only love. Can you not give me one word of joy? Some comfort, Nurse, please.

**NURSE** (*taking a moment to think about it*)
Here it is, child. Kino is banished. He can't step back into this town without risking his death. You must consider what's best for yourself, and I think it best you marry Don Juan de Vargas.

**TERESA** (*taken aback*)
What you speak comes from the heart?

**NURSE**
And my soul, too; else, beshrew them both.

**TERESA**
Well, you have comforted me marvelous much. Leave me and tell my mother that I've gone to see Fray Olvera. Having displeased my father, I think it wise to make confession and to be absolved.

**NURSE**
I think you are wise to do so, my child. I'll tell your mother.

> *The NURSE walks out, leaving TERESA to fume.*

**TERESA**
Ancient damnation! O most wicked fiend! Go, counselor! Henceforth, you shall be separated from my trust. The only one I can turn to now is the good Fray Olvera. I pray he can tell me what to do. Otherwise, my life is for naught.

# Scene 8

> *In the church. FRAY OLVERA is in the middle of talking to VARGAS.*

**FRAY OLVERA**
Tomorrow, Don Diego? The time is very short for planning a wedding, especially after all the tragedy that has befallen the family.

**TERESA** (*offstage*)
Fray Olvera?

> *FRAY OLVERA and VARGAS turn to see TERESA rushing in through the door. She stops in her tracks, not expecting to see VARGAS.*

**VARGAS**

Ah, here she is. The lovely girl who will make my son the happiest man on earth. Come you to make confession to Fray Olvera?

**TERESA**

To answer that, I should have to make confession to you.

**VARGAS**

Clever girl. I'll leave you then. Tomorrow, I shall welcome you to my family.

*VARGAS kisses TERESA on the forehead, then heads out the door. As soon as he does, TERESA bursts into tears.*

**TERESA**

O, Father, I know not what to do. I'm past hope, past care, past help!

**FRAY OLVERA**

I already know of thy grief, child. It strains me past the compass of my wits to hear that tomorrow, without delay, thou must marry Don Juan de Vargas.

**TERESA**

Is there nothing you can do?

**FRAY OLVERA**

How I wish there was, but I fear the Lord's wisdom is in short supply right now.

**TERESA**

If your wisdom can do me no favors, then all is lost. Perhaps the only favors that can be done for me are with this —

*TERESA suddenly reaches for a dagger on FRAY OLVERA's table.*

**FRAY OLVERA**

No!

*FRAY OLVERA immediately takes away the dagger.*

Death is never the answer, only an escape.

*As FRAY OLVERA puts the dagger back on the table, he pauses to look at all his potions and herbs. It gives him an idea.*

Listen, daughter. I do spy a kind of hope. Fraught with risk it is, but if thou hast the strength of will to slay thyself, then it is likely thou wilt undertake a thing that looks like death to save thyself.

**TERESA**

Tell me what to do, Father, and I will do it without fear or doubt.

*FRAY OLVERA picks up from the table a small vial.*

**FRAY OLVERA**

Go home, give consent to marry Don Juan. Then, tonight, being in bed, take this vial and drink it. It will make thee appear as though thy mortal coil has been shed. When thy parents in the morning come to rouse thee, they will find thee thus dead. Instead of a wedding, there will be a funeral. Kino by my letters shall know our plan, and he and I will go to your family's mausoleum to watch thy waking, and that night shalt thou both hie thee hence to Taos to live as husband and wife. What say you?

**TERESA**

I'll do it, Father — anything to be reunited with my love.

**FRAY OLVERA**

Then, I'll dispatch Fray García to Taos, with letters to thy lord. Go now.

**TERESA**

My love gives me the strength of a thousand suns. Farewell.

*TERESA runs out of the church, leaving FRAY OLVERA, who looks like he's not sure whether he has done the right thing.*

# Scene 9

*Inside Teresa's chamber. TERESA, wearing her nightgown, anxiously sits on her bed, looking at the vial.*

**TERESA**

The course I set tonight will change the rest of my life. All I've ever known will soon come to an end, but I will begin anew with a love that will always be true.

**MADRID** (*offstage*)

Where is that headstrong child of mine?

*As soon as she hears her father's voice, TERESA quickly hides the vial. MADRID enters.*

The Nurse said you sent for me. She said you went to see Fray Olvera to make confession.

**TERESA**

Yes, father. I have learnt me to repent the sin of disobedient opposition to you and am enjoined by holy Fray Olvera to fall prostrate here and beg your pardon. Henceforward, I am ever ruled by you. Thus, tomorrow, I will become the wife of Don Juan de Vargas.

**MADRID**

Ah, this is well. Stand up, querida. This is as it should be. I'll send word to the Governor. I'll have this knot knit up by tomorrow morning. This reverend holy friar — all of Santa Fe is very much bound to him.

**TERESA**

Sí, papá. Now, I wish to go to bed early so that tomorrow I will be well rested for the happiest day of my life.

**MADRID**

I'm very proud of you, my sweet flower. Take care then till morning.

*MADRID exits. TERESA holds up the vial.*

**TERESA**

For the power of this thing called love, what would I not do? What things, both fearless and foolish — all in return for a sensation that causes as much pain as pleasure. I drink to thee, love. And to my love's love, I drink to Kino.

*TERESA drinks from the vial. After a moment, she drowsily slides into her bed.*

## Scene 10

*A corridor in the Madrid household. MADRID enters, accompanied by JUAN, looking determined.*

**MADRID**

Please come in, Don Juan. I wasn't expecting you this early in the morning.

**JUAN**

It's my w-w-wedding day. I w-wanted to m-make sure everything is in order.

**MADRID**

Nurse!

*The NURSE rushes onstage.*

See to it that Teresa is roused from her bed. It's time for her to get ready.

**NURSE**

Yes, my lord. Mistress, sweet mistress! It's time you wakened.

*The NURSE goes into Teresa's chamber.*

**JUAN**

D-Don Madrid, I r-r-realize I've only kn-known your d-d-daughter f-for a short time, b-b-but I p-p-promise you I'll m-m-make her happy.

**MADRID**

I hope so. For your father hasn't the power to stay an unhappy father-in-law.

*Suddenly, the NURSE screams and runs back out into the corridor.*

**NURSE**

O my god! She's dead! My lady is dead! Don Lorenzo! O such tragedy!

*MADRID and JUAN are shocked. CATALINA comes onstage.*

My lord, she's dead!

**MADRID**

What are you nattering about, you fool! She can't be dead!

*MADRID and CATALINA run inside while the weeping NURSE remains outside. The incredulous JUAN rushes to the door.*

**JUAN**

Don Lorenzo! Speak! Is she ill? Shall I s-s-send for a d-doctor?

*CATALINA slowly walks out of the room, in a state of shock and grief.*

**CATALINA**

It's too late, Don Juan. Death lies on her like an untimely frost.

*The anguished MADRID walks out of the room.*

**MADRID**

Accursed, unhappy, wretched, hateful day! My last child, my only hope, my only reason for living! Cruel death has snatched her with this vial of poison.

*MADRID holds up the vial and sinks to his knees in despair. JUAN is shocked.*

# Scene 11

*Outside Taos Pueblo. An old Indian man, frail, impoverished, and wrapped in a blanket, sits on a tree stump in silent contemplation. Though he was wearing a hood when we first saw him, this is the MEDICINE MAN, the ethereal presence from the beginning of the story. NICOLÁS enters, looking very distressed.*

**NICOLÁS**

I beg your pardon, sir, but I am looking for the house of the Gomez family.

**MEDICINE MAN**

The people of Taos Pueblo are very wary of those in uniform, especially Indians in uniform. What do you want with them, soldier boy?

**NICOLÁS**

A friend of mine is staying with them, in hiding. I've come all the way from Santa Fe to deliver some urgent news.

*A happy KINO then comes onstage to greet his cousin.*

**KINO**

Nicolás! I wasn't expecting you to come here so soon, cousin. Do you have news from Santa Fe? How fares my lady Teresa?

**NICOLÁS** (*his eyes starting to well up with tears*)

I came as soon as I could. It is with great sadness I tell you this, cousin. Your lady lives no longer. She is dead.

**KINO**

What? If this be a cruel jest —

**NICOLÁS**

If only it were. Your Teresa, rather than marry Don Juan de Vargas, took poison. Her body was laid to rest this afternoon at the tomb of the Madrid family.

*Looking as if he's had the wind knocked out of him, KINO sits down on the ground. He pounds his fist into the dirt.*

**KINO**

No, no, no! Our love has survived so much already. This is not the way it was meant to pass. I curse you, stars! I must see her. Nicolás, ready my horse.

*NICOLÁS goes offstage, and KINO gets up and turns to the old Indian man.*

You — they say you are a medicine man.

**MEDICINE MAN**

I heard your friend say that your love is dead. A medicine man I may be, but even I cannot cure death.

**KINO**

I don't want you to cure death, wise one. I want you to induce it. Tonight, I intend to lie with my Teresa so that we may walk through the heavens together.

**MEDICINE MAN**

You intend to walk through the heaven of the Spaniards? You're an Indian man. Are you sure they'll let you in?

**KINO**

I don't have time to argue religious philosophies with you. What I require is a poison that will send my immortal soul off to wherever immortal souls go.

**MEDICINE MAN**

Spaniards I will gladly kill, but not Indians.

*KINO reaches into his pocket and pulls out a couple of silver coins.*

**KINO**

When's the last time you had a full meal, old man?

*The MEDICINE MAN licks his lips, then reaches into his blanket and pulls out a collection of herbs wrapped in a small bundle. He hands it to KINO.*

**MEDICINE MAN**

My poverty, not my will, consents.

**KINO**

Then this is for your poverty, not your will.

**MEDICINE MAN**

Put these herbs in any liquid and drink it off. If you had the strength of twenty men, it would dispatch you straight.

**KINO**

Here's your silver — worse than poison.

> *KINO exits. On the opposite side of the stage, enter FRAY GARCÍA, a pouch around his shoulder. He looks around and walks up to the old man.*

**FRAY GARCÍA**

I've been sent by Fray Olvera. I bring an important letter for Kino.

**MEDICINE MAN** (*regarding him with intense contempt*)

I have nothing to say to a Spanish priest. Except in my own language.

> *The old man spews out a Pueblo curse. He then gets up and walks away, leaving FRAY GARCÍA to look around by himself for KINO.*

# Scene 12

> *Inside the mausoleum. Holding flowers, JUAN steps up to TERESA's body.*

**JUAN**

To the only love I knew, with flowers thy bridal bed I strew. With a vial of poison you left the world. I can't help but think you did it so you wouldn't have to marry me. I beg you to forgive me for all my failings, and I swear now on your grave I will do something to make you proud of me.

> *He hears something.*

Somebody comes.

> *JUAN quickly hides in the shadows to watch as KINO enters, carrying a lantern. NICOLÁS trails behind.*

**NICOLÁS**

Kino, the watch could come at any time. I'll stay out here and stand guard.

**KINO**

No, my friend. I intend to spend a length of time to grieve for my beloved. Please, go.

*NICOLÁS nods and exits. KINO walks through the crypt until he comes upon the body of TERESA resting on a slab. He rushes over to her.*

O Teresa, my wife, my love! Look at you — death has sucked the honey out of your breath, but it has had no power upon your beauty. As lovely as the night we met. How could you go on to the next world and leave behind my heart?

**JUAN**

¡Indio!

*Startled, KINO turns around to see that JUAN has stepped out of the shadows and has unsheathed his sword.*

Y-y-you are the reason T-Teresa d-did not want to m-marry me? You are the reason she k--k-killed herself! Now you shall p-p-pay!

**KINO**

I beseech you, gentle youth, tempt not a desperate man. Put not another sin upon my head by urging me to fury. For I come armed against myself.

*KINO reveals his dagger.*

**JUAN**

I defy you, Indian!

*JUAN launches an attack with his sword, but he is not a skilled swordsman. KINO easily steps out of the way, and JUAN trips and falls. KINO brings his dagger up to JUAN's throat.*

**KINO**

There has been too much death today, most of it brought by the hatred between our peoples. It doesn't have to be this way. One lesson I learned from Fray Olvera about the teachings of Christ is that all men are brothers. So, on this day, remember that an Indian spared your life, the life of a Spaniard.

*KINO pulls JUAN to his feet.*

Hereafter say an Indian's mercy bid thee run away. Be gone!

*JUAN runs off. KINO turns back to look at TERESA.*

Three days ago, we knew nothing of each other. But I feel I've known you my entire life. And now that you've gone on to the spirit world, I will follow you.

*He takes out his vial of poison.*

Come, unsavory guide, and escort me to my love. Here's to our journey.

*He drinks the poison.*

Thus with a kiss I die.

*KINO kisses her. He waits for a moment, then drowsily lays himself on the ground and dies. After a moment, FRAY OLVERA enters, carrying a lantern.*

**FRAY OLVERA**
Kino? I thought I heard your voice. If he received my letters, he shall be here at this appointed hour, for Teresa will awaken at any moment. Ah, there she is, that sweet child.

*FRAY OLVERA walks over to TERESA. As he does, he catches sight of KINO's fallen body. He immediately rushes over to him.*

Kino? Has he fallen asleep? Awaken, my boy! The time is almost at hand!

*FRAY OLVERA tries to wake him up, but to no avail. He then sees the empty vial in KINO's hand.*

What is this? A dram of poison? But why, Kino? He came here to die with his lady love, not knowing that she was not dead. O what unkind hour is guilty of this lamentable chance?

**TERESA**
Fray Olvera? Is that you?

*FRAY OLVERA sees that TERESA has just awakened and is beginning to stir. He immediately goes up to her to shield her view of the fallen KINO.*

Your plan worked, Father, just as you said. Where is my Kino?

**FRAY OLVERA**
Señora, let's away from this nest of death, contagion, and unnatural sleep. A greater power than we can contradict hath thwarted our intents.

**WATCHMAN** (*offstage*)
Who's in there?

**FRAY OLVERA**
The watch is coming. We must go now.

> *TERESA looks around, and, as she does, she sees the fallen KINO at the base of the slab. She rushes over to him.*

**TERESA**
Kino? What happened?

**FRAY OLVERA**
He's dead, señora. Please, stay not to question, for the watch is coming.

**TERESA**
Dead? How can this be?

**FRAY OLVERA**
Please, my lady. I dare no longer stay!

**TERESA**
I will not away! I shall never abandon my husband's side. Go, friar! Leave me!

**WATCHMAN** (*offstage, but coming closer*)
Who's in there?

**FRAY OLVERA**
I dare no longer stay!

> *With nothing else he can do, FRAY OLVERA flees offstage.*

**TERESA** (*distraught*)
O Kino! How could this have happened?

> *TERESA sees the vial of poison and picks it up.*

A dram of poison I see has been his timeless end. All drunk with no friendly drop left to help me follow? Perhaps some poison still stains your lips. I will kiss them.

> *TERESA kisses KINO. Her eyes fill with tears.*

How could you take your own life, my husband? Did you not think I'd come back to you? Now, you've left me behind. Perhaps we were never meant to be. Yet I cannot see myself living another tomorrow without you, Kino.

> *Suddenly, the WATCHMAN, a Spaniard, has entered, looking around, carrying a lantern.*

**WATCHMAN**
Who has violated this sacred tomb?

**TERESA**
Quickly — what shall I do so that I may walk with you hand in hand to the next world?

*TERESA thinks and quickly unsheathes KINO's dagger.*

Till the end of time we will be joined, even in death as we were in life.

*TERESA stabs herself and falls, her body resting with KINO's.*

# Scene 13

*Outside the Governor's Palace. On stage right, KINO's body is laid out, prepared for burial, surrounded by his family and friends, including CHISTOE, ANIERI, and NICOLÁS. On stage left, TERESA's funeral wrapped body is surrounded by her family and friends, including MADRID, CATALINA, and the NURSE. MADRID is a coiled powder keg of emotions, ready to explode at any moment. He paces around like a caged lion.*

**MADRID**
I can't bear waiting any longer for the Governor's pronouncement. There can only be one verdict possible — guilty and a sentence of death for Felipe Chistoe. I should have killed that traitorous coward years ago.

**CATALINA**
Please, husband, stop. We have lost so much already.

**MADRID**
My blood boils when I think of my daughter consorting with that Indian boy, defiled by him. All the while, laughing at me.

*He whips out his sword.*

Chistoe! You have dishonored my family for the last time!

**CHISTOE**
And you have hurt my family for the last time! I have always tried to be a man of peace, but if you choose to end the peace, so be it.

**MADRID**

So be it!

*Swinging his sword, MADRID charges at CHISTOE, who barely has time to defend himself, unsheathing his sword and blocking the attack. The two old men go at each other until —*

**VARGAS**

¡Basta!

*VARGAS arrives on the scene, looking sad and disgusted. He is followed by JUAN. The families pull the men apart.*

Look at what your hate has wrought upon these two innocent souls, yet still you don't have the decency to stop your fighting. I do hereby place Don Lorenzo and Don Felipe under arrest. I put forth that whoever drew the two swords, their lives would pay the forfeit of the peace, and so shall you now. You will both be put to death, as an example for all those who dare violate the peace!

**CATALINA**

Don Diego, no! My husband is grieving!

**ANIERI**

Is this Spanish justice? My husband was only defending himself!

*A commotion erupts as both families protest. Suddenly, a voice booms.*

**JUAN**

S-stop this! PLEASE!

*The commotion dies down as all eyes turn to JUAN.*

P-please, father, don't do this. An act such as this can only breed more hate.

**VARGAS**

This is none of your affair, boy! Hold your place.

**JUAN**

No! Teresa was to be my wife. And when I found out she was in love with an Indian, I gave into the hate. But the Indian Kino spared my life. He spared your son. He showed that hate didn't have to be the way. Why not learn from him and spare these two men, so they can go back to their families? Let them learn from your forgiveness so that, one day, maybe they can learn to forgive each other. And isn't that what you've always wanted, for them to live in peace?

*VARGAS takes a moment to calm down and think. He walks over to*
*CHISTOE and MADRID.*

**VARGAS**

My son is a wise man. Go, Don Felipe. Go, Don Lorenzo. Go grieve for your
children in peace.

*VARGAS proudly puts his arm around JUAN, and the father and*
*son exit. They are followed by MADRID and his family. NICOLÁS*
*also exits. The only ones left onstage are CHISTOE and ANIERI who*
*stand over the bodies of KINO and TERESA.*

**CHISTOE**

The time has come for us to bury our son.

**ANIERI**

The time has come for us to avenge our son. I want you to contact the other
Pueblos, send message, even the Navajos and Apaches.

**CHISTOE**

For what purpose?

**ANIERI**

To tell them we will join them in an all-out attack on Santa Fe. With our combined forces, we'll kill the Spaniards and finally take back our land.

**CHISTOE**

I will not hear of such a horrific plot. The Governor could have me put to
death, but he pardoned me as an example for us all to put our hatred aside.

**ANIERI**

What do you expect from me, sweet tears of gratitude? The only tears I will
shed are for my dead son. And I will not rest until all the Spanish are made
to pay!

**CHISTOE**

They're paying, we're paying, all of us are paying! You do what you must, my
wife, but not with my help. It's best I leave you here with your hate to be your
only friend. It has made you so blind that you can't see it has caused you to lose
a son … and now a husband.

**ANIERI**

Then go, you coward! Leave me!

*CHISTOE exits, leaving ANIERI the only one onstage. She is totally alone and wretched, standing over the body of her son. With vengeance still on her mind, she turns and exits.*

*Lastly, the MEDICINE MAN walks onstage, wearing his blanket like a cloak. He sadly gazes down at the bodies of KINO and TERESA.*

**MEDICINE MAN**

A glooming peace this morning with it brings. The sun for sorrow will not show its head. For never was there a story of more woe than our Teresa and her Kino.

*The MEDICINE MAN whips his blanket over his head, assuming his hooded role as the specter of the spirit world. He bids KINO and TERESA to rise, which they do. They follow him hand in hand into eternity. Curtain falls.*

**FINIS**

# Introduction to Seres Jaime Magaña's
# *The Tragic Corrido of Romeo and Lupe*

Seres Jaime Magaña's *The Tragic Corrido of Romeo and Lupe* is a bilingual adaptation of *Romeo and Juliet* that was first performed in 2018 at the Pharr Community Theater in Pharr, Texas, under the direction of Pedro Garcia. Nearly all of the characters in *The Tragic Corrido* are Mexican American. Some have deep roots in the Rio Grande Valley, and some are immigrants, both documented and undocumented. Romeo's mixed-race Anglo and Mexican American family owns the Campbell Irrigation Company, while the majority of Lupe's family members are recent Mexican immigrants who work in the fields. *The Tragic Corrido* situates *Romeo and Juliet*'s treatment of love, identity, and justice within the Rio Grande Valley, foregrounding colonialism, environmental destruction, and labor rights. Magaña provocatively appropriates *Romeo and Juliet* for a border context, using it not as an oppressive mold in which to fit life en La Frontera, but as a malleable frame that can be transformed by the region's hybrid cultures, languages, and art forms. In his appropriation of Shakespeare's famous tragedy, Magaña centers the voices, histories, and ways of knowing of fronterizos, fashioning the theater as a space in which the community can forge collective responses to common challenges.

*The Tragic Corrido of Romeo and Lupe* is set during the early twentieth century in Pharr, which is connected by bridge to its sister city of Reynosa in Tamaulipas, Mexico. This geographical specificity is highlighted from the beginning of the play, which the bilingual corrido singer, analogous to Shakespeare's Chorus, opens by welcoming the audience to "Cage Boulevard here in the city of Pharr" (1.2). This sense that the play is situated within the community is augmented by its intense focus on the broader region of the Rio Grande Valley, which for the most part constitutes the world of the play. The Río Bravo itself plays a critical role in a play whose central conflict revolves around who has rights to the water that sustains the Valley's land and culture. In this way, the original production run of *The Tragic Corrido* was aligned with the Pharr Community Theater's 2018 season theme of water politics, which highlighted the importance of the river to the region and its inhabitants.

Set "in an alternate timeline in a growing Republic of Texas," the play's temporality is somewhat unstable. *The Tragic Corrido* engages with the agricultural economics and labor politics of the 1940s as World War II looms in the background. It is also reliant on later twentieth-century contexts in its staging of Chicanx identity, engaging deeply with the tradition of protest and the return to Indigenous symbolism that was embraced by the United Farm Workers and the Chicano Movement of the 1960s and 70s. This shifting temporality permits Magaña to engage with legacies of colonization that include racism, labor exploitation, and environmental injustice, as well as the militarization of the border and forced deportations that continue in the present century. This speculative, transhistorical approach makes apparent the mutating but always present systems of oppression that have impacted the lives of Valley residents. The play implicitly links, for example, the Bracero Program of the 1940s, in which Mexican agricultural workers were encouraged to come to the United States to ameliorate labor shortages, with today's forced deportations of undocumented people, including those who have been exploited to serve U.S. capitalism. This expansive historical vista connects to, and in a sense justifies, Magaña's choice to appropriate an early modern European play: the colonialism that began in the region in the sixteenth century continues to affect it today.

These aftereffects can be seen in the way that *The Tragic Corrido* critiques the role that agribusiness played in shaping the Rio Grande Valley. The Campbell Irrigation Company is buying up land so that it can expand its pipelines. As such, the Campbells promote a vision of the region as the "Magic Valley," which María Herrera-Sobek explains is "the nickname its chamber of commerce seductively imagined for it."[1] Driven by the desire to extract wealth from the land and its people, the Campbells exploit the Valley's natural and human resources. As the corridista explains in her role as narrator, "nothing can stop their visions, as they build their dreams through refugees, as they build their dreams through people's homes" (1.2).

Reflecting the political aims of the play, and its roots in the theatrical tradition that began with the Teatro Campesino during the farmworkers movement of the 1960s, Romeo and Lupe meet at a protest that interrupts a party. Staged at the Birthday of the Magic Valley, an event intended as a celebration of agricultural abundance from which the Campbells profit, this protest takes the form of an acto, or a short skit, featuring models dressed as fruit who attest to the devastation inflicted upon the region. In addition, Lupe's cousin Ramón raps about how the duplicity of white landowners has led to poverty and oppression: "we worked

---

1    María Herrera-Sobek, "Gloria Anzaldúa, Place, Race, Language, and Sexuality in the Magic Valley," *PMLA* 121, no. 1 (2006): 266, https://doi.org/10.1632/003081206 X129800.

this earth first you returned it to us cursed / your handshake agreement is but double cross coerce / your logic is rehearsed and your compassion is even worse" (2.4). His "Tejano lament" draws on the Indigenous heritage of Valley campesinos to cast the Campbells as colonizers. His use of a Black American poetic and musical form highlights the influence of the African diaspora in Borderlands culture and within discourses of resistance and social justice. When interrupted by the Campbells' security guards, the protestors chant, "We do not want your segregation, your discrimination, your dreams. Esta tierra no te quiere aqui. This is not your magic valley, this is the RGV. This is not your magic valley, this is the RGV" (1.6). The RGV, in contrast to the Magic Valley, is fashioned as a space that centers the lives and labor of border residents and that acknowledges the racial and class-based inequalities that shape the region. Romeo and Lupe's love arises from these fraught contexts, emphasizing that the feud between their families is far from senseless but rather is rooted in centuries of oppression and therefore has extremely high stakes.

*The Tragic Corrido* responds to these colonial conflicts through a collective, intertextual approach to storytelling and artmaking. Aspects of *Romeo and Juliet*, translated and adapted by Magaña into a mixture of Spanish, English, and Spanglish, are integrated into the tradition of the Mexican corrido, or dramatic ballad. A Spanish form that has evolved within the Mexico–U.S. border region, the genre is known both for its malleability and for its frequent themes of border crossing and immigration.[2] According to Herrera-Sobek, "Corridos have been the voice of the Mexican and Mexican American people narrating their history, love stories, and tragedies; the exploits of famous bandits, deeds of revolutionary heroes and heroines, and any other newsworthy event."[3] It is a music for the people that reflects the lived realities of border residents. Magaña uses the form throughout the play, in both the actual songs of the corridista and the broader depiction of Romeo and Lupe's love story as one that would be told in a corrido.

Similarly, Romeo and Lupe privilege hybridity over the divisions that consume their family members. As Lupe articulates early in the play, "Somos de ambos lados, y de ninguno" (2.8). The lovers translanguage throughout the play, seamlessly moving between Spanish and English. Romeo approaches Lupe first in English, commenting on her beauty hidden under a veil. Lupe then responds with "Buen peregrino, you do wrong your hand too much. Qué clase de devoción

---

2   Américo Paredes, *"With His Pistol in His Hand": A Border Ballad and Its Hero* (Austin: University of Texas Press, 1958).

3   María Herrera-Sobek, "The Border Patrol and Their Migra Corridos: Propaganda, Genre Adaptation, and Mexican Immigration," *American Studies Journal* 57 (2012): para. 8, https://doi.org/10.18422/57-06.

es esta?" (1.6). The word "peregrino," a direct translation of Shakespeare's "pilgrim," acquires added resonance in a border context characterized by migration and attempts to impede it. Romeo is a "peregrino" not in the sense that he has crossed national borders but because he has abandoned his familial allegiance to learn more about the protestors' cause. Romeo and Lupe's mixture of Spanish and English is complemented by a sense of religious hybridity, captured in Lupe's name, which invokes la Virgen de Guadalupe, Mexico's most famous symbol of the interweaving of Christian and Indigenous traditions. Her likeness was even framed above Lupe's bed in the Pharr Community Theater production. Similarly, the lovers' exchanges integrate Indigenous myth and geography with the Christian references in Shakespeare's text. In one striking example, Romeo references the snow of Iztaccíhuatl, one of two volcanoes whose formation is explained by a legend about a Tlaxcala princess and a Chichimeca warrior. Iztaccíhuatl and her lover, Popocatépetl, are often referred to as the Mexican Romeo and Juliet because their love story has a similarly tragic ending brought about by rivalry, miscommunication, and grief. Magaña's invocation of this myth, which predates Shakespeare's play, raises questions of influence and power, and it disrupts colonial timelines as well as Shakespeare's perceived supremacy as a "universal" storyteller.

Indigenous spirituality, furthermore, informs Magaña's depiction of the Valley. Like Friar Lawrence, Padre Lauro's apothecary work is grounded in the land. He makes allusions to curanderismo and draws his treatments from local plants such as sábila, or aloe. Rather than using political constructs such as the Magic Valley, the RGV, the Republic of Texas, or Aztlán to name the region, Romeo and Lupe emphasize the richness of the natural environment. Magaña replaces Shakespeare's references to various plants and animals with species found in the Valley, whether they are indigenous or have been transported there. Like Juliet, Lupe references animals to prolong her night with Romeo, saying, "Ese no fue el gallo, el que perforó tu tímpano. Listen, la chicharra still sings, cada noche canta mientras reposa sobre el mezquite. While it sings, time is ours" (2.8). Romeo responds, "That is not the chicharra. That is the green jay, and the great kiskadee, and the crow that waits for our final consequence. I must go" (2.8). The play's emphasis on the sacredness of the earth and its connection to love is also linked to histories of resistance in the Borderlands, and the land itself is depicted as resisting colonial violence.

In *The Tragic Corrido*, Magaña weaves together narratives of Chicanx labor, love, and land to rewrite Shakespeare's classic play within a colonized setting, placing struggles against oppression at the center. In this context, the tragic deaths of Romeo and Lupe cannot fully resolve the tensions between their families, which are shaped by complex conflicts between Chicanxs and Anglos, between farm owners and fieldworkers, and between irrigation companies and those forced off their land to clear space for pipelines. Nevertheless, *The Tragic Corrido* presents the Rio Grande Valley as a generative Borderlands space where, given more just circumstances, Romeo and Lupe's love might thrive.

— KATHERINE GILLEN, ADRIANNA M. SANTOS,
AND KATHRYN VOMERO SANTOS

# The Tragic Corrido of Romeo and Lupe

SERES JAIME MAGAÑA

Adapted from Shakespeare's *Romeo and Juliet*
Original music and lyrics by Seres Jaime Magaña, Veronique Medrano, and Arnulfo Daniel Segovia

SETTING: Our tale is set in an alternate timeline in a growing Republic of Texas, where events from throughout history are all clashing at once around the love story of Romeo and Lupe.

## CHARACTERS

| | |
|---|---|
| **MR. CAMPBELL** | Owner of the Campbell Irrigation Company |
| **MRS. CAMPBELL** | Wife of Mr. Campbell |
| **ROMEO** | Son of Mr. and Mrs. Campbell and heir to the Campbell Irrigation Company |
| **NELSON** | Romeo's cousin and son of the Campbell Irrigation Company General Sales Director |
| **STELLAN** | Son of the Campbell Irrigation Company General Sales Manager |
| **BALTI** | Romeo's childhood friend and a farmworker born in the Rio Grande Valley |
| **MERCUTIO** | Republic of Texas soldier stationed in the Rio Grande Valley and son of the Town Judge |
| **DON DÍAZ** | Patriarch of the Díaz family |
| **LUPE** | Daughter of Don Díaz |
| **TÍA MARLA** | Lupe's aunt |
| **DELMA** | Lupe's cousin and her most trusted friend |
| **RAMÓN** | Lupe's cousin |

| | |
|---|---|
| **PLÁCIDO** | Lupe's cousin and a farmworker and activist |
| **DÍAZ 1** | Lupe's cousin |
| **PADRE LAURO** | Botanist and priest from Mexico |
| **CORRIDO SINGER** | Chorus |
| **TOWN JUDGE** | |
| **PROTESTORS** | |
| **MODEL 1** | |
| **MODEL 2** | |
| **CUSTOMER** | |
| **POLICE OFFICER** | |
| **PARAMEDIC** | |
| **MAIL CARRIER** | |
| **FUNERAL HOME CARETAKER** | |

# ACT 1
# Scene 1

**CORRIDO SINGER**

Damas y caballeros. Ladies and gentlemen. Les traigo un consejo.

(*singing*)

> No le digas no al amor
> No hagas tanto coraje
> Este es mi mensaje
> Don't say no to love

> Here in the Magic Valley
> In the Republic of Texas
> On these fertile lands
> Of opportunity
> Covered in blood and strife
> Blooms a forbidden love

> No le digas no al amor
> No hagas tanto coraje
> Este es mi mensaje
> Don't say no to love

> Sabes de la antigua discordia
> Aquí en el Valle Mágico
> La gente se levanta en protesta
> Contra los visionarios

> No le digas no al amor
> No hagas tanto coraje
> Este es mi mensaje
> Don't say no to love

> Only love can free a soul
> Take heed of this true story
> Don't say no to love

Rivals equal in dignity,
Civil blood makes civil hands unclean.
From the fatal loins of these foes

A pair of star-crossed lovers,
Who could not love freely, end their life.
Now we turn back the clock and revive this
Tragic Corrido of Romeo and Lupe.

# Scene 2

**CORRIDO SINGER**

Welcome to Cage Boulevard,
Here in the city of Pharr.
A big night just 'round the corner,
The Birthday Party they call it,
A display of the valley's reward.
People are coming from miles around.
They're looking to know what all the chisme is about.

> *The TOWN JUDGE enters with MR. CAMPBELL.*

That man there is Mr. Campbell, followed by the town judge. He owns Campbell Irrigation. He is respected by most and most detested by some. The locals show their affection, writing his name across cardboards. They tell him to leave, to rot, to die, to never return anymore. You ask, why the reputation? The thing about Campbells is this: they are ambitious dreamers, nothing can stop their visions, as they build their dreams through refugees, as they build their dreams through people's homes. So as you can see, it's easy to tell why they dislike him so. The Campbells live across the valley, but tonight they are here in town. That is because the boss is here with us, and he is looking to lure in some buyers.

**MR. CAMPBELL**

It has worked marvelously. I sent out flyers all over the Republic announcing our land sale. And we have received a fantastic response. It's going to be a great night.

> *MR. CAMPBELL and the TOWN JUDGE exit.*

**CORRIDO SINGER**

The Campbells have prepared for so many nights just as the protestors who are about to enter have prepared for today's protest. Yet regardless of all their preparation, they'll be too late to turn their wrongs right.

*MR. CAMPBELL exits. The CORRIDO SINGER's guitar is suddenly accompanied by drums, adding a rap beat to the melody. RAMÓN enters.*

**RAMÓN** (*rapping*)
        to my ancestors
        Magic Valley fame
        since before northern investors
        the Republic of Texas
        brought the growth and strife
        got me feeling life is conflict
        so I brought my knife
        tried to tear us down like weeds
        didn't know that we was seeds
        land of opportunity but the infantry exceeds
        our greatest protests
        my words are true I confess
        we tryna keep our way
        but don't know what it means
        Aztec Tejano flow my life is so supreme
        like a young Cuauhtemoc destined to be the king
        but heavy is the head that wears the crown
        kissed by the sun, that's why my people is brown
        we've got our own rules, we've got our own tools
        our own ways of living, and we won't be made fools
        I got the spirits of the ancients,
        and they telling me be patient
        but I soaked up the old ways,
        now I'm gonna make my statement
        what is buried is the conflict in the food we pick
        breathing in chemical vapors, it make us sick
        like two sides to a coin,
        I'm calling you to join
        in breaking every chain,
        in channeling this pain
        as it pumps through my veins
        and expels in my verse
        siphoning my life's curse
        till I'm rolling in the hearse
        then return me to the earth,

lay me in the corn fields
cuz even in the afterlife I still be keeping it real
cuz even in the afterlife my people still on the battlefield
so let me tell you the deal:
I bare culture, I bare pain,
both Turtle Island and Spain
I'm like the smell of the earth after a summer a rain
planting seeds like prodigy
is this Tejano's odyssey
you oughta see like the dreamers we naive,
it's not exactly how it seems
depending on the version you read of the history
but I would bleed for this land,
I'm extending out my hand
I'm telling you to fight,
till we return to sand.

*NELSON, STELLAN, and BALTI enter. RAMÓN is joined by PLÁ-
CIDO and DÍAZ 1.*

**RAMÓN**

Hey, Campbells, I got something for ya! You looked, vato! You looked!

**NELSON**

What's wrong with you?

**RAMÓN**

I get to punch you.

**NELSON**

Don't you dare lay a finger on me.

**STELLAN**

I don't quite follow you. Why do you say you get to punch him?

**RAMÓN**

That's the rule. I make an "O" with my fingers below the waistline — if you
look through it, I get to punch you. You looked. Now I punch you.

**NELSON**

I don't have time for this stupidity.

**RAMÓN**

But that's the rule, vato. It's the law around here. Right, primo?

**PLÁCIDO**

The law is on our side.

**NELSON**

Are you looking for a quarrel?

**RAMÓN**

Do I hear a voice that tells me not to fight? No, not a voice is there.

**PLÁCIDO**

Don't worry, primo. We are not looking for a fight. We are only looking to keep our ways. Because here we have our own rules. Our own way of living. And you want to come here and make this your home. Well, the rule is you get a punch if you look. You looked. Ponte.

**RAMÓN**

There might have been a voice in my head that talked of peace, but now there is a louder voice, the voice of violence.

*He brings out a pocketknife. MERCUTIO enters.*

**MERCUTIO**

Well, I'm glad that voice is speaking, because I'm its best listener.

**NELSON & STELLAN**

Mercutio?

**MERCUTIO**

I've returned. But more about that later over a drink at the Shamrock. You can also tell me the details of this quarrel, but for now . . .

*They fight. The TOWN JUDGE enters from inside Padre Lauro's Botica.*

**TOWN JUDGE**

Stop! Rebellious subjects, enemies to peace, profaners who stain the streets of our promising Magic Valley with your neighbors' blood. Will you not listen? Or are you like a beast, quenching the fire of your pernicious rage with the red fountains that issue from each other's veins? In respect for the law of our Republic, control your tempers and throw down your weapons! Díaz! Withdraw at once to your homes. If you do transgress like this upon the peace of our valley again, I will have to start putting somebody under arrest. Mercutio! With me son.

**MERCUTIO**
Anything for your majesty.

**PLÁCIDO**
Vámonos.

> *The TOWN JUDGE, MERCUTIO, PLÁCIDO, DÍAZ 1, and RAMÓN exit as MR. CAMPBELL and MRS. CAMPBELL enter.*

**MR. CAMPBELL**
That man Plácido is really starting to distemper me. I don't care who started this. Learn to act civil. Something like this again and I will be forced to start letting some of you go. I don't care if you are my family . . .

> *He is interrupted by a charro yell. ROMEO enters singing "Amorcito Corazón" by Pedro Infante, not noticing his parents.*

**NELSON**
In love?

**ROMEO**
Out.

**STELLAN**
Out of love?

**ROMEO**
Out of her favor where I am in love. Love that is so sweet in appearance, when in actuality it is tyrannous and cruel.

**NELSON**
Love is blind. And even so it still finds pathways for its lust.

**ROMEO**
Balti! Oh my dear camarada, my heart is heavy with the love of my life, Rosalina. You've seen her. The daughter of Don Pérez. ¡Esta chula!

> *BALTI tries to direct ROMEO's attention to his father using his eyes, and clearing his throat, but with no success. ROMEO tries to hand BALTI a drink.*

**ROMEO**

Here. This will clear your throat.

**BALTI**

No bebo mientras trabajo.

**ROMEO**

But you must drink. You must celebrate. Celebrate our friendship. Oh, how I thank you for being in my life, dear Balti. You saved my life when we were boys, when I was about to drown, and although my judgmental jerk of a father does not completely approve of our friendship, you don't know how much I absolutely love you, and you don't know how much I thank you for saving my life that day. Because if I had died, I would not have drank all that tequila, and I would not have had these lips lay on the beautiful tender pink lips of Rosalina!

**MR. CAMPBELL**

That's enough, Romeo.

> *ROMEO turns around and notices his parents.*

**ROMEO**

Father.

**MR. CAMPBELL**

Drinking in the morning, son?

**ROMEO**

Is the day so young? I thought I saw the moon out. What happened here? You all had a fight? Sure it has much to do with hate, but more to do with love. Hateful love, loving hate, anything of nothing first created, heavy lightness, selfless selfishness, chaos of seemingly well-shaped forms, bright smoke, cold fire, sick health, reality sown of daydreams. Don't you laugh at these ironies?

**NELSON**

Rather, I weep.

**ROMEO**

At what?

**NELSON**

At your mind's loss of sense.

*ROMEO and NELSON wrestle.*

**MRS. CAMPBELL**
¡Peleoneros! I don't even know why I cook for you if you all would just rather be dead. All you Campbells are so impulsive.

*MR. CAMPBELL raises his hand with annoyance to indicate to his wife to be quiet.*

**ROMEO**
Mom is right.

**MR. CAMPBELL**
Both of you, back to the hotel. Now!

*ROMEO and MRS. CAMPBELL exit.*

**MR. CAMPBELL** (*to the rest*)
Get on with your day.

*All exit except NELSON and MR. CAMPBELL.*

**MR. CAMPBELL**
Nelson. Come here. Who is this Rosalina?

**NELSON**
She works out in the fields. Many a day has Romeo been seen there, with tears augmenting the fresh morning's dew, adding to clouds more clouds with his deep sighs, all the time howling like a mad dog, "Rosalina, let me in your heart!"

**MR. CAMPBELL**
Black and ill must this humor prove. Unless good counsel may the cause remove. It's time I have a proper talk with my son.

*They exit.*

# Scene 3

*ROMEO and MR. CAMPBELL enter the living room area of their suite.*

**MR. CAMPBELL**

What is the point? What is the point of all this we work so hard to build? There are times, son, that my heart beams with pride when I see your natural talent to be the heir to this company. Then there are times that you make me afraid that I will regret ever handing such a proud achievement to somebody of such low estimation. Your mind gets the best of you. You can't hold a thought before chasing after a new delusion. You prove to me again and again that I can't rely on you.

**ROMEO**

If you would just listen to what is in my heart . . .

**MR. CAMPBELL**

What is in your heart has clouded your mind, and I expect you to get yourself in order. Your inconsistency is ridiculous. One minute, you are the best asset to the company. A man worth the name. And at another minute, you are drunk and drooling over some farm girl! You lack pride! You lack dignity! You are the future owner of the Campbell Irrigation Company. You are an important man. You must earn the respect of people and always keep yourself above them, so they will know their place. You can't be embarrassing yourself as you did today.

**ROMEO**

That's the problem, father. That you look down on everyone. Just like you look down on my mother for being mexicana.

**MR. CAMPBELL**

Enough! I have given you and your mother a better life than anyone could have asked for. You are nobody to judge me. What do you have to say for yourself? Nothing! You're just a young fool living off your father's money. You have no idea what it means to struggle for what you want. You have no character, no mettle. I'm sick and tired of this. I don't care if you are my son, you will not inherit what you have not earned. I will not place the future of this company, of all my hard work, in the hands of somebody so incompetent. More of this and I will be sending you away to the military to earn your honor. Either that, or you can live on the street.

**ROMEO**

I'm sorry, father. I don't know what came over me. I will do better.

**MR. CAMPBELL**

Actions speak louder than words.

*MR. CAMPBELL exits.*

**ROMEO**

What's the point of actions speaking if the world is deaf?

*ROMEO exits.*

# Scene 4

*DELMA is at the Díaz house. She hears voices approaching and realizes that it's DON DÍAZ and TÍA MARLA. She quickly hides to spy on their conversation.*

**DON DÍAZ**

Mi sobrino solo hace lo que hace para defender su hogar. Tan solo la semana pasada esos Campbells sacaron al Pepe y su familia de su casa, que para excavar un canal.

**TÍA MARLA**

Ambos tú y el señor Campbell son señores muy honrados. El problema con lo que pasó ahora fue un pleito de jóvenes. Alguien tiene que controlar a estos muchachos. ¿Pero dime, hermano, qué dices a lo que te ofrezco?

**DON DÍAZ**

Mi respuesta es no. Mi Lupita nunca ha salido del valle. No conoce el mundo. Tiene sólo catorce años.

**TÍA MARLA**

Dos veranos más y será adulta. ¿Qué quieres? ¿Que termine casada con algún campesino? ¿O con algún cholo, o un pobretón? Deja llevármela a México conmigo. Yo la haría tal dama, que un hombre no la escogerá, ella escogerá a un hombre.

**DON DÍAZ**

Mi Lupita no está en edad para estar pensando en matrimonios. ¿De qué hablas? Más, sus primos la tienen bien cuidada.

**TÍA MARLA**

Sus primos son unos vagos. Más, ellos no la pueden cuidar a todas horas, tienen sus vagancias que atender. Hermano, hay muchachitas más jóvenes que ella en este vecindario que ya son madres. De eso tienes que tener cuidado.

**DON DÍAZ**

Tienes razón. Cuando murió su madre, la tierra se tragó mi felicidad, y la poca que me quedo, se la debo a mi Lupita. Odiaría ver a mi muchachita maltratada por algún pelado.

**TÍA MARLA**

Vez lo que te digo.

**DON DÍAZ**

Pero tienes que convencerla. Mi consentimiento es tan solo una parte. La cosa es que ella quiera ir.

**TÍA MARLA**

Vendrá, si sabe lo que es bueno para ella. Yo a su edad me hubiera encantado esta oportunidad. Recibir el consejo de una mujer con experiencia. De alguien que me haya podido guiar y advertir. Más, la casa de mi difunto esposo es muy grande tan solo para mí. Me gustaría la compañía de una mujer. Ya tendría más o menos la edad de Lupe mi hija si hubiera nacido. Eso fue hace tanto tiempo. Piénsalo. Lupe es una muchacha muy atractiva, y necesita una buena educación. Aquí se va a ser una naquita pocha. A menos de que se case con uno de estos Campbells que dices, o algún . . .

**DON DÍAZ**

De ninguna manera. Esa clase de gente se cree mejor que los demás. Desde que te casaste con ese ricachón, que descanse en paz, y te fuiste de la casa y lejos de la vida del campo, se te olvidó tu humildad. Lupe se merece el cielo y las estrellas. Que la traten como lo más majestuoso y esencial de la vida.

**TÍA MARLA**

Pues no se me haría raro que se junte con alguien que la humille, ya que ella se humilla a ella misma.

**DON DÍAZ**

¿Qué habladurías dices?

**TÍA MARLA**

Sí, el otro día las escuche a ella y a Delma hablando en inglés entre ellas. ¿Para que hablen en inglés si ellas son mexicanas? ¿Que acaso le da vergüenza ser quien es? Hasta luego, hermano.

*TÍA MARLA exits.*

**DON DÍAZ**

¡Lupe! ¡Lupe! ¿Dónde está esa niña? ¡Lupe!

*DELMA exits from her hiding place while DON DÍAZ isn't looking. He turns around just in time to see her by the door and thinks she's just entered.*

**DON DÍAZ**

Delma, mija, que bueno que llegas. ¿Dónde está tu prima? Ayúdame a buscarla.

**DELMA & DON DÍAZ**

¡Lupe! ¡Lupe!

*DON DÍAZ exits and LUPE enters. She is distracted, folding an elegant dress and placing it suspiciously under a drawer.*

**DELMA**

Lupe, hazme caso. ¿Para qué es ese vestido?

**LUPE**

Para esta noche.

**DELMA**

¿No me digas que estás planeando ir a la protesta?

**LUPE**

No hay de otra. Tú sabes que tengo que ir.

**DELMA**

¿Y de dónde sacaste el vestido? No me digas que . . . ¡No!

**LUPE**

Sí, lo tomé del cuarto de Tía Marla.

**DELMA**

Que loca estás. Acaso tengo que recordarte que Tía Marla lleva estos vestidos cada año al altar que tiene en su casa para su bebé que perdió en parto. Si aún recuerdo cuando tenía yo doce años y Tía Marla vino a visitarnos, y me enseñó el primer vestidito amarillo de bebe, seguido por otros catorce, uno por cada año. Y cuando su muertita cumplió quince años le llevó un vestido de quinceañera al altar con una corona. Y a la corona le puso velo, ya ves que con sus vestidos siempre lleva un turbante, que para que el sol no moleste el descanso de su muertita.

**LUPE**

Es por eso que es perfecto, porque esconderá mi rostro. Y no es un vestido que he usado antes, o que usualmente usaría. Nadie me reconocerá.

**DELMA**

Pero no vas a un velorio. Esta es una Fiesta de Cumpleaños del Magic Valley.

**LUPE**

Ah nadie le va a importar.

> *DON DÍAZ enters. They don't notice him.*

**DELMA**

Lástima que sea verde. Parece moco.

**DON DÍAZ** (*aside*)

Escúchalas. Sí hablan en español. Su tía está equivocada.

**DELMA**

Pero no crees que . . .

> *She notices DON DÍAZ standing close to them.*

Be careful what you say, your father is here.

**LUPE**

He is right behind me, isn't he?

**DELMA**

Yeah. Tía Marla was talking to him. She wants to take you to Mexico with her.

**LUPE**

No way!

**DON DÍAZ**

¿Por qué cambiaron de español a inglés así cuando llegue yo? ¿Están escondiendo lo que dicen? Tu tía Marla tiene razón. ¡Tiene razón! Necesitas que alguien te corrija, Lupe. Desde que tu madre murió, mi corazón es débil, y no logró imponer mi carácter sobre ti como debo. Es por eso que he decidido que te marcharas con . . .

**LUPE**

Ay, papá, ¿cómo crees que vamos hablar en inglés para esconder las cosas de ti? Tú sabes que hemos crecido aquí, y el inglés es tan parte de nosotras como el español. Si quieres hasta te enseño inglés. Cualquier cosa para pasar más tiempo con mi papito chulo que lo quiero tanto.

**DON DÍAZ**

¡Ya, párale, ya! Tienes razón, mija. Que estoy pensando. Yo no te quiero lejos. Más me recuerdas tanto a tu madre, que en paz descanse. Te he platicado el cuento de la carreta y el alazán.

**LUPE**

Tú sabes que me encanta ese cuento. Platícame de nuevo.

**DELMA**

Sí, tío, ándale.

**DON DÍAZ**

Fue cuando tú eras una bebita. Los tiempos eran difíciles para campesinos como nosotros, y vivíamos con el Jesús en la boca por la falta de dinero. Aun así, esos fueron los años más felices de mi vida. Pues tenía el apoyo de tu madre, y mi vida brillaba con la luz de mi chiquitita. En esos días yo era dueño de un hermoso alazán. Pero me hacía falta una silla de montar. Tu madre cuidaba mucho de una carreta muy útil que ella solita armó. Desafortunadamente, ella batallaba mucho con el viejo buey que jalaba su carreta, el cual en cualquier momento iba a estirar la pata. Así que poco antes de llegar nuestro aniversario, yo subí al norte por unos meses para trabajar, pero en realidad buscaba vender mi alazán y comprarle a tu madre una mula nueva y fuerte para su carreta. Tu madre tomó la oportunidad y contigo en sus brazos se dirigió al sur a vender su carreta y comprarme una silla mexicana para mi alazán. Cuando me fui, me despedí de un valle con caminos abiertos y regresé a una frontera cerrada. Lo debimos haber visto venir. Pues poco a poco después de la guerra civil se empezó a construir una cerca, que para que no cruzara el ganado con sus piojos. Después, la República de Texas comenzó a exigir exámenes para poder pasar. Fue así que la frontera nos cruzó a nosotros y no nosotros a la frontera. Para cuando regresé a casa, con las nuevas mulas para tu madre, todo había cambiado, y ahora mi familia no podía poner pie aquí sin que se les diga ilegales. Donde yo anduve tranquilo a pie, ahora mis sobrinos andan escondidos y arrastrándose por la tierra.

**DELMA**

Tranquilo, tío. No se enoje. Yo se como es eso. Aún tengo las cicatrices de las espinas del nopal en la planta de mis pies, de cuando yo cruce.

**DON DÍAZ**

Tu madre se había quedado del lado mexicano y yo del estadounidense. Nos empezamos a comunicar por medio de cartas. Cuando aprendí que ella había ido al sur a vender su carreta para comprar mi silla y ella que yo fui al norte a vender mi alazán para comprar sus mulas, nos dio tanta risa. ¿Qué íbamos a hacer? ¡Andar montados en una mula!

**LUPE**

Me encanta esa historia. Que los dos hayan estado dispuestos a sacrificar lo que más atesoran para demostrarse lo tanto que se aman. Espero algún día encontrar un amor así.

**DON DÍAZ**

Tú estás muy jovencita para andar pensando en el amor.

**LUPE**

Ay, ya papá.

**DON DÍAZ**

Te quiero mucho, mija. Jamás quiero volver a sentir lo que sentí al perder a tu madre. Le diré a tu tía que te quedarás conmigo. Yo quiero disfrutar cuanto tiempo pueda con mi hija. Aún recuerdo el día que el río te trajo de regreso a mí, el mismo río que se llevó la vida de tu madre.

*PLÁCIDO enters.*

**DON DÍAZ**

Ah, sobrino. Ya no se ande metiendo usted en pleitos, mijo. Que no ve que lo queremos mucho y no queremos que le pase nada. Ande con cuidado. Los quiero tanto a todos.

*DON DÍAZ exits.*

**PLÁCIDO**

Lupita, I came to tell you to please . . .

**LUPE**

¿Que no me meta en tus pleitos? Plácido, the judge already warned you what will happen next time something like today breaks out. If you do this protest tonight, tomorrow you will either be arrested or hiding out someplace. Please don't do it.

**PLÁCIDO**

I don't understand how you can ask me to turn my back on my duty.

**LUPE**

Then let me go with you.

**PLÁCIDO**

No way, Lupe. It will be dangerous.

**LUPE**

That's why I want to go.

**DELMA**

You don't fight when Lupe is around.

**PLÁCIDO**

That's because I'm scared of my primita getting hurt. But tonight is an important night, so we can't go easy on them. You have to stay home, Lupita. I'll be fine. I will be doing what I have to do for mi gente.

**LUPE**

Nobody should be in danger of getting hurt. These are peaceful protests, remember? Keep that in mind.

**PLÁCIDO**

If it comes to violence, I'm not to blame. But if they want a fight, we'll give them one back. Be safe, primita.

*PLÁCIDO exits.*

**LUPE**

I must go. Enter the party in a disguise. Once he delivers his protest message, I will reveal myself and persuade him to withdraw. Hopefully he will listen.

*LUPE grabs the dress and exits.*

**DELMA**

I know mi prima. She is going to try to cut off the protest before it escalates — that much is true — but I know that's not the only reason why. Go on, Lupe, seek happy nights to happy days!

*DELMA exits.*

# Scene 5

*STELLAN, NELSON, BALTI, and ROMEO hang out in their suite at the Pharr Hotel.*

**STELLAN**

It's almost time for the birthday party.

**NELSON**

And we will not go like a blindfolded cupid, or beheaded chickens, frightening the ladies like scarecrows. Let them measure us by what we are. I, Nelson Campbell, future Sales Director of Campbell Irrigation, learning the ways of my father. Stellan Caudwell, son of our Sales Manager. Balti, the musician. And Romeo Campbell, son of our Company Director, future heir to all his father's land and riches.

**STELLAN**

Such prolixity is outdated. Let them measure us by what they will.

**NELSON**

I'll measure them a measure and be gone.

**ROMEO**

I'm not up for this.

**BALTI**

Is there something on your mind, Romeo?

**ROMEO**

I'm thinking of a dream I had last night.

**BALTI**

Let go of yesterday's dreams and welcome tonight's.

**NELSON**

Yes, just focus on the party.

**ROMEO**

I will not be going to the party.

**STELLAN**

Mercutio will be there.

**ROMEO**

Mercutio is in town?

>   *There is a knock at the door. NELSON opens it.*

**NELSON**

Speak of the devil.

>   *MERCUTIO enters. ROMEO jumps out of his chair to greet him.*
>   *The two longtime friends are happy to see each other after so many*
>   *months apart.*

**ROMEO**

It's been such a long time, Mercutio.

**MERCUTIO**

That's funny. I would say the hours were cut short. I feel like I left yesterday, and I'm already back in this wretched valley.

**ROMEO**

To me, hours are long. For I don't have that which, otherwise if I had, would make the hours fly by unnoticed. But what made you come back? And what is this you're wearing?

**MERCUTIO**

I did not come back, I was sent back. Yes, as you guess, I'm with one of the infantries stationed here. As destiny has it, there is no escaping my father and this nauseating place. As you know, I left, looking for anything really. I reached the great cities north of our Republic. I was thinking of going into the stock business. But next thing I know, everybody is panicking about a stock market crash, banks are in mayhem, people are going broke. Father told me to come back home, and I, thinking nothing could force me out of the valley more than a uniform, joined the military. Then what happens? I'm stationed right here in the Magic Valley! Under the shadow of my father, my drill sergeant, and don't forget, dear Uncle Sam. God, Romeo, you're a mess. All you're going to attract looking like that is a mule. Since when is dear Romeo so careless and unready for a night to dance? Hurry up and get ready, it's getting late.

**NELSON**

I should inform you — our dear Romeo does not want to join us at the party tonight.

**MERCUTIO**

No? What are you, sick?

**ROMEO**

I got a hundred tequila worms eating my heart.

**STELLAN**

This time her name is Rosalina.

**ROMEO**

What do you mean this time?

**MERCUTIO**

Now I understand the reason for my friend looking like such a mess. He is being delirious about another of his romances gone astray. No way, we must have Romeo dance tonight.

**ROMEO**

My heart is heavy, which makes my whole body heavy. I can't move.

**MERCUTIO**

You are a lover. Borrow cupid's wings.

**NELSON**

Yes. And soar with them above common ground.

**ROMEO**

I am too wounded by one of his arrows to soar with his light feathers, and, so bound, were I a singer, I could not sing a note above dull sadness. I sink under love's heavy burden.

**MERCUTIO**

And by sinking you will burden love: too great an oppression for a tender thing.

**ROMEO**

Is love a tender thing? It is too rough, too rude, too selfish, and it pricks like a thorn.

**MERCUTIO**

If love is rough with you, be rough with love. We are wasting time!

**ROMEO**

No. It would not be wise to go.

**MERCUTIO**

And why not?

**ROMEO**

I had a dream.

**MERCUTIO**

So did I.

**ROMEO**

What was yours?

**MERCUTIO**

That dreamers often lie.

**ROMEO**

In bed asleep while they dream things true.

**MERCUTIO**

Then I see you've eaten a button off her crown. From it blossoms a flower of fair pink petals. It is no bigger than a hand palm and lays on the bronze head of an alderwoman. She is the fairest midwife. Sowing sights and feels with a team of little atoms as it drizzles them over men's dormant heads. She has a spider's legs, and whistles like the white noise from a grasshopper. She draws the thinnest spider web made of moonshine's watery beams; she has a whip made from a cricket's backbone. Her chariot is unlike an Englishman's Queen Mab, which is like an empty hazelnut; instead, her chariot is a dripping lemon. She gallops night by night through lovers' brains and makes them dream of love, and thus, love is but the effects of her dreamlike web on their cerebrum. This is she —

**ROMEO**

Settle down, Mercutio. You talk about nothing.

**MERCUTIO**

True, I talk about dreams. And what are dreams, both the ones we sit on and the ones we set after, if not children of an idle brain, conceived of nothing but vain fantasy, which is as thin a substance as the air, and more inconstant than the changing wind that swirls us around in any direction like fallen leaves. In fact, every dream is a nightmare.

**ROMEO**

You talk about dreams as if they've sickened you.

**MERCUTIO**

And so you hit it right — dreams are a sickness of the brain, for a dream's nature depends on what we insert in our minds, what's in our blood, our bellies, and most of all, it depends on the state of our humor. Don't be so high up in your mind, Romeo, or else your humor turns cold. This Rosalina that you're lamenting, like a rose she will shrivel up, and at this pace you are shriveling up with her. No, dear friend, you and I are young! And we can't waste our youth in dreams, in wondering. I've wasted enough time that way. I want to live. Feel alive. For while you sit here in the peace of the Magic Valley, in your bubble of dreams, other corners of the world are not as quiet. The depression ravages the North, the world war rises. In one place people starve, in another people are murdered, and in another happy wealthy families sit together rotting in their own hypocrisy. It's a ticking clock, this train you're riding called life, and the shadow of death lurks over every second.

**NELSON**

It's past eight. We should start heading down to the lobby.

**STELLAN**

There is a mob gathering outside.

**MERCUTIO**

Guess I was wrong. Not even the valley is quiet. See what I mean? Wake up, Romeo. Life is but a glimpse, and you are too late.

**ROMEO** (*aside*)

To me it appears I'm much too soon. For so much of tonight is so like my dream, where I foresaw Mercutio's arrival and this protest. My mind misgives some consequence hanging in the stars, which will bitterly begin its fearful turn toward the expiration of this life that beats through me. But he that steers my course directs my sail forward.

**NELSON**
So will you be coming?

**ROMEO**
Yes. Mercutio, I am happy for your return, dearest friend. Let me get a change of clothes.

**MERCUTIO**
Now you're talking sense. Here, take a button from her crown.

**ROMEO**
No, Mercutio. Tonight, I keep a clear head.

> ROMEO exits into his room. All others exit into the Pharr Hotel lobby, where the party is beginning.

# Scene 6

> At the party, LUPE wears a dress and a hat with a veil that covers her face. She crosses the party unnoticed by ROMEO.

**MERCUTIO**
Taste this stuff, it is amazing.

**ROMEO**
My appetite is not up to it.

**MERCUTIO**
And does your peon want a plate?

**BALTI**
No se me antoja. I personally love tortillas, and here there is only bread.

> MERCUTIO exits. ROMEO walks across the room to his father.

**ROMEO**
Dad, I wanted to ask you a question.

**MR. CAMPBELL**
What is it, Romeo? I'm busy.

**ROMEO**
Where is mom?

**MR. CAMPBELL**

She was feeling sick.

**ROMEO**

I don't recall her being sick.

**MR. CAMPBELL**

Enough, Romeo. I won't have it tonight. Gentlemen, let's make sure those cabbage crates are ready to catch the train.

*ROMEO returns with BALTI.*

**BALTI**

Is everything okay? You look upset.

**ROMEO**

Father left mother at home. Wouldn't want people to find out he has a Mexican wife.

**BALTI**

Pay no heed to it.

**ROMEO**

What kind of jerk do you have to be to marry a person, and go to the extent of having children with them, just so you could own the land they inherited? Look at him. How unhappy a man. To never love.

**BALTI**

I daresay he does love your mother. But he can't help who he is. Your father has chosen a difficult position to uphold.

**ROMEO**

And what is more important: position or love? What is the point of upholding such an "honorable" position with a hollow heart? I try to see my father's vision, but he lies, he cheats these people, and he steals from them. Agh! I can't tolerate it!

**BALTI**

Your grievance with him is so great. You should join the protestors.

**ROMEO**

Balti, that is an excellent idea.

**BALTI**

No, it's not. Do you know who you are? They'll tear you apart.

**ROMEO**

I'll not be Romeo tonight. I will go in a disguise. Seriously. This is so boring. The real party is over there with them. Lend me some of your work clothes.

**BALTI**

Are you sure about this?

**ROMEO**

Of course I am.

 *ROMEO and BALTI exit.*

**MR. CAMPBELL**

Good evening, ladies and gentlemen. I want to thank everybody for traveling such a long way down to discover the magic of our valley. Welcome to this year's party and fashion show, celebrating the birthday of our beautiful Magic Valley. It's an enchanting night. The moon sets high over our beautiful palm trees looming over our rich harvests: cotton, cane, grapefruit, carrot, broccoli. You name it!

 *ROMEO enters dressed as a farmworker.*

A life of prosperity awaits you here. That same life of ensured liberty and prosperity that the founding fathers of our Republic envisioned. Tranquility for your family and the promise of never-ending growth. Once again, I want to thank everybody. And give a big round of applause for our beautiful models.

 *MODEL 1 enters dressed representing grapefruits.*

**MODEL 1**

This valley here is a grapefruit. Anywhere you make a cut, the nectar from the land spills out like an open wound. You cut deep into it. And you drain it of its soul. Sister, where were you?

 *MODEL 2 enters dressed representing grapes.*

**MODEL 2**

I was hungry and wandering, when I saw a woman eating grapes. I told her, "Please, give me one for my child." She said, "Go away. Your feet are muddy, and I despise your stare."

**MR. CAMPBELL** (*aside*)
What is this? Security!

**MODEL 2**
I saw her husband sucking on a sugar cane like a thumb. All the time he cries, "I want more."

**MODELS 1 & 2**
We do not want your segregation, your discrimination, your dreams. Esta tierra no te quiere aquí. This is not your Magic Valley, this is the RGV. This is not your Magic Valley, this is the RGV.

> *PLÁCIDO enters followed by protestors. He recites the chant along with the MODELS.*

**LUPE**
You've made your point. Let's go home.

**PLÁCIDO**
What are you doing here? I told you we were not going to go easy on them. Take her home!

> *Suddenly a fight breaks out. While being taken away, LUPE takes advantage of the distraction and releases herself, managing to get away from her primos while dodging people fighting in the crowd. She is pushed by PLÁCIDO's opponent, and ROMEO, who is close by, catches her.*

**ROMEO**
Who are you who hides behind this veil?

> *He picks up her veil and is captivated by her. They get separated. The fight freezes as ROMEO continues to walk about.*

Oh, does she teach the torches to burn bright. It seems she hangs upon the cheek of night, as a rich jewel in the skin of the Guadalupana. Beauty too rich for use, for earth too dear. Did my heart love until now? Forswear it, sight, for I ne'er saw true beauty until this night.

> *The fight continues. Lupe returns to where ROMEO is standing. The fight freezes as ROMEO and LUPE talk.*

If I profane with my unworthiest hand this holy shrine by lifting up your veil, the gentle sin is this: my lips, two blushing pilgrims, ready stand to smooth that rough touch with a tender kiss.

*LUPE puts the veil down.*

**LUPE**

Buen peregrino, you do wrong your hand too much. ¿Qué clase de devoción es esta? Saints have hands that pilgrims' hands do touch. And palm to palm is a pilgrim's kiss.

*She offers a handshake. ROMEO grabs her hand and pulls her away from RAMÓN's grasp.*

**ROMEO**

¿Y qué acaso los santos no tienen labios como los peregrinos?

**LUPE**

Yes, pilgrim, lips that they must use in prayer.

**ROMEO**

Oh, then, dear saint, let lips do what hands do. Rezan. Grant me this prayer, unless faith turns to despair.

**LUPE**

Los santos son estatuas — they don't move.

**ROMEO**

A statue? I see no statue. Before me stands the essence of life itself. Your fingers are the petals of the dahlia, your words a hummingbird's flight, your eyes a volcano that awakens, like Iztaccíhuatl melting down her snow. If you are like a statue, perhaps it is because you sleep. Then here is my prayer's effect: con un poco de tu brillo alumbrare la pasión que mueve este beso . . .

*He kisses her.*

. . . y ahora así es como despiertas con la luz que emanas de ti misma.

**LUPE**

¿Y qué hay de tu pecado?

**ROMEO**

My sin, from my lips, by your lips, is purged.

**LUPE**
Then have my lips the sin that they have took?

**ROMEO**
A sin from my lips? Trespass sweetly urged! Give me back my sin again.

*He kisses her again. The action around them resumes.*

**MERCUTIO**
Predator! Can't put a mexicana in front of you without you trying to eat her.

**RAMÓN**
Lupe! Let's go.

*ROMEO and LUPE get pulled away from each other and off stage.*

**ROMEO** (*while exiting*)
Where is she?

# Scene 7

*The next morning on Cage Boulevard. The CORRIDO SINGER enters.*

**CORRIDO SINGER**
But this will become more than a simple crush,
As you all will see.
Passion lends them power, time means, to meet,
Tempering extremities with extreme sweet.

**BALTI**
Good morning, Romeo.

**ROMEO**
It's a sweet Wednesday morning, Balti. Did you see that girl last night?

**BALTI**
Of course.

**ROMEO**
Wasn't she the most beautiful star you have seen?

**BALTI**

One good thing is that your father will approve more of this romance than the last.

**ROMEO**

Why do you say that?

**BALTI**

She is not a Mexican.

**ROMEO**

She is. Picking up that veil, I saw it right away, el sol de bronce en sus ojos.

**BALTI**

Ah, no me digas. Está seguro que no era algún foco reflejado en sus pupilas.

*LUPE enters from the opposite side of the stage.*

**LUPE**

I wonder who that boy I met last night could be. I've never seen him before. Maybe he works for the Smiths or Campbells. Oh, I wonder if I'll ever see him again. What if he came and went with the party?

**LUPE & ROMEO** (*simultaneously*)

Where could (s)he be?

*They turn a corner and end up facing each other.*

**ROMEO**

Hello.

**LUPE**

Hi.

*ROMEO closes the gap between their lips. They kiss.*

**LUPE**

You kiss by the book.

*DELMA enters.*

**DELMA**

Prima! What do you think you're doing? Vámonos! Tu papá me mandó. Plácido is looking for you.

**ROMEO**

¿Plácido? Is she a Díaz?

**LUPE**

Who is that man? I have not seen him before.

**DELMA**

Don't you recognize him? That is Romeo Campbell, one of the men our primo Plácido is fighting against.

**LUPE**

Campbell? Mi amor florece de donde está mi odio. Lo conocí demasiado temprano sin saber la verdad, y ahora sé la verdad demasiado tarde. Que monstruosidad parece este amor recién nacido, pues me enamorado de un enemigo.

*All exit. PLÁCIDO, RAMÓN, DÍAZ 1, and PROTESTORS enter.*

**PLÁCIDO**

Amigos, last night was a great achievement. Though I wish it did not have to end in blood, our message got across, and what happened will not be soon forgotten. ¡Aquí, los que mandan, somos nosotros!

*They all cheer.*

**RAMÓN**

That's right! And what happened last night couldn't have been done without you. ¿Verdad, amigos? ¡Que viva Plácido Díaz!

**PROTESTORS**

¡Viva!

**DÍAZ 1**

¡Viva! Look at these! They are putting them all over town.

*He holds up a "WANTED" flyer with PLÁCIDO's picture on it.*

**PLÁCIDO**

Good. Means that they're scared.

**DÍAZ 1**

We must keep our eyes open. Not all are on our side. There are mexicanos who want you to stop doing what you're doing. They call you a troublemaker. They say that they got good relations with the gringos, and you're stirring up problems where there are none.

**PLÁCIDO**

Let their low-wage complacency blind them; it works no charm on us. We want nothing with their coin. We want the gringos out. Let's move on, lest they find me. I must hide until I figure out my next move.

*PLÁCIDO, RAMÓN, and DÍAZ 1 exit. MR. CAMPBELL,*
*MRS. CAMPBELL, the TOWN JUDGE, and ROMEO enter.*

**MR. CAMPBELL**

It will take us a long time to recover from last night. I want that man under control.

**TOWN JUDGE**

I've talked to the authorities, and they are doing what they can to find him.

**MR. CAMPBELL**

I need to talk to the new arrivals at once and persuade them before they are completely uninterested. Helena, for tonight's dinner, please don't make anything spicy.

*MR. CAMPBELL and the TOWN JUDGE exit.*

**MRS. CAMPBELL**

Ay, Romeo, siempre andas bien ojerudo.

**ROMEO**

Me siento de maravilla. Tengo que encontrarla, mamá. Tengo que encontrarla y descubrir quién es.

**MRS. CAMPBELL**

Recuerda lo que siempre te he dicho. Al hombre se le enamora con los ojos, y a la mujer por los oídos. Dile cosas lindas. Declárale versos de amor. Hazla sentirse querida.

**ROMEO**

Y mi papá alguna vez te ha hecho sentir esas cosas.

**MRS. CAMPBELL**

Tu papá es como es para aconsejarte. No lo conoces. Sí, tu papá es bien cariñoso. Impulsivo como todos ustedes. Ahorita porque es el "Dueño de Campbell Irrigation Company," pero cuando éramos jóvenes, él era muy diferente.

**ROMEO**
No lo creo.

**MRS. CAMPBELL**
El amor puede pasar en cualquier lugar. Hay un dicho que decía mi madre, "toda paciencia tiene su límite." Hace años, un muchacho del norte de la república llegó a trabajar en un rancho del valle. Y parecía que la tierra no lo quería aquí. Las vacas lo pateaban cuando le tocaba ordeñarlas, los perros le ladraban más a él que a las ovejas, y al montar, los caballos lo sacudían. Era la carilla de todos. El dueño del rancho era el que más se divertía, y lo traía como burro. Y él aguantaba y completaba sus tareas. Lo que nadie sabía es que el joven del norte estaba de lo más enamorado de la hija del dueño. Un día vino un señor de mucha influencia a pedir su mano, queriendo usar sus riquezas para atraerla. Y al oír esto, el joven ya no aguantó, y como el dicho que te comenté, su paciencia se agotó. Declaro la verdad. Que él amaba a la hija del dueño. Que no solo la amaba, pero que ella lo amaba a él. Y confesó que llevaban ya meses casados en secreto. El señor encontró la ocasión tan chistosa, y la paciencia y lealtad del muchacho tan sorpréndete que les prometió que usaría su fuerte influencia para convencer al dueño del rancho de abrir su corazón a su matrimonio. ¡Y así fue! Hasta se hizo una gran fiesta para celebrarlos. Un año después comenzó la guerra, el norte de la república peleaba contra el sur, y el joven luchó. Cuando ganó el norte, regresó a casa, pero todo era diferente. A él la guerra lo hizo frío y duro. El dueño del rancho había muerto, y la guerra tomó a su hijo, así que su hija y él heredaron el rancho. Y no pudo ser más conveniente, pues había conocido a un hombre en la guerra quien tenía grandes planes de hacer una compañía de irrigación en el valle. Decidieron hacerse socios. Una gran ambición se cosechó en él, pues la tierra que de joven tanto rechazaba ahora resultó ser un gran tesoro. Comenzó a vender terreno, a construir un pueblo, y enriqueció. Hizo de la tierra algo suyo. Trajo a su gente del norte, trajo palmas, trajo máquinas, y se volvió parte de un sueño que de pronto emergió, ese de construir un valle mágico, que no sea de aquí ni de allá, pero auténticamente tejano.

**ROMEO**
¿Estás diciendo que el joven de esa historia es mi padre?

**MRS. CAMPBELL**
Así es.

**ROMEO**
No lo puedo creer.

**MRS. CAMPBELL**

No le digas que te dije.

**ROMEO**

¿Cómo es que nunca me entere de esto?

**MRS. CAMPBELL**

Nadie lo sabe. Está olvidado.

**ROMEO**

Pues la tierra aun lo sigue rechazando. ¿Qué crees que son estas protestas?

**MRS. CAMPBELL**

Romeo.

**ROMEO**

Nomás digo. Piensa en lo que me dijiste. Toda paciencia tiene su límite. La gente de esta tierra se agota de lo que mi papá está haciendo. ¿Y se casaron en secreto?

**MRS. CAMPBELL**

Ya vez lo lejos que tu papá está dispuesto a llegar por el amor. Y yo, hijo mío, haría lo mismo por él.

**ROMEO**

Siempre pensé que mi padre tenía el corazón vacío.

**MRS. CAMPBELL**

No es que tenga el corazón vacío, es que ha endurecido sus paredes. Ahora, tengo que apurarme a cocinar la cena.

> *MRS. CAMPBELL exits as the sun begins to set.*

**ROMEO**

I wonder what Lupe is doing right now. Does she look from somewhere in the east at the falling sun in the west, waiting for it to sweep under our feet and rise over her home again . . . or does she live in the south, looking northward upon that line where night and day blend? Ah Lupe, where in this town do you live? I know an hour on the clock awaits, reigning upon the moment of our reunion. It won't be an ordinary hour, for it will have shed its fears and oppressions; it will be an hour like a glimpse through the looking glass, into our very souls, an hour to let go and be held in each other's words, and perchance to kiss as if it were the last time, for anytime it might just be so. I know life tends to go in directions that are not of our own design, but stick around and talk to me for this one hour. I believe that you and I can make it. Yeah, sure, I have my flaws. But nothing that can't be worked out. We met amidst a storm, and we were blown away. Have you forgotten me? Because I can't forget your eyes. I'll search through the valley, whether it be cold and raining, regardless of what others might say. Even if you were an apparition that has left me forever, I will hold on to the hope of finding you. Hermosa Guadalupe, where in the Magic Valley do you live?

> *The CORRIDO SINGER clears her throat.*

Do you know Lupe Díaz?

**CORRIDO SINGER**
I certainly do.

**ROMEO**
Where does she live?

**CORRIDO SINGER**
On the corner of Cage and Polk.

**ROMEO**
You are an angel who comes where a bridge has gone missing and carries the pilgrims across so they may carry on. What beautiful wings are your melodies! Thank you!

> *ROMEO and the CORRIDO SINGER exit.*

# Scene 8

> *LUPE stands on her patio.*

**LUPE**
Que linda noche.

> *ROMEO enters, unnoticed by LUPE.*

**ROMEO**
Like morning breaking through the clouds, a light breaks through the starlit curtain. If midnight has a sun, she rises here. Lupe, you are that fair sun! Arise and kill this envious moon that is so sick and pale with grief, wanting nothing

more than to be as free and beautiful as you are. Cast off the night — the seeds
in the fields won't spur their roots without your touch. Burn away this veil of
dreams. It is like unripe fruit, incomplete and unfulfilled. Rise, querida Lupe,
and awaken me.

*LUPE moves closer.*

Here comes my love! How I wish she knew that she is. She speaks yet says
nothing — what of that? Those eyes seem to be saying something. I'll answer
them. I'm too bold. It's not to me she speaks. Some star in heaven does entreat
her eyes, twinkling there with such brightness. And if that star were her eyes,
and her eyes were that star, its light would then shine so bright through her
head, as sunlight through a lamp. All the birds that cross this yard would be
singing, thinking it's no longer night. Such is the way she encompasses my
thoughts, so completely, like sunlight on the face of a full moon.

**LUPE**
¡Ay me!

**ROMEO**
She speaks. Speak, bright star, for you are as glorious to this night as a messenger from heaven that over mortals' heads causes them to fall back in awe as
they gaze upon its wings sailing on the bosom of the air.

**LUPE**
¿Romeo, por qué eres Romeo? Niega a tu padre, y rechaza tu nombre. O si no
lo harás, negaré el mío, si tan solo juras que me amas.

**ROMEO**
Should I speak at this or keep listening?

**LUPE**
It's only your name that is my enemy. You are yourself, whether you are a
Campbell or not. What is a "Campbell"? It is not your hand, or your face
— it's only a word. Like the words we give to name flowers: whether we call
these poinsettias or nochebuenas, they would still be as red. The same way,
if Romeo was named anything else, he would still retain that dear perfection
which he possesses without that title. Romeo, cast away your name, and, in its
place, take all of me.

**ROMEO**

¡Así será, querida Lupe! Llámame "amor mio" y seré bautizado nuevamente con el nombre. Henceforth, I will never be called Romeo.

**LUPE**

¿Qué clase de hombre eres? Cubierto por la noche y espiando mis pensamientos.

**ROMEO**

By my name, I don't know how to tell you who I am. Aborrezco mi nombre, porque es tu enemigo. Si yo lo hubiera escrito, arrancaría la palabra.

**LUPE**

My ears have not yet drunk a hundred of your words, yet I know the sound. Aren't you Romeo, and a Campbell?

**ROMEO**

Neither, si ninguno de los dos te agrada.

**LUPE**

If my primos see you, they will kill you.

**ROMEO**

There is more danger in your eyes than in twenty of your primos.

**LUPE**

Someone's coming!

**ROMEO**

¡Que vengan! My life better ended by their hate than death prolonged, wanting of your love.

**LUPE**

Who told you where to find my apartment?

**ROMEO**

No one — other than love itself. Love lent me its wings. I lent love my eyes. I am no pilot, but even if you were beyond the sea, I would still find you.

**LUPE**

¡Hay que pena! The mask of night is on my face, or else you would see my cheeks blush for that of which you heard me speak a while ago. Negaría mis palabras. Dime, ¿me amas? I know you'll say that you do love me, and I'll take your word for it. But if you swear, you might prove false, or else the tides will somehow take you from me. I've heard it said that God laughs at our plans, so God may laugh at our promise. O Romeo, if you love me, si de verdad me amas, dilo. Say it truly. Pronúncialo con toda tu bondades. Or if you think that my heart is easily won, then I'll end this and won't speak to you aunque me chilles. But on the contrary, if you do love me, then I won't leave your side for the world. La verdad, querido Campbell, es que me encantas, y es por eso que quizás encuentres mi comportamiento un poco ligero. But trust me, I'll prove more true than all those people who act distant. I should have been more distant, but you heard me speak my mind.

**ROMEO**
Querida Lupe, by this blessed moon I vow, that tips with silver these treetops.

**LUPE**
Don't swear by the moon — the moon is always changing. Unless you prove to be as inconstant.

**ROMEO**
Then what do I swear by?

**LUPE**
No jures. Or if you must swear, swear on yourself, and I'll believe you.

**ROMEO**
I swear, por todo el amor que hay en mi . . .

**LUPE**
Don't swear. I'm happy you're here, but this exchange of vows isn't right. It's too rash, too sudden. It's like lighting, gone before you realize it lit the night. Buenas noches, dulce Romeo. Estas raíces que aquí nacen quizás crecerán a una cosecha cuando nos volvamos a ver. Buenas noches, que la dulce calma esté en tu corazón como en mi pecho.

**ROMEO**
Will you leave me so unsatisfied?

**LUPE**
What type of satisfaction can you have tonight?

**ROMEO**
The exchange of your love's faithful vow for mine.

**LUPE**

I gave you mine before you asked for it. If I still had it, I would give it to you again. The more love I give you, the more love I feel, pues amar es un verbo infinito, boundless as the sky, es una sustancia inexhausta, es para siempre.

**DELMA** (*offstage*)

Lupe?

**LUPE**

Me están llamando. Adiós.

(*to DELMA*) ¡Ya vengo!

(*turning back to ROMEO*) Dulce, Romeo, sé honesto en tu amor. Espera, no te vayas, ahora vuelvo.

> *LUPE exits.*

**ROMEO**

Oh, dear night, don't let this be a dream. I'm afraid that any moment I will awaken.

> *LUPE returns.*

**LUPE**

Dos palabras, dulce Romeo, y buenas noches. If your love is honorable, propose marriage. Let me know tomorrow where and when you will perform the rite, and I will be there, to follow you until the end of the world.

**DELMA** (*offstage*)

Lupe!

**LUPE**

A thousand times goodnight.

> *She kisses him and exits.*

**ROMEO**

A thousand times the worse to want your light.

> *LUPE returns.*

**LUPE**

Romeo!

**ROMEO**

What is it, love?

**LUPE**

Que siempre estuvieras aquí con solo pronunciar tu nombre. I forgot what I called you back for.

**ROMEO**

Let me stand here until you remember.

**LUPE**

No, it's almost morning. You have to go. At what time will I see you tomorrow? I do pass by the hotel on my way back from work. Will you be leaving already, now that the party has passed?

**ROMEO**

I should be staying a bit longer. Either way, my house is not far from here. I would drive a thousand miles and more every morning to be at your side. At what time should I expect to see you?

**LUPE**

At one.

**ROMEO**

I'll be there.

**LUPE**

Buenas noches. Decir adiós es algo tan triste, tener que decir buenas noches y no vernos hasta el amanecer.

**ROMEO**

Descansa, amor mío.

> *ROMEO leaves and doesn't see RAMÓN enter from the other side.*

**RAMÓN**

Romeo, you are a dead man. Plácido will know of this.

> *RAMÓN exits.*

# Scene 9

*At the Botica, PADRE LAURO and a CUSTOMER enter.*

**PADRE LAURO**
I know your prescription said to give you something else, but trust me, this simple remedy will work just as well, and it will cost half as much. It's a mix of eucalyptus, peppermint, lavender, rosemary, coconut, and tea tree oils. In most cases, a garden will give you most remedies.

**CUSTOMER**
Tiene algo para el rasponcito que se hizo mi hijo.

**PADRE LAURO**
Nomás pongale sábila. Tenga. That is why I keep a garden, and because it preserves life. Times are changing, both in terms of industry and in the way we think, and change brings conflict and war as we see with this depression in the north and the war rising across the seas. In such times, innocent things like plants suffer the consequences. And once a certain flower is gone, all it is — its nectar and beauty — is gone with it. That part of life can never be replaced. Listen to me go on. Pay me when you have the money. I pray you get better.

**CUSTOMER**
Muchas gracias, Padre. Fue un gusto platicar con usted.

**ROMEO**
Buenos días, Padre Lauro!

**PADRE LAURO**
Cualli Tlanecic! What early tongue so sweet greets me this Thursday morning? Young son, it argues a distempered head to rise so early from your bed. An old man keeps a careful eye and so he doesn't sleep. But in your young mind, unbruised, there golden sleep reigns. You wouldn't be here so early if you weren't up to no good. I know you were not awakened by some nightmare. You are like the moon that stays awake at night and day. Lo veo en tus ojeras, Romeo has not seen his bed tonight.

**ROMEO**
That last is true; the sweeter rest was mine.

**PADRE LAURO**

¿Estabas con Rosalina?

**ROMEO**

Rosalina! Good heaven, Padre, no! I've forgotten that name.

**PADRE LAURO**

That's good, son. ¿Entonces, dónde estabas? Did you get yourself caught in that protest?

**ROMEO**

Yes, Padre, and I was wounded. And only your holiness has the remedy.

**PADRE LAURO**

Be plain and direct in what you are here to tell me, son. Riddled confessions find riddled absolutions.

**ROMEO**

Then know my heart is set on Lupe Díaz. As mine on hers, so hers is set on mine, and all combined. Except what you must combine, dear Padre, in holy marriage. While we eat our breakfast, I'll tell you the details of when and how we met, but I pray to you, you must consent to marry us today.

**PADRE LAURO**

Is Rosalina, that you loved so dearly, so soon tirada al grano? Young men's love, then, lies not truly in their hearts, but in their eyes. Jesús María, andabas como cachorrito tras esa Rosalina. Now you tell me you've forgotten her.

**ROMEO**

Yes! Didn't you chastise me so many times about her?

**PADRE LAURO**

For doting, not for loving, Romeo.

**ROMEO**

I love Lupe. No me regañe, Padre. I love her, so I will marry her today. I did not love Rosalina. I would not have come this far for her.

**PADRE LAURO**

Oh, believe me. She knew that. But I do see a sudden resolution in you, son, which might prove true. I'll assist you, for this alliance may so happy prove to turn your households' rancor to pure love. And in these times, we can't afford to be divided, for terrible things loom in the horizon: the depression, the world war that escalates. Although it is far from the Magic Valley now, its whip will be felt, as young men are taken from their families to fight and die . . . but only love can make us strong for what's to come.

**ROMEO**
Wonderful. Let's get started at once!

**PADRE LAURO**
Wisely and slow; they stumble that run fast.

*ROMEO and PADRE LAURO exit.*

# ACT 2
# Scene 1

*DELMA is alone on stage.*

**DELMA**

Lupe has done nothing else but talk about that Romeo. ¡Ya me tiene mareada! This whole business sure is bringing her a whole lot of trouble. Plácido found out from Ramón that Romeo was with Lupe last night, right under their very noses. Now he has our primos watching over her to make sure she can't get out and Romeo can't come in. He even made her cancel her shift at work! "You stay here until I settle this!" he said, "Or I will tell your father, and you know that this is the last thing my tío needs. It would break his heart." It's a very unfortunate love story, this story of Romeo and Lupe. What are the chances you fall in love with your family's rival? And I say love, because I suspect there really is love there. Just the other night, when we met Romeo at the party, I did see something spark in her eye, and in Romeo's as well. And I know it was in her eye for certain, because love is blind. When she met him dressed in those clothes, she didn't recognize him. Given that she can't leave but needs to make contact with her sweetheart, she asked me to stop by the Botica on my way back to work and have a word with Romeo. Find out if he is really serious about her or not, for he will either propose or withdraw. And I'm sure he will propose. How romantic! I do think this is true love.

*DELMA exits. MERCUTIO, STELLAN, and NELSON enter, coming from the Pharr Hotel.*

**MERCUTIO**

Where the hell is this Romeo?

**NELSON**

Came he not to his suite last night?

**STELLAN**

I didn't see him.

**MERCUTIO**

He must be with that Mexican girl we caught him with at the party.

**NELSON**

Or with that other wench, Rosaline, Rosalina, whatever she is called.

**STELLAN**

Have you heard? That guy who's been leading the protests, Plácido Díaz, is out looking for Romeo. Turns out that girl from the party is Plácido's cousin, and he is furious.

**NELSON**

That might explain why our Romeo isn't here. He is hiding.

**MERCUTIO**

My friend is no coward. He is a lover, but not a coward. Unless, of course, he is dead, killed by a wench, stabbed in the ear by a love song, making him as dull as a withered corpse. If so, then I doubt he'll be a challenge for this Plácido. Who is this Plácido anyways?

**NELSON**

Some protester.

**MERCUTIO**

Oh, I see. A righteous man! Protesting what?

**STELLAN**

They say they are defending their land.

**NELSON**

They are getting in the way of *our* land's progress. This land is ours. We earn it fair and square through all the hard work we put into our vision. All we are doing is in fact serving the valley. It's true! We have brought technology unlike any this place has seen. You wait a couple of years and just watch how much this place grows. It's soil for promises to bloom. They fight against what is good for this land.

**MERCUTIO**

And fight against one they'll never beat.

**STELLAN**

Here comes Romeo.

**NELSON**

He looks exceedingly happy, doesn't he? I don't like it.

**ROMEO**

Good morning!

**MERCUTIO**

Too late for good morning. Where have you been?

**ROMEO**

Sorry, gentleman, I've had great business to attend to.

> *DELMA enters.*

**DELMA**

Romeo?

**ROMEO**

Yes?

**MERCUTIO**

A third wench? At three Romeo is surely dead. Remove the fan from your face, sweet madam, your lips are much better bare.

**DELMA**

Goodbye, caballeros.

**MERCUTIO**

You say goodbye as if you're saying good night. Yet the hand on the dial is on the prick of noon.

**DELMA**

Who do you think you are?

**MERCUTIO**

I am a man God made to be as I see fit to be.

**DELMA**

Eso ya veo. May I speak to you, Romeo?

**ROMEO**

Of course.

> *ROMEO and DELMA step aside.*

**DELMA**

¿Quién es ese grosero?

**ROMEO**

A gentleman who likes the sound of his own voice too much for his own good. You say Lupe sent you? Where is she?

**DELMA**

My name is Delma, and Lupe is my cousin. Plácido has found out about your little adventure. He is keeping her under careful watch while he is out looking for you. I'm surprised he hasn't found you.

**ROMEO**

I need to go see her at once.

**DELMA**

Espérate, cálmate. Don't be so reckless! Now let me tell you this: if you lead her into some fool's paradise, y te comportas tan majadero como tus amiguitos, that would be a very disgusting thing on your part. Now that we have addressed that — yes, as I told you, my cousin asked me to come look for you. I trust you have news for her.

**ROMEO**

Tell my dear love that I propose . . .

**DELMA**

I will tell her immediately.

**ROMEO**

But you haven't heard me out.

**DELMA**

I know what you're going to say. Where and when?

**ROMEO**

At Padre Lauro's church. At three today. There Lupe and I will be wedded.

*He offers her money.*

Here. For your trouble.

**DELMA**

Oh, no, really, not a penny.

**ROMEO**

Go on — I say you take it.

**DELMA**

¡Ya! No estoy trabajando, no tienes por qué pagarme. Esto es un gesto entre amigos, o entre primos más bien. Le daré la noticia a Lupita de inmediato.

**ROMEO**

Gracias, Delma. Es un verdadero gusto conocerte.

**DELMA**

El gusto es mío, siempre y cuando no me disguste. Pórtese bien, Romeo.

*DELMA exits.*

**MERCUTIO**

Done killing yourself?

**ROMEO**

Love isn't suicide.

**MERCUTIO**

All things in excess are suicide. Now let's go drown at the Shamrock.

*They all exit.*

# Scene 2

*At the Díaz House, LUPE waits impatiently for DELMA to come back, pacing back and forth and looking at the time on her phone. Finally, DELMA enters.*

**LUPE**

¿Delma? ¿Qué es esa mueca de tristeza sobre tu rostro? Aunque las noticias sean tristes, dímelas con alegría. Si la noticia es buena, causa pena que arruines su dulce canto con un gesto tan amargo. Ándale, si esto es broma, es de mal gusto.

**DELMA**

Estoy cansadísima. Déjame descansar tantito.

**LUPE**

Descansa mientras me platicas lo que pasó.

**DELMA**

¿Cuál es la prisa? ¿Qué no ves que me hace falta aire?

**LUPE**

¿Cómo te falta el aire cuando tienes suficiente aire para decirme que te falta aire? Tardas más en dar tus excusas. Solo dime si las noticias son malas o buenas.

**DELMA**

Pues te diré. Tiras muy bajo. No sabes cómo escoger a un hombre.

**LUPE**

¿Y tú sí? Si eres más chica que yo.

**DELMA**

Y eso que. Yo no me ando fijando en hombrecitos como Romeo. Digo, de que está guapo, está guapo. Su cara está mejor formada que la mayoría de los hombres, y sus piernas, y sus brazos, su cuerpo, aunque no valga la pena mencionarlo, está mejor que la mayoría de los hombres del valle. No es tan caballero que digamos, pero ha de ser tan cariñoso como un cachorrito. ¿Oye, que comiste? ¿Traigo un hambre tremenda?

**LUPE**

¡Hay no! Dices puras cosas que ya sé. ¿Qué dice Romeo sobre nuestra boda?

**DELMA**

Pero como me duele la cabeza. Traigo náuseas.

**LUPE**

Lo siento que no te sientas bien. Dime que dice mi amor.

**DELMA**

Romeo dice, como todo un hombre, caballeroso, honesto, cortés, y dulce, y guapo, que . . . ¿Dónde está tu papá?

**LUPE**

Romeo dice, "¿Dónde está tu papá?"

**DELMA**

¿Dónde está? No quiero que me oigas.

**LUPE**

Está en su cuarto. No nos puede oír.

**DELMA**

Muy bien. Pero antes de decirte . . . ¿me das un masaje?

**LUPE**

¡Ya! Dime qué dice Romeo.

> *DELMA laughs. Then, she hears the sound of DON DÍAZ so she lowers her voice.*

**DELMA**

You think Plácido will let you go to confession?

**LUPE**

He can't keep me here forever.

**DELMA**

Then go to Padre Lauro's, where a husband waits to make you a wife. The fire returns to your cheeks. I'm so happy for you, prima. I'll keep the boys busy. Don't worry.

> *They exit in opposite directions.*

# Scene 3

> *At the Botica. The CORRIDO SINGER plays guitar music fit for a wedding.*

**PADRE LAURO**

These violent delights, so rash in their behavior, have violent ends, and in their triumph die, like fire and powder which, as they kiss, consume. May heaven smile on this holy act, that after hours with sorrow chide us not.

**ROMEO**

Amen. But even if something terrible happens, it cannot countervail the exchange of joy that one short minute gives me in her sight. Close our hands with your holy words, then let death do what it dare — this love can't be done apart, Padre.

**PADRE LAURO**

Here comes the lady.

*The CORRIDO SINGER switches to the wedding march with Spanish guitar.*

**PADRE LAURO**

Lupe, do you take this man to be your lawfully wedded husband? Romeo, do you take this woman to be your lawfully wedded wife?

**LUPE**

I accept.

**ROMEO**

Acepto, con todo mi ser.

*They kiss. BALTI enters.*

**BALTI**

Romeo! Forgive me. I know this is supposed to be the happiest moment of your life, but you must come. Mercutio and the others are heading to Plácido's apartment. They are there to respond to his threats to your name.

**ROMEO**

I must break this quarrel apart before it begins. Else, something terrible might happen that will destroy what has been accomplished here. Their adversity might intensify such that a consequence will surface that might render our marriage impossible in the eyes of our families and friends. And though I don't mind living as an outcast at your side, we must try to seize this chance at a peaceful life together in the Magic Valley. Lupe, I must end this at once.

*ROMEO kisses LUPE and exits. Thunder sounds.*

**DELMA**

¡Qué demencia es esta de dejarte así en el altar, justo después de unirse en matrimonio! Vamos.

**PADRE LAURO**

Go home and wait there.

*Thunder sounds again.*

I'm afraid heaven disapproves of what has been done here, and dreadful consequences begin thundering the sky like a knock at the door from that most feared visitor — fate.

# Scene 4

*MERCUTIO, NELSON, and RAMÓN gather outside PLÁCIDO's home.*

**MERCUTIO**

Plácido Díaz! Come out so I can rip from you the name of day. I am here to shut your flame, and leave you cold and empty.

**NELSON**

I beg you, Mercutio. Let's quit this. Our heads are hotter than this day, and on these hot days, the mad blood is stirring.

**MERCUTIO**

Oh, Nelson. You're like a man who enters a cantina and puts his blade away thinking he'll have no need of it. Then barely by the second drink, he'll be slashing and poking at whatever nonsense, when in fact he was initially right: there was no need for his blade.

**STELLAN**

Hm, am I like such a fellow?

**MERCUTIO**

No. If we had two of those, we would have none shortly, because one would kill the other. This one here will quarrel with a man that has one hair more or one hair less in his beard than he has. Yet you will counsel me not to fight.

**NELSON**

If I were so apt to fight as you are, you could bet on me at the Luchas Libres.

**MERCUTIO**

Lucha Libre?

**STELLAN**

Here come the Díazes.

**NELSON**

They have weapons.

**MERCUTIO**

I don't care.

**RAMÓN** (*rapping*)

    what is a man without a name to his own land
    what is a man with no spine to where he can't even stand
    what is a man's labor that can't feed his fam
    and what's man's right besides bronze skin tanned
    I remember working this earth with both hands
    I remember laying bricks while dreaming future plans
    this is our barrio, you are not welcome at our home
    cast you out of this place after battering your dome
    death before discrimination, dishonor, and discontent
    we begin our descent into resistance segments
    one hundred percent is this Tejano lament
    we worked this earth first you returned it to us cursed
    your handshake agreement is but double cross coerce
    your logic is rehearsed and your compassion is even worse

**NELSON** (*rapping*)

    it's survival of the fittest
    what you think we didn't live it
    family destined for greatness,
    since birth I always knew it
    heirs to the throne,
    the future has already come to be shown
    the Campbell legacy and empire
    will remain beyond us as known
    as the beacon the light, right, and might
    upon the South Texas strife
    the curators of development, growth,
    the masters of the elements
    bending nature to our will,
    our cup runneth over but never spill
    so we welcome the chill, frost, freeze,
    never labor on our knees
    rose up from the ground destroyed the trees
    and cashed the cheese
    this is the development decree,
    cast out resistance enemies
    and squeeze resources into surplus
    to kick our feet up by the furnace
    our policies is stern but fair,

> disciplined at a level so rare
> so beware with your protests
> when they're broke and turn to confess
> retreating back to your nest,
> your threats are only beating your chest
> and crying out "oppressed"
> because you slacked at the get-go
> but even so, take note by example
> and don't test us toe-to-toe.

*PLÁCIDO enters.*

**PLÁCIDO**

I'll talk to them.

**RAMÓN**

I'll be right here if you need me, carnal, pa' tirarte esquina.

**PLÁCIDO**

I want to have a word with one of you Campbells. Where is that coward Romeo?

**MERCUTIO**

A word? Why not make it a word, and a punch?

*He makes a circle with his index finger and his thumb.*

**PLÁCIDO**

You'll find me ready for that.

**MERCUTIO**

Tell your friends to back away. Rule is I give you a punch, remember. You must take it without giving.

*MERCUTIO takes out a gun and points it at PLÁCIDO. Laughing, he puts it away.*

**RAMÓN**

"Friends"? Ese, we are not "friends," we are homies. Ready to die for each other. Can you say the same about these vatos backing you up? Here comes Romeo.

*ROMEO enters.*

**DÍAZ 1**

Followed by Balti, backstabber of his gente.

**PLÁCIDO**

Peace be with you. Here comes my man.

**MERCUTIO**

I'll be hanged before he becomes any type of servant to you as your people are to him. If he follows you in one of your senseless protests, you may call him "my man."

**PLÁCIDO**

That I remember, he did in fact mix himself in one of my protests. But even then, Romeo, I have no better word to call you than this: villain. I know the type of man you are, you are like your father, get with a mexicana just so you can get what you want out of her — her land, the land of her parents — or in the case of you and mi prima, just to get what a pelado wants. You chose the wrong mexicana, cabrón!

**ROMEO**

Plácido, the reason I have to love you does excuse this behavior. I am no villain. I see you don't know me. We will leave from here. Farewell.

**MERCUTIO**

Leave?

**PLÁCIDO**

This does not excuse the injuries that you have done to me.

**ROMEO**

I've done no harm to you. I respect you more than you can understand. We must set aside our grievances and love each other as the brothers we have become.

**PLÁCIDO**

¿De qué hablas? You and I will never be brothers.

*PLÁCIDO attacks ROMEO.*

**MERCUTIO**

Oh, passive, dishonorable, disgusting submission!

*MERCUTIO enters the fight.*

**PLÁCIDO**

¿Qué quieres conmigo?

**MERCUTIO**

If you were a cat, I would only want one of your nine lives.

**ROMEO**

Stop, Mercutio! Your father has warned us against this. Nelson, Stellan, stop this outrage.

**PLÁCIDO**

You always have others fight your fights, Romeo?

**ROMEO**

Things must not be this way between us.

**PLÁCIDO**

Cállate, I will not try to reason with you.

> *PLÁCIDO stabs MERCUTIO.*

**MERCUTIO**

I am hurt.

**ROMEO**

Mercutio, are you okay?

**MERCUTIO**

Damn it! Bring me a surgeon!

**ROMEO**

The hurt can't be that bad?

**MERCUTIO**

You're right. It's only a scratch. Not too deep, not too wide, but it'll do. Ask for me tomorrow and you'll find me a grave man. Guess I'm meant to die in the valley. Ironic destiny: I left the valley so that I would live and was sent right back here to die. Our lives are but a joke to God. A curse on all of you. You've made worms' meat out of me. A curse on all of you. A curse on this valley.

**ROMEO**

The love I feel for Lupe softened me up, and I lost my courage. But this grievance will not go unchecked. This day's black fate begins the pain that must be put to an end in the hours to come. If you must die today, dear Mercutio, your blood will not be shed alone. Plácido!

*ROMEO picks up the bloody knife that was used on MERCUTIO.*

Hasta la muerte — either you, or I, or both, must go with him.

**PLÁCIDO**
You will be joining your friend on the ground.

**ROMEO**
This will determine that.

*They fight. ROMEO stabs PLÁCIDO. As his adversary bleeds out, ROMEO seems to awaken suddenly from his fit of violence.*

I am fortune's fool.

*A PARAMEDIC enters.*

**PARAMEDIC**
Where is the man who hurt this soldier?

**NELSON**
Plácido Díaz. There.

**PARAMEDIC**
Take these two to get treated.

*A POLICE OFFICER enters and arrests ROMEO.*

**POLICE OFFICER**
You have the right to remain silent.

*All exit.*

# Scene 5

**LUPE**
Tonatiuh, dios del sol, reposa el xiuhuitzolli en la cama del oeste, esa corona que marca el paso de los días y nuestros destinos. Sumérgete en las entrañas de tu tierra y que despierte el sol de medianoche, el que emerge del pecho cuando los amantes en la oscuridad se sostienen entre brazos y platican con el calor

de su alma. Trae a mi Romeo entre mis brazos, para escuchar en su calor el testimonio de sus actos de este día. No me importa lo que digan que él con odio lastimó a mi primo Plácido. Lo escucharé del mismo. Noche, tú que divides el día, como la campana que cuenta las horas, haz que recorra el tiempo hasta la hora del llegar de mi amor. Así es noche, tráeme a mi Romeo. Y el día que me muera, no hagas de el tierra, si no un vapor que flote fuera de esta atmósfera y se desplace por el universo, creando mil y un millón de estrellas en el cielo, embelleciendo la noche de tal manera que el mundo jamás volverá a desear el sol. Noche, dame a mi Romeo. Pues lo espero con la ansiedad con que una casa espera convertirse en hogar. Este anillo es una casa vacía hasta su llegar. Me siento como una niña llena de emoción por un nuevo vestido sin poder estrenarlo.

*DELMA enters.*

**LUPE**
¿Qué noticias me traes?

**DELMA**
He's been deported. Poor Plácido, my dearest friend, they are revoking his residency and sending him back to Mexico. Anger clouded their minds, and the consequences of this day are costly. All that was accomplished is undone.

**LUPE**
Can God be so cruel?

**DELMA**
The cruelty is Romeo's. Who would have thought it? Romeo! He is dead.

**LUPE**
What are you saying, Delma?

**DELMA**
The Romeo you married is dead, prima. In looking to undo Plácido's life, he undid his own. He destroyed the man who made marriage vows to you this afternoon. That man was free and innocent, this man is condemned and guilty.

**LUPE**
Romeo is innocent. He went there to break up the fight. You heard him. I was told he yielded and did not attack my cousin until his friend had been injured.

**DELMA**

Whether he yielded at first, no importa, he did not yield at last. You must bury him, bury his memory.

**LUPE**

Not until I find out what really happened. I must see him. He is my husband.

**DELMA**

Here comes your father.

> *DON DÍAZ enters.*

**DON DÍAZ**

¡Lo deportaron! Nos han arrebatado a nuestro Plácido. Este es el hogar de su familia. Pero desde que estos visionarios llegaron aquí nosotros no tenemos hogar. Hacen lo quieren. Y a aquel gringo que le enterró la navaja, ni lo castigaron. Lo dejaron ir. Fueron ellos los que vinieron a molestarlos. ¡Yo los vi! Esta es la justicia que nos espera en esta que una vez fue nuestra tierra. ¡Malditos! ¡Desgraciados! Deseo lo peor de lo peor sobre todos ellos, en especial a ese tal Romeo.

**LUPE** (*to DELMA*)

These words from my father tear at my heart. Either way, I see he is suffering so much I'm afraid his heart might fail him. I shouldn't leave him. Go find Romeo. He must be with Padre Lauro. Tell him that he must come see me.

**DON DÍAZ**

¿Por qué hablan en inglés?

**LUPE**

Anda.

> *DELMA exits.*

**LUPE**

Ven, papá, vamos a tomar un poco de aire.

> *LUPE and DON DÍAZ exit.*

# Scene 6

*ROMEO is having his wounds taken care of by PADRE LAURO*
*at the Botica.*

**ROMEO**

How fares Mercutio?

**PADRE LAURO**

He is being taken care of by the medics at his base. I also have the fortunate news that the young man, Plácido, will recover as well. They both will live. Your hands remain clean of blood, son.

**ROMEO**

I wonder what verdict will be laid on me.

**PADRE LAURO**

Here comes your father to answer that question.

*MR. CAMPBELL enters.*

**MR. CAMPBELL**

I've talked to the judge. Your record and Mercutio's will remain clean. Your harm to Plácido will be regarded as self-defense, given that Plácido had been looking for you. We found that the simplest thing to do is deport him. That troublemaker has been a real nuisance riling up the mob, and our judge will not have his son go to trial over this. This is easiest for everyone. I doubt that Plácido would rather be behind bars than across the border. Now, about this girl, Lupe. I found out about your endeavor with her. Nelson told me that he overheard you talking to a cousin of the girl and that in your delirium you had even proposed marriage. Although I'm glad fate intervened in that account, I do lament that you haven't the aptitude not to find yourself in this situation. Therefore, I have decided that you have exhausted your chances at proving your ability to cope and act accordingly, and so I must send you away to the military, where you will refine your character. I myself served, and I have to thank those years of harsh discipline for making me the man I am today. Tomorrow morning we leave to head back home, and on Monday you will enlist. Nelson will accompany you, as his father also sees fit that he be taught a lesson.

**ROMEO**

Perhaps I'll bring you back a medal and wear it on my corpse.

**MR. CAMPBELL**

Only if you honorably earn it. We leave first thing in the morning.

*MR. CAMPBELL exits.*

**ROMEO**

This service that I'm forced to give is a disservice to my soul. Sent away from Lupe! I would rather die.

**PADRE LAURO**

How blind you must be to mistake this blessing for a curse. The young Plácido could have been dead, and you would have been put in jail. That would have ruined your good name, yet in service your name will receive honor. Sent away from the Magic Valley you are. But be patient. The world is wide and the paths are many.

**ROMEO**

There is no world for me beyond the Magic Valley as long as this is Lupe's home. Only paths that lead to purgatory, to hell itself! You say my name will receive honor? What honor is there in wearing a name that every time uttered it rings hollow, what honor in living falsely?

**PADRE LAURO**

Malagradecido. This is an opportunity, and you don't see it. El alma nace del cielo, y no de la tierra como el cuerpo, y en cualquier esquina del cielo puede encontrar su hogar. Tu alma no es de aquí, ni de allá. Nuestro cuerpo se hace polvo, pero nuestra alma es de Dios. No pierdes nada mientras no pierdas la fe. And there is certainly honor in serving, because although your soul is God's, your name is your country's. Once this country registers your name, it gives that name purpose. It gives it background, and your name carries the weight of your nation, as your nation carries the weight of your name. Romeo Campbell is the Republic of Texas, and the Republic of Texas is Romeo Campbell.

**ROMEO**

Then why is it that now the Republic is my enemy? If the Republic was not my enemy, then I could love Lupe freely.

**PADRE LAURO**

Your family and her family come from very different universes. The world is
yet learning to know itself. God did not make wisdom a given thing, rather
a thing acquired. We must suffer and fall into ashes, individuals and nations
alike, yet from these ashes we rise and are reborn in freedom. The time will
come when your grievances must be amended. The story of the Rio Grande
Valley belongs to all whose lives form a part of it. Mark my words, tragedy will
strike us if we do not learn to co-exist.

*DELMA knocks.*

**DELMA**

I come on behalf of Lupe. Is Romeo here?

**PADRE LAURO**

Come in. He sits there drowning in his tears.

**DELMA**

He and Lupe alike. ¡Par de chillones! ¡Párate! Stand up! For hers and your
sake.

**ROMEO**

Delma . . .

**DELMA**

Alguien les ha de ver hecho ojo a ti y a mi prima, porque estan bien salados.
Les hubiera venido mejor una limpia, que una boda.

**ROMEO**

You say Lupe also drowns in tears? Tears of what sort? Of hate or sadness?
Does she think of me as a murderer, who stained our love with blood from her
own? Or does she still think of me as she did before, as her other half, as one
to whom her heart opens naturally and overflows with love?

**DELMA**

She is broken apart. At one moment she'll cry "Romeo," at another "Plácido."

**ROMEO**

Plácido, that name killed us.

**DELMA**

Nonsense. You're paying for your own actions.

**ROMEO**

Ay, you're right! I detest the suffering that I bring to Lupe. I'll set her free from our troublesome fates.

*ROMEO picks up a knife as if to stab himself.*

**PADRE LAURO**

Settle down, Romeo! Was I robbed off my senses when I thought I saw determination in you, boy? Muchacho impulsivo. You've been doing nothing but acting out of impulse this whole time. Things have become grave. You need to start acting with sense. And now, go see Lupe, for the new-wed wife must be impatiently waiting to hear from her husband. Leave early in the morning so that you won't be caught. And listen to me closely now, Romeo: do your service, obey, do your time, and patiently wait to hear from me. I will find a solution. Go on, son.

**ROMEO**

Farewell, Padre.

*ROMEO and PADRE LAURO exit.*

## Scene 7

*At the Díaz home.*

**DON DÍAZ**

No puede ser verdad lo que me dices. ¿Mi hija?

**TÍA MARLA**

Así es.

**DON DÍAZ**

¿Y mi sobrino ha perdido todo, porque mi hija andaba de aflojada con un gringo?

**TÍA MARLA**

Así es.

**DON DÍAZ**

¡Ay! Marla, con estas noticias has acabado de destrozar esa pared frágil en mí, que quedo cuarteada con la muerte de mi esposa, y ahora acaba su colapso total, y se desborda todo el dolor que por años he luchado contra su invasión total de mi ser, lo he dejado reposar, haciéndose bilis en mi estómago, y ahora en este dolor desbordado, me hundiré. No habrá paso atrás. La pena será mía por el resto de mis días, pues los dos amores de mi vida han muerto, mi difunta esposa y Lupe. Pues con lo que me dices, ella está muerta para mí. Jamás podré perdonarla, mirarla a los ojos, y saber que por su imprudes, tanto se tiró a la basura. Llévatela, no la quiero aquí. Que se vaya contigo a México. Es ella a la que debieron de deportar. Pues ella cometió los daños, ella los debe de pagar.

**TÍA MARLA**

No creo que sea posible. Yo tenía planeado irme mañana. A menos de que estés dispuesto en partir tan rápido de ella.

**DON DÍAZ**

Entre lo más pronto mejor.

*DON DÍAZ exits.*

**TÍA MARLA**

Estoy de acuerdo. Estos tiempos que en la juventud se desmorona la conservación de nuestros principios, no hay tiempo para andarse con rodeos.

*TÍA MARLA exits.*

# Scene 8

*LUPE and ROMEO enter the patio outside her room.*

**LUPE**

¿Ya te vas? The sky is still dark. Ese no fue el gallo, el que perforó tu tímpano. Listen, la chicharra still sings, cada noche canta mientras reposa sobre el mezquite. While it sings, time is ours.

**ROMEO**

That is not the chicharra. That is the green jay, and the great kiskadee, and the crow that waits for our final consequence. I must go.

**LUPE**

That light isn't sunlight. It is a light of the night, a comet, a shooting star. To be a torchbearer and guide you in your way. Therefore, stay! You must not leave yet.

**ROMEO**

No light will I follow that leads me away from you. It would be like following a light into a lightless place, deeper into the night. Yes, you are right, Lupe. That is not the sun, el sol eres tú, and that outside the window is but a lamplight that comes and goes over the ever-sleeping world. Yet into that night I must go, lit with a false sun whilst I will remain nocturnal, lit with the sun of ambitions that aren't mine whilst I hold to that dream of you in my mind until its time comes to materialize. I must go. Farewell, until that shooting star guides me back to you, querida Lupe.

**LUPE**

More light and light, more dark and dark our life. Someone comes. Go! Go!

> *DELMA enters.*

**DELMA**

¡Lupe!

**LUPE**

¿Qué pasa?

**DELMA**

Your father is coming. He is furious!

**LUPE**

Does he know Romeo is here?

**DELMA**

No, but get him out of here before he finds out.

> *DELMA exits.*

**LUPE**

¿Ya te has ido, amor mío?

**ROMEO**

Sigo aquí.

**LUPE**

I wish you didn't have to go.

**ROMEO**

Then I'll stay and we'll face the world. I'm suddenly so ready.

**LUPE**

No, we must not continue to act rashly. Oh, let fortune be fickle, and, as it took you away, send you back to me.

*ROMEO wants to kiss her, but LUPE stops him.*

**LUPE**

Guardaré este beso. Y por ahora, sostenme en un abrazo, y así me quedaré con un pedazo de tu calor, de tu alma.

**ROMEO** (*holding her in a close embrace*)

I promise you, Lupe. No moriré sin ese beso en mis labios. Goodbye, amor mío, hasta que el destino nos vuelva a reunir.

*ROMEO exits.*

**DON DÍAZ** (*offstage*)

¡Lupe!

*DON DÍAZ enters infuriated, crying heavily, sweating, and trembling. He grabs LUPE by the arm and sits her down.*

Tu primo ha perdido todo en su vida, porque tú te andabas besuqueando con un pillo. Peleo teniendo que defender tu honor, ya que no lo supiste defender por ti misma. ¡Ya me dijeron todo! Me dijeron que Ramón lo vio aquí. ¡Aquí! ¡En mi propia casa!

**LUPE**

Papá . . .

**DON DÍAZ**

¡Te largas a México! A ser una dama o a ser una mujerzuela, eso a mí no me importa. Yo no te quiero a ti como hija. Te largas con tu tía, y te olvidas de todo. Te olvidas de mí, del valle, y de tu romance con ese pelado.

**LUPE**

De ninguna manera. Romeo no es ningún pelado. Papá, quiero que lo conozcas.

**DON DÍAZ**

¡Mocosa estúpida! A la gente como ellos, la gente como nosotros les valemos madres. Te está usando.

**LUPE**

No es verdad. El me ama. Y yo lo amo. Lo amo, papá.

**DON DÍAZ**

¡Te largas a México!

**LUPE**

¡No!

**DON DÍAZ**

¿Me contestas a mi así? ¿A tu padre? ¿Yo que te he dado todo? Harás lo que te digo, y estarás agradecida.

**LUPE**

¡Cómo puedo estar agradecida por algo que aborrezco!

**DON DÍAZ**

Niña chiqueada, ahora si vas a ver. Harás lo que te digo. Se acabó.

> *DON DÍAZ turns to leave.*

**LUPE**

De menos déjame pedirle perdón a Dios por mi pecado. Dame permiso de ir a confesarme. Niégame como tu hija, pero no me niegues la virtud te arrepentirme ante Dios.

**DON DÍAZ**

¡Solo a confesarte! Delma, Ramón, acompáñenla.

**DELMA**

A mí me traen aquí, que para que saque papeles y me haga tejana, y a ti te quieren mandar allá por ser demasiado tejana y hacerte más mexicana. ¿Pues quién les entiende?

**LUPE**

Somos de ambos lados, y de ninguno.

**RAMÓN**

Ready to go?

> *DON DÍAZ exits. DELMA wants to start talking to LUPE, but RAMÓN gets close to them, so they remain quiet.*

# Scene 9

*PADRE LAURO and TÍA MARLA enter the church.*

**PADRE LAURO**
¿Pero el jueves? Sí, eso es mañana. No piensa usted que es demasiado rápido. No le da oportunidad ni siquiera de despedirse.

**TÍA MARLA**
Su padre no la quiere en la casa. El insistió que me la llevara inmediatamente. Para mí entre más pronto, mejor. Aquí Guadalupe pierde lo mexicana, debe regresar a sus tradiciones.

**PADRE LAURO** (*aside*)
¿Regresar a sus tradiciones, dice ella? He aquí que continúa la cultura. Y la tradición, cual es conservativa en su naturaleza, busca atraparla, y en eso cesa de ser cultura, y se convierte en una estatua, inmóvil, melancólica, orgullosa, egoísta. Pero la cultura es algo que crece, a toda hora cultivándose, y descubre en las fronteras nuevos amores.

*LUPE, DELMA, and RAMÓN enter.*

**TÍA MARLA**
¿Cómo estás, Lupita? Espero ya escuchaste la noticia. Es por tu bien, hija. Ya verás que serás muy feliz.

**LUPE**
Quizás así sea.

**TÍA MARLA**
Así será. Nos vamos el jueves.

**LUPE**
Lo que será, será.

**TÍA MARLA**
De eso no hay duda.

*TÍA MARLA exits. LUPE turns to PADRE LAURO.*

**LUPE**
Vengo a confesarme, Padre.

**PADRE LAURO**
Wait for us outside.

*DELMA and RAMÓN exit.*

**LUPE** (*breaking into tears*)
What am I going to do?

**PADRE LAURO**
Lupe, ya escuché de tu dolor. Hace que se me tuerza el alma.

**LUPE**
How can destiny pull me and Romeo apart this way? If the future of our love is here? En la frontera. Where his and my world met into this beautiful happening. Must our worlds go on to be separate? Like the sun and the moon are always at opposite ends of the sky. Was this instant we had together nothing but a passing eclipse? Yet, in spite of their distance from each other, the sun and the moon are in fact one. Yes. For they become one over the earth, as their power blends into the mixture of life. So do his and my world blend! When we touch, we create universes with every kiss. Yet our families always treat their problems with one another in isolation. They can never see eye to eye, the way me and Romeo have looked into each other's souls. I wish I could fall into a deep sleep and wake up to find that the world has moved on and next to me is my querido Romeo, and together we enter a new world where we love one another por toda la eternidad.

**PADRE LAURO**
Then, Lupita, that is exactly what you must do. Hold on, hija mia.

*He looks in his medicines.*

I do spy a kind of hope, and desperate times may call for desperate measures. Tomorrow morning, before Delma wakes you from bed to bid you farewell, you must drink this vial, and this distilling liquor will make a cold and drowsy humor run through your veins. There will be no pulse, no heat, and all the color will fade from your cheeks. Your eyes' windows will fall like death when it shuts up the day of life. Like death you will appear, and in this state you will remain for twenty-four hours, and then awake as from a pleasant sleep. Romeo will not be enlisting until Monday. I will write to his home at the other end of the Magic Valley, and by my letters he will know our drift, and hither shall he come, and he and I keep watch for your waking. That very night you and Romeo will go to Aztlán where I was born. There's a family to welcome you. This will free you from your present shame. You must not fear.

**LUPE**

El amor me hace fuerte, y prosperaré en mi propósito.

**PADRE LAURO**

Lo sé, hija mía. My thought that your marriage could bring peace to this conflict in our valle was infantile. But who am I to say that our circumstances are testimonies of heaven's disapproval? This can all very well be the devil's doing. For how can God ever withhold love, love that is as true as it is present here? I will not fall under the errors of our valle, of your parents and your cousins, for I see truth in your love and I place my faith upon it. Save your love, Lupe. Y que no te importe, que te valga, it's not worth losing so much. Save your love, Lupe. Save yourselves. Le escribiré a Romeo de inmediato. Anda a casa.

**LUPE**

Farewell, Padre.

*She exits.*

# Scene 10

*The stage is divided into two rooms. Half is Lupe's room, half is the kitchen. LUPE enters her room.*

**LUPE**

¿Qué es más esencial, el ser, o el estar? ¿La realización del alma, o la posición en la vida? ¿Qué es más esencial, darle la espalda al mundo por amor, o negar el amor por lo que exige el mundo? ¿Pero cómo he de estar sin ser? ¿Cómo darle al mundo, sin amar? El alma, sin realizarse, desaparece. Esa muertita a quien Tía Marla quiere que reemplace no soy yo, y ahí no pertenezco, ahí no daré nada. Y que tan sencillo es resolverlo, solo beber y dormir. Dormir, dormir, y quizás despertar junto a mi Romeo. Sé que quizás no estará ahí, pues tanto puede pasar, pero aun así no me atormenta la cobardía. Sé quién soy, y sé dónde quiero estar.

*LUPE drinks the liquor and falls asleep. DON DÍAZ and DELMA enter the kitchen.*

**DON DÍAZ**

El segundo gallo cantó, devorando en sí la última estrella de la noche. Y con ella terminan los sueños, y regresa la realidad y nuestro deber a ella. Si ayer soñé que mi Plácido estaba aquí, y que mi hijita jamás conoció a ese Romeo.

Pero ese sueño, como las estrellas, los devora el amanecer. Despierta a Lupe. Comprendo su tardanza, pero nada me hará cambiar de opinión. Esto se tiene que hacer.

> *TÍA MARLA enters.*

**DON DÍAZ**

Buenos días, Marla.

**TÍA MARLA**

¿Dónde está Lupita? ¡No me digas que sigue dormida! Despiértenla. No cambias, hermano, sigues siendo igual de mano blanda con ella. Su disciplina comienza hoy. Despiértenla, y díganle que la quiero aquí en quince minutos. ¡Ándale, Delma, te debería de llevar a ti también!

**DELMA**

¡Ay, no! Lupe es la joya de la familia. A mi déjenme. ¡Lupe, despiértate! Lupe, ándale, levántate, que Tía Marla ya hasta me anda queriendo llevar a mí. Anda, Lupe, se cómo te lastima esto, pero ya verás que con el tiempo te acostumbraras al cambio, y después hasta te andas conociendo a otro guapetón por allá, y quizás uno que no sea tan menso. Ándale, Lupe. Lupe.

> *LUPE is unresponsive.*

¡Tío! ¡Tía! ¡Vengan rápido!

**DON DÍAZ**

¡Hija! ¡Lupita! Despiértate.

**TÍA MARLA**

¿Qué le pasa?

**DON DÍAZ**

¡Está muerta! ¡No! ¡Mi hija está muerta! ¡Marla, Marla, mi hija está muerta!

**DELMA**

No. Lupe.

**DON DÍAZ**

Qué es esto en su mano. Se envenenó. Se quitó la vida.

> *In shock, he holds the vial in his hand.*

Esto es culpa mía. Su muerte está en mis manos. ¡Maldita muerte! Despreciable sombra que acecha y roba todo lo que amo. Primero mi esposa, ahora mi hija. Ay, Catrina, llévame a mi desgraciada.

    *PADRE LAURO enters.*

**PADRE LAURO**
¿Qué desgracia ha pasado aquí?

**DON DÍAZ**
Mi hija se ha suicidado.

    *PADRE LAURO walks up to take LUPE's pulse.*

**PADRE LAURO**
¿Porque lo haría?

**DON DÍAZ**
Por confusión, un güero que le . . . su cabeza . . . estoy seguro que él tiene que ver con esto. Cuando lo vea lo voy a matar al maldito. Y quizás al que debería de castigar es a mí mismo. Pues fueron tan dolorosas mis palabras y mi decisión, también tengo culpa.

    *PADRE LAURO makes the sign of the cross on LUPE's forehead.*

**PADRE LAURO**
Que Dios la cuide en su viaje.

**DON DÍAZ**
¿Y a donde ira? ¿Acaso su agresión a ella misma tendrá perdón de Dios?

**PADRE LAURO**
No es ella la que debe de pedir perdón de Dios. Ella como una flor extinguida, perdida jamás la recuperaremos. Pero ya, paremos esta angustia, y démosle paz al alma de esta pobre criatura de Dios.

# Scene 11

*PADRE LAURO crosses the stage and runs into BALTI.*

**BALTI**

¡Hola, Padre! ¿Qué pasa, Padre? Se ve preocupado.

**PADRE LAURO**

Not now, hijo mío. The young girl Lupe Díaz acaba de tomarse la vida.

*PADRE LAURO continues on his way off stage.*

**BALTI**

How this news will shatter my friend's heart. Yet a true friend would not hold such truths back. I must write to him. May the news of her death not destroy my good friend.

*He exits.*

# Scene 12

*NELSON and ROMEO enter.*

**NELSON**

Excited to visit the recruitment office this Monday, Romeo?

**ROMEO**

I dread the day.

**NELSON**

I dread the beds. Last night was my first good sleep in a while. Those Pharr Hotel beds are as firm as tile, and once we are enlisted, who knows how long I'll be sleeping on another terrible mattress.

**ROMEO**

If I may trust the flattering truth of sleep, my dreams presage some joyful news at hand. I dreamed that mi amada came and found me dead — strange dream that gives a dead man leave to think — and breathed such life with kisses in my lips that I revived and was an emperor.

*The doorbell rings. A MAIL CARRIER enters.*

**MAIL CARRIER**

Good evening. A letter for Romeo Campbell.

**ROMEO**

Thank you.

*The MAIL CARRIER exits.*

**ROMEO**

A letter from Balti? I was expecting news from Padre Lauro.

*He opens the letter. As he reads, he breaks into tears.*

Lupe has died. Is this so? Then I deny you, stars!

**NELSON**

Things like this happen, and when they do, one must simply forget and move on.

**ROMEO**

Forget? How to vanish a memory? How to live through, to endure the days that will seem eternal, when God denies us what we love? How? It would be like stealing the sun from the night and leaving the face of the moon dark. In darkness, life withers and great empires are laid under the ice. I must leave at once.

**NELSON**

You can't leave. I won't let you.

**ROMEO**

Would you stop the river from flowing to the sea, or the moon from beaming with its reflected sunlight over the night creatures? Out of the way. I must return to my wife.

*NELSON stands in the way. They fight. ROMEO knocks out NELSON and exits. MR. CAMPBELL and MRS. CAMPBELL enter.*

**MR. CAMPBELL**

Get up! What happened here?

**NELSON**

Romeo did this to me. He received a letter from Balti with the news that Lupe died. Romeo has gone into a fit of distress and ran off to see for himself.

**MR. CAMPBELL**
We must go after him.

**NELSON**
Uncle. I heard him call Lupe his "wife."

**MR. CAMPBELL**
Are you sure of this?

(*turning to his wife*) Did you know of this?

**MRS. CAMPBELL**
Only that he met someone.

**MR. CAMPBELL**
If this is true, then my son has lost a wife.

> MR. CAMPBELL exits. The others follow.

# Scene 13

> PADRE LAURO enters.

**PADRE LAURO**
Returned mail? This is the letter I sent to Romeo. He has no knowledge of the events that have passed. Que patraña a planeado el diablo esta vez. I must drive to his house right away and deliver the news personally.

> PADRE LAURO exits.

# Scene 14

> At a funeral home. ROMEO approaches and tries to break in.
> Then the FUNERAL HOME CARETAKER enters.

**CARETAKER**
Where do you think you are going? A esta hora, solo los muertos deben de estar aquí.

**ROMEO**
He venido aquí a morir. Déjame pasar, o terminaré mi vida aquí mismo.

**CARETAKER**

Muchacho, tú estás loco. No se viene a la funeraria a morir, se viene muerto. Y usted se ve muy vivo. Largo de mi ultratumba, regresa al mundo, o llamaré a la policía y dejaré que la ley de nuestra república se encargue de ti.

**ROMEO**

Ni el mundo ni la ley de nuestra república son amigos vuestros. I see that you are poor — take this money.

**CARETAKER**

I, my friend, am never poor. I'm the richest there is.

(*Pointing at the graves*) I only take care of the dead. Who am I to say how the living should die? And with your coin I hold off death for another day. I'll let you pass.

　　*ROMEO enters the funeral home and kneels by LUPE's altar.*

**ROMEO**

Lupe, you are yet so fair. Should I believe that unsubstantial death is amorous and that the abhorred monster keeps you here in the dark to be his lover? For fear of that, I will remain here with you and never again depart from this dim palace. I have brought this vile poison, a swift canoe to death's lodging.

　　*He drinks some of the poison, leaving some behind.*

My heart skips a beat, my pulse flattens, my eyes begin to close, and my breathing is slowing, stopping. Where will this drift take me? No matter, as long as it lays me on the bed on which you sleep. Ay, Lupe, why did fortune give you to me, then so soon take you? I know you're here, in the afterlife. I've felt its touch in sleepless nights. I will go there now, and I know, querida Lupe, you are there waiting for me.

　　*LUPE wakes up.*

**ROMEO**

You are alive.

**LUPE**

Amor mío. Amor? What is this? Poison? No, what happened? Did you not receive the news? I was only sleeping. I was to wake and we were to run away together.

**ROMEO**

Mi hermosa Lupe. Mi sol. I fall into my sleep too early, and you wake too late.

**LUPE**

No. Our timing is perfect. This is just as planned. I woke, and you are here, to take me to a world where our love can be free.

*LUPE drinks the rest of the poison.*

**ROMEO**

Don't Lupe. Why?

**LUPE**

Because I, like you, will give everything up for us.

*She kisses him.*

**ROMEO**

It is just as I dreamed. With a kiss, I die.

*They close their eyes and enter everlasting sleep. All the main characters enter except PLÁCIDO.*

**JUDGE**

Look at what verdict is set upon your hate. Because of your conflicts. I almost lost a son. Plácido Díaz, by my lawful verdict, lost the life that he built here. All are punished.

**DON DÍAZ**

Perdí a mi hija dos veces, primero la perdí en el alma y la segunda en la vida. Y ahora en esta segunda vez, ya no la recuperaré. Perdí a mi hija la primera vez cuando cerré mi corazón a ella, la segunda cuando su último suspiro se escapó de su boca. Esa boca que tantas veces sonrió, que tantas veces besó esta mejilla. Bendita eres Lupita, que vas al cielo con los que amas. Descansa en paz al lado de tu madre y tu Romeo.

**MR. CAMPBELL**

I could not come to see what was in my son's heart, forgetting that I have loved as he did. I regret my insensitivity. But I can't regret my severity with him. I've only done what was right. I raised him as I saw best. Life is a very difficult place, and it's eat or be eaten, for life only smiles on those who know how to mind their wealth. I've done everything I can in my life to make a good living, yet all I did was try to teach him to live as a Campbell. My son saw wealth in love, otherwise there was poverty. He dies being Romeo, the man who loved Lupe above all other things.

**BALTI**

It's true that the way life works is a mystery. I saved Romeo when he was a child and now, by sending my letter, I caused this misunderstanding and therefore his death. Perhaps he wasn't meant to die back then. I saved him, just to deliver him on Lupe's deathbed.

**NELSON**

I see that with Romeo's death, there might now be a vacancy to take his position as future owner of the Campbell Irrigation Company.

(to RAMÓN) I promise that whether or not I gain that office, I will not dismiss the love that Romeo felt for your cousin. Our cousins did marry, after all, and now we are family. From now on I will persuade our parents to negotiate, and if need be, find other routes for our irrigation systems. We will continue to grow, yet grow as neighbors and brothers.

**RAMÓN**

Estoy de acuerdo. This Rio Grande Valley is in fact un valle mágico, "Magic Valley" like you call it. Because only in a magical place can love like this happen. And we didn't see it. We are carnales, and we must work together and learn to see eye to eye.

*NELSON and RAMÓN shake hands.*

**PADRE LAURO**

See here that war destroys the most innocent and beautiful of creatures. In these times of change we fight for what we love, yet we focus so much on our hate that when the opportunity for love to flourish shows itself, we miss it. And indeed I know their love has made Romeo and Lupe eternal in heaven, but their love much too quickly to our world is lost. And what is lost, can never be replaced. This flame that was born between them, if it is born amongst us again, may it glow across the Rio Grande Valley.

*PADRE LAURO drops a rose before the dead couple, followed by the others, who all also drop roses. MR. CAMPBELL joins the hands of the dead lovers with his rose and exits. The CORRIDO SINGER enters.*

**CORRIDO SINGER**
Now as time returns to its course
May you heed the warning of this old consejo:

> *The CORRIDO SINGER begins to sing "No le digas no al amor."*

> No le digas no al amor
> No hagas tanto coraje
> Este es mi mensaje
> Don't say no to love
> Only love can free a soul
> Take heed of this true story
> Don't say no to love

**END OF PLAY**

# Introduction to Tara Moses's
## *Hamlet El Príncipe de Denmark*

In the bilingual *Hamlet, El Príncipe de Denmark*, director and adaptor Tara Moses (Seminole Nation of Oklahoma, Mvskoke) places the events of *Hamlet* in colonial Mexico during the ritual of Día de los Muertos, a context in which the appearance of the spirit of Hamlet's father is interpreted through Indigenous frameworks. The play was first performed in 2018 by telatúlsa, a Latinx and Native theater company in Tulsa, Oklahoma. The production was staged in the round at Living Arts of Tulsa as part of its annual Día de los Muertos festival, which included crafts, a screening of the film *Coco*, and a roundtable discussion on the decolonization of death. Audiences were encouraged to arrive at the venue early to learn about the Indigenous origins and ceremonies of Día de los Muertos and to view the altars that would become part of the performance. As Moses explains, "The play opens with three people placing ofrendas (offerings) on the altars of their loved ones, and while you are watching the actors on stage, you're surrounded by altars built by people in our community here in Tulsa."[1] By honoring Indigenous cultures and local communities in these ways and facilitating experiences for learning, Moses's *Hamlet* participates in the decolonial, educational, co-created work common in many Borderlands Shakespeare productions.

The geographies and temporalities of *Hamlet, El Príncipe de Denmark* are palimpsestic and thus reflect the overlapping colonial and Indigenous legacies that shape the region. Setting *Hamlet* in colonial Mexico also illuminates the colonial dynamics within Shakespeare's play and in the U.S.–Mexico Borderlands today. Tellingly, Moses revises the role of England in her adaptation. Hamlet journeys there not to be executed but to find a better life, invoking the illusion of the "American Dream" and inviting audiences to consider the complex conditions that drive migration. Fortinbras is from England, not Norway,

---

1  James D. Watts, Jr., "Arts Scene: First Friday Hosts Art Market After Dark; Beethoven Gets Exposed," *Tulsa World*, October 28, 2018, https://tulsaworld.com/entertainment/arts-scene-first-friday-hosts-art-market-after-dark-beethoven-gets-exposed/article_aadd8f42-5488-541c-9244-ff07f1b99440.html.

and his takeover of the "Danish" throne represents ongoing European colonialism in the Americas as well as the dominance of the Anglosphere. Moreover, in keeping with the twenty-first century politics that inform the adaptation and its initial performance, many characters speak Spanish rather than an Indigenous language. The colonial language in this context is English, and the script merges the text of Shakespeare's play with lines from Spanish translations and contributions of Moses's own creation.

As in many Borderlands Shakespeare plays, linguistic choices reflect the relationships among characters and the regional power dynamics that shape them. Indicating his allegiance to Mexican ways of life, the ghost of King Hamlet, for instance, refuses to speak English. When Hamlet asks the ghost to answer him, Horatio advises him to speak "[e]n su lengua" (1.4). It is only when Hamlet speaks in Spanish that the ghost tells his story and demands vengeance. Both Hamlet and Ophelia frequently speak Spanish and Spanglish, a tendency that reflects their status as hybrid colonial subjects. Claudius, Gertrude, and Polonius, by contrast, speak only English, though they understand Spanish, and their linguistic choices signal their alliance with corrupt power structures. When Ophelia sees Hamlet distraught and exclaims to her father, "¡Que he tenido un susto muy grande!" Polonius responds, "With what, i' th' name of God? In English, child!" (2.1). Later, when Ophelia objects in Spanish to Claudius's plan for Laertes to avenge Polonius's death, Claudius dismisses her, saying, "Enough of this! Your words matter not!" (2.2) These exchanges suggest that speaking Spanish is improper or frivolous in this setting.

In response, Hamlet mobilizes Spanish and Spanglish as languages of resistance to such imperial domination. By speaking Spanish in the Anglocentric court and mixing Spanish and English in his performance of madness, he actively subverts the colonial power structure that insists upon a clear division between the languages of colonizer and colonized. For these reasons, Claudius refuses to recognize Hamlet when he speaks Spanish. The following example is illustrative:

**CLAUDIUS**

How fares our cousin Hamlet?

**HAMLET**

Muy bien. Me mantengo del aire como el camaleón engorda con esperanzas. No podrás así a tus capones.

**CLAUDIUS**

I have nothing with this answer, Hamlet. These words are not mine. (3.2)

Claudius rejects Hamlet's words not only because of the sarcastic nature of Hamlet's comment about a chameleon fattened with hope but also because he will not countenance Spanish being spoken at his court. Hamlet's use of Spanish thus makes his dissembling madness even more subversive and threatening.

In much the same way that the Spanish language disrupts colonial power in Moses's play, Indigenous Mexican worldviews destabilize Shakespeare's treatment of death and the afterlife. Hamlet objects to Claudius and Gertrude's failure not only to adequately mourn his father's death but also to properly observe the ritual of Día de los Muertos. In Hamlet's mind, they have betrayed his father as well as Mexican culture and spirituality. He is outraged, for instance, when Claudius suggests that Gertrude wipe her calavera makeup off her face. Hamlet's anger seems to stem, in part, from his own uncertainty about how to understand death. Powerfully, Hamlet's "To be or not to be" soliloquy—which takes place in a mixture of English and Spanish—reflects his ambivalence about both Christian and Indigenous beliefs about the afterlife:

Ser o no ser, esa es la cuestión.
¿Cuál más digna acción del ánimo:
Sufrir los tiros penetrantes de la fortuna injusta,
U oponer las armas a este torrente de calamidades,
Y darles fin con atrevida resistencia? To die, to sleep —
No more — and by a sleep to say we end
The heartache and the thousand natural shocks
That flesh is heir to — 'tis a consummation
Devoutly to be wished. To die, to sleep —
To sleep, perchance to dream. Ay, there's the rub. (3.1)

This linguistic composition of the famous speech amplifies Hamlet's uncertainty about death, allowing space for Indigenous beliefs in which time and life are cyclical. As in Shakespeare's play, Hamlet's speech suggests the potential for something after death—it is not a Christian afterlife in this case, however, but the return of the spirits associated with Día de los Muertos.

Moses's treatment of Ophelia's death also reflects these Indigenous traditions, as she remains an active participant in the play even after she has died. It is King Hamlet who guides Ophelia to the spirit world, beckoning her with "Es hora, mi niña," as she attempts to paint her face as a calavera one last time (4.3). Ophelia's spirit returns in the graveyard scene in which Hamlet responds to her recent death. She hands Hamlet a skull for him to contemplate, and she observes as Hamlet and Laertes fight in her grave, wondering at their inability to understand that death is not final. She asks the ghost of King Hamlet about their behavior, inquiring, "Ellos no entienden, ¿verdad?," to which he responds, "No entienden" (5.1). What they do not understand is that both Ophelia and King Hamlet inhabit an Indigenous afterlife — a recognition that would potentially alter Hamlet's perception of their deaths.

This emphasis on the wisdom of the spirit world is especially prominent in the play's conclusion. The spirits of King Hamlet and Ophelia are present for the final duel, as they "perch on either side of the stage awaiting what is to come" (5.2). Although Fortinbras will treat the bodies, as Horatio remarks, "[i]n your Christian ways unlike ours," Hamlet ultimately enters an Indigenous Mexican afterlife (5.2). While music plays, King Hamlet helps him get up and walk off stage. "¿Entiendes ahora?" he asks Hamlet (5.2). Hamlet thus completes his spiritual journey as he is guided into the afterlife by his father. Like Hamlet, audience members and readers are left with a reverence for Indigenous beliefs and lifeways.

— Katherine Gillen, Adrianna M. Santos,
and Kathryn Vomero Santos

# Hamlet, El Príncipe de Denmark

Tara Moses

SETTING: November 2nd in colonized Mexico.

## CHARACTERS

| | |
|---|---|
| **HAMLET** | Prince of Denmark and son of the late King Hamlet and Queen Gertrude. He is bilingual. |
| **BERNARDO** | A guard. |
| **HORATIO** | A close friend of Hamlet. |
| **GHOST** | The ghost of King Hamlet. He speaks only Spanish. |
| **KING CLAUDIUS** | The brother of the late King Hamlet. |
| **QUEEN GER-TRUDE** | Queen of Denmark. |
| **POLONIUS** | A councilor to King Claudius and father of Laertes and Ophelia. |
| **LAERTES** | The brother of Ophelia. |
| **OPHELIA** | The girlfriend of Hamlet. She is bilingual. |
| **GUILDENSTERN** | A friend of Hamlet. |
| **ROSENCRANTZ** | A friend of Hamlet. |
| **DANCER** | |
| **PLAYERS** | Playing several roles including King, Queen, Poisoner, Lucianus, and Prologue. |
| **DOCTOR** | |
| **GRAVEDIGGER** | |
| **COMPANION** | Companion to the Gravedigger. |
| **LORD** | |
| **FORTINBRAS** | Prince of England. |
| **MESSENGER** | |
| **WOMEN** | Women who engage in rituals throughout the play. |

**A NOTE ON CASTING:** All characters should be played by Indigenous, Mexican, and/or Latinx actors.

**A NOTE ON LANGUAGE:** Reflecting the double colonization of the Borderlands, Spanish is used in this play as a proxy for Indigenous Mexican languages. English represents the language of the colonizer. The language use of the characters varies depending on their relationship to colonial power.

**A NOTE ON THE TEXT:** The playtext is adapted from the Folger Shakespeare Library edition of *Hamlet* and Editorial Porrúa's reprinting of Leandro Fernández de Moratín's 1798 Spanish translation of *Hamlet*.

# ACT 1
## Scene 1

*The early hours of November 2nd, Día de Muertos. The play opens in a graveyard with three tombstones and three small altars. HAMLET and two WOMEN enter. The WOMEN's faces are painted as calacas, and they are wearing hooded shawls. The three enter with ofrendas. Instrumental Mexican music is playing. In synchronized motion, they lay their offerings onto the tombstones, and they each light a candle. It's a ritual. As soon as HAMLET's candle is lit, the music abruptly goes out as howling wind and rolling thunder are heard. The WOMEN, frightened, exit. HAMLET, perplexed, stays behind for a few beats. He exits when he hears BERNARDO enter.*

**BERNARDO**
Who's there? Nay, answer me. Stand and unfold yourself.

*Enter HORATIO.*

I think I hear them. — Stand ho!

**HORATIO**
Long live the King!

**BERNARDO**
Say, what, is Horatio there?

**HORATIO**
A piece of him.

**BERNARDO**
Hola, Horatio. Why are you out so late at night?

**HORATIO**
Un paseo, mi amigo.

**BERNARDO**
A stroll at this hour? You jest. Speak the truth.

**HORATIO**
Curiosity plagues me. Has this thing appeared again tonight?

**BERNARDO**
I have seen nothing. What drives your curiosity?

**HORATIO**
A belief takes hold of me
To watch the minutes of this night,
That, if again this apparition come,
We may speak to it
On this eve of All Souls Day tonight.
Cuéntame sobre el fantasma.

**BERNARDO**
Sit down awhile,
And let me once again assail your ears,
That are so fortified against my story,
What I have two nights seen.
Last night of all,
When yond same star that's westward from the pole
O'er the sounds of celebrations
During Día de Todos los Santos
The bell then beating one —

   *Enter GHOST.*

**HORATIO**
Calla, mírale por dónde viene otra vez.

**BERNARDO**
In the same figure like the King that's dead!
Speak to it, Horatio!

**HORATIO**
It harrows me with fear and wonder.

**BERNARDO**
Háblale, Horatio.

**HORATIO**
What art thou that usurp'st this time of night,
Together with that fair and warlike form
In which the majesty of buried Denmark
Did sometimes march? By heaven, I charge thee, speak.

**BERNARDO**

It is offended. See, it stalks away.

**HORATIO**

Stay! Speak! Speak! I charge thee, speak!

> *GHOST exits.*

**BERNARDO**

How now, Horatio, you tremble and look pale.

**HORATIO**

Por Dios, que nunca lo hubiera creído sin la sensible y cierta demostración de mis propios ojos.

**BERNARDO**

Is it not like the King?

**HORATIO**

As thou art to thyself.

**BERNARDO**

Thus twice before, and jump at this dead hour,
With martial stalk hath he gone by my watch.

**HORATIO**

In what particular thought to work I know not,
But this bodes some strange eruption to our state.

> *Enter GHOST.*

But soft, behold! Lo, where it comes again!
I'll cross it though it blast me. — Stay, illusion!

> *GHOST spreads his arms.*

If thou hast any sound or use of voice,
Speak to me.
If there be any good thing to be done
That may to thee do ease and grace to me,
Speak to me.
If thou art privy to thy country's fate,
Which happily foreknowing may avoid,
O, speak!

*A rooster crows. Day break.*

Stay and speak! — Stop it, Bernardo!

**BERNARDO**
Shall I strike it with my partisan?

**HORATIO**
'Tis here.

*GHOST exits.*

**HORATIO**
'Tis gone.
We do it wrong, being so majestical,
To offer it the show of violence,
For it is as the air, invulnerable,
And our vain blows malicious mockery.

**BERNARDO**
It was about to speak when the cock crew.

**HORATIO**
So have I heard and do in part believe it.
Let us impart what we have seen tonight
Unto young Hamlet; for, upon my life,
This spirit, dumb to us, will speak to him.
Do you consent we shall acquaint him with it
As needful in our loves, fitting our duty?

**BERNARDO**
Let's do 't, I pray, and I this morning know
Where we shall find him most convenient.

*They exit.*

# Scene 2

*Music plays as OPHELIA, GERTRUDE, and another WOM-AN enter in bright dresses with their faces painted as calacas. They dance for the final day of celebrations. KING CLAUDIUS, POLONIUS, and HAMLET watch. As the dance and music end, applause erupts, and KING CLAUDIUS begins to address the crowd.*

**KING CLAUDIUS**
How wonderful! Thank you, dancers!
Everyone, please sit.
Though yet of Hamlet our dear brother's death
The memory be green, and that it us befitted
To bear our hearts in grief, and our whole kingdom
To be contracted in one brow of woe,
Yet so far hath discretion fought with nature
That we with wisest sorrow think on him
Together with remembrance of ourselves.
Therefore our sometime sister, now our queen,
Have we taken to wife. Nor have we herein barred
Your better wisdoms, which have freely gone
With this affair along. For all, our thanks.

*He hands GERTRUDE a wipe to clean her face of the makeup.*

Farewell to our past as we celebrate our future.

*She wipes her face to HAMLET's dismay as LAERTES enters.*

And now, Laertes, what's the news with you?

**LAERTES**
My dread lord,
Your leave and favor to return to France,
From whence though willingly I came to Denmark
To show my duty in your coronation,
Yet now I must confess, that duty done,
My thoughts and wishes bend again toward France
And bow them to your gracious leave and pardon.

**KING CLAUDIUS**

Have you your father's leave? What says Polonius?

**POLONIUS**

He hath, my lord, wrung from me my slow leave
By laborsome petition, and at last
Upon his will I sealed my hard consent.
I do beseech you give him leave to go.

**KING CLAUDIUS**

Take thy fair hour, Laertes. Time be thine,
And thy best graces spend it at thy will. —
But now, my cousin Hamlet and my son —

**HAMLET** (*aside*)

Algo más que deudo y menos que amigo.

**KING CLAUDIUS**

How is it that the clouds still hang on you?
Today we celebrate!

**HAMLET**

Not so, my lord; I am too much in the sun.

**QUEEN GERTRUDE**

Good Hamlet, cast thy nighted color off,
And let thine eye look like a friend on Denmark.
Do not forever with thy vailèd lids
Seek for thy noble father in the dust.
Thou know'st 'tis common; all that lives must die,
Passing through nature to eternity.

**HAMLET**

Ay, madam, it is common.

**QUEEN GERTRUDE**

If it be,
Why seems it so particular with thee?

**HAMLET**

"Seems," madam? Nay, it is. I know not "seems."
'Tis not alone my inky cloak, good mother,

Nor customary suits of solemn black,
Nor windy suspiration of forced breath,
No, nor the fruitful river in the eye,
Nor the dejected behavior of the visage,
Together with all forms, moods, shapes of grief,
That can denote me truly. These indeed "seem,"
For they are actions that a man might play;
But I have that within which passes show,
These but the trappings and the suits of woe.

**KING CLAUDIUS**
'Tis sweet and commendable in your nature, Hamlet,
To give these mourning duties to your father.
But you must know your father lost a father,
That father lost, lost his, and the survivor bound
In filial obligation for some term
To do obsequious sorrow. But to persevere
In obstinate condolement is a course
Of impious stubbornness. 'Tis unmanly grief.
For your intent in going back to school in Wittenberg,
It is most retrograde to our desire,
And we beseech you, bend you to remain
Here in the cheer and comfort of our eye,
Our chiefest courtier, cousin, and our son.

**QUEEN GERTRUDE**
Let not thy mother lose her prayers, Hamlet.
I pray thee, stay with us. Go not to Wittenberg.

**HAMLET**
I shall in all my best obey you, madam.

**KING CLAUDIUS**
Why, 'tis a loving and a fair reply.
Be as ourself in Denmark. — Madam, come.
This gentle and unforced accord of Hamlet
Sits smiling to my heart. Come away.

*All but HAMLET exit.*

**HAMLET**
O, that this too, too sullied flesh would melt,
Thaw, and resolve itself into a dew,
Or that the Everlasting had not fixed
His canon 'gainst self-slaughter! O God, God,
How weary, stale, flat, and unprofitable
Seem to me all the uses of this world!
Fie on 't, ah fie! 'Tis an unweeded garden
That grows to seed. Things rank and gross in nature
Possess it merely. That it should come to this:
But two months dead — nay, not so much, not two.
So excellent a king, so loving to my mother
That he might not beteem the winds of heaven
Visit her face too roughly. Heaven and Earth,
Must I remember? Why, she would hang on him
As if increase of appetite had grown
By what it fed on. And yet, within a month
(Let me not think on 't; frailty, thy name is woman!),
A little month, or ere those shoes were old
With which she followed my poor father's body,
Like Niobe, all tears — why she, even she
(O God, a beast that wants discourse of reason
Would have mourned longer!) married with my uncle,
My father's brother, but no more like my father
Than I to Hercules. Within a month,
Ere yet the salt of most unrighteous tears
Had left the flushing in her gallèd eyes,
She married. O, most wicked speed, to post
With such dexterity to incestuous sheets!
It is not, nor it cannot come to good.
But break, my heart, for I must hold my tongue.

*Enter HORATIO.*

**HORATIO**
Buenos días, señor.

**HAMLET**
Horatio — or I do forget myself!

**HORATIO**

The same, my lord, and your poor servant ever.

**HAMLET**

Sir, my good friend. I'll change that name with you.
And what make you from Wittenberg, Horatio?

**HORATIO**

A truant disposition, good my lord.

**HAMLET**

I know you are no truant.
But what is your affair in Elsinore?
We'll teach you to drink deep ere you depart.

**HORATIO**

My lord, I came to see your father's funeral.

**HAMLET**

I prithee, do not mock me, fellow student.
I think it was to see my mother's wedding.

**HORATIO**

Indeed, my lord, it followed hard upon.

**HAMLET**

Thrift, thrift, Horatio. The funeral baked meats
Did coldly furnish forth the marriage tables.
Would I had met my dearest foe in heaven
Or ever I had seen that day, Horatio!
My father — methinks I see my father!

**HORATIO**

Where, my lord?

**HAMLET**

In my mind's eye, Horatio.

**HORATIO**

My lord, I think I saw him yesternight.

**HAMLET**

Saw who?

**HORATIO**
My lord, the King your father.

**HAMLET**
The King my father?

**HORATIO**
Two nights together had this gentleman,
Bernardo, on his watch,
In the dead waste and middle of the night,
Been thus encountered: a figure like your father
Appears before them and with solemn march
Goes slow and stately by them.

**HAMLET**
Two nights?

**HORATIO**
The first on Día de Todos los Santos.

**HAMLET**
That night you swear?

**HORATIO**
Yes, my lord, as Bernardo reported. 'Twas that night.

**HAMLET**
But where was this?

**BERNARDO**
My lord, upon the platform where they watch.

**HAMLET**
Did you not speak to it?

**HORATIO**
My lord, I did,
But answer made it none.
But even then the morning cock crew loud,
And at the sound it shrunk in haste away
And vanished from our sight.

**HAMLET**

Indeed, sir, but this troubles me.
Hold you the watch tonight?

**HORATIO**

I can, my lord.

**HAMLET**

What, looked he frowningly?

**HORATIO**

A countenance more in sorrow than in anger.

**HAMLET**

Pale or red?

**HORATIO**

Nay, very pale.

**HAMLET**

And fixed his eyes upon you?

**HORATIO**

Most constantly.

**HAMLET**

I would I had been there.

**HORATIO**

It would have much amazed you.

**HAMLET**

I will watch tonight.
Perchance 'twill walk again.

**HORATIO**

I warrant it will.

**HAMLET**

If it assume my noble father's person,
I'll speak to it, though hell itself should gape
And bid me hold my peace. I pray you,
If you have hitherto concealed this sight,

Let it be tenable in your silence still;
And whatsoever else shall hap tonight,
Give it an understanding but no tongue.
I will requite your love. So fare you well.
Upon the platform, 'twixt eleven and twelve,
I'll visit you.

**HORATIO**
My duty to your Honor.

**HAMLET**
Your loves, as mine to you. Farewell.

> *HORATIO exits.*

My father's spirit — in arms! All is not well.
I doubt some foul play. Would the night were come!
Till then, sit still, my soul. Foul deeds will rise,
Though all the earth o'erwhelm them, to men's eyes.

> *HAMLET exits.*

# Scene 3

> *OPHELIA is at a mirror removing her makeup and taking the
> flowers out of her hair. LAERTES enters.*

**LAERTES**
My necessaries are embarked. Farewell.
And, sister, as the winds give benefit
And convey is assistant, do not sleep,
But let me hear from you.

**OPHELIA**
Do you doubt that?

**LAERTES**
For Hamlet, and the trifling of his favor,
Hold it a fashion and a toy in blood,
A violet in the youth of primy nature,
Forward, not permanent, sweet, not lasting,

The perfume and suppliance of a minute,
No more.

**OPHELIA**

No more but so?

**LAERTES**

Think it no more.
If he says he loves you,
It fits your wisdom so far to believe it.
However, weigh what loss your honor may sustain
If with too credent ear you list his songs
Or lose your heart or your chaste treasure open
To his unmastered importunity.
Fear it, Ophelia; fear it, my dear sister,
And keep you in the rear of your affection,
Out of the shot and danger of desire.
The chariest maid is prodigal enough
If she unmask her beauty to the moon.

**OPHELIA**

I shall the effect of this good lesson keep
As watchman to my heart. But, good my brother,
Do not, as some ungracious pastors do,
Show me the steep and thorny way to heaven,
Whiles, like a puffed and reckless libertine,
Himself the primrose path of dalliance treads
And recks not his own rede.

**LAERTES**

O, fear me not.

*POLONIUS enters.*

I stay too long. But here my father comes.
A double blessing is a double grace.
Occasion smiles upon a second leave.

**POLONIUS**

Yet here, Laertes? Aboard, aboard, for shame!
The wind sits in the shoulder of your sail,
And you are stayed for. There, my blessing with thee.

**LAERTES**

Most humbly do I take my leave, my lord.

**POLONIUS**

The time invests you. Go, your servants tend.

**LAERTES**

Farewell, Ophelia, y acuérdate bien de lo que te he dicho. Farewell.

*He exits.*

**POLONIUS**

What is 't, Ophelia, he hath said to you?

**OPHELIA**

So please you, something touching the Lord Hamlet.

**POLONIUS**

Marry, well bethought. I must tell you
You do not understand yourself so clearly
As it behooves my daughter and your honor.
What is between you? Give me up the truth.

**OPHELIA**

He hath, my lord, of late made many tenders
Of his affection to me.

**POLONIUS**

Affection, puh! You speak like a green girl
Unsifted in such perilous circumstance.
Do you believe his "tenders," as you call them?

**OPHELIA**

I do not know, my lord, what I should think.

**POLONIUS**

Marry, I will teach you. Think yourself a baby,
Tender yourself more dearly,
Or (not to crack the wind of the poor phrase,
Running it thus) you'll tender me a fool.

**OPHELIA**

My lord, he hath importuned me with love

In honorable fashion —

**POLONIUS**

Ay, "fashion" you may call it. Go to, go to!

**OPHELIA**

And hath given countenance to his speech, my lord,
With almost all the holy vows of heaven.

**POLONIUS**

Do not believe his vows, for they are brokers,
Not of that dye which their investments show,
But mere implorators of unholy suits.
I would not, in plain terms, from this time forth
Have you so slander any moment leisure
As to give words or talk with the Lord Hamlet.
This above all: to thine own self be true.

**OPHELIA**

I shall obey, my lord.

> *They exit.*

# Scene 4

> *In the transition to the graveyard, HAMLET enters in a hurry,*
> *passing OPHELIA as she exits.*

**HAMLET**

¡Con prisa!

> *HORATIO enters.*

**HORATIO**

¡Estoy corriendo! ¡O, hace tanto frío!

**HAMLET**

The air bites shrewdly.

**HORATIO**

It is a nipping and an eager air.

**HAMLET**

What hour now?

**HORATIO**

I think it lacks of twelve.

>    *A flourish of trumpets and two pieces goes off.*

What does this mean, my lord?

**HAMLET**

The King doth wake tonight and takes his rouse.

**HORATIO**

Is it a custom?

**HAMLET**

Ay, marry, is 't to this land,
But, to my mind, though I am native here
And to the manner born, it is a custom
More honored in the breach than the observance.
The dram of evil
Doth all the noble substance of a doubt to his own scandal.

>    *Enter GHOST.*

**HORATIO** ·

Look, my lord, it comes!

**HAMLET**

Angels and ministers of grace, defend us!
Be thy intents wicked or charitable,
Thou com'st in such a questionable shape
That I will speak to thee. I'll call thee "Hamlet,"
"King," "Father," "Royal Dane." O, answer me!

**HORATIO**

En su lengua.

**HAMLET**

Dime, ¿por qué dejaste tu tumba? ¿Cuál puede ser la causa de que tu difunto cuerpo, del todo armado, vuelva otra vez a ver los rayos pálidos de la luna, añadiendo a la noche horror? Di. ¿Por qué es esto? ¿Por qué? ¿O qué debemos hacer nosotros?

*GHOST beckons.*

**HORATIO**

It waves you to a more removèd ground.
But do not go with it.

**HAMLET**

It will not speak. Then I will follow it.

**HORATIO**

Do not, my lord.

**HAMLET**

Why, what should be the fear?
I do not set my life at a pin's fee.
And for my soul, what can it do to that,
Being a thing immortal as itself?
It waves me forth again. I'll follow it.

**HORATIO**

What if it tempt you toward the flood, my lord?
Or to the dreadful summit of the cliff
That beetles o'er his base into the sea,
And there assume some other horrible form
Which might deprive your sovereignty of reason
And draw you into madness? Think of it.

**HAMLET**

It waves me still. — Go on, I'll follow thee.

**HORATIO**

You shall not go, my lord.

*They restrain HAMLET.*

**HAMLET**

Hold off your hands.

**HORATIO**

Be ruled. You shall not go.

**HAMLET**

My fate cries out as I am called.

Unhand me, gentlemen!
By heaven, I'll make a ghost of him that lets me!
I say, away! — Go on. I'll follow thee.

*GHOST and HAMLET exit.*

**HORATIO**
Something is rotten in the state of Denmark.
I'll follow him.

*He exits.*

# Scene 5

*HAMLET and GHOST enter.*

**HAMLET**
Whither wilt thou lead me? Speak. I'll go no further.

**GHOST**
Mírame.

**HAMLET**
I will.

**GHOST**
Casi es ya llegada la hora en que debo restituirme a las sulfúreas y atormentadoras llamas.

**HAMLET**
Alas, poor ghost!

**GHOST**
No me compadezcas: presta solo atentos oídos a lo que voy a revelarte. Luego que me oigas, prometerás venganza.

**HAMLET**
Promise revenge?

**GHOST**
Soy el alma de tu padre, destinado a pasar un cierto tiempo de noche, y encarcelado en fuego durante el día, hasta que sus llamas purifiquen los pecados

que cometí en el mundo. ¡Asistir, asistir, ahora! ¡Asistir! Si tuvieras amor por tu tierno padre . . .venga su muerte; venga su homicidio cruel y atroz.

**HAMLET**

Murder?

**GHOST**

Sí. Homicidio cruel, como todos lo son; pero el más cruel y el más injusto y el más aleve.

**HAMLET**

Most foul, strange, and unnatural.
Haste me to know't, that I, with wings as swift
As meditation or the thoughts of love,
May sweep to my revenge.

**GHOST**

Escúchame ahora, Hamlet. Tú debes saber que la serpiente que mordió a tu padre hoy ciñe su corona.

**HAMLET**

My uncle!

**GHOST**

Ay, aquel incestuoso, aquel monstruo adúltero, valiéndose de su talento diabólico, valiéndose de traidores dádivas . . .o! Talento y dádivas malditas, ¡que tal poder tiene para seducir! Supo inclinar a su deshonesto apetito la voluntad de la reina mi esposa que yo creía tan llena de virtud. O, Hamlet, ¡cuán grande fue su caída! Yo, cuyo amor para con ella fue tan puro. Yo siempre tan fiel a los solemnes juramentos que en nuestro desposorio la hice, yo fui aborrecido, y se rindió a aquel miserable, cuyas prendas eran en verdad harto inferiores a las mías. Pero ya me parece que percibo el ambiente de la mañana. Debo ser breve. Dormía yo una tarde en mi jardín según lo acostumbraba siempre. Tu tío me sorprendió en aquella hora de quietud, y trayendo consigo una ampolla de licor venenoso, derramó en mi oído su ponzoñosa destilación, la cual, de tal manera es contraria a la sangre del hombre, que semejante en la sutileza al mercurio, se dilata por todas las entradas y conductos del cuerpo, y con súbita fuerza le ocupa, cuajando la más pura y robusta sangre, como la leche con las gotas ácidas. Este efecto produjo inmediatamente en mí, y el cutis hinchado, comenzó a despegarse a trechos con una especie de lepra en ásperas y asquerosas costras. Así fue que estando durmiendo, perdí a manos de mi hermano mismo, mi corona, mi esposa y mi vida a un tiempo. O, ¡maldad horrible, horrible! Si oyes la voz de la naturaleza, no sufras, no, que el tálamo real de Dinamarca sea el lecho de la lujuria y abominable incesto. Pero de cualquier modo que dirijas la acción, no manches con delito el alma, previniendo ofensas a tu madre. Adiós. Ya la luciérnaga, amortiguando su aparente fuego, nos anuncia la proximidad del día. Adiós, adiós. Acuérdate de mí.

*He exits.*

**HAMLET**
O most pernicious woman!
O villain, villain, smiling, damnèd villain!
My tables — meet it is I set it down
That one may smile and smile and be a villain.
At least I am sure it may be so in Denmark.
So, uncle, there you are. Now to my word.
It is "adieu, adieu, remember me."
I have sworn 't.

*HORATIO enters.*

**HORATIO**
My lord, my lord!

**HAMLET**
Hola, ho, ho, boy! Come, bird, come!

**HORATIO**
What news, my lord?

**HAMLET**
O, wonderful!

**HORATIO**
Good my lord, tell it.

**HAMLET**
No, you will reveal it.

**HORATIO**
Not I, my lord, by heaven.

**HAMLET**
There's never a villain dwelling in all Denmark
But he's an arrant knave.

**HORATIO**
There needs no ghost, my lord, come from the grave
To tell us this.

**HAMLET**
Why, right, you are in the right.
And so, without more circumstance at all,
I hold it fit that we shake hands and part,
You, as your business and desire shall point you
(For every man hath business and desire,
Such as it is), and for my own poor part,
I will go pray.

**HORATIO**
These are but wild and whirling words, my lord.

**HAMLET**
Give me one poor request.

**HORATIO**
What is 't, my lord? I will.

**HAMLET**
Never make known what you have seen tonight.

**HORATIO**
My lord, I will not.

**HAMLET**
Nay, but swear 't.

**HORATIO**
In faith, my lord, not I.

**HAMLET**
Upon my sword.

**GHOST** (*offstage*)
Júrenlo.

**HAMLET**
   Consent to swear.

**HORATIO**
   Propose the oath, my lord.

**HAMLET**
   Never to speak of this that you have seen,
   Swear by my sword.

**GHOST** (*offstage*)
   Júrenlo.

**HAMLET**
   Lay your hands again upon my sword. Swear by my sword
   Never to speak of this that you have heard.

**GHOST** (*offstage*)
   Júrenlo por su espada.

**HORATIO**
   O day and night, but this is wondrous strange.

**HAMLET**
   There are more things in heaven and earth, Horatio,
   Than are dreamt of in your philosophy.

**GHOST** (*offstage*)
   Júrenlo.

**HAMLET**
   Rest, rest, perturbèd spirit
   The time is out of joint. O, cursèd spite
   That ever I was born to set it right!
   So, gentleman, let's go together.

   *They exit.*

# ACT 2
## Scene 1

*HAMLET, still shaking from the anger of his discovery, comes across OPHELIA in the courtyard.*

**OPHELIA**
My dearest —

*He grabs her by her wrist. She winces in pain.*

**HAMLET** (*out of it*)
How can you be so cheerful
When you know not?

**OPHELIA**
Hamlet! What is in thine eyes?
I beseech you! Let go of me!

*He gets overwhelmed and shakes her. He pauses, sighs, and then lets her go.*

**HAMLET**
I must go. Forgive me,
There is much to know.

**OPHELIA** (*calling after him*)
Hamlet!

*He's gone. POLONIUS enters walking while reviewing some materials. OPHELIA runs after him.*

**OPHELIA**
¡Papá!

**POLONIUS**
How now, Ophelia, what's the matter?

**OPHELIA**
¡Que he tenido un susto muy grande!

**POLONIUS**
With what, i' th' name of God? In English, child!

**OPHELIA**

My lord, Lord Hamlet, with his doublet all unbraced,
And with a look so piteous in purport
As if he had been loosèd out of hell
To speak of horrors — se presentó delante de mí.

**POLONIUS**

Mad for thy love?

**OPHELIA**

My lord, I do not know,
But truly I do fear it.

**POLONIUS**

Come, go with me. I will go seek the King.
This is the very ecstasy of love,
Whose violent property fordoes itself
And leads the will to desperate undertakings
As oft as any passion under heaven
That does afflict our natures. I am sorry.
What, have you given him any hard words of late?

**OPHELIA**

No, my good lord, but as you did command,
I did repel his letters and denied
His access to me.

**POLONIUS**

That hath made him mad.
Come, go we to the King.
This must be known, which, being kept close, might move
More grief to hide than hate to utter love.
Come.

> *They exit.*

# Scene 2

*Enter KING CLAUDIUS, QUEEN GERTRUDE, ROSEN-CRANTZ, and GUILDENSTERN.*

**KING CLAUDIUS**

    Welcome, dear Rosencrantz and Guildenstern.

    Something have you heard

    Of Hamlet's transformation, so call it,

    Since not th' exterior nor the inward man

    Resembles that it was. What it should be,

    More than his father's death, that thus hath put him

    So much from th' understanding of himself

    I cannot dream of. I entreat you both

    To draw him on to pleasures, and to gather

    So much as from occasion you may glean,

    Whether aught to us unknown afflicts him thus

    That, opened, lies within our remedy.

**QUEEN GERTRUDE**

    Good gentlemen, he hath much talked of you,

    And sure I am two men there are not living

    To whom he more adheres. If it will please you

    To show us so much gentry and goodwill

    As to expend your time with us awhile

    For the supply and profit of our hope,

    Your visitation shall receive such thanks

    As fits a king's remembrance.

**ROSENCRANTZ**

    Both your Majesties

    Might, by the sovereign power you have of us,

    Put your dread pleasures more into command

    Than to entreaty.

**GUILDENSTERN**

    But we both obey,

    And here give up ourselves in the full bent

    To lay our service freely at your feet,

    To be commanded.

**KING CLAUDIUS**

Thanks, Rosencrantz and gentle Guildenstern.

**QUEEN GERTRUDE**

Thanks, Guildenstern and gentle Rosencrantz.
And I beseech you instantly to visit
My too much changèd son. — Go, some of you,
And bring these gentlemen where Hamlet is.

**GUILDENSTERN**

Heavens make our presence and our practices
Pleasant and helpful to him!

**QUEEN GERTRUDE**

Ay, amen!

> *ROSENCRANTZ and GUILDENSTERN exit as POLONIUS enters.*

**POLONIUS**

Th'ambassadors from Norway, my good lord,
Are joyfully returned.

**KING CLAUDIUS**

Thou still hast been the father of good news.

**POLONIUS**

Have I, my lord? I assure my good liege
I hold my duty as I hold my soul,
Both to my God and to my gracious king,
And I do think, or else this brain of mine
Hunts not the trail of policy so sure
As it hath used to do, that I have found
The very cause of Hamlet's lunacy.

**KING CLAUDIUS**

O, speak of that! That do I long to hear.
My dear Gertrude, he hath found
The head and source of all your son's distemper.

**QUEEN GERTRUDE**

I doubt it is no other but the main —
His father's death and our o'erhasty marriage.

**POLONIUS**

I will be brief. Your noble son is mad.
"Mad" call I it, for, to define true madness,
What is 't but to be nothing else but mad?
But let that go.

**QUEEN GERTRUDE**

More matter with less art.

**POLONIUS**

Madam, I swear I use no art at all.
That he's mad, 'tis true; 'tis true 'tis pity,
And pity 'tis 'tis true — a foolish figure,
But farewell it, for I will use no art.
I have a daughter (have while she is mine)
Who, in her duty and obedience, mark,
Hath given me this. Now gather and surmise.

(*reading*) To the celestial, and my soul's idol, the most beautified Ophelia —

(*to QUEEN GERTRUDE*) That's an ill phrase, a vile phrase; "beautified" is a vile phrase. But you shall hear. Thus:

(*reading*) In her excellent white bosom, these, etc. —

**QUEEN GERTRUDE**

Came this from Hamlet to her?

**POLONIUS**

Good madam, stay awhile. I will be faithful.

(*reading*)

> Doubt thou the stars are fire,
> Doubt that the sun doth move,
> Doubt truth to be a liar,
> But never doubt I love.

O dear Ophelia, I am ill at these numbers. I have not art to reckon my groans, but that I love thee best, O most best, believe it. Adieu.

This, in obedience, hath my daughter shown me,
And more above, hath his solicitings,

As they fell out by time, by means, and place,
All given to mine ear.

**KING CLAUDIUS**
But how hath she received his love?

**POLONIUS**
What do you think of me?

**KING CLAUDIUS**
As of a man faithful and honorable.

**POLONIUS**
I would fain prove so. But I prescripts gave her,
That she should lock herself from his resort,
Admit no messengers, receive no tokens;
Which done, she took the fruits of my advice,
And he, repelled (a short tale to make),
Fell into a sadness, then into a fast,
Thence to a watch, thence into a weakness,
Thence to a lightness, and, by this declension,
Into the madness wherein now he raves
And all we mourn for.

**KING CLAUDIUS** (*to QUEEN GERTRUDE*)
Do you think 'tis this?

**QUEEN GERTRUDE**
It may be, very like.

**POLONIUS**
Hath there been such a time (I would fain know that)
That I have positively said 'tis so,
When it proved otherwise?

**KING CLAUDIUS**
How may we try it further?

**POLONIUS**
You know sometimes he walks four hours together
Here in the lobby.

**QUEEN GERTRUDE**
So he does indeed.

**POLONIUS**
At such a time I'll loose my daughter to him.

(*to KING CLAUDIUS*) Be you and I behind an arras then.
Mark the encounter. If he love her not,
And be not from his reason fall'n thereon,
Let me be no assistant for a state,
But keep a farm and carters.

**KING CLAUDIUS**
We will try it.

*Enter HAMLET reading a book.*

**QUEEN GERTRUDE**
But look where sadly the poor wretch comes reading.

**POLONIUS**
Away, I do beseech you both, away.
I'll board him presently. O, give me leave.

*They exit.*

How does my good Lord Hamlet?

**HAMLET**
Bien, a Dios gracias.

**POLONIUS**
Do you know me, my lord?

**HAMLET**
Perfectamente. You are a fishmonger.

**POLONIUS**
Not I, my lord.

**HAMLET**
Así fueras honrado.

**POLONIUS**
Honest, my lord?

**HAMLET**

Ay, sir. El ser honrado, según va el mundo, es lo mismo que ser escogido uno entre diez mil.

**POLONIUS**

That's very true, my lord.

**HAMLET**

For if the sun breed maggots in a dead dog, being a good kissing carrion — ¿No tienes una hija?

**POLONIUS**

I have, my lord.

**HAMLET**

Let her not walk i'th' sun. La concepción es una bendición del cielo, pero no del modo en que tu hija podrá concebir. Cuida mucho de esto, amigo.

**POLONIUS** (*aside*)

How say you by that? Still harping on my daughter. Yet he knew me not at first; he said I was a fishmonger. He is far gone. And truly, in my youth, I suffered much extremity for love, very near this. I'll speak to him again.

(*to HAMLET*) What do you read, my lord?

**HAMLET**

Palabras, palabras, todo palabras.

**POLONIUS**

What is the matter, my lord?

**HAMLET**

Between who?

**POLONIUS**

I mean the matter that you read, my lord.

**HAMLET**

De calumnias; for the satirical rogue says here that old men have gray beards, las caras con arrugas, que vierten de sus ojos ámbar abundante y goma de ciruela, and that they have a plentiful lack of wit, together with most weak hams; all which, sir, though I most powerfully and potently believe, yet I hold it not honesty to have it thus set down; for yourself, sir, shall grow old as I am, si le fuera posible andar hacia atrás como el cangrejo.

**POLONIUS** (*aside*)
Though this be madness, yet there is method in't. — Will you walk out of the air, my lord?

**HAMLET**
¿A la sepultura?

**POLONIUS**
Indeed, that's out of the air.

(*aside*) How pregnant sometimes his replies are! I will leave him and suddenly contrive the means of meeting between him and my daughter.

(*to HAMLET*) My lord, I will take my leave of you.

**HAMLET**
No me puedes pedir cosa que con más gusto te conceda — except my life, except my life, except my life.

**POLONIUS**
Fare you well, my lord.

**HAMLET** (*aside*)
These tedious old fools.

> *ROSENCRANTZ and GUILDENSTERN enter.*

**POLONIUS**
You go to seek the Lord Hamlet. There he is.

**ROSENCRANTZ** (*to POLONIUS*)
God save you, sir.

> *POLONIUS exits.*

**GUILDENSTERN**
My honored lord.

**ROSENCRANTZ**
My most dear lord.

**HAMLET**

My excellent good friends! How dost thou, Guildenstern? Ah, Rosencrantz! Good lads, how do you both?

**ROSENCRANTZ**

As the indifferent children of the earth.

**GUILDENSTERN**

Happy in that we are not overhappy. On Fortune's cap, we are not the very button.

**HAMLET**

Nor the soles of her shoe?

**ROSENCRANTZ**

Neither, my lord.

**HAMLET**

Then you live about her waist, or in the middle of her favors?

**GUILDENSTERN**

Faith, her privates we.

**HAMLET**

In the secret parts of Fortune? O, most true! She is a strumpet. What news?

**ROSENCRANTZ**

None, my lord, but that the world's grown honest.

**HAMLET**

Then is doomsday near. What have you, my good friends, deserved at the hands of Fortune that she sends you to prison hither?

**GUILDENSTERN**

Prison, my lord?

**HAMLET**

Denmark's a prison.

**ROSENCRANTZ**

Then is the world one.

**HAMLET**

A goodly one, in which there are many confines, wards, and dungeons, Denmark being one o' th' worst.

**ROSENCRANTZ**

We think not so, my lord.

**HAMLET**

Why, then, 'tis none to you, for there is nothing either good or bad but thinking makes it so. To me, it is a prison.

**ROSENCRANTZ**

Why, then, your ambition makes it one. 'Tis too narrow for your mind.

**HAMLET**

No such matter. I will not sort you with the rest of my servants, for, to speak to you like an honest man, I am most dreadfully attended. But, in the beaten way of friendship, what make you at Elsinore?

**ROSENCRANTZ**

To visit you, my lord, no other occasion.

**HAMLET**

Beggar that I am, I am even poor in thanks; but I thank you, and sure, dear friends, my thanks are too dear a halfpenny. Were you not sent for? Is it your own inclining? Is it a free visitation? Come, come, deal justly with me. Come, come; nay, speak.

**GUILDENSTERN**

What should we say, my lord?

**HAMLET**

I know the good king and queen have sent for you.

**ROSENCRANTZ**

To what end, my lord?

**HAMLET**

That you must teach me. But let me conjure you by the rights of our fellowship, by the consonancy of our youth, by the obligation of our ever-preserved love, and by what more dear a better proposer can charge you withal: be even and direct with me whether you were sent for or no.

**ROSENCRANTZ** (*to GUILDENSTERN*)
What say you?

**HAMLET** (*aside*)
Nay, then, I have an eye of you.

(*to GUILDENSTERN*) If you love me, hold not off.

**GUILDENSTERN**
My lord, we were sent for.

**HAMLET**
I will tell you why, so your secrecy to the King and Queen molt no feather. I have of late, but wherefore I know not, lost all my mirth, forgone all custom of exercises, and, indeed, it goes so heavily with my disposition that this goodly frame, the earth, seems to me a sterile promontory. Man delights not me, no, nor woman neither, though by your smiling you seem to say so.

**ROSENCRANTZ**
My lord, there was no such stuff in my thoughts.

**HAMLET**
Why did you laugh, then, when I said, "man delights not me"?

**ROSENCRANTZ**
To think, my lord, if you delight not in man, what Lenten entertainment the players shall receive from you. We coted them on the way, and hither are they coming to offer you service.

**HAMLET**
What players are they?

**ROSENCRANTZ**
Even those you were wont to take such delight in, the tragedians of the city.

**HAMLET**
How chances it they travel? Their residence, both in reputation and profit, was better both ways.

**ROSENCRANTZ**
I think their inhibition comes by the means of the late innovation.

**HAMLET**
Do they hold the same estimation they did when I was in the city? Are they so followed?

**ROSENCRANTZ**
No, indeed are they not.

> *The PLAYERS enter.*

**GUILDENSTERN**
There are the players.

**ROSENCRANTZ** (*to GUILDENSTERN*)
Only three?

**GUILDENSTERN** (*to ROSENCRANTZ*)
We're on a budget.

**HAMLET**
Players, you are welcome to Elsinore. But my uncle-father and aunt-mother are deceived.

**GUILDENSTERN**
In what, my dear lord?

**HAMLET**
I am but mad north-north-west. When the wind is southerly, I know a hawk from a handsaw.

> *POLONIUS enters.*

**POLONIUS**
Well be with you, gentlemen.

**HAMLET**
Oye, Guillermo, y tú también . . .un oyente a cada lado. ¿Ven aquel vejestorio que acaba de entrar? Pues aún no ha salido de mantillas.

**GUILDENSTERN** (*aside*)
Guillermo?

**ROSENCRANTZ**
Haply he is the second time come to them, for they say an old man is twice a child.

**HAMLET**

I will prophesy he comes to tell me of the players; mark it. — You say right, sir, a Monday morning, 'twas then indeed.

**POLONIUS**

My lord, I have news to tell you.

**HAMLET**

Tengo que darle una noticia. Cuando Roscio era actor en Roma ...

**POLONIUS**

The actors are come hither, my lord.

**HAMLET**

Buzz, buzz.

**POLONIUS**

Upon my honor —

**HAMLET**

¡Cada actor viene caballero en burro!

**POLONIUS**

The best actors in the world, either for tragedy, comedy, history, pastoral, pastoral-comical, historical-pastoral, tragical-historical, tragical-comical-historical-pastoral, scene individable, or poem unlimited. Seneca cannot be too heavy, nor Plautus too light. For the law of writ and the liberty, these are the only men. A suggestion I leave you with.

**HAMLET**

Understood. Adiós, amigo.

**POLONIUS** (*aside*)

Mad he truly be!

**HAMLET**

We'll hear a play tomorrow!

> *POLONIUS exits.*

Dost thou hear me, old friend? Can you play "The Murder of Gonzago"?

**FIRST PLAYER**

Ay, my lord.

**HAMLET**

We'll ha 't tomorrow night. You could, for a need, study a speech of some dozen or sixteen lines, which I would set down and insert in't, could you not?

**FIRST PLAYER**

Ay, my lord.

**HAMLET**

Very well. Follow that lord — and look you mock him not. My good friends, I'll leave you till night. You are welcome to Elsinore.

**ROSENCRANTZ**

Good my lord.

**HAMLET**

Ay, so, good-bye to you.

*All but HAMLET exit.*

Now I am alone.
O, what a rogue and peasant slave am I!
¿Soy cobarde yo?
¿Quién se atreve a llamarse villano, o a insultarme en mi presencia,
Arrancarme la barba, soplármela al rostro,
Asirme de la nariz, o hacerme tragar lejía
Que me llegue al pulmón?
Bloody, bawdy villain!
Remorseless, treacherous, lecherous, kindless villain!
O vengeance!
Why, what an ass am I! This is most brave,
That I, the son of a dear father murdered,
Prompted to my revenge by heaven and hell,
Must, like a whore, unpack my heart with words
And fall a-cursing like a very drab,
A stallion! Fie upon 't! Foh!
About, my brains! — Hum, I have heard
That guilty creatures sitting at a play
Have, by the very cunning of the scene,
Been struck so to the soul that presently
They have proclaimed their malefactions;
I'll have these players
Play something like the murder of my father

Before mine uncle. I'll observe his looks;
I'll tent him to the quick. If he do blench,
I know my course. The spirit that I have seen
May be a devil, and the devil hath power
T' assume a pleasing shape; yea, and perhaps,
Out of my weakness and my melancholy,
As he is very potent with such spirits,
Abuses me to damn me. I'll have grounds
More relative than this. The play's the thing
Wherein I'll catch the conscience of the King.

*He exits.*

# ACT 3
## Scene 1

*KING CLAUDIUS, QUEEN GERTRUDE, POLONIUS, ROSEN-*
*CRANTZ, and GUILDENSTERN enter.*

**KING CLAUDIUS**
And can you by no drift of conference
Get from him why he puts on this confusion,
Grating so harshly all his days of quiet
With turbulent and dangerous lunacy?

**ROSENCRANTZ**
He does confess he feels himself distracted,
But from what cause he will by no means speak.

**GUILDENSTERN**
Nor do we find him forward to be sounded,
But with a crafty madness keeps aloof
When we would bring him on to some confession
Of his true state.

**QUEEN GERTRUDE**
Did he receive you well?

**ROSENCRANTZ**
Most like a gentleman.

**GUILDENSTERN**
But with much forcing of his disposition.

**QUEEN GERTRUDE**
Did you assay him to any pastime?

**ROSENCRANTZ**
Madam, it so fell out that certain players
We o'erraught on the way. Of these we told him,
And there did seem in him a kind of joy
To hear of it. They are here about the court,
And, as I think, they have already order
This night to play before him.

**POLONIUS**
'Tis most true,
And he beseeched me to entreat your Majesties
To hear and see the matter.

**KING CLAUDIUS**
With all my heart, and it doth much content me
To hear him so inclined.
Good gentlemen, give him a further edge
And drive his purpose into these delights.

**ROSENCRANTZ**
We shall, my lord.

*They exit as OPHELIA enters.*

**KING CLAUDIUS**
Sweet Gertrude, leave us too,
For we have closely sent for Hamlet hither,
That he, as 'twere by accident, may here affront Ophelia.

**QUEEN GERTRUDE**
I shall obey you.
And for your part, Ophelia, I do wish
That your good beauties be the happy cause
Of Hamlet's wildness.

**OPHELIA**
Madam, I wish it may.

*QUEEN GERTRUDE exits.*

**POLONIUS**
Ophelia, walk you here.

**KING CLAUDIUS** (*aside*)
O, 'tis too true!
How smart a lash that speech doth give my conscience.
The harlot's cheek beautied with plast'ring art
Is not more ugly to the thing that helps it
Than is my deed to my most painted word.
O heavy burden!

**POLONIUS**

I hear him coming. Let's withdraw, my lord.

*They withdraw as HAMLET enters.*

**HAMLET**

Ser o no ser, esa es la cuestión.
¿Cuál más digna acción del ánimo:
Sufrir los tiros penetrantes de la fortuna injusta,
U oponer las armas a este torrente de calamidades,
Y darles fin con atrevida resistencia? To die, to sleep —
No more — and by a sleep to say we end
The heartache and the thousand natural shocks
That flesh is heir to — 'tis a consummation
Devoutly to be wished. To die, to sleep —
To sleep, perchance to dream. Ay, there's the rub,
For in that sleep of death what dreams may come,
When we have shuffled off this mortal coil,
Must give us pause. There's the respect
That makes calamity of so long life.
Esta previsión nos hace a todos cobardes:
Así la natural tintura del valor
Se debilita con los barnices pálidos de la prudencia;
Las empresas de mayor importancia
Por esta sola consideración mudan camino,
No se ejecutan, y se reducen a designios vanos.
Pero — soft you now,
The fair Ophelia! Nymph, in thy orisons
Be all my sins remembered.

**OPHELIA**

Good my lord,
How does your Honor for this many a day?

**HAMLET**

I humbly thank you, well.

**OPHELIA**

My lord, I have remembrances of yours
That I have longèd long to redeliver.
I pray you now receive them.

**HAMLET**

Ha, ha, are you honest?

**OPHELIA**

My lord?

**HAMLET**

Are you fair?

**OPHELIA**

What means your Lordship?

**HAMLET**

That if you be honest and fair, your honesty should admit no discourse to your beauty.

**OPHELIA**

Could beauty, my lord, have better commerce than with honesty?

**HAMLET**

Ay, truly, for the power of beauty will sooner transform honesty from what it is to a bawd than the force of honesty can translate beauty into his likeness. This was sometime a paradox, but now the time gives it proof. I did love you once.

**OPHELIA**

Indeed, my lord, you made me believe so.

**HAMLET**

You should not have believed me, for virtue cannot so inoculate our old stock but we shall relish of it. I loved you not.

**OPHELIA**

I was the more deceived.

**HAMLET**

Get thee to a nunnery. Why wouldst thou be a breeder of sinners? I am myself indifferent honest, but yet I could accuse me of such things that it were better my mother had not borne me: I am very proud, revengeful, ambitious, with more offenses at my beck than I have thoughts to put them in, imagination to give them shape, or time to act them in. What should such fellows as I do crawling between earth and heaven? We are arrant knaves all; believe none of us. Go thy ways to a nunnery. Where's your father?

**OPHELIA**

At home, my lord.

**HAMLET**

Let the doors be shut upon him that he may play the fool nowhere but in 's own house. Farewell.

**OPHELIA**

O, help him, you sweet heavens!

**HAMLET**

If thou dost marry, I'll give thee this plague for thy dowry: be thou as chaste as ice, as pure as snow, thou shalt not escape calumny. Get thee to a nunnery, farewell. Or if thou wilt needs marry, marry a fool, for wise men know well enough what monsters you make of them.

*HAMLET exits.*

**OPHELIA**

¡O! ¡Qué trastorno ha padecido esa alma generosa! Y yo, la más desconsolada e infeliz de las mujeres porque él es el hombre más infeliz. ¡O! ¡Cuánta, cuánta es mi desdicha de haber visto lo que vi para ver lo que veo!

**KING CLAUDIUS**

Love? His affections do not that way tend;
Nor what he spake, though it lacked form a little,
Was not like madness. There's something in his soul
O'er which his melancholy sits on brood.
He shall with speed to England
For the demand of our neglected tribute.
What think you on 't?

**POLONIUS**

It shall do well. But yet do I believe
The origin and commencement of his grief
Sprung from neglected love. — How now, Ophelia?
You need not tell us what Lord Hamlet said;
We heard it all. — My lord, do as you please,
But, if you hold it fit, after the play
Let his queen-mother all alone entreat him
To show his grief. If she find him not,

To England send him, or confine him where
Your wisdom best shall think.

**KING CLAUDIUS**
It shall be so.
Madness in great ones must not unwatched go.

*They exit.*

# Scene 2

*Enter HAMLET, ROSENCRANTZ, GUILDENSTERN, and the three PLAYERS.*

**HAMLET**
Speak the speech, I pray you, as I pronounced it to you, trippingly on the tongue; but if you mouth it, as many of our players do, I had as lief the town-crier spoke my lines. Nor do not saw the air too much with your hand, thus, but use all gently; for in the very torrent, tempest, and, as I may say, whirlwind of your passion, you must acquire and beget a temperance that may give it smoothness.

**FIRST PLAYER**
I warrant your Honor.

**HAMLET**
Be not too tame neither, but let your own discretion be your tutor.

**SECOND PLAYER**
I hope we have reformed that indifferently with us, sir.

**HAMLET**
O, reform it altogether. Go make you ready.

*The PLAYERS exit.*

**HAMLET**
Will you two help to hasten them?

**ROSENCRANTZ**
Ay, my lord.

*A trumpet flourish sounds.*

**HAMLET**
Ya viene a la función; vuelvo a hacerme el loco.

*KING CLAUDIUS, QUEEN GERTRUDE, POLONIUS, and
OPHELIA enter.*

**KING CLAUDIUS**
How fares our cousin Hamlet?

**HAMLET**
Muy bien. Me mantengo del aire como el camaleón engorda con esperanzas.
No podrás así a tus capones.

**KING CLAUDIUS**
I have nothing with this answer, Hamlet. These words are not mine.

**HAMLET**
Be the players ready?

**ROSENCRANTZ**
Ay, my lord. They stay upon your patience.

**QUEEN GERTRUDE**
Come hither, my dear Hamlet, sit by me.

**HAMLET**
No. Aquí hay un imán de más atracción para mí.

*HAMLET sits by OPHELIA.*

**POLONIUS** (*to KING CLAUDIUS*)
O, ho! Do you mark that?

**HAMLET**
Lady, shall I lie in your lap?

**OPHELIA**
No.

**HAMLET**
I mean, my head upon your lap?

**OPHELIA**
Ay, my lord.

**HAMLET**
Do you think I meant country matters?

**OPHELIA**
I think nothing, my lord.

**HAMLET**
That's a fair thought to lie between maids' legs.

**OPHELIA**
¿Qué dice, señor?

**HAMLET**
Nada.

**OPHELIA**
You are merry, my lord.

**HAMLET**
Who, I?

**OPHELIA**
Ay, you.

**HAMLET**
What should a man do but be merry? For look you how cheerfully my mother looks, and my father died within 's two hours.

**OPHELIA**
Nay, 'tis twice two months, my lord.

**HAMLET**
So long? O heavens, die two months ago, and not forgotten yet? Then there's hope a great man's memory may outlive his life half a year.

> *Music plays. The PLAYERS enter in folk masks. They move around the stage in a traditional, physical manner. A PLAYER as the King and a PLAYER as the Queen embrace very lovingly. She kneels and makes a show of protestation unto him. He takes her up and declines his head upon her neck. He lies him down upon a bank of flowers.*

> *She, seeing him asleep, leaves him. Anon comes in a PLAYER as*
> *Poisoner, and he takes off the King's crown, kisses it, pours poison*
> *in the sleeper's ears, and leaves him. The Queen returns, finds the*
> *King dead, makes passionate action. The Poisoner comes in again*
> *and seems to condole with her. The dead body is carried away. The*
> *Poisoner woos the Queen with gifts. She seems harsh awhile but in*
> *the end accepts his love. They exit.*

**OPHELIA**
What means this, my lord?

**HAMLET**
Anuncia grandes maldades.

> *Enter a PLAYER as the Prologue.*

**OPHELIA**
Will he tell us what this show meant?

**PROLOGUE**
For us and for our tragedy,
Here stooping to your clemency,
We beg your hearing patiently.

> *He exits.*

**HAMLET**
Is this a prologue or the posy of a ring?

**OPHELIA**
'Tis brief, my lord.

**HAMLET**
As woman's love.

> *Enter PLAYER KING and PLAYER QUEEN.*

**PLAYER KING**
Full thirty times hath Phoebus' cart gone round
Neptune's salt wash and Tellus' orbèd ground,
And thirty dozen moons with borrowed sheen
About the world have times twelve thirties been
Since love our hearts and Hymen did our hands
Unite commutual in most sacred bands.

**PLAYER QUEEN**
So many journeys may the sun and moon
Make us again count o'er ere love be done!
But woe is me! You are so sick of late,
So far from cheer and from your former state,
That I distrust you. Yet, though I distrust,
Discomfort you, my lord, it nothing must.
For women fear too much, even as they love,
Now what my love is, proof hath made you know,
And, as my love is sized, my fear is so:
Where love is great, the littlest doubts are fear;
Where little fears grow great, great love grows there.

**PLAYER KING**
Faith, I must leave thee, love, and shortly too.
My operant powers their functions leave to do.
And thou shall live in this fair world behind,
Honored, beloved; and haply one as kind
For husband shalt thou —

**PLAYER QUEEN**
O, confound the rest!
Such love must needs be treason in my breast.
In second husband let me be accurst.
None wed the second but who killed the first.

**HAMLET**
¡Esto es zumo de ajenjos!

**PLAYER QUEEN**
The instances that second marriage move
Are base respects of thrift, but none of love.
A second time I kill my husband dead
When second husband kisses me in bed.

**PLAYER KING**
The violence of either grief or joy
Their own enactures with themselves destroy.
So think thou wilt no second husband wed,
But die thy thoughts when thy first lord is dead.

**PLAYER QUEEN**

Both here and hence pursue me lasting strife,
If, once a widow, ever I be wife.

**HAMLET**

Si ella no cumpliese lo que promete …

**PLAYER KING**

'Tis deeply sworn. Sweet, leave me here awhile.
My spirits grow dull, and fain I would beguile
The tedious day with sleep.

 *He sleeps.*

**PLAYER QUEEN**

Sleep rock thy brain,
And never come mischance between us twain.

 *She exits.*

**HAMLET**

Y bien, señora, ¿qué tal le va pareciendo la pieza?

**QUEEN GERTRUDE**

The lady doth protest too much, methinks.

**HAMLET**

O, pero lo cumplirá.

**KING CLAUDIUS**

Have you heard the argument? Is there no offense in 't?

**HAMLET**

No, no, they do but jest, poison in jest. No offense i' th' world.

**KING CLAUDIUS**

What do you call the play?

**HAMLET**

"The Mousetrap." Marry, how? Tropically. This play is the image of a murder done in Vienna. Gonzago is the duke's name, his wife Baptista. You shall see anon. 'Tis a knavish piece of work, but what of that? Your Majesty and we that have free souls, it touches us not. Let the galled jade wince; our withers are unwrung.

*Enter another PLAYER as Lucianus.*

This is one Lucianus, nephew to the king.

**OPHELIA**
You are as good as a chorus, my lord.

**HAMLET**
So you mis-take your husbands. — Begin, murderer. Pox, leave thy damnable faces and begin. Come, the croaking raven doth bellow for revenge.

**LUCIANUS**
Thoughts black, hands apt, drugs fit, and time agreeing,
Confederate season, else no creature seeing,
Thou mixture rank, of midnight weeds collected,
With Hecate's ban thrice blasted, thrice infected,
Thy natural magic and dire property
On wholesome life usurp immediately.

*LUCIANUS pours the poison in the PLAYER KING's ears.*

**HAMLET**
He poisons him i' th' garden for his estate. His name's Gonzago. The story is extant and written in very choice Italian. You shall see anon how the murderer gets the love of Gonzago's wife.

*KING CLAUDIUS rises.*

**OPHELIA**
The King rises.

**HAMLET**
What, frighted with false fire?

**QUEEN GERTRUDE**
How fares my lord?

**POLONIUS**
Give o'er the play.

**KING CLAUDIUS**
Give me some light. Away!

**POLONIUS**
Lights, lights, lights!

*All but HAMLET exit.*

**HAMLET**
For if the King like not the comedy,
Why, then, belike he likes it not, perdy.
¡Un cobarde, él es!

*ROSENCRANTZ and GUILDENSTERN enter.*

**GUILDENSTERN**
Good my lord, vouchsafe me a word with you.

**ROSENCRANTZ**
The King, sir —

**HAMLET**
Ay, sir, what of him?

**GUILDENSTERN**
Is in his retirement marvelous distempered.

**ROSENCRANTZ**
The Queen your mother, in most great affliction of spirit, hath sent me to you.

**GUILDENSTERN**
Thus she says: your behavior hath struck her into amazement and admiration.

**ROSENCRANTZ**
She desires to speak with you in her closet ere you go to bed.

**HAMLET**
We shall obey, were she ten times our mother.

*POLONIUS enters.*

**POLONIUS**
My lord, the Queen would speak with you, and presently.

**HAMLET**
¿No ves allí aquella nube que parece un camello?

**POLONIUS**

By th' Mass, and 'tis like a camel indeed.

**HAMLET**

Pues ahora me parece una comadreja.

**POLONIUS**

It is backed like a weasel.

**HAMLET**

O como una ballena.

**POLONIUS**

Very like a whale.

**HAMLET**

Pues al instante iré a ver a mi madre.

(*aside*) They fool me to the top of my bent.
Déjenme solo, amigos.

> *All but HAMLET exit.*

Este es el espacio de la noche, apto a los maleficios.
Esta es la hora en que los cementerios se abren,
Y el infierno respira contagios al mundo.
Ahora podría yo beber caliente sangre,
Ahora podría ejecutar tales acciones,
Que el día se estremeciese al verlas.
Now to my mother.
Let me be cruel, not unnatural.
I will speak daggers to her, but use none.
My tongue and soul in this be hypocrites:
How in my words somever she be shent,
To give them seals never, my soul, consent.

> *He exits.*

# Scene 3

*Enter KING CLAUDIUS and POLONIUS.*

**POLONIUS**
My lord, he's going to his mother's closet.
Behind the arras I'll convey myself
To hear the process. I'll warrant she'll tax him home.
And, as you said (and wisely was it said),
'Tis meet that some more audience than a mother,
Since nature makes them partial, should o'erhear
The speech of vantage. Fare you well, my liege.
I'll call upon you ere you go to bed
And tell you what I know.

**KING CLAUDIUS**
Thanks, dear my lord.

*POLONIUS exits.*

O, my offense is rank, it smells to heaven;
It hath the primal eldest curse upon 't,
A brother's murder. Pray can I not.
My fault is past. But, O, what form of prayer
Can serve my turn? "Forgive me my foul murder?"
That cannot be, since I am still possessed
Of those effects for which I did the murder:
My crown, mine own ambition, and my queen.
May one be pardoned and retain th' offense?
In the corrupted currents of this world,
Shown to me by ways of Spain and England,
And oft 'tis seen the wicked prize itself
Buys out the law. O wretched state!
Help, angels! Make assay.
Bow, stubborn knees, and heart with strings of steel
Be soft as sinews of the newborn babe.
All may be well.

*As KING CLAUDIUS kneels, HAMLET enters.*

**HAMLET**

Esta es la ocasión propicia. Ahora está rezando, ahora lo mato …

*He draws his sword.*

Y asi se irá al cielo . . .¿Y es ésta mi venganza? No, reflexionemos. Un malvado asesina a mi padre, y yo, su hijo único, aseguro al malhechor la Gloria:
¿No es esto, en vez de castigo, premio y recompensa? ¿Quién sabe, sino Dios,
la estrecha cuenta que hubo de dar? Pero, según nuestra razón concibe, terrible ha sido su sentencia. Cuando esté ocupado en el juego, cuando blaspheme
colérico, o duerma con la embriaguez, o se adónde a los placeres incestuosos
del lecho, o cometa acciones contrarias a su salvación, hiérele entonces, caiga
precipitado al profundo, y su alma quede negra y maldita, como el infierno
que ha de recibirle.

*He sheathes his sword.*

Mi madre me espera. Malvada esta medicina, que te dilate la dolencia, pero no
evitará tu muerte.

*He exits.*

**KING CLAUDIUS** (*rising*)

My words fly up, my thoughts remain below;
Words without thoughts never to heaven go.

*He exits.*

# Scene 4

*QUEEN GERTRUDE and POLONIUS enter.*

**POLONIUS**

He will come straight. Look you lay home to him.
Tell him his pranks have been too broad to bear with,
And that your Grace hath screened and stood between
Much heat and him. I'll silence me even here.
Pray you, be round with him.

**QUEEN GERTRUDE**

I'll warrant you. Fear me not.
Withdraw, I hear him coming.

> *POLONIUS hides as HAMLET enters.*

Hamlet, thou hast thy father much offended.

**HAMLET**
Madre, muy ofendido tienes al mío.

**QUEEN GERTRUDE**
Come, come, you answer with an idle tongue.

**HAMLET**
Go, go, you question with a wicked tongue.

**QUEEN GERTRUDE**
Have you forgot me?

**HAMLET**
No, by the rood, not so.
You are the Queen, your husband's brother's wife,
And (would it were not so) you are my mother.

**QUEEN GERTRUDE**
Nay, then I'll set those to you that can speak.

**HAMLET**
Come, come, and sit you down; you shall not budge.
You go not till I set you up a glass
Where you may see the inmost part of you.

**QUEEN GERTRUDE**
What wilt thou do? Thou wilt not murder me?
Help, ho!

**POLONIUS** (*behind the arras*)
What ho! Help!

**HAMLET**
¿Qué es esto? ¿Un ratón? Murió . . .un ducado a que ya está muerto.

> *He kills him by thrusting a rapier through the arras.*

**POLONIUS** (*behind the arras*)
O, I am slain!

**QUEEN GERTRUDE**

O me, what hast thou done?

**HAMLET**

Is it the King?

**QUEEN GERTRUDE**

O, what a rash and bloody deed is this!

**HAMLET**

A bloody deed — almost as bad, good mother,
As kill a king and marry with his brother.

**QUEEN GERTRUDE**

As kill a king?

**HAMLET**

Ay, lady, it was my word.
Thou wretched, rash, intruding fool, farewell.
I took thee for thy better. Take thy fortune.
Thou find'st to be too busy is some danger.

**QUEEN GERTRUDE**

What have I done, that thou dar'st wag thy tongue
In noise so rude against me?

**HAMLET**

Such an act
That blurs the grace and blush of modesty,
Calls virtue hypocrite, takes off the rose
From the fair forehead of an innocent love
And sets a blister there, makes marriage vows
As false as dicers' oaths — Heaven's face does glow
O'er this solidity and compound mass
With heated visage, as against the doom,
Is thought-sick at the act.

**QUEEN GERTRUDE**

O, speak to me no more!
These words like daggers enter in my ears.
No more, sweet Hamlet!

**HAMLET**
A murderer and a villain!

**QUEEN GERTRUDE**
No more!

**HAMLET**
A king of shreds and patches —

*GHOST enters.*

Sálvame y vuela sobre mí con tus alas, ¡guardias celestiales! ¿Cuál sería su gracia?

**QUEEN GERTRUDE**
Alas, he's mad.

**HAMLET**
On him, on him! Look you how pale he glares.
His form and cause conjoined, preaching to stones,
Would make them capable.

*(to GHOST)* No me mires así, no sea que ese lastimoso semblante destruya mis designios crueles, no sea que al ejecutarlos equivoque los medios y en vez de sangre se derramen lágrimas.

**QUEEN GERTRUDE**
To whom do you speak this?

**HAMLET**
Do you see nothing there?

**QUEEN GERTRUDE**
Nothing at all; yet all that is I see.

**HAMLET**
Why, look you there, look how it steals away!
My father, in his habit as he lived!
Look where he goes even now out at the portal!

*GHOST exits.*

**QUEEN GERTRUDE**
This is the very coinage of your brain.

This bodiless creation ecstasy
Is very cunning in.

**HAMLET**

Ecstasy?
My pulse as yours doth temperately keep time
And makes as healthful music. It is not madness
That I have uttered. Bring me to the test,
And I the matter will reword, which madness
Would gambol from. Mother, for love of grace,
Lay not that flattering unction to your soul
That not your trespass but my madness speaks.
Good night. But go not to my uncle's bed.
Assume a virtue if you have it not.

**QUEEN GERTRUDE**

What shall I do?

**HAMLET**

Not this by no means that I bid you do:
Let the bloat king tempt you again to bed.

**QUEEN GERTRUDE**

Be thou assured, if words be made of breath
And breath of life, I have no life to breathe
What thou hast said to me.

**HAMLET**

Buenas noches, madre.

*They exit, HAMLET tugging on POLONIUS.*

# ACT 4
## Scene 1

*KING CLAUDIUS enters, still troubled and tormented by the revelation of his act. Powerful Indigenous music begins to play, startling him. The lights dim as we hear GHOST enter.*

**GHOST**

Él sabe. Todo el mundo sabe. Obtendrá lo que merece porque olvidó quiénes somos y lo que creemos. La venganza es ahora.

**KING CLAUDIUS** (*overlapping with GHOST's line*)

Hamlet? No. No. You're dead! Stop! Enough! *ENOUGH!*

*On his last "enough," the music abruptly stops, and the lights change back to normal. QUEEN GERTRUDE enters.*

**QUEEN GERTRUDE**

Ah, mine own lord, what have I seen tonight!

**KING CLAUDIUS**

What, Gertrude? How does Hamlet?

**QUEEN GERTRUDE**

Mad as the sea and wind when both contend
Which is the mightier. In his lawless fit,
Behind the arras hearing something stir,
Whips out his rapier, cries "A rat, a rat,"
And in this brainish apprehension kills
The unseen good old man.

**KING CLAUDIUS**

O heavy deed! Where is he gone?

**QUEEN GERTRUDE**

To draw apart the body he hath killed,
O'er whom his very madness, like some ore
Among a mineral of metals base,
Shows itself pure: he weeps for what is done.

**KING CLAUDIUS**

O Gertrude, come away!

The sun no sooner shall the mountains touch
But we will ship him hence; and this vile deed
We must with all our majesty and skill
Both countenance and excuse. — Ho, Guildenstern!

*HAMLET enters with ROSENCRANTZ and GUILDENSTERN.*

**GUILDENSTERN**
He's here, my lord.

**KING CLAUDIUS**
Now, Hamlet, where's Polonius?

**HAMLET**
Ha ido a cenar.

**KING CLAUDIUS**
At supper where?

**HAMLET**
No adonde coma, sino adonde es comido, entre una numerosa congregación de gusanos. El gusano es el monarca supremo de todos los comedores. Nosotros engordamos a los demás animales para engordarnos, y engordamos para el gusanillo que nos come después. El rey gordo y el mendigo flaco son dos platos diferentes, pero se sirven a una misma mesa. En esto para todo.

**KING CLAUDIUS**
What dost thou mean by this?

**HAMLET**
Nada más que manifestar cómo un rey puede pasar progresivamente a las tripas de un mendigo.

**KING CLAUDIUS**
Where is Polonius?

**HAMLET**
En el cielo. Le olerán sin duda al subir los escalones de la galería.

**KING CLAUDIUS**
Rosencrantz, seek him there.

*ROSENCRANTZ exits.*

**KING CLAUDIUS**
Hamlet, this deed, for thine especial safety
Must send thee hence with fiery quickness.
Therefore prepare thyself for England.

**HAMLET**
For England?

**KING CLAUDIUS**
Ay, Hamlet.

**HAMLET**
Bien.

*He exits.*

**KING CLAUDIUS** (*to GUILDENSTERN*)
Follow him at foot; tempt him with speed aboard.
Delay it not. I'll have him hence tonight.

*All but KING CLAUDIUS exit.*

And England, if my love thou hold'st at aught,
You will bring the present death of Hamlet.
Do it, England,
For like the hectic in my blood he rages,
And thou must cure me. Till I know 'tis done,
Howe'er my haps, my joys will ne'er begin.

# Scene 2

*LAERTES enters with a distraught OPHELIA.*

**LAERTES**
Where is my father?

**KING CLAUDIUS**
Dead.

**OPHELIA**
No!

**LAERTES**

How came he dead? I'll not be juggled with.
To hell, allegiance! Vows, to the blackest devil!
Conscience and grace, to the profoundest pit!
I dare damnation. To this point I stand,
That both the worlds I give to negligence,
Let come what comes, only I'll be revenged
Most throughly for my father.

**OPHELIA**

¡No haga! ¡O, miseria! ¡Cielos! ¡Torpeza villana! ¿Qué tipo de empresas de alta
suerte? Bueno, todos los regalos falsos, dice indignada: antes de que mirara en
tus brazos apretados, para convertirme en tu esposa, me di una palabra. Y al
abrir las puertas entró la niña que vino virgen y regresó desflorada.

**KING CLAUDIUS**

How now, what noise is that?

**LAERTES**

A document in madness: thoughts and remembrance fitted.

**KING CLAUDIUS**

Good Laertes,
If you desire to know the certainty
Of your dear father, is 't writ in your revenge
That, swoopstake, you will draw both friend and foe,
Winner and loser?

**LAERTES**

None but his enemies.

**KING CLAUDIUS**

Laertes, I must commune with your grief,
So seek Hamlet and unleash your revenge
As your father's death be it unnatural
Deserves justice.

**OPHELIA**

¡No! ¡No hagas esto!

**KING CLAUDIUS**

Silly, girl. You know not.

**OPHELIA**

Una vida no traerá otra. No tendré a nadie y estaré sola en tristeza por el resto de mi vida. ¿No soy importante para ti?

**KING CLAUDIUS**

Enough of this! Your words matter not!
Laertes, what say you?

**LAERTES**

Let this be so.
His means of death, his obscure funeral
(No trophy, sword, nor hatchment o'er his bones,
No noble rite nor formal ostentation)
Cry to be heard, as 'twere from heaven to earth,
That I must call 't in question.

**KING CLAUDIUS**

So you shall
And where th' offense is, let the great ax fall.
I pray you, go with me.

> *They exit.*

# Scene 3

> *It starts to rain and thunder. Lightning strikes as OPHELIA walks up to the river. We can hear the rushing of the waters as soft, solemn music plays. She is sobbing. As she walks up to the bank, she pulls out her makeup. In a ritualistic motion, she attempts to paint her face like a calaca one last time. She finishes, throws her remaining makeup into the river, and stands.*

**OPHELIA**

Si no me quieren en la vida, tal vez me amarán en la muerte.

> *Enter GHOST.*

**GHOST**

Es hora, mi niña.

> *He takes OPHELIA's hand.*

# ACT 5
## Scene 1

*The GRAVEDIGGER and his COMPANION enter. During the exchange GHOST leads OPHELIA in. OPHELIA lingers as GHOST exits.*

**GRAVEDIGGER**

Is she to be buried in Christian burial, when she willfully seeks her own salvation?

**COMPANION**

I tell thee she is. Therefore make her grave straight. The crowner hath sat on her and finds it Christian burial.

**GRAVEDIGGER**

How can that be, unless she drowned herself in her own defense?

**COMPANION**

Why, 'tis found so.

**GRAVEDIGGER**

It must be *se offendendo*; it cannot be else. For here lies the point: if I drown myself wittingly, it argues an act, and an act hath three branches — it is to act, to do, to perform. Argal, she drowned herself wittingly. Go thee then and fetch me some drink if you will.

*His COMPANION exits. The GRAVEDIGGER digs and sings "Historia de un Amor"[1] as HAMLET and HORATIO enter.*

> Ya no estás a mi lado, corazón,
> En el alma sólo tengo soledad
> Y si ya no puedo verte,
> Porque Dios me hizo quererte
> Para hacerme sufrir más ...

**HAMLET**

¡Qué poco siente ese hombre lo que hace, que abre una sepultura y canta!

---

1    This popular song was written by Panamanian songwriter Carlos Eleta Almarán and has been performed and recorded by many artists.

**HORATIO**

Custom hath made it in him a property of easiness.

**GRAVEDIGGER** (*singing*)

> Siempre fuiste la razón de mi existir,
> Adorarte para mí fue religión.
> Y en tus besos yo encontraba
> El calor que me brindaba,
> El amor y la pasión.

*He digs up a skull.*

**HAMLET**

Aquella calavera tendría lengua en otro tiempo, y con ella podría también cantar.

**HORATIO**

Bien puede ser.

**GRAVEDIGGER** (*singing*)

> Que me hizo comprender,
> Todo el bien, todo el mal,
> Que le dio luz a mi vida,
> Apagándola después.
> ¡Ay, qué vida tan oscura, corazón,
> Sin tu amor no viviré!

*He digs up more skulls. HAMLET is intrigued by them. OPHELIA hands him a skull.*

**HAMLET**

Y esa otra, ¿por qué no podría ser la calavera de un letrado? ¿Adónde se fueron sus equívocos y sutilezas, sus litigios, sus interpretaciones, sus embrollos? ¿Por qué sufre ahora que ese bribón grosero le golpee contra la pared con el azadón lleno de barro? ¡Y no dirá palabra acera de un hecho tan criminal! Este sería, quizás, mientras vivió un gran comprador de tierras, con sus obligaciones y reconocimientos, transacciones, seguridades mutuas, pagos, recibos . . .¡O! Ya su opulento sucesor tampoco le quedará más. Voy a hablar con este compañero —

Whose grave's this, sirrah? What man dost thou dig it for?

**GRAVEDIGGER**
For no man, sir.

**HAMLET**
What woman then?

**GRAVEDIGGER**
For none, neither.

**HAMLET**
Who is to be buried in 't?

**GRAVEDIGGER**
One that was a woman, sir, but, rest her soul, she's dead.

**HAMLET**
¡Qué absoluto es el bribón! Debemos hablar por la tarjeta, o la equivocación nos deshará — How long hast thou been grave-maker?

**GRAVEDIGGER**
Of all the days i' th' year, I came to 't that day that our last King Hamlet overcame Fortinbras.

**HAMLET**
How long is that since?

**GRAVEDIGGER**
Cannot you tell that? Every fool can tell that. It was that very day that young Hamlet was born — he that is mad and sent into England.

**HAMLET**
How came he mad?

**GRAVEDIGGER**
Very strangely, they say.

**HAMLET**
How "strangely"?

**GRAVEDIGGER**
Faith, e'en with losing his wits.

**HAMLET**
Upon what ground?

**GRAVEDIGGER**
Why, here in Denmark. I have been sexton here, man and boy, thirty years.

**HAMLET**
How long will a man lie i' th' earth ere he rot?

> *KING CLAUDIUS, QUEEN GERTRUDE, LAERTES, and a*
> *DOCTOR enter. They are holding Ophelia's "corpse." OPHELIA*
> *looks on and follows them.*

¡Aquí viene el rey, la reina, los grandes . . .¿A quién acompañan? Ocultémonos un poco y observa.

> *They hide as the GRAVEDIGGER exits.*

**LAERTES**
What ceremony else?

**HAMLET**
Laertes?

**LAERTES**
What ceremony else?

**DOCTOR**
Her obsequies have been as far enlarged
As we have warranty. Her death was doubtful,
And, but that great command o'ersways the order,
She should in ground unsanctified been lodged
Till the last trumpet.

**LAERTES**
Must there no more be done?

**DOCTOR**
No more be done.
We should profane the service of the dead
To sing a requiem and such rest to her
As to peace-parted souls.

**LAERTES**
Lay her i' th' earth,
And from her fair and unpolluted flesh
May violets spring! I tell thee, churlish priest,
A minist'ring angel shall my sister be
When thou liest howling.

**HAMLET** (*to HORATIO*)
¿Qué? ¿La hermosa Ophelia?

**QUEEN GERTRUDE** (*scattering flowers*)
I hoped thou shouldst have been my Hamlet's wife;
I thought thy bride-bed to have decked, sweet maid,
And not have strewed thy grave.

**LAERTES**
O, treble woe
Fall ten times treble on that cursèd head
Whose wicked deed thy most ingenious sense
Deprived thee of! — Hold off the earth awhile,
Till I have caught her once more in mine arms.

**HAMLET** (*advancing*)
¿Quién es el que da a sus penas idioma tan enfático? Yo soy Hamlet.

**LAERTES**
The devil take thy soul!

> *They fight as OPHELIA watches, speaking over one another.*

**HAMLET**
¡Quita esos dedos de mi cuello! ¡Quita de ahí esa mano!

**KING CLAUDIUS**
Pluck them asunder.

**QUEEN GERTRUDE**
Hamlet! Hamlet!

**ALL**
Gentlemen!

**HORATIO**

Good my lord, be quiet!

> *HAMLET and LAERTES are pulled apart. GHOST returns for OPHELIA.*

**HAMLET**

¡No! ¡Por causa tan justa lidiaré con él, hasta que cierre mis párpados la muerte!

**OPHELIA**

Ellos no entienden, ¿verdad?

**GHOST**

No entienden.

**QUEEN GERTRUDE**

O my son, what theme?

**HAMLET**

Yo he querido a Ophelia, y cuatro mil hermanos juntos no podrán con su amor exceder al mío. What wilt thou do for her?

**OPHELIA**

No hiciste nada.

**GHOST**

Vamos, mi hija.

> *They exit.*

**KING CLAUDIUS**

O, he is mad, Laertes!

**QUEEN GERTRUDE**

For love of God, forbear him.

**HAMLET**

El gato maullará y el perro quedará vencedor.

> *HAMLET breaks free from HORATIO and exits.*

**QUEEN GERTRUDE**

This is mere madness!

**KING CLAUDIUS**

  I pray thee, good Horatio, wait upon him.

  *HORATIO exits.*

  (*to LAERTES*) Strengthen your patience in our last night's speech.
  We'll put the matter to the present push. —
  Good Gertrude, set some watch over your son. —
  This grave shall have a living monument.
  An hour of quiet thereby shall we see.
  Till then in patience our proceeding be.

  *They exit.*

# Scene 2

  *HAMLET and HORATIO enter.*

**HAMLET**

  So much for this, sir. Now shall you see the other.
  You do remember all the circumstance?

**HORATIO**

  Remember it, my lord!

**HAMLET**

  For he that hath killed my king and whored my mother,
  England was his faithful tributary,
  As love between them like the palm might flourish.

**HORATIO**

  What be the issue of the business there in England?

**HAMLET**

  Por la posibilidad de una vida perfecta.
  Uno enraizado en el mal y el cancro …
  Sólo me disgusta, amigo Horatio,
  El lance ocurrido con Laertes,
  En que olvidado de mí mismo,
  No vi en mi sentimiento la imagen
  Y semejanza del suyo al igual que el mal del rey.

**HORATIO**

Peace, who comes here?

*A LORD enters.*

**LORD**

My lord, his Majesty sends to know if your pleasure hold to play with Laertes, or that you will take longer time.

**HAMLET**

In happy time.

*They exit.*

**HORATIO**

You will lose, my lord.

**HAMLET**

Si el hombre al terminar su vida ignora siempre lo que podría ocurrir después, ¿qué importa que la pierda tarde o presto? Sepa morir.

*Music plays. KING CLAUDIUS enters with drinks, followed by QUEEN GERTRUDE, LAERTES with a sword, GHOST, and OPHE-LIA. GHOST hands HAMLET a sword. As they are distracted, KING CLAUDIUS poisons one cup. The spirits perch on either side of the stage awaiting what is to come.*

**KING CLAUDIUS**

Come, Hamlet, come and take this hand from me.
You know the wager?

**HAMLET**

Muy bien, mi señor.

*They prepare to fight.*

**KING CLAUDIUS**

Set me the stoups of wine upon that table.
If Hamlet give the first or second hit
Or quit in answer of the third exchange,
Let all the battlements their ordnance fire.
The King shall drink to Hamlet's better breath,
And in the cup an union shall he throw,
Richer than that which four successive kings

In Denmark's crown have worn. Give me the cups,
And let the kettle to the trumpet speak,
The trumpet to the cannoneer without,
The cannons to the heavens, the heaven to earth,
"Now the King drinks to Hamlet." Come, begin.
And you, the judges, bear a wary eye.

**HAMLET**
Vamos, señor.

**LAERTES**
Come, my lord.

> *They fight.*

**HAMLET**
Uno.

**LAERTES**
No.

**HORATIO**
A hit, a very palpable hit!

**LAERTES**
Well, again.

**KING CLAUDIUS**
Stay, give me drink. — Hamlet, this pearl is thine.
Here's to thy health.

> *KING CLAUDIUS drinks and attempts to hand HAMLET the poisoned cup.*

Drink.

**HAMLET**
Quiero dar este bote primero. Vamos . . .otra estocada.

**LAERTES**
A touch, a touch. I do confess 't.

**KING CLAUDIUS**
Our son shall win?

**QUEEN GERTRUDE**
Here, Hamlet, take my napkin; rub thy brows.
The Queen carouses to thy fortune, Hamlet.

*She lifts the cup.*

**KING CLAUDIUS**
Gertrude, do not drink.

**QUEEN GERTRUDE** (*drinking*)
I will, my lord; I pray you pardon me.

**KING CLAUDIUS** (*aside*)
It is the poisoned cup. It is too late.

*LAERTES wounds HAMLET. HAMLET then wounds LAERTES.*

Part them. They are incensed.

**HAMLET**
¡No, ven de nuevo!

*QUEEN GERTRUDE falls.*

**HORATIO**
Look to the Queen there, ho!

**LAERTES**
How does the Queen?

*HAMLET fatally wounds him.*

**QUEEN GERTRUDE**
No, no, the drink, the drink! O, my dear Hamlet!
The drink, the drink! I am poisoned.

*She dies.*

**HAMLET**
¡O villanía! Cierren las puertas. ¡Traición! Busquen por todas partes.

*He hurts KING CLAUDIUS.*

**ALL**
Treason, treason!

**KING CLAUDIUS**

O, yet defend me, friends! I am but hurt.

**HAMLET**

¡Malvado, incestuoso asesino! Bebe esta ponzoña, acompaña a mi madre.

*He forces KING CLAUDIUS to drink the poison and he dies.*

**LAERTES**

He is justly served.
It is a poison tempered by himself.
Exchange forgiveness with me, noble Hamlet.
Mine and my father's death come not upon thee, nor thine on me.

*He dies. HORATIO rushes to him.*

**HAMLET**

El cielo te hace libre de eso. Yo te sigo.
Estoy muerto, Horatio. Reina miserable, adiós.
Dame la copa envenenada.

*OPHELIA brings him the cup. He drinks, then hears a march far off
and a shot within.*

**HORATIO**

What warlike noise is this?

*A MESSENGER enters.*

**MESSENGER**

Young Fortinbras, with conquest come from Poland,
To th' ambassadors of England gives
This warlike volley.

**HAMLET**

Yo expiro, Horatio —
La activa ponzoña sofoca mi aliento.
No puedo vivir para saber nuevas de Inglaterra.
Para mí solo queda ya — silencio eterno.

*He dies.*

**HORATIO**

Now cracks a noble heart. Good night, sweet prince,
And flights of angels sing thee to thy rest.

*March within.*

Why does the drum come hither?

*FORTINBRAS enters. He speaks with an English accent.*

**FORTINBRAS**
Where is this sight? The sight is dismal,
And our affairs from England come too late.

**HORATIO**
He never gave commandment for their death.
But since, so jump upon this bloody question,
You from the Polack wars, and you from England,
Are here arrived, give order that these bodies
High on a stage be placed to the view,
In your Christian ways unlike ours
And let me speak to th' yet unknowing world
How these things came about. So shall you hear
Of carnal, bloody, and unnatural acts,
Of accidental judgments, casual slaughters,
Of deaths put on by cunning and forced cause,
And, in this upshot, purposes mistook
Fall'n on th' inventors' heads. All this can I
Truly deliver.

*They bend over to examine the bodies. Lights change, and they freeze
in a tableau. Soft Indigenous music plays. The spirits make their way
downstage.*

**OPHELIA**
Pero ahora que los ánimos están en peligroso movimiento, no se dilate la eje-
cución un instante solo, para evitar los males que pudieran causar la maligni-
dad o el terror. This above all: to thine own self be true.

*GHOST helps HAMLET up.*

**GHOST**
¿Entiendes ahora?

*The three exit into the light. Blackout.*

**END OF PLAY**

# Introduction to Josh Inocéncio's *Ofélio*

Josh Inocéncio's one-act play *Ofélio* draws on Shakespeare's *Hamlet* to tell the story of a queer Latino undergraduate who visits a medical clinic after having been sexually assaulted by his instructor, a white male graduate student. Before any dialogue is spoken, the doctor pulls a "little purple flower" from the mouth of Ofélio, the eponymous protagonist, thus affirming his connection to Ophelia, who is often associated with the flowers she wears and distributes. *Ofélio* reflects the concerns of Inocéncio's larger body of theatrical work, which addresses the intersections of his queer and ethnic identities.[1] In a 2016 essay titled "Mixing the Culture Pot: Growing Up Gay and Austro-Mexican in Houston," Inocéncio explains the importance of reclaiming stories from the traditions of his ancestors in Austria and Mexico:

> [T]hese cultures and their myths — from countries much older than the United States — also shepherded my sexual orientation as a gay man. While living away from Houston in the swampy Florida flatlands during graduate school, I learned to embrace my sexuality as a cultural core that bound together my ethnicities.[2]

These intersections of ethnicity and sexuality are especially apparent in *Ofélio*, where Inocéncio calls attention to the sexual violence faced by Shakespeare's heroine and also addresses the racism and homophobia that threaten the lives of LGBTQIA2+ people of color.

*Ofélio* premiered at the Midtown Arts and Theater Center Houston in 2017 as part of a sexual violence prevention campaign organized by the T.R.U.T.H. Project, whose mission is to "educate and mobilize LGBTQ communities of color and their allies through social arts that promote mental, emotional and sexual

---

1 For an overview of Inocéncio's work, see Trevor Boffone, "Queering Machismo from Michoacán to Montrose: *Purple Eyes* by Josh Inocéncio," *Howl Round*, July 14, 2016, https://howlround.com/queering-machismo-michoacan-montrose.

2 Josh Inocéncio, "Mixing the Culture Pot: Growing Up Gay and Austro-Mexican in Houston," *OutSmart Magazine*, September 1, 2016, https://www.outsmartmagazine.com/2016/09/mixing-the-culture-pot-growing-up-gay-and-austro-mexican-in-houston/.

health."[3] Embracing this community-oriented ethos, Inocéncio grounds *Ofélio* firmly in the experiences of queer communities of color in Houston neighborhoods such as Montrose and the East End, thus demonstrating his commitment to a "more localized theatre that cultivates sustainable living opportunities for homegrown playwrights and other theatre artists."[4] As he notes, "There's no reason why Houston and other cities can't be theatre hubs like NYC or Chicago."[5]

In the play, Inocéncio transforms Ophelia's victimization into a story of embattled survivorship. Resisting the whiteness of both mainstream queer politics and Shakespeare performance, Inocéncio takes possession of *Hamlet* by placing it within the community-oriented frameworks of Chicanx theater and within the tradition of Chicanx healing stories. As Adrianna M. Santos contends, such stories "articulate subjectivities beyond victimization" for survivors of interpersonal violence and structural oppression, and they emphasize "collective struggle and storytelling as radical acts of cultural survival."[6] Inocéncio participates in this tradition in *Ofélio*, suggesting that queer people of color can appropriate — and speak back to — Shakespeare in the interests of personal survival and collective liberation, as he brings Mexican frameworks to bear on Ophelia's story in order to recast queer sexuality in a positive light.

In *Ofélio*, the protagonist is violated both by the white queer graduate assistant, representative of academic institutions, and by the medical establishment, which is shaped by both whiteness and heteronormativity. By aligning Hamlet and the graduate instructor, Inocéncio forces audiences to reckon with the fact that sexual violence — not rape, but Hamlet's mistreatment of Ophelia and deeply misogynist diatribes — lies at the heart of a play that is often considered the premier work of Western literature. The doctor's inability to understand Ofélio's needs as a queer Latino re-traumatizes him and intensifies his sense of violation. Inocéncio thus critiques the sexual and racial politics of *Hamlet* while also drawing on the play to imagine new modes of queer Latinx survivorship.

Like many queer and feminist revisions of Ophelia's story, Inocéncio returns to the moment of Ophelia's death and reworks Gertrude's idealized portrait of it.[7] As Gertrude explains to her fellow members of the court:

3   *The T.R.U.T.H Project.* Telling Real Unapologetic Truth Through Healing, (T.R.U.T.H.), Inc. Project. Accessed June 16, 2022, https://truthprojecthtx.org.
4   Adam Szymkowicz, "I Interview Playwrights Part 931: Joshua Inocéncio," April 30, 2017, http://aszym.blogspot.com/2017/04/i-interview-playwrights-part-931-joshua.html.
5   Szymkowicz, "I Interview Playwrights Part 931: Joshua Inocéncio."
6   Adrianna M. Santos, "Surviving the Alamo, Violence Vengeance, and Women's Solidarity in Emma Pérez's *Forgetting the Alamo, Or, Blood Memory,*" *The Journal of Latina Critical Feminism* 2, no. 1 (2019): 38.
7   For feminist and queer appropriations of Ophelia, see Kaara L. Peterson and Deanne Williams, eds., *The Afterlife of Ophelia* (New York: Palgrave MacMillan, 2012).

There is a willow grows askant the brook
That shows his hoary leaves in the glassy stream;
Therewith fantastic garlands did she make
Of crowflowers, nettles, daisies, and long purples
That liberal shepherds give a grosser name
But our cold maids do dead men's fingers call them.
There on the pendent boughs her crownet weeds
Clamb'ring to hang, an envious sliver broke,
When down her weedy trophies and herself
Fell in the weeping brook. Her clothes spread wide
And mermaid-like awhile they bore her up,
Which time she chanted snatches of old lauds
As one incapable of her own distress,
Or like a creature native and endued
Unto that element. But long it could not be
Till that her garments, heavy with their drink,
Pulled the poor wretch from her melodious lay
To muddy death. (4.4.165–82)

In Gertrude's rendering, Ophelia is elegantly framed, objectified, and removed from the patriarchal dynamics that led to her "muddy death," with her placid "mermaid-like" body surrounded by flowers. Inocéncio's *Ofélio* rejects this image of the cleansing death in which the white woman is purified and instead interrogates the sexual and racial politics influencing both Gertrude's elegy and the many artistic renderings based on it.

Rather than idealizing and restoring the purity of the assault victim, Inocéncio presents Ofélio as intensely embodied and refuses to participate in discourses of purification. Ofélio's "naked body" is dug "in deep," mired in mud that is both elemental and metaphoric, reflecting the related degradations of sexual assault and white supremacist heteropatriarchy. Inocéncio insists, however, that Ofélio (and perhaps Ophelia as well) need not be sanitized, disembodied, or whitewashed in order to have value. In contrast to dominant associations of mud with filth, Ofélio draws on Indigenous healing traditions to recast it as a kind of balm, healing him from the "brush fire" of sexual assault:

i coat myself in
mud.
i cool myself with
the earth's
soil.

my armor against the
elements so that he
doesn't
burn
me anymore.

Ofélio imagines the mud as soothing, providing him with cooling armor against the ravaging fire. Like Ophelia, Ofélio is closely associated with nature; however, he infuses *Hamlet*'s Western paradigm with a more Mesoamerican understanding of nature as salutary. Channeling the wisdom of curanderismo, Ofélio transforms himself into what Gertrude describes in her speech as "a creature native and endued / Unto that element," though, in his case, that element is mud, not water. This is not an ethereal, white Ophelia but rather one who is embodied and integrated with the earth, drawing wisdom from Indigenous roots.

The play's ending gestures toward the arduous journey Ofélio must undertake to heal from sexual assault and navigate a racist, heterosexist world. Ofélio does not imagine that he can return to a virginal purified state or that he can fully escape from trauma and oppression. Instead, he wonders:

maybe if i inhale only
water and mud
i can grow more
flowers.

maybe the other faggots won't
choke on the
pansies
as easily as me.

Ofélio's resistance is painful, but it also contains seeds of hope and the potential for rebirth. Ofélio's flower, his sense of self, is not reducible to Ophelia's early modern virginity, and he has not been irrevocably "deflowered." Although mud and water never cease to be suffocating, and may even ultimately kill Ofélio, they are nonetheless generative, potentially facilitating the growth of more flowers and permitting beautiful queer lives to flourish.

— KATHERINE GILLEN, ADRIANNA M. SANTOS,
AND KATHRYN VOMERO SANTOS

# Ofélio

Josh Inocéncio

SETTING: A clinic in Houston, and an apartment near campus; 2010s. The set should easily transform from one location to the other, almost in a dreamlike way.

CHARACTERS

| | |
|---|---|
| **OFÉLIO** | An undergraduate student at a local university. Latino, male, queer. |
| **DOCTOR** | Works at Planned Parenthood, mostly examines women. Female, any race or ethnicity. |
| **GRAD STUDENT** | A Ph.D. student at the same local university. White, male, queer. |

*OFÉLIO walks alone on a sidewalk to a clinic, his mouth tightly shut.*
*OFÉLIO stops walking. He stands there nearly motionless as the*
*DOCTOR approaches him. He opens his mouth, and she pulls*
*out a little purple flower. He drops everything he's carrying. As*
*OFÉLIO begins his poetic monologue, the DOCTOR stands, fac-*
*ing another direction, and asks him about his medical history.*

**OFÉLIO**
what can grow in
the wake
of his
brush
fire?

        **DOCTOR**
        If you could fill out this form here . . .

**OFÉLIO**
i coat myself in
mud.
i cool myself with
the earth's
soil.

        **DOCTOR**
        Who's your insurance provider?

**OFÉLIO**
my armor against the
elements so that he
doesn't
burn
me anymore.

        **DOCTOR**
        Do you have a regular physician?

**OFÉLIO**
under the force of his
chest he
pressed me deeper into this
mud.

not by choice but by
reality.

>            DOCTOR
>            When's the last time you visited a clinic?

OFÉLIO

into my own little
cave under the
ground.

>            DOCTOR
>            Are you up to date on all your vaccines?

OFÉLIO

he dug my
naked body in
deep.

>            DOCTOR
>            Are you on any medications currently?

OFÉLIO

i heave
caked on the ground after
he finishes and walks
away.

>            DOCTOR
>            Are you allergic to any medications that you know of?

OFÉLIO

left in pieces
scattered
all over his floor ready
to give a final
exhale.

>            DOCTOR
>            Are you sexually active?

**OFÉLIO**
and i wonder if
a purple pansy can
ever grow
again?

     **DOCTOR**
     Where are you coming from today?

    *OFÉLIO begins to acknowledge the DOCTOR.*

**OFÉLIO**
I asked for a male doctor.

**DOCTOR**
Well, the other doctor is on vacation. I'd say you could wait until next week, but you've described this appointment as urgent.

    *Beat.*

**DOCTOR**
Where are you coming from today?

**OFÉLIO**
Montrose.

**DOCTOR**
Do you live there?

**OFÉLIO**
No, no. Was in the neighborhood. I'm a student. I live in the East End with a couple roommates.

**DOCTOR**
What brings you here today?

    *Beat.*

**DOCTOR**
STI testing? HPV vaccine? Education on PrEP?

**OFÉLIO** (*on edge*)
Why do you assume I'm gay? That I need the little blue pill?

**DOCTOR**

I don't, sir. But you're not giving me a lot of information. And I assume you aren't here for an abortion or a breast cancer screening.

**OFÉLIO**

Right.

> *Beat.*

**OFÉLIO**

I had sex last night. For the first time.

**DOCTOR**

With a man or woman?

**OFÉLIO**

Another guy. From the university.

**DOCTOR**

Did you use protection?

**OFÉLIO**

. . . No.

**DOCTOR**

Well, I'm sure you've had this lecture before, but I must advise you, even if you and your sexual partner have nev —

**OFÉLIO**

He isn't my partner.

**DOCTOR**

Well. More important, then, for you to use condoms or consider getting on PrEP. And even if you don't see this particular individual again, we should get you tested.

**OFÉLIO**

Okay.

**DOCTOR**

Sexual health is health. And there's no shame in that.

**OFÉLIO**

There was a little blood.

**DOCTOR**

That's perfectly normal if it was your first time, as long as it wasn't excessive —

**OFÉLIO**

There was blood. Still. Dried into my boxers this morning. Blood on the toilet paper, on my fingers.

*Beat.*

I didn't want to do it. I asked him to stop. Because it was painful.

*Beat.*

**DOCTOR**

Did you report this? To the campus police?

**OFÉLIO**

No. No. No. I can't do that. He's a friend.

**DOCTOR**

Look, he's not really a friend if he —

**OFÉLIO**

I feel nothing. But a searing pain here (*indicating his lower abdomen*).

**DOCTOR** (*gentle, but insistent*)

Let's get you checked out, then. We'll schedule an STI testing — but an HIV infection wouldn't show up for at least thirty days. But I can give you an examination. Just to make sure everything's okay.

> *Mechanically, OFÉLIO unbuttons his jeans as the DOCTOR instructs and lets them fall to his ankles, standing there in his boxers. He bends over but not without a degree of resistance and begins reliving the night before. The DOCTOR stands behind him and puts on a rubber glove. She proceeds to examine him. She dissolves and the GRAD STUDENT appears.*

**GRAD STUDENT**

You just hit it too hard tonight. It's the end of the semester, exams are finished. You can sleep it off here. I'll even take you to breakfast in the morning.

**OFÉLIO**

Ay! I didn't start drinking until a few months ago. Still a bit of a lightweight.

**GRAD STUDENT**

It shows. But no shame in that. You're a good boy. Focused on your studies. But believe me, a few glasses of wine goes a long way when you're a graduate student like me.

**OFÉLIO**

Oh yeah?

**GRAD STUDENT**

Sure. And once you're a seasoned drinker, you won't jump on coffee tables and tear your shirt off, shouting about queer takeovers and utopias!

> *They laugh.*

**OFÉLIO**

Thanks for rescuing me. I don't think I said that. Things could've gone much worse.

**GRAD STUDENT**

It was getting late. You needed a safe couch.

**OFÉLIO**

I still can't believe my roommate just left with that random math major. Especially after we agreed on a "no boys" policy tonight! But I can't blame her. He was cute.

**GRAD STUDENT**

It's the end of the semester! She needed to celebrate too, I bet. So about that no guys rule. She broke it — are you still hanging on?

> *OFÉLIO smirks. They kiss. They remove each other's shirts, but then the GRAD STUDENT fondles OFÉLIO's crotch.*

**OFÉLIO**

I, uh, I haven't exactly done anything before. I'm a . . . a . . . virgin, you know.

**GRAD STUDENT** (*delighted*)

Oh, Ofélio. There's no such thing as virginity. Didn't you pay any attention when you took my course? Get your head out of the patriarchal past.

**OFÉLIO**

I don't know if I'm ready yet! Look, I'm just an intellectual queer boy. All the theory, none of the experience.

**GRAD STUDENT**

You don't have, like, some Southern Baptist — or Catholic — hang-up do you?

**OFÉLIO**

No, no, no, no! It's definitely not that. I just, uh, I don't know . . . I don't know what my hang-ups are or why it's taken me so long. I've definitely wanted to — and, and it's not like guys here aren't interested —

**GRAD STUDENT**

I'll go slow, Ofélio. I don't want to hurt you. I just want to take you to a place where we can escape the rules, where we can live up to that queer future you're always talking about. A place where simple sex acts are revolutionary.

> *The GRAD STUDENT disappears, and the DOCTOR stands behind OFÉLIO again.*

**OFÉLIO**

undignified
her cold plastic hand in
me.

for sanitation i
know
but only then
did i feel
dirty.

don't breathe my
lungs.
fill yourself with
mud and
water.

maybe if i inhale only
water and mud
i can grow more
flowers.

maybe the other faggots won't
choke on the
pansies.
as easily as me.

**THE END**

# Introduction to Olga Sanchez Saltveit's *¡O Romeo!*

Olga Sanchez Saltveit conceived and devised *¡O Romeo!* in 2014 for the annual Día de los Muertos festival at the Milagro Theatre, the premier Latinx theater company in Portland, Oregon. The play, co-created with the Milagro cast, takes place in 1616 as Shakespeare is on his deathbed. While the historical Shakespeare died in April, the death of Sanchez Saltveit's Shakespeare aligns with celebrations of Día de los Muertos, opening the possibility for understanding the concepts of life and death as well as the legacies of Shakespeare's works through Indigenous frameworks. *¡O Romeo!* takes a humorous approach to such serious topics, using satire and absurdity to make a trenchant anticolonial critique while also reflexively commenting on the politics of Shakespeare's afterlives.

The play's central conceit is that Shakespeare is writing what he hopes will be his most important work: a play about Mexico. His source is a series of letters that his housekeeper Rifke—a Jewish woman from Spain who fled the Inquisition—has received from her brother, a missionary in the "Nuevo Mundo" (1.1). Shakespeare's in-process play relates the love story of Don Armando, a Spanish conquistador, and Xochiquetzal, a woman from Tenochtitlán, the ancient capital upon which Mexico City was built. In *¡O Romeo!*, Shakespeare's creative process reflects his curiosity about Mexica (commonly known as Aztec) culture, but it also reveals his limited cultural awareness and the appropriative impulses he shares with many other European writers. Shakespeare is eager for new knowledge from the Americas. He enthusiastically learns Spanish from Rifke and presses her for information about Mexica culture. He marvels at the "mystical potion" xocalatl, or chocolate, and he takes Rifke's advice to incorporate a hummingbird, which was "very important para los Aztecas" into his play, leading to a line about a "huitzilin that sips the flower's dew" (1.1). However, Shakespeare naïvely believes that his art can transform colonization into a benign process of cultural exchange, and he hopes to write a story in which Xochiquetzal "[i]ntegrat[es] her life and her faith with" those of Don Armando (1.1). Rifke reminds him that this is not the reality of colonization. "Los conquistadores no integran, imponen," she insists (1.1). Conquistadors do not integrate, they impose.

*¡O Romeo!* emphasizes the persistent power of Mexica spirituality, even in Shakespeare's colonial imagining of Mexico. Xochiquetzal, who is named after the goddess of beauty, sexual love, and fertility, has a transformative effect on Don Armando and his worldview. Don Armando is further swayed by the power of Coatlicue, "creation's fire, / La madre of all gods and stars and moon" (2.2). When Don Armando experiences her wrath in response to his attempts to build a cathedral on the grounds of her temple, he agrees not to impede the sacrificial rituals that occur at the sacred site, including the sacrifice of Xochiquetzal. Connecting her death to the rituals of Día de los Muertos, Xochiquetzal explains to Don Armando, "Año tras año, yo visitaré / A mi ofrenda, decorada con / Flores de cempasúchitl" (2.2). Following her death, Don Armando does create an altar to her, thus suggesting that his faith has been expanded to incorporate hers and that Mexica beliefs endure despite colonization.

The tradition of Día de los Muertos, moreover, gives Shakespeare the opportunity to reconcile with his deceased son Hamnet and to confront his own mortality. Rifke creates an altar that she hopes will help Shakespeare connect to Hamnet. She succeeds in calling spirits to the altar, not only of Hamnet but also of Shakespeare's characters, who are, as Titania insists, "sus hijos, born of his spirit" as well (1.2). Shakespeare initially confuses his own son with Romeo, giving the play its title and further compounding Hamnet's sense that his father loved his work more than he loved his children. Shakespeare is remorseful, regretting that he "was in London, at the theatre, when [his] son died" and questioning whether his "rolls of ink-stained pages" were worth the time he spent away from his family (1.5). Once the spirits perform Shakespeare's Mexican play, Shakespeare recognizes Hamnet as his son and as a talented poet, and he asks him for forgiveness. Shortly thereafter, Shakespeare realizes that it is his birthday, which modern audiences also recognize as his death-day, and the spirits mark these milestones with a round of "Las Mañanitas," welcoming Shakespeare not only to the day of his birth but to a new morning in the afterlife. Ultimately, as in the story of Xochiquetzal and Don Armando, Mexica spirituality prevails, its sustaining power evident in the celebration of Día de los Muertos that *¡O Romeo!* commemorates.

*¡O Romeo!* won a Drammy Award for Outstanding Achievement in Devised Work in 2015, and Sanchez Saltveit's commitment to community work is clear in her approach to the devising process in which "rehearsals began without a script" and in which she gave a great deal of control to the actors in developing the play.[1]

---

1    Olga Sanchez Saltveit, "*¡O Romeo!* Shakespeare on the Altar of Día de los Muertos," in *Shakespeare and Latinidad*, eds. Trevor Boffone and Carla Della Gatta (Edinburgh: Edinburgh University Press, 2021), 39, https://doi.org/10.1515/9781474488501-005.

As with many Chicanx plays that draw on the teatro traditions of caricature and satire, *¡O Romeo!* uses humor to approach political issues. In particular, the co-created play parodies Shakespeare and his outsized stature in order to emphasize resistance to colonial structures and oppression.[2] The improvisational ethos of teatro is also evident in the performance of Shakespeare's Mexican play by the spirits of his characters, who see the play as an opportunity to advance their own agendas. The villains believe that they have been defamed in Shakespeare's plays and, like Hamnet, have been "neglected, disregarded, abandoned" (1.4), and they hope that a bad enactment of Shakespeare's Mexican play will cause him to burn his corpus. The "good" characters, on the other hand, hope that the performance will help Shakespeare see the value of his work.

*¡O Romeo!* thus uses Shakespeare's theatrical experiment to comment on connections between colonization and the politics of artistic representation and appropriation. As Sanchez Saltveit remarks, her play "used Shakespeare's penchant for writing from extant sources to illustrate the history of colonialisation that cultivated modern-day Día de Muertos traditions."[3] By highlighting Shakespeare's own appropriative impulses and giving voice to Mexica deities, Sanchez Saltveit and her collaborators remind us that Shakespeare's plays are not his exclusive property, as they were created collectively and appropriated from several sources, including—as in the case of *The Tempest*—from the trauma of Indigenous people. The plays, it follows, constitute material that can be recuperated by Indigenous playwrights and other playwrights of color. Although Sanchez Saltveit implicates Shakespeare in the appropriative "colonising forces that sought (and seek) to eradicate Indigenous traditions," her play also reverses expected colonial power dynamics.[4] It is not the Mexica who need to be civilized or educated by Shakespeare but rather Shakespeare who needs Mexican spirituality and his Mexican play in order to heal.

The politics of language play a role in this rebalancing of power. Sanchez Saltveit's Shakespeare fumbles through his newly acquired Spanish, and the play contains not only dialogue in Spanish and Nahuatl but also Shakespearean lines translated into other languages, such as Russian, French, and Korean, thus prefiguring Shakespeare's global reach and highlighting the work of translators

---

2  On Chicanx uses of humor, see Carl Gutiérrez-Jones, "Humor, Literacy, and Trauma in Chicano Culture," *Comparative Literature Studies* 40, no. 2 (2003): 112–26, https://doi.org/10.1353/cls.2003.0014.

3  Sanchez Saltveit, "*¡O Romeo!*," 38.

4  Sanchez Saltveit, "*¡O Romeo!*," 43.

and adaptors in making Shakespeare communal property.[5] By sprinkling translations throughout the play, Sanchez Saltveit shows how, 450 years after his birth, Shakespeare's writing has reached a much broader audience than the one for which it was originally intended. *¡O Romeo!* thus invites future students and scholars to examine what Shakespearean translations and adaptations can reveal about imperialism and colonialism throughout history.

The play also invites audiences to see Shakespeare — a figure who has been made larger than life in the cultural imagination — as a human who is subject to the same forces of death as everyone else. As Sanchez Saltveit writes of her play, "the revered Bard is levelled . . . by mortality, remorse and cultural ineptitude."[6] Removed from the rarified space of the canon, Shakespeare is free to work with artistic collaborators in an egalitarian, rather than oppressive, way. When Shakespeare arises from the afterlife to visit his own altar, he gives Rifke a pen and ink so that she can finish his masterpiece, symbolically handing off his craft to others, including those from different cultural, religious, and linguistic backgrounds. *¡O Romeo!* ultimately suggests that artists around the world will continuously transform Shakespeare through their appropriations, achieving a more truly diverse, intercultural vision than the historical Shakespeare himself was able to achieve.

— KATHERINE GILLEN, ADRIANNA M. SANTOS,
AND KATHRYN VOMERO SANTOS

---

5   In keeping with the collaborative spirit of the production, some lines were directly translated by cast members. The Korean translations, for example, were done by Heath Hyun Houghton, the actor who played Hamlet.
6   Sanchez Saltveit, "*¡O Romeo!*," 38.

# ¡O Romeo!

## Olga Sanchez Saltveit

Portions of the text by William Shakespeare
Conceived and penned by Olga Sanchez Saltveit
Devised with the Milagro Theatre cast

SETTING: In Shakespeare's bed chambers. 1616.

## CHARACTERS

| | |
|---|---|
| **SHAKESPEARE** | An English playwright, on his deathbed. |
| **RIFKE** | Shakespeare's Spanish housekeeper. |
| **HAMLET** | Spirit of the Danish prince, title character of *Hamlet*. |
| **OPHELIA** | Spirit of Hamlet's tragic love interest. |
| **RICHARD III** | Spirit of King of England, from Shakespeare's *Richard III*. |
| **LADY M** | Spirit of Lady Macbeth, wife of the title character of *Macbeth*. |
| **POLONIUS** | Spirit of Ophelia's father, courtier. |
| **YORICK** | Spirit of a court jester whose skull Hamlet uses to contemplate the meaning of life. |
| **TITANIA** | Spirit of the Queen of the faeries in *A Midsummer Night's Dream*. |
| **HAMNET** | Spirit of Shakespeare's son. |

# Prologue

**ALL**

El mundo es un gran teatro,
Y los hombres y mujeres son actores.
El mundo es un gran teatro,
Y los hombres y mujeres son actores.
All the world's a stage,
And all the men and women merely players. [1]

**TITANIA**

Amigos, bienvenidos a nuestro cuento,
A trifle of a work about reunion.
One household, ubicada en Inglaterra,
Set within this humble wooden M. [2]
Un escritor famoso, William Shakespeare
Himself, lives here but near the gates of death.
He is not well, él tiene un catarro.
We'll catch his spirit at his dying breath.
El mundo es un gran teatro . . .

**ALL**

Y los hombres y mujeres son actores.
El mundo es un gran teatro . . .

---

1   *As You Like It*, 2.7.139
2   This is a reference to the Milagro Theatre, for which this play was devised.

# ACT 1
## Scene 1

**SHAKESPEARE**

*The Tragical Story of Love and Demise of Xochiquetzal of Tenochtitlán and Don Armando, an Aztec Maiden and the Conquistador who Conquered her Heart* . . . no. This is my most important work — the title must reflect its purpose. *The Mystical Story of Love and Reunion of Xochiquetzal, the Aztec Maiden, and the Spanish Conquistador, Don Armando.*

*He coughs, then recovers.*

Act Two, Scene One:

Xochiquetzal, Armando's dearest love,
Conqueror of his heart yet faith pulls strong

Sounds like the rubbish of Cervantes! Rifke! Something warm to drink! Rifke!

**RIFKE**

Ah, I'm so glad to see you are out of the bed! I was just putting the final touches on your birthday pudding. I'm making it with three milks.

**SHAKESPEARE**

Three milks?

**RIFKE**

Tres leches, sí. We are celebrating your birthday today! ¿Qué está pasando?

**SHAKESPEARE**

He has professed his love to her. Listen:

First light of dawn that broke as my heart soared,
A morning bird that sips the flower's dew

**RIFKE**

¡Qué lindo! But perhaps . . .

**SHAKESPEARE**

¿Qué?

**RIFKE**

Bueno, si recuerdo bien, let me look, my brother wrote that the hummingbird is very important para los Aztecas . . .

*She looks through her notebook.*

**SHAKESPEARE**

Ah! So . . .

A hummingbird that sips the flower's dew

**RIFKE**

Dónde está . . . la palabra para colibrí . . .

**SHAKESPEARE**

Colibrí?

**RIFKE**

Hummingbird, in Spanish. The word in Nahuatl . . .

**SHAKESPEARE**

Nahuatl . . . the language of the Aztecs

**RIFKE**

Sí . . . ¡aquí está! La palabra es . . . huitzilin!

**SHAKESPEARE**

A huitzilin that sips the flower's dew

**RIFKE**

Yes! This shows that he is learning her language! ¡Eso es amor!

**SHAKESPEARE**

Ah, not everyone learns a language because they are in love, Rifke! A mi simplemente me encantan los . . . languages.

**RIFKE**

Idiomas, maestro. Sí, yo sé.

**SHAKESPEARE**

Los idiomas. Y Don Armando, le enseña el español a Xochiquetzal, as you have taught me, in his attempt to convert her. Integrating her life and her faith with his!

**RIFKE**

Los conquistadores no integran, imponen. ¿No has oído lo que escribe mi hermano?

*She goes about picking up the pages he has written on, to hang them to dry.*

**SHAKESPEARE**

This is fiction, Rifke. This is love.

**RIFKE**

But you place the story in the New World! ¡Todo es diferente allá!

**SHAKESPEARE**

So true! The people! Adoran a los muertos, and they believe the spirits are close at hand, ready to mingle at any moment with the living. And no matter how Spain tries, nunca conquistará la fe de los indígenas.

**RIFKE**

De eso mismo escribió mi hermano, como los indígenas están cambiando las tradiciones religiosas de los conquistadores en este Nuevo Mundo.

**SHAKESPEARE**

The New World. It sounds promising, does it not? Rifke, I know I am dying, but I will finish this work!

**RIFKE**

Sí, maestro.

**SHAKESPEARE**

You must thank your brother for me. His letters are invaluable sources of information.

**RIFKE**

Ay, mi hermano, Tubal. I miss him terribly. I can't believe it's been twenty-two years since we left Spain.

*SHAKESPEARE coughs.*

Oh! My brother promised to send a gift of crushèd beans.

**SHAKESPEARE**

Crushed beans?

**RIFKE**

Crushed beans, sí. Me escribió que son una maravilla, le da buena salud, energía, y más. With them a beverage is prepared that cures all ills!

**SHAKESPEARE**

¿Cómo se llama?

**RIFKE**

Se llama . . . xocolatl.

**SHAKESPEARE**

Xocolatl. Ah, an idea! Xochiquetzal brings a cup of this mystical potion to the Conquistador Don Armando while he is overseeing the construction of a magnificent cathedral, and its healing properties melt his heart.

**RIFKE**

¿No dijiste que Don Armando es un guerrero?

**SHAKESPEARE**

Sí. ¡Es un conquistador!

**RIFKE**

According to my brother, the ones who oversee the construction are Franciscan priests.

**SHAKESPEARE**

Fine. We change it. Dare I make him, instead of a soldier, a priest?

**RIFKE & SHAKESPEARE**

Forbidden love!

**RIFKE**

Those are your best stories!

**SHAKESPEARE**

What human heart has not felt the pangs of forbidden love?

**RIFKE**

¡Romeo y Julieta!

**SHAKESPEARE**

Altars!

**RIFKE**

¿Maestro?

**SHAKESPEARE**

You mentioned Romeo and Juliet, I thought of weddings, then remembered altars . . .

**RIFKE**

¡Ay, qué mente!

**SHAKESPEARE**

Your brother wrote of altars for the dead?

**RIFKE**

Oh yes. Tienen un sistema en el cual ellos les dan regalos que llaman a los espíritus . . .

**SHAKESPEARE**

In English, please.

**RIFKE**

Sí maestro. They honor their dead with gifts that summon the spirits close. Es una ofrenda. Candles, comida, things they love . . . When you place them on the altar, the spirits return!

**SHAKESPEARE**

. . . llaman a los espíritus . . .

**RIFKE**

And they have a flower . . .

  *TITANIA and OPHELIA appear.*

**TITANIA**

Cempasúchitl.

**RIFKE & SHAKESPEARE**

Cempasúchitl.

**OPHELIA**

For remembrance!

**SHAKESPEARE**

Rifke, is there a spirit you would remember?

**RIFKE**

¿Un espíritu que desearía ver otra vez?

**SHAKESPEARE**

Sí.

**RIFKE**

Ay maestro, sería el niño.

**SHAKESPEARE**

The boy?

**RIFKE**

I have lived long, y he perdido muchos, but I would love to see your son, Hamnet. Ay, mi Neto! Qué sonrisa. His face, when I would sing to him, "A la nanita nana, nanita ella, nanita ella." He died so young. Grief fills up the room of my absent child.[3]

**SHAKESPEARE**

Please let us return to the letter from your brother that describes the altars.

**RIFKE**

Me gustaría verlo hecho todo un joven. He would be seventeen years of age now. A married man! Tan buen mozo.

**SHAKESPEARE**

What is mozo?

**RIFKE**

It means handsome young man. Oh, so handsome!

**SHAKESPEARE**

Enough! Tell me more of this ritual. Does it not include symbols of the four elements?

**RIFKE**

Fire, water . . . do you wish to build an altar?

**SHAKESPEARE**

I wish to write a play.

---

3  *King John*, 3.4.93

**RIFKE**

I think it is very easy to honor his memory.

*She pulls out the letter.*

Necesitamos algo suyo, una vela, ah . . .

*She pulls out a jacket.*

Wouldn't it be wonderful if this would bring him close to us? Maestro . . .

**SHAKESPEARE**

Where have you been hiding that?

**RIFKE**

No lo he escondido. I took it from him before he fell ill, to mend it. Oh, his poor little body.

**SHAKESPEARE**

Prithee, peace, speak no more of him.

**RIFKE**

Perdón.

*She places the jacket on the chest.*

Tell me more of the lovers in the New World.

**SHAKESPEARE**

In Act Five, there is a battle giving us the opportunity for swordplay with the Grand Inquisitor. Don Armando is killed and Xochiquetzal builds an altar hoping he will return!

**RIFKE**

Or, better, Xochiquetzal is killed and Don Armando builds an altar to her!

**SHAKESPEARE**

Denying his faith?

**RIFKE**

Expanding his faith! The ceremony grows to include both religions, Catholic and Aztec. He does it out of love!

**SHAKESPEARE**

Love transcends faith.

**RIFKE**

Love conquers death.

**SHAKESPEARE** (*writing*)

. . . love conquers death . . .

>*He coughs.*

**RIFKE**

I'll bring you your drink.

>*She leaves. SHAKESPEARE brings the candle over to the jacket, singing a little bit . . .*

**SHAKESPEARE**

Nana nanita nana . . .

>*He stops and then goes back to his writing table.*

# Scene 2

>*Sounds of a conch shell, rattles, and drums reflecting traditional Aztec music transform the room. HAMNET enters, visits the nascent altar, and examines the clothing placed there by RIFKE.*

**HAMNET**

A gift from my father, mended by Rifke. They told me we would meet again.

**SHAKESPEARE**

. . . meet again . . .

**HAMNET**

My father . . .

**SHAKESPEARE**

La muerte no existe para mí . . .

**HAMNET**

Hello sir. Sir William Shakespeare. Dost thou not hear my voice? Dost thou not know thy son?

**SHAKESPEARE**

Rifke, are there guests? Who is talking there?

**HAMNET**

The time is nigh, father. Dost thou hear music? It is the sounds of the world you have yet to know. The world I can finally share with you.

**SHAKESPEARE**

Rifke! ¿Quién está allí?

**HAMNET**

He does not believe.

> *The music stops.*

Titania!

> *She appears.*

He does not see me!

**TITANIA**

Oh, young lord, inténtelo otra vez.

> *HAMNET touches SHAKESPEARE's shoulder. SHAKESPEARE recoils.*

**SHAKESPEARE**

Halt!

**HAMNET**

I've waited so many years for him, Titania.

**TITANIA**

And he is very close. Shall I place a spell on him?

**HAMNET**

No. He rarely saw me in life . . . perhaps he will not see me in death.

**TITANIA**

Oh, young master Hamnet.

**HAMNET**
Don't call me that. He cared more for the revision, Ham-let, than he ever cared for me. Tantas horas que pasó con esa obra. I was a sickly child and then I died. Not an interesting story, I guess.

**TITANIA**
Hamnet.

**HAMNET**
My name is Neto.

**TITANIA**
Neto?

**HAMNET**
That was Rifke's name for me.

**SHAKESPEARE**
Why is it so warm in this chamber?

**RIFKE** (*returning with his tea*)
It is the change of seasons, master. Perhaps I added too much wood to the fire.

**HAMNET**
Rifke.

**RIFKE** (*not seeing HAMNET, to SHAKESPEARE*)
Is it good?

**SHAKESPEARE**
Too warm.

   *TITANIA summons YORICK.*

**YORICK**
What is wrong, young master? Need you some good cheer?

**HAMNET**
Yorick, fellow of infinite jest.[4] Yes, laughter.

---

4  *Hamlet*, 5.1.166–67

**YORICK**

¡Bueno! You know me well. There once was a man from Gloucester, who visited food carts on Foster, he far —

**TITANIA**

Yorick!

**YORICK**

Strings! Oh, how long it has been! I have a reasonably good ear for music. I will play!

> *He plays and sings "Aires Vascos."*

> > Viva la gente del pueblo (¡Que viva!)
> > Viva la gente torera (¡Olé!)
> > Viva todo aquel que diga (¡La uva!)
> > Salga el sol por donde quiere . . .

**OPHELIA**

Hamlet? Is Hamlet there with you? He loves music!

**TITANIA**

Only master Hamnet is here.

**HAMNET**

My name is not Hamnet anymore, it's Neto!

**OPHELIA**

My lord! My lord! I have been so affrighted![5]

**YORICK**

Ophelia's madness doth indeed outdo my own.

**SHAKESPEARE**

Rifke! What is brewed in this drink?

**RIFKE**

Hibiscus. Jamaica del Nuevo Mundo.

> *YORICK tickles her. She exits.*

---

5   *Hamlet*, 2.1.72

**SHAKESPEARE**
No me siento bien.

**OPHELIA**
What ails you, my lord?

**TITANIA**
He's so close to death, and Neto . . .

**OPHELIA**
Neto?

**TITANIA**
Neto is here to welcome him. Pero el maestro no lo ve.

**OPHELIA**
There's rosemary, que es bueno para la memoria. Pray you, love, remember. And there is pansies, que son para los pensamientos. There's fennel for you, and columbines. Esta es una margarita.[6]

**SHAKESPEARE**
¿Dónde están mis anteojos? They were right here . . .

**POLONIUS**
Ophelia, you do not understand yourself so clearly
As it behooves my daughter and your honor.[7]

**TITANIA**
Be kind and courteous to this gentleman! Brincad a su paso, ante él dad vueltas.[8]

**OPHELIA**
I'm trying to be of service to young Hamnet!

**HAMNET**
Neto!

**OPHELIA**
Neto.

---

6   *Hamlet*, 4.2.174–77
7   *Hamlet*, 1.3.95–6
8   *A Midsummer Night's Dream*, 3.1.146–47

**SHAKESPEARE**

I am dizzied.

**POLONIUS**

Ophelia, we are all here to help our dear young Hamnet, but you must return Master Shakespeare his due.

**OPHELIA** (*handing SHAKESPEARE's glasses to him*)

Sus anteojos.

**SHAKESPEARE**

Angels and ministers of grace defend me![9] Ophelia?

**OPHELIA**

He sees me! ¡Me ve! That's a start!

**SHAKESPEARE**

And . . . Polonius?

> *RIFKE returns.*

**RIFKE**

¿Maestro?

**POLONIUS**

Ever at your service, my lord.

**SHAKESPEARE**

How are you here? You are dead!

**RIFKE**

¡Maestro! ¡Yo estoy viva! ¡Una mujer muy viva!

**POLONIUS**

I am dead, my lord, killed at the hand of Prince Hamlet.

**SHAKESPEARE & OPHELIA**

Hamlet?

**POLONIUS**

He hovers ever near my daughter, sir.

---

9   *Hamlet*, 1.4.39

**TITANIA**
But says not a word to her.

**SHAKESPEARE**
Titania?

**HAMLET**
What dost thou study, 아버지 (*ah-pá-jee*)?

**SHAKESPEARE**
Words, words, words.[10] Texts of the New World.

**YORICK**
Seek you adventure? Travels abroad? To go we know not where?

**POLONIUS**
Alas, Yorick, not so sudden your boundless spirit! You will fright our master Shakespeare.

**OPHELIA**
Father, must you counsel everyone you meet?

**SHAKESPEARE**
Yorick!?

**RIFKE**
Maestro, ¿a quién le hablas?

**SHAKESPEARE**
You don't see them?

**RIFKE**
No señor.

**SHAKESPEARE**
Estoy loco.

**RIFKE**
Ya regreso.

*She exits to fetch a cold washcloth for his forehead.*

---

10  *Hamlet*, 2.2.189

**LADY M**
Mad? Yes, welcome madness, father.

**SHAKESPEARE**
What thing of darkness[11] lurks behind me? A shadow speaks. A monster . . . ?

**LADY M**
¡Monstruo! I would be queen! Richard, Richard! He calls us monsters!

**RICHARD III**
Esto se puede hacer más fácil . . . Put out the light![12]

**TITANIA**
¡No!

**LADY M**
Oh you and your spells vex me so, Titania!

**RICHARD III**
He deserves no mercy, nunca me dio su misericordia.

**LADY M**
He despises us.

**TITANIA**
Somos sus hijos, born of his spirit, su imaginación nos creó.

**HAMNET**
I was born of his flesh.

**SHAKESPEARE**
I have only two children. Daughters.

**HAMNET**
Father.

**SHAKESPEARE**
O! Romeo!

**SPIRITS**
Romeo?!

---

11  *The Tempest*, 5.1.278–79
12  *Othello*, 5.2.7

**OPHELIA**
He's not Romeo, he's . . .

*HAMNET stops her.*

**HAMNET**
You see me? I will be as you see me, father. For now.

**SHAKESPEARE**
Rifke! Rifke!

**RIFKE** (*returning*)
Master William!

**SHAKESPEARE**
I see spirits, figments . . . the characters of my plays: Romeo, Ophelia, Polonius, Hamlet, Titania, Yorick, Richard the Third, Lady Macbeth!

**RIFKE**
There are spiders about, master, muchas arañas!

**LADY M**
Spiders, figments, again!

**POLONIUS**
We've come on him too suddenly, too abruptly.

**OPHELIA**
I know what 'tis to bear a broken heart.

**HAMLET**
His heart's not broken, but he is confused.

**YORICK**
Confusion is a threshold to the truth.

**TITANIA**
He needs a tea of hollyhocks and thyme.

**LADY M**
His madness is a product of his guilt.

**RICHARD III**
He knows he served us wrong, and he regrets.

**HAMNET**

Father is a frail and dying man!

**SHAKESPEARE**

Estoy loco. ¡Ayúdame, Rifke! I see dead people.

**RIFKE**

No, no, no, Master William. Tal vez nos cayó un poco de peyote en este té. Deberías dormir, maestro.

**SHAKESPEARE**

Sleep? How can I sleep with these visions before me?

**POLONIUS**

Our mistress Rifke is wise. Sleep heals.

**HAMLET**

아마도금울구겠지 (*ah mah doh geum ool goo geht ji*), to sleep, perchance to dream, and by a sleep to say we end the heartache and the thousand natural shocks that flesh is heir to.[13]

**SHAKESPEARE**

You wish to kill me, all of you! Be gone!

**RIFKE**

¡Maestro, no!

**SHAKESPEARE**

You are not real. You are inventions, notions, creations, ideas! ¡Dejádme en paz!

**TITANIA**

Quiere que nos vayamos. We must do as he says, young master.

*All SPIRITS but HAMNET exit.*

---

13 *Hamlet*, 3.1.59–64

# Scene 3

**RIFKE**

Maestro, estás muy cansado y muy débil. ¿Por qué no duermes?

**SHAKESPEARE**

How can I sleep? My mind toys with me. Hell is empty and all the devils are here. [14]

**RIFKE**

Descansa, señor, y pronto ¡celebraremos tu cumpleaños!

**SHAKESPEARE**

Why is it so cold in here?

**RIFKE**

Now it is cold?

**SHAKESPEARE**

Rifke, stoke the fire!

**RIFKE**

Sí, señor.

> *RIFKE tends to the fire and tries to make SHAKESPEARE comfortable.*

**SHAKESPEARE**

Birthday, indeed.

**RIFKE**

Sleep master, let me sing you to sleep . . .

> *She begins "A la Nanita Nana," and the SPIRITS join in. SHAKE-SPEARE falls asleep.*

> A la nanita nana, nanita ella, nanita ella
> Mi niña tiene sueño, bendito sea, bendito sea
> A la nanita nana, nanita ella, nanita ella
> Mi niña tiene sueño, bendito sea, bendito sea

---

14  *The Tempest*, 1.2.214–15

Fuentecita que corre clara y sonora
Ruiseñor que en la selva, cantando y llora
Calla mientras la cuna se balancea

A la nanita nana, nanita ella, nanita ella
A la nanita nana, nanita ella, nanita ella
Mi niña tiene sueño, bendito sea, bendito sea

# Scene 4

*The villains, LADY M and RICHARD III, sneak in.*

**LADY M**

Look at him sleep.

**RICHARD III**

So sickly.

*He coughs.*

Helpless, is he?

**LADY M**

Hamnet is convinced his time is near.

**RICHARD III**

¡Quiere que lo llamemos Neto!

**LADY M**

Neto. His obsession with his father. No lo entiendo.

**RICHARD III**

Oh?

**LADY M**

Shakespeare does not deserve such devotion.

**RICHARD III**

Neto es un inocente.

**LADY M**

So strange.

*They laugh.*

**RICHARD III**

Ah well, we all have our parts to play.[15] I am determined to prove a villain[16] until my name is cleared. Descubrirán mis huesos y me verán como el héroe deforme que intentó salvar a Inglaterra.

**LADY M**

Someday I will be seen as nothing more or less than a loving, supportive wife.

**RICHARD III**

It will come. A time for us, at last, to shine.

**LADY M**

His versions of our stories are cruel.

**RICHARD III**

Nunca escribió como me gusta cantar.

**LADY M**

Nor mentioned my musical qualities either.

**RICHARD III**

O, to be released of his slanderous portrait.

**LADY M**

We are bound to those pages for eternity.

**RICHARD III**

Abandoned to the misinterpretation of the future. For as long as those texts exist.

**LADY M**

Neto is like us in this case — neglected, disregarded, abandoned.

**RICHARD III**

Neto sufre de todas las indignidades que nosotros hemos sufrido.

**LADY M**

And then he died. Poor baby, so young.

---

15  *The Merchant of Venice*, 1.1.78
16  *Richard III*, 1.1.30

**RICHARD III**

And what did the Bard do to commemorate him? Nothing! Not a piece of writing or a play. Pobre niño, lo enojado que debe estar.

**LADY M**

That's the problem: Neto never gets mad! He waits for his father to arrive like a loyal pup! Tenemos que protegerlo — protect his heart from further disappointment!

**RICHARD III**

It's the writing.

**LADY M**

The plays?

**RICHARD III**

The plays, the poems, the sonnets . . . Neto no para de leerlos.

**LADY M**

They fuel his obsession. Destroy them, and Shakespeare's spell is broken!

**RICHARD III**

Destroy them, and our names are cleared as well!

    *They sing "The Villains' Duet."*

> (R) Now is the winter of our discontent
> Made glorious summer by this son[17] of Will
> (R) Stop up the access and passage to remorse,
> That no compunctious visitings of nature
> Shake my fell purpose[18]
> (M) To beguile the time, look like the time; bear welcome in your
>     eye,
> Your hand, your tongue: look like the innocent flower,
> But be the serpent underneath.[19]
> (M) Para engañar al mundo, (R) Parécete al mundo,
> (M) lleva la bienvenida (R) en los ojos, (M) las manos, (R) la lengua.
> (M) Parécete a la cándida flor,
> Pero sé la serpiente que hay debajo (R) debajo (M) debajo.

---

17  *Richard III*, 1.1.1–2
18  *Macbeth*, 1.5.43
19  *Macbeth*, 1.5.63–64

(R) And thus we clothe our villainy (M) villania
(R) with old odd ends stolen out of holy writ;
And seem a saint, when most we play the devil.[20]
(M) Parecemos un par de santos cuando más hagamos el diablo.

**SHAKESPEARE**
What devilry? Who art thou?

**LADY M**
Misery acquaints a man with strange bedfellows,[21] does it not?

**RICHARD III**
Master William, no venimos a espantarlo.

**LADY M**
We come in peace, to soothe your worries.

**RICHARD III**
We understand how shocking this recent visitation must be for you.

**SHAKESPEARE**
Shocking, to say the least. You are figments of my imagination.

**LADY M**
Not exactly. You wrote about us, but you did not invent us.

**RICHARD III**
I was the King of England.

**SHAKESPEARE**
That is true.

**RICHARD III**
But you turned me into a loveless villain.

**LADY M**
And me into a childless villainess.

**SHAKESPEARE**
You are here to bring me to my early death!

---

20  *Richard III*, 1.3.334
21  *The Tempest*, 2.2.37

**RICHARD III**

¿Nosotros? Nous? ¿Cómo se puede imaginar que nosotros queremos hacerle daño?

**LADY M**

We would never harm you.

**RICHARD III & LADY M**

That's not the real "us."

*They smile.*

**SHAKESPEARE**

¿Qué quieren de mí?

**LADY M**

¿Qué quiere usted, maestro?

**SHAKESPEARE**

To receive no visitations from spirits.

**RICHARD III**

Hmmmmmmm.

**SHAKESPEARE**

¿Qué?

**RICHARD III**

Debe de haber algo que nos atrae a usted.

**LADY M**

Something that draws us to you, but what could it be?

**SHAKESPEARE**

Mis textos.

**LADY M**

Of course! Your scripts!

**RICHARD III**

¡Sus obras me enloquecen!

**LADY M**

They are irresistible.

**RICHARD III**
But we're always here.

**LADY M**
Why is it you're seeing us only now?

**RICHARD III**
Because you're dying!

**LADY M**
Of course, with all that work!

**RICHARD III**
Lo vemos sufrir tanto con ese trabajo de escribir y escribir día y noche.

**LADY M**
Would it not please to have such weight lifted from your shoulders?

**RICHARD III**
Sería muy saludable dejar todas estas preocupaciones dramáticas.

**LADY M**
Might even extend your life.

**SHAKESPEARE**
¿Mi vida?

**RICHARD III**
You've given so much of yourself.

**LADY M**
Your very essence.

**RICHARD III**
Su pura alma y corazón.

**SHAKESPEARE**
Each work I've written contains a piece of me. Es verdad.

**LADY M**
And as you near the end, you need your strength.

**RICHARD III**
Está claro. You must decide: your work or your life.

*LADY M and RICHARD III exit.*

# Scene 5

**SHAKESPEARE**
Rifke, Rifke!

**RIFKE**
¿Sí señor?

**SHAKESPEARE**
Gather my manuscripts . . .

**RIFKE**
Do you wish to work?

**SHAKESPEARE**
Work? No! ¡Este trabajo me ha enfermado! Bring me all of my manuscripts!

**RIFKE**
¿Todas las obras?

**SHAKESPEARE**
I am ill.

**RIFKE**
Yes, Master William.

*She begins to remove the works from the wooden chest by the window.*

¡Tanto papel!

**SHAKESPEARE**
My life's work, rolls of ink-stained pages. The totality of my worth.

**RIFKE**
¡Poesía!

**SHAKESPEARE**
¡Sueños! And these dreams have cost me dearly!

**RIFKE**
Maestro, ¡te han hecho un hombre rico!

**SHAKESPEARE**

And to whom shall I leave my fortune?

**RIFKE**

De seguro se me ocurre alguien . . .

**SHAKESPEARE**

I was in London, at the theatre, when my son died.

**RIFKE**

You sustained your family with your work! Your good work brought you fame! Your good name!

**SHAKESPEARE**

What's in a name[22] if never spoken to a son?

**RIFKE**

Neto loved your plays . . .

**SHAKESPEARE**

Rifke . . .

**RIFKE**

. . . se aprendía todas las palabras.

**SHAKESPEARE**

Rifke!

**RIFKE**

Neto! Neto! Neto! 'Tis but his name that is your enemy.[23]

**SHAKESPEARE**

My work is my enemy.

**RIFKE**

No, maestro, has escrito por muchos años sin ningún problema. You have reached the sixth age, that is all. Enflaquecido en zapatillas, lentes en las napias y bolsa al costado.[24]

---

22 *Romeo and Juliet*, 2.1.85
23 *Romeo and Juliet*, 2.1.80
24 *As You Like It*, 2.7.158–9

**SHAKESPEARE** (*looking over the texts*)
All this is meaningless. Meaningless!

> *The SPIRITS enter.*

**RIFKE** (*reading the titles*)
*¡Sueño de una noche de verano* . . . qué obra más divina! *Richard III*, oh, such villainy, chilling. *Macbeth*, I appreciated the complexity of the female lead. *Hamlet!* True, it is very long, but it contains some of your finest words . . . ¡Oh! Si esta demasiada, demasiada sólida masa de carne pudiera ablandarse y liqui-darse . . .[25] ¡Y *Romeo y Julieta*!

**HAMNET & RIFKE**
My bounty is as boundless as the sea,
My love as deep; the more I give to thee,
The more I have, for both are infinite.[26]

**SHAKESPEARE**
I must burn them.

**RIFKE & SPIRITS**
Burn them?!

**SHAKESPEARE**
This work is the cause of my frailty.

**RIFKE**
Maestro, you are fifty-two years of age. That is the cause of your frailty!

**SHAKESPEARE**
This work led me astray! Give me my texts!

**RIFKE**
¿Para quemarlos? ¡No!

> *She gathers up the scripts back into the wooden chest, closes the lid, and sits on it.*

**SHAKESPEARE**
Thou canst not guard it in perpetuity.

---

25 *Hamlet*, 1.2.129–130
26 *Romeo and Juliet*, 2.1.175–77

**RIFKE**
Try me, master. (*pause*) A new letter arrived from my brother.

**SHAKESPEARE**
I care not.

**RIFKE**
Me envió la letra de una canción.

**SHAKESPEARE**
A song?

**RIFKE**
De una mujer que llora.

**SHAKESPEARE**
Why does she weep?

**RIFKE**
She cries for her lost children.

**SHAKESPEARE**
¿Están muertos?

**RIFKE**
Sí. Jóvenes, como Neto.

**SHAKESPEARE**
No more. Let me sleep now since you are immovable.[27]

**RIFKE**
You never wish to speak of your son.

**SHAKESPEARE**
Speaking of the dead will not bring them back to life!

*He ducks under the covers.*

**RIFKE**
If what my brother says is true, the spirits are with us always. Not frightening like your ghosts, but warm and loving. Qué lindo sueño.

*She finds a blanket and lies down to sleep.*

---

27  *The Taming of the Shrew*, 2.1.197

# Scene 6

*The SPIRITS enter.*

**HAMLET**
He wishes to destroy the texts?

**OPHELIA**
Our stories.

**YORICK**
If he burns the texts, do we die? Again?

**RICHARD III**
¡Claro que no!

**LADY M**
There's nothing for us to fear.

**HAMLET**
I am not so sure of that.

**OPHELIA**
Every time an actor speaks my lines, I live again. I feel the heat of a flame.

**LADY M**
Out, out, brief candle!

**RICHARD III**
Life's but a walking shadow, a poor player
That struts and frets his hour upon the stage
And then is heard no more.

**LADY M**
It is a tale
Told by an idiot, full of sound and fury,
Signifying nothing.[28]

**POLONIUS**
I dread for certain the loss of his writing.

---

28 *Macbeth*, 5.5.23–28

*Pause.*

**HAMNET**

He cannot. He must not.

**TITANIA**

Child?

**HAMNET**

I only know my father through his words. He's spoken to me more through his plays than he ever did in life. I know the world through his words. I know all of you. I know life.

**OPHELIA**

We know what we are, but know not what we may be.[29]

**HAMLET** (*singing*)

>    What a piece of work is a man!
>    How noble in reason, how infinite in faculty!
>    In form and moving, how express and admirable!
>    In action how like an angel,
>    In apprehension how like a god!
>    The beauty of the world.
>    The paragon of animals.[30]

**POLONIUS**

*Hamlet*, Act Two, Scene Two. The boy is right. We must save the texts.

**TITANIA**

His writing will endure centuries.

**YORICK**

This is true. Alas, I was just a skull, but everyone claims to know me well![31]

**POLONIUS**

The wheel is come full circle![32]

---

29 *Hamlet*, 4.2.45–45
30 *Hamlet*, 2.2.264–68. The song based on these lines is from *Hair*, lyrics by Gerome Ragni and James Rado and music by Galt Macdermot.
31 *Hamlet*, 5.1.166.
32 *King Lear*, 5.3.167

*The word "circle" sparks an idea! Everyone grabs their instruments!*
*The SPIRITS begin to sing "The Circle of Life."*[33]

**SPIRITS** (*singing*)

> It's the circle of life
> And it moves us all
> Through despair and hope
> Through faith and love . . .

*SHAKESPEARE wakes up.*

**SHAKESPEARE**

Peace, you ungracious clamours! Peace, rude sounds! Fools on both sides![34]

**POLONIUS**

Master, we are remarking on your legacy, which long outlives your life.

**SHAKESPEARE**

A thousand twangling instruments![35]

**TITANIA**

This song is from a movie that will be inspired by Hamlet's story.

**SHAKESPEARE**

A movie? What's a movie?

**YORICK**

It's like a talking fairy tale, and this one is a musical, where people break into song and dance for no apparent reason but the swelling of their hearts!

**SPIRITS** (*singing*)

> When you're a Jet, you're a Jet all the way
> From your first cigarette till your last dyin' day
> When you're a Jet, if the spit hits the fan
> You got brothers around, you're a family man
> You're never alone
> You're never disconnected
> You're home with your own
> When company's expected

---

33  A song from *The Lion King*; lyrics by Tim Rice and music by Elton John.
34  *Troilus and Cressida*, 1.1.85
35  *The Tempest*, 3.2.130

You're well protected
Then you are set with a capital J
Which you'll never forget till they cart you away
When you're a Jet
You stay a Jet![36]

**SHAKESPEARE**
They burn.

**SPIRITS**
No puede.

**SHAKESPEARE**
If this is what becomes of my writing, it is far better to spare mankind. I shudder to think what else might come.

**HAMLET**
Your work will be studied at university.

**SHAKESPEARE**
Studied? This is theatre, not literature! What next, will they add punctuation?

*A collective gasp of horror from the SPIRITS.*

**POLONIUS**
Your works will be translated into the dominant Western cultures' languages.

**RIFKE** (*in her sleep*)
¡Ser, o no ser, esa es la cuestión![37]

**SHAKESPEARE**
¿Para que lo presenten en cualquier lugar? In a park for hounds? By a milepost far from town? In a space no bigger than a shoebox?[38] Anon it moves[39] me to tears to think on't!

**YORICK**
Master William, there is no limit to the inspiration your writing engenders!

---

36 A song from *West Side Story*; lyrics by Stephen Sondheim and music by Leonard Bernstein.
37 *Hamlet*, 3.1.55
38 Reflecting the original production of *¡O Romeo!*, these are references to locations in which Shakespeare's works are often performed in Portland, Oregon. For your production, feel free to invent descriptions for your local community to create an inside joke with your audience.
39 *The Winter's Tale*, 5.3.61

**OPHELIA**
*Julius Caesar,* con solo mujeres actuando . . .

**RIFKE** (*in her sleep*)
быть или не быть вот в чем вопрос . . . [40]

**POLONIUS**
With scrolls in hand, unrehearsed!

**TITANIA**
Or, a multilingual story ¡en celebración del Día de los Muertos!

**SHAKESPEARE**
¡Qué milagro! Would that be based on *The Mystical Story of Love and Reunion of Xochiquetzal, the Aztec Maiden, and the Spanish Conquistador, Don Armando?*

**RIFKE** (*in her sleep, recalling lines from Shakespeare's play*)
Xochiquetzal, el amor de Don Armando. Conquistadora de mi corazón, pero la fe domina mi vida.

**HAMNET**
Father, you must finish this play on the New World.

**SHAKESPEARE**
Must? Must? Who are you to urge "must"?

**HAMNET**
Yo soy . . . muy importante.

**SHAKESPEARE**
You are a dream, que no significa nada![41]

**LADY M**
How he discredits you!

**RICHARD III**
Es un insulto, joven, que no debes aguantar.

**LADY M**
Después de todo su descuido.

---

40 *Hamlet,* 3.1.55
41 *Macbeth,* 5.5.28

**RICHARD III**
No es justo.

**HAMNET**
You are right. Finish, don't finish, burn them, don't burn them. I will care no longer what you do, Father.

> *Pause.*

**SHAKESPEARE**
And why shouldst thou care?

**HAMNET**
I know what it cost you, what sacrifices were made for your art. Destroy them all and be left with naught if you so wish.

**SHAKESPEARE**
I do wish.

**HAMNET**
Fine.

**SHAKESPEARE**
Fine.

**HAMNET**
Fine.

**SHAKESPEARE**
Fine.

**OPHELIA**
It ends like this?

**YORICK**
Aye, without much ado at all. [42]

**LADY M**
Ha pausado. Father, may we be of service?

**RICHARD III**
Surely there's a tinderbox at hand.

---

42 A reference to Shakespeare's comedy *Much Ado About Nothing.*

**POLONIUS**
The pause is wise. They stumble that run fast.[43]

**HAMLET**
Yes, perhaps you should wait before you decide to burn . . . or not to burn.

**SHAKESPEARE**
He decidido. Los quemo.

**RICHARD III**
"Romeo" doesn't care, so why should we?

**TITANIA**
He cares. We know he cares.

**YORICK**
He reads those texts as if they were love letters.

**OPHELIA**
To him they are.

**LADY M**
He's not a child anymore . . . He'll get over this easily.

**OPHELIA**
I know what 'tis to have a broken heart.

**HAMLET**
Ophelia's right.

**POLONIUS**
We must save the texts for Master "Romeo's" sake.

**TITANIA**
We need time. Father, if your mind is fixed, then it must be done with ceremony, for in your pause I sense the gravity of this act.

**YORICK**
We shall prepare a rightly occasion, appropriate and true.

**OPHELIA**
One that will honor the burning of your scrolls.

---

43 *Romeo and Juliet*, 2.3.94

**HAMLET**

Before you actually burn them.

**TITANIA**

Will you give us three days to prepare?

**SHAKESPEARE**

You have three hours. Go!

> *The SPIRITS exit, and SHAKESPEARE goes back to his bed.*

They burn with the chimes at midnight![44]

# Scene 7

> *RIFKE wakes up as SHAKESPEARE turns away.*

**RIFKE**

Está determinado a quemar sus obras. Qué triste. He will burn our tale of Xochiquetzal and Don Armando, to be sure. It's not even finished! Oh, and my brother's song would have been perfect!

> *She finds her brother's letter with the song and begins to read "La Llorona."*

(*reading out of rhythm*)

> Todos me dicen el negro, Llorona
> Negro pero cariñoso

(*reading in rhythm*)

> Todos me dicen el negro, Llorona
> Negro pero cariñoso

(*reading with guitar*)

> Yo soy como el chile verde, Llorona
> Picante pero sabroso

---

44  *2 Henry IV*, 3.2.193; also a reference to the Orson Welles 1966 film *Chimes at Midnight*.

*(singing)*

    Yo soy como el chile verde, Llorona
    Picante pero sabroso
    Ay de mí, Llorona, Llorona
    Llorona llévame al río
    Ay de mí, Llorona, Llorona
    Llorona llévame al río
    Tápame con tu rebozo, Llorona
    Porque me muero de frío
    Tápame con tu rebozo, Llorona
    Porque me muero de frío

*OPHELIA, LADY M, and TITANIA re-enter and harmonize with RIFKE.*

    Ay de mí, Llorona, Llorona de ayer y hoy
    No creas que porque canto, ay Llorona
    Tengo el corazón alegre
    No creas que porque canto, ay Llorona
    Tengo el corazón alegre
    También de dolor se canta, ay Llorona
    Cuando llorar no se puede
    También de dolor se canta, ay Llorona
    Cuando llorar no se puede

    Ay de mí, Llorona, Llorona de ayer y hoy
    Ayer maravilla fui, Llorona
    Y ahora ni sombra soy
    Ayer maravilla fui, Llorona
    Y ahora ni sombra soy
    Ayer maravilla fui, Llorona
    Y ahora ni sombra soy
    Ay. Such a good song.

# ACT 2
# Scene 1

*RICHARD III and LADY M enter stealthily while SHAKE-SPEARE and RIFKE sleep.*

**LADY M**
Estuvimos tan cerca.

**RICHARD III**
We're not that far off yet, madam.

**LADY M**
He stood by the fire . . . we could have easily handed him a sheet to burn.

**RICHARD III**
¿Por qué pausó?

**LADY M**
I think he was tempted by the idea of eternal legacy. That movie that Titania spoke of.

**RICHARD III**
*Julius Caesar* performed with all women. ¡Absurdo!

**LADY M**
Or unrehearsèd, with scroll in hand! He will roll in his grave.

**RICHARD III**
Roll in his grave! (*pause*) Think ye what I am thinking?

**LADY M**
If we can show him the fiascos of his so-called legacy . . .

**RICHARD III**
Una horrible versión de su trabajo. Él va a destruir sus obras . . .

**LADY M**
. . . so that no one ever touches them. He'll destroy the works . . .

**LADY M & RICHARD III**

. . . swifter than arrow from the Tartar's bow![45]

**LADY M**

¡Y seremos libres! You, me, and Neto, free . . . which of his plays should we mangle first?

**RICHARD III**

This new, unfinished play of his . . .

**LADY M**

His "most important" work. Ha! We all know which play that is . . .

**RICHARD III**

Yes we do.

> *TITANIA enters.*

**TITANIA**

There you are! We've been looking for you everywhere! Tenemos unas ideas para convencer a Shakespeare a no quemar sus obras. But you two always have such effective ideas . . .

**RICHARD III**

Nosotros también hemos pensado en esto. ¡Qué horrible que quiera quemar sus obras!

**LADY M**

¡Es una tragedia!

**RICHARD III**

We've come up with an idea.

**TITANIA**

I knew that you two were team players! I'll summon the rest!

> *She shakes a rattle. The other SPIRITS enter.*

**TITANIA**

Well met, fellows! Lady Macbeth and Richard III have an idea to share with us. Lady Macbeth?

---

45  *A Midsummer Night's Dream*, 3.2.101

**LADY M**

Richard and I think we should perform the Bard's newest play.

**RICHARD III**

His most mature piece of work . . . so modern . . .

**LADY M**

Ethnic and relevant . . .

**RICHARD III**

Romantically tragic . . .

**POLONIUS**

Why don't we perform *The Comedy of Errors*?

**ALL**

Eh . . . no.

**OPHELIA**

*The Mystical Story of Love and Reunion* . . .

**HAMLET**

I don't know . . . are we sure it's good?

**RICHARD III**

Of course it's good . . .

**RICHARD III & LADY M**

It's Shakespeare!

**YORICK**

Let's do the play!

**TITANIA**

That's the spirit! Yorick — here, you can play the role of Manuel!

**YORICK**

If I do it, let the audience look to their eyes. I will move storms. I will con-
dole in some measure. Yet my chief humour is for a tyrant: I could play Don
Armando rarely.

> The raging rocks
> And shivering shocks

> Shall break the locks
> Of prison gates! [46]

I also like the part of the goddess . . .

**TITANIA**

I will be the goddess. Hamlet! You shall play Don Armando.

**HAMLET**

Me? A romantic lead? Why not Romeo?

**TITANIA**

No, you're the perfect choice!

(*to LADY M*) And you, you can play the Grand Inquisitor! This role is devious. The Grand Inquisitor is in reality a woman pretending to be a man!

**LADY M**

Unsex me [47] now.

**TITANIA**

Richard, you are best suited for the role of Don Xavier, the father of Don Armando. Polonius, you shall assume the role of Don Apolonio, Don Armando's trusted confidante.

**POLONIUS**

I shall endeavor to tender sage advice.

**TITANIA**

Ophelia, the role of Citlali, the Aztec high priestess . . .

> *OPHELIA bursts into tears and wanders away sobbing over not getting the part she wanted.*

**TITANIA**

Ophelia! Child, you'll drown yourself in a river of tears.

> *OPHELIA mumbles incoherently.*

**TITANIA**

You may play . . . Xochiquetzal . . .

---

46 *A Midsummer Night's Dream*, 1.2.24–27
47 *Macbeth*, 1.5.39

**OPHELIA**
I shall!

**TITANIA**
. . . and Citlali, the Aztec high priestess.

**OPHELIA**
That sounds complicated.

**TITANIA**
Young lord Hamnet, you can play Esquincle, the younger brother of Xochiquetzal.

**ALL**
Esquincle!

**HAMNET**
I don't know . . .

**TITANIA**
Haven't you always wanted to be a part of one of your father's plays?

**HAMNET**
What does Esquincle do?

**TITANIA**
Why he is the hero who saves the day at the end of the play.

**POLONIUS**
You're a natural.

**YORICK**
If the young lord wish not, why, I could take on that role. I could play every single one of these characters! With grandiosity! With fervor! Allow me . . .

**TITANIA**
Yorick, I think you should play the most important role of all! The narrator, Manuel, El Borracho!

**YORICK**
Ich mag es!

**TITANIA**
¡A mí me gusta también!

# Scene 2

*The SPIRITS go to wake up SHAKESPEARE.*

**OPHELIA**
Father, it's time for your ceremony!

**YORICK**
Wake up!!

*They make a clamor.*

**SHAKESPEARE**
Neighbors, you are tedious![48]

**TITANIA**
We have prepared a wondrous surprise for you!

**YORICK**
But we need you to remove yourself from your bedding.    .

*They lead him to a seat.*

**LADY M**
This is going to be my worst performance ever.

**RICHARD III**
You think your play was cursed . . . wait 'til he sees what we do with this one!

**OPHELIA**
. . . and please don't block the front row.

*The actors arrange the furniture. LADY M and RICHARD III step to one side.*

**TITANIA**
Alright, everyone! Let's take two minutes to look over your scripts and prepare.

**EVERYONE**
Thank you, two!

*The actors stretch and practice tongue twisters.*

---

48 *Much Ado About Nothing*, 3.5.16

**TITANIA**
Places!

**ALL**
Gracias. Places.

**POLONIUS**
Master William, in honor of your decision to burn all of your works, we have decided to present your latest play.

**SHAKESPEARE**
But it is unfinished! It is but a skeleton of a play!

**POLONIUS**
It will be wonderful.

**OPHELIA**
*The Mystical Story of Love and Reunion, of Xochiquetzal, the Aztec Maiden, and the Spanish Conquistador, Don Armando . . .*

**YORICK** (*as Manuel, playing the guitar*)
¡Saludos! Yo soy Manuel, El Borracho, para servirles. Hoy les contaré un cuento del Nuevo Mundo. A tale that will rivet you, move you, ascend you to the apex of the Aztec pyramids! Lend me your ears[49] as we venture to Tenochtitlán . . .

Act One, Scene One, in which Don Xavier introduces his son, Don Armando, to the Grand Inquisitor.

> *RICHARD III, playing Don Xavier, shoves HAMLET, playing*
> *Don Armando, toward LADY M, playing Gertrudis, the Grand*
> *Inquisitor. LADY M will recite all her lines in the most stilted iambic*
> *pentameter.*

**RICHARD III** (*as Don Xavier*)
Excelencia, mi hijo adorado, a su servicio.

**LADY M** (*as Gertrudis, the Inquisitor*)
Don Armando!
He is the very reason I fled Spain!

---

49 *Julius Caesar*, 3.2.71

**HAMLET** (*as Don Armando*)
> Grand Inquisitor, I am your slave.
> Tenochtitlán is new and strange to me.

**LADY M** (*as Gertrudis, the Inquisitor*)
> A priest, I see by your holy vestments.

**HAMLET** (*as Don Armando*)
> Sí, soy sacerdote, noble señor.
> I humbly ask permission from your grace
> En nombre del divino rey Carlos
> That I might build a glorious cathedral
> To awe and move the hearts of pagan souls.

**LADY M** (*as Gertrudis, the Inquisitor*)
> He crush'd my heart, but I cannot resist,
> Adoring his commitment to the faith!
> Tienes permiso joven buen mozo.

**SHAKESPEARE** (*correcting her mispronunciation*)
> MO-zo, buen MO-zo!

> *While exiting, RICHARD III stops by SHAKESPEARE.*

**RICHARD III**
> I notice Don Xavier has very few lines, rather mostly exits and entrances. I think that's a flaw in the script.

**SHAKESPEARE**
> We all have our entrances and exits . . .[50]

**YORICK** (*as Manuel*)
> Act One, Scene Two. Don Armando viaja al sitio de la nueva catedral, but is met with the challenging Citlali, the Aztec high priestess.

**OPHELIA** (*looking over the script*)
> I don't think I can pronounce this!

**SHAKESPEARE**
> It is Nahuatl, the language of the people. Rifke taught me the words sent by her brother.

---

50 *As You Like It,* 2.7.141

**RICHARD III**

¡Entonces Rifke es la única que los puede pronunciar! Then only she can play the role. Oh! Such a shame she sleeps so soundly. Ah well, cancel the show and on to the bonfire!

**TITANIA**

I can cast a spell to wake her without waking.

**LADY M**

¡Eso es imposible!

**TITANIA**

I am a spirit of no common rate.[51] She will play her part to perfection . . .

*TITANIA casts a spell on RIFKE.*

**RIFKE** (*as Citlali*)

Huitzilopochtli, papalotl, elote, tecolote . . .

**HAMLET** (*as Don Armando*)

Excellency, on this site must I build
A grand cathedral honoring our king,
Though on the grounds of your sacred retreat
And temple to the goddess Coatlicue.

**RIFKE** (*as Citlali*)

Coyote, ocelote, aguacate, tácate, nopal . . .

**HAMLET** (*as Don Armando*)

I will simply have to take that chance.

**RIFKE** (*as Citlali*)

Guatemala, Yucatán, Jalisco, Mazatlán . . .

**HAMLET** (*as Don Armando*)

One more sacrifice, that cannot be!

**TITANIA** (*as Coatlicue*)

Yo soy Coatlicue, creation's fire,
La madre of all gods and stars and moon!
How dare they put an end to sacrifice?

---

51  *A Midsummer Night's Dream* 3.1.136

¿No saben la importancia del ritual?
The corn they eat grows from a nourished soil
For which with grateful hearts they should give their lives!
These Spanish warlords come to kill Aztecas
Y a enterrar a mis pirámides
Beneath a Catholic temple for their King.
If these oppressors, or conquistadores,
Put not an end to dominance and strife,
I will send them to death and to Mictlán
With great volcanoes spewing fire and ash!

**RIFKE** (*as Citlali*)
Peyote, xocolatl . . .

**HAMLET** (*as Don Armando*)
I sense impending doom. I know not how
You have convinced me, Priestess. We will wait
For the completion of your final rite.

**YORICK** (*as Manuel*)
Act One, Scene Three. The maiden Xochiquetzal wins Don Armando's heart
through her xocolatl and piety.

**OPHELIA** (*as Xochiquetzal*)
Le traigo xocolatl, mi señor,
A healing bev'rage warmed to thank your heart.
Your willingness to grant us due respect
Means I will serve Coatlicue in this rite,
Sacrificing my life for my people.
Es gran honor servir al pueblo hoy.

**HAMLET** (*as Don Armando*)
I do not understand your ways, maiden.

**OPHELIA** (*as Xochiquetzal*)
Me llamo, mi señor, Xochiquetzal.

**HAMLET** (*as Don Armando*)
Xochiquetzal.

**OPHELIA** (*as Xochiquetzal*)
Xochiquetzal.

Our ways are holy. My death is a gift
To please our jealous goddess Coatlicue.
La muerte no existe para mí.
My sacrifice will bring me to the land
Of Ichantona-tiu-hilhuicatl.
Año tras año, yo visitaré
A mi ofrenda, decorada con
Flores de cempasúchitl.

> *Love strikes.*

**YORICK**

I don't know about you, but I really like that scene . . . makes me hungry. Act One, Scene Four. Don Armando confides in Don Apolonio.

**SHAKESPEARE**

That scene has but one line!

**YORICK**

Not to worry, Nuncle!

> *Dumb show: HAMLET, as Don Armando, confides in POLONIUS, as Apolonio.*

**POLONIUS** (*as Apolonio*)

Noooooooooooooooooooooooooooooooooooooooooooooooooooooooooooo!

**YORICK** (*as Manuel*)

End of Act One.

> *Applause.*

Act Two, Scene One: The Pyramid Scheme.

**SHAKESPEARE**

Pyramid SCENE!

**YORICK**

Apologies, nuncle.

(*as Manuel*) Don Armando visits Xochiquetzal at the base of the Temple of the Moon. El templo de la luna . . .

**HAMLET** (*as Don Armando*)

First light of dawn that broke as my heart soared,

A huitzilin that sips the flower's dew,
Xochiquetzal, Armando's dearest love,
Conqueror of my heart, yet faith pulls strong.

**OPHELIA** (*as Xochiquetzal*)
¿Don Armando?

**HAMLET** (*as Don Armando*)
Xochiquetzal.

**OPHELIA** (*as Xochiquetzal*)
Don Armando.

**HAMLET** (*as Don Armando*)
Xochiquetzal.

**OPHELIA** (*as Xochiquetzal*)
Don Armando.

**HAMLET** (*as Don Armando*)
Xochiquetzal.

> *All look at SHAKESPEARE.*

**SHAKESPEARE**
It's a first draft!

**OPHELIA** (*as Xochiquetzal*)
This morning is the last I'll ever know,
The last I shall behold my one true love.

**HAMLET** (*as Don Armando*)
¡Ojos, dadle la última mirada!
Arms, take your last embrace![52]

> *They kiss.*

**YORICK** (*as Manuel*)
Act Two, Scene Two. Don Apolonio le cuenta al Gran Inquisidor del amor prohibido entre Don Armando y Xochiquetzal.

---

52 *Romeo and Juliet*, 5.3.112–113

**POLONIUS** (*as Apolonio*)
Grand Inquisitor, what I must reveal
Is overwhelming. I can hardly breathe.

**LADY M** (*as Gertrudis, the Inquisitor*)
Speak, my child.

**POLONIUS** (*as Apolonio*)
It is a shameful, forbidden love!

**LADY M** (*as Gertrudis, the Inquisitor*)
¿Y los nombres?

**RICHARD III** (*coaching POLONIUS*)
Zonkey pretzel.

**POLONIUS** (*as Apolonio*)
Zonkey pretzel and . . . Don Armando!

**LADY M** (*as Gertrudis, the Inquisitor*)
No-oo-oo-oo-oo-oo-oo-oo-oo-oo!

**SHAKESPEARE**
Ay, ay, ay, ay, ay, ay, ay, ay, ay!

**LADY M** (*as Gertrudis, the Inquisitor*)
Against his faith he loves an infidel?
Armando said I lacked true piety;
I gave up womanhood to prove him wrong.
What I could never have, she will not get.

**YORICK** (*as Manuel*)
Act Three, Scene One! The Grand Inquisitor visits Xochiquetzal!

**OPHELIA** (*as Xochiquetzal*)
¿Quién eres tú?

**LADY M** (*as Gertrudis, the Inquisitor*)
You dare speak rudely, you who have brought sin
To Spain's most noble son, Don Armando.
You face, heathen, the Grand Inquisitor.

**OPHELIA** (*as Xochiquetzal*)
¿Qué es eso?

**LADY M** (*as Gertrudis, the Inquisitor*)
No questions more! You must cease this affair!

**OPHELIA** (*as Xochiquetzal*)
¡Pero, mi señora . . . !

**LADY M** (*as Gertrudis, the Inquisitor*)
I am not a woman. ¡Yo soy hombre!

**OPHELIA** (*as Xochiquetzal*)
¡No con esas chichis! ¡No hay forma!

**LADY M** (*as Gertrudis, the Inquisitor*)
If you tell anyone what thou think'st thou know'st . . .

**OPHELIA** (*as Xochiquetzal*)
What do you think'st I think'st I know'st?

**LADY M** (*as Gertrudis, the Inquisitor*)
Thou know'st what I think'st thou think'st thou know'st.

**OPHELIA** (*as Xochiquetzal*)
I don't know'st, but I think'st thou know'st what I think'st I know'st.

**LADY M** (*as Gertrudis, the Inquisitor*)
If thou reveal'st my secret, thou art deadest!

**OPHELIA** (*as Xochiquetzal*)
I shall die'st but not by your hand.

**YORICK** (*as Manuel*)
Well, that was pretty titillating! Act Four, Scene One. Xochiquetzal is sacrificed by Citlali to the goddess Coatlicue.

*HAMLET, as Don Armando, watches from a distance.*

**RIFKE** (*as Citlali*)
Ándale, niña . . .

*OPHELIA, as Xochiquetzal, lies down on the bench. RIFKE, as Citlali, performs a cleansing ritual, then begins the sacrifice.*

**OPHELIA** (*as Xochiquetzal*)
¡Espera!

> *RIFKE stops the ritual. She then resumes.*

¡Espera, espera!

> *She sneezes.*

**RIFKE** (*as Citlali, with speed*)
¡Nili, wili, vanili!

> *RIFKE, as Citlali, extracts Xochiquetzal's heart and presents it to
> TITANIA, as Coatlicue, who takes a bite. OPHELIA, as Xochiquet-
> zal, rises and is walked off.*

**YORICK** (*as Manuel*)
Act Five, Scene One. Don Armando builds an altar to Xochiquetzal.

**HAMLET** (*as Don Armando*)
Oh! ¡Mi corazón!

**OPHELIA** (*as Xochiquetzal, sings "La Llorona"*)
> Dicen que no tengo duelo, Llorona
> Porque no me ven llorar
> Dicen que no tengo duelo, Llorona
> Porque no me ven llorar

**HAMLET** (*as Don Armando*)
Xochiquetzal . . .

**OPHELIA** (*as Xochiquetzal, singing*)
> Hay muertos que no hacen ruido, Llorona
> Y es más grande su pena.
> Hay muertos que . . .

**LADY M** (*as Gertrudis, the Inquisitor, interrupting*)
¡Don Armando! ¿Qué haces?

**HAMLET** (*as Don Armando*)
Honoring the woman I love.

**LADY M** (*as Gertrudis, the Inquisitor*)
¡Que blasfemia!

**HAMLET** (*as Don Armando*)
Love transcends doctrine.

**LADY M** (*as Gertrudis, the Inquisitor*)
You've crossed the line, Armando, with this fling.
Although she's dead, your transgression lives on,
And by my sword, empowered by our King,
Your body must release your sinful soul!

**HAMLET** (*as Don Armando*)
Sir, no sin exists. Love is not love
Which alters when it alteration finds
Or bends with the remover to remove.
O no, it is an ever-fixèd mark,
That looks on tempests and is never shaken![53]
Your challenge I accept, for love is pure.
The goddess take my heart, that it may serve.

> *Sword fight!*

**HAMLET** (*as Don Armando, recognizing Sor Gertrudis*)
Sor Gertrudis!

**LADY M** (*as Gertrudis, the Inquisitor*)
Now you see me as I truly am.

**HAMLET** (*as Don Armando*)
I see your vengeful heart beneath your cloak.

**LADY M** (*as Gertrudis, the Inquisitor*)
I wanted this to be a time for us.
But you have forced my hand. Now you must die.

> *HAMLET, as Don Armando, is pinned, and HAMNET, as Esquin-
> cle, stops the fight just before his death . . .*

**HAMNET** (*as Esquincle*)
Halt!

> *Pause.*

---

53 Sonnet 116

**TITANIA**
Continue, young lord!

**HAMNET**
There's nothing more written here. Look: the rest is blank.

*All look at SHAKESPEARE.*

**SHAKESPEARE**
It's unfinished!

**RICHARD III**
Well, time to burn the scripts!

**TITANIA**
Young lord, finish it yourself . . .

**OPHELIA**
Say more!

**POLONIUS**
Indeed!

**YORICK**
Say anything!

**HAMNET** (*as Esquincle*)
Honoring Xochiquetzal, my sister,
By building an ofrenda in her name,
Don Armando blended our two worlds.
The Old and New will never be the same.
No border lies between your faith and mine;
We all await reunion with our dead.
You must spare his life!

> *Gertrudis, played by LADY M, kills Don Armando, played by HAMLET.*

**LADY M** (*as Gertrudis, the Inquisitor*)
Goodnight, sweet prince. [54]

> *She congratulates HAMNET.*

---

54  *Hamlet*, 5.2.337

**RICHARD II**
Well done indeed, Romeo!

**RIFKE**
That's not Romeo, that's . . .

> *TITANIA returns RIFKE to her sleep.*

**SHAKESPEARE**
I never intended Don Armando's death!

**LADY M**
I am a villain. What else would I have done?

**RICHARD III**
Sí, la villanía es consistente. Así nos creaste, así somos.

**SHAKESPEARE**
But this is the New World, a place of better human nature, of infinite potential. A place where we might have learned from our mistakes before it's too late . . .

**RICHARD III**
That is a lofty dream.

**SHAKESPEARE**
It is not a dream, it is a vision. But now he lies dead.

**LADY M**
You love him.

**SHAKESPEARE**
I love all of you.

**HAMNET**
Father . . .
You think that death has won but are mistaken.
Death will not kill their love. Although they met
But briefly while on earth, they now possess
Eternity's embrace. They laugh at death.

**SHAKESPEARE**

Yes! Eternity's embrace! Well done! Romeo, I am amazed. You are so young — where did you find such poetry to finish?

**HAMNET**

I learned from the best. I read every story you wrote, every sonnet, every poem, every word.

**SHAKESPEARE**

¿Por qué?

**HAMNET**

I wanted to know you. They told me we would meet again. I wanted to be ready.

**SHAKESPEARE**

They?

**HAMNET**

Your creations. They are my friends.

**SHAKESPEARE**

En la muerte.

**HAMNET**

Sí.

**SHAKESPEARE**

You are not Romeo.

**HAMNET**

No.

**SHAKESPEARE**

Methinks I should know you. Yet I am doubtful.[55]

**HAMNET**

Do not doubt.

**SHAKESPEARE**

Hamnet?

---

55 *King Lear*, 4.7.61–62

**HAMNET**

Yes.

**SHAKESPEARE**

My son! I know not by what magic you appear nor will I question it. A thousand thoughts, a thousand words would I speak. But what first springs is what has weighed on my heart since the instant I lost you.

**HAMNET**

Father . . .

**SHAKESPEARE**

I beg your forgiveness. For the years I was distant, for my absence at your bedside when you were sick. Had I been there, a father's rightful place, perhaps I might have saved your life!

**HAMNET**

No, father, my time had come. It could not be rewritten.

**SHAKESPEARE**

Is this my time? Is this why you are here?

**HAMNET**

Yes. This is finally the time for us.

**SHAKESPEARE**

I'm not ready. Today is my birthday!

**SPIRITS**

¡Su cumpleaños!

> *They begin to sing "Las Mañanitas."*

Estas son las mañanitas,
Que cantaba el rey David,
Hoy por ser día de tu santo,
Te las cantamos a ti.

Despierta, William, despierta,
Mira que ya amaneció,
Ya los pajarillos cantan
La luna ya se metió.

**SHAKESPEARE**
But what a wonderful present!

*SHAKESPEARE dies.*

**HAMNET**
Father!

*Music for the song "Full Fathom Five" begins. HAMNET places
SHAKESPEARE's glasses on the altar. SHAKESPEARE stands in
death, then returns to his bed. The SPIRITS exit, singing:*

Put out the light, then put out the light. [56]

Full fathom five thy father lies;
Those are pearls that were his eyes;
Hourly ring his knell. Ding dong.
Hark, now I hear them. Ding dong, bell. [57]
Escucha ahora la campana,
Escucha ahora la campana,
Put out the light, then put out the light. [58]

El mundo es un gran teatro, teatro,
Y los hombres y mujeres son actores.

# Scene 3

*RIFKE wakes up alone, recalling her dream.*

**RIFKE**
When my cue comes, call me, and I will answer. My next is "Coyote, ocelote,
aguacate, nopal . . . " He tenido una vision tan rara. Tuve un sueño — past the
wit of man to say what dream it was. [59]

. . . Maestro?

*She discovers his death.*

---

56  *Othello*, 5.2.7
57  *The Tempest*, 1.2.395–97; 401–4
58  *Othello*, 5.2.7
59  *A Midsummer Night's Dream*, 4.1.202–3

When thou reviewest this, thou dost review
The very part was consecrate to thee:
La tierra sólo tierra posee, pues esto merece,
Mas mi espíritu es tuyo, lo mejor de mí.
So then thou hast but lost the dregs of life,
The prey of worms, my body being dead;
El valor es, por tanto, lo que contiene,
And that is this, and this with thee remains.[60]

> *At a loss, she begins to clean up the room. She moves the bed, the*
> *window seat, and the bench and inadvertently creates an altar with*
> *the items left behind by the SPIRITS during the play. The SPIRITS*
> *return to her and sing "A Time for Us"[61] as she builds the altar.*

**TITANIA**
Nuestra hora si llegará cadenas rotas por valor d'un libre amor.

**HAMLET**
A time when dreams

**OPHELIA**
Negados sueños brillarán

**HAMLET**
so long denied can flourish

**OPHELIA**
Mostrando

**HAMLET & OPHELIA**
amor del interior con su fervor.

> *GROUP A and GROUP B begin singing in a round.*

**GROUP A**
Al fin / la'hora / cuando / vemos / la libertad para todos

**GROUP B**
A time / for us / at last / to see / a life / worthwhile / for you / and me.

---

60  Sonnet 74
61  "Love Theme from *Romeo and Juliet*," written by Nino Rota for the 1968 film directed by Franco
    Zefferelli; English lyrics by Larry Kusik and Eddie Snyder.

**RICHARD III**

> Y el amor

**LADY M**

> And with our love / through tears and thorns

**RICHARD III**

> que sanará

**LADY M**

> we will endure

**TITANIA**

> con fuerza'y paz

**OPHELIA**

> la heridas

**RICHARD III**

> toutes les tempêtes

**HAMLET**

> через каждый шторм

*Pause.*

*As Group A and B sing in a round, RIFKE sees the spirit of SHAKE-SPEARE and then the spirit of HAMNET approaching her. It is the first time she has seen HAMNET since his death.*

**GROUP A**

> A time for us

**GROUP B**

> Nuestra hora si llegará

**GROUP A**

> someday there'll be a new world, a

**GROUP B**

> nuevo mundo

**GROUP A**

> world of shining hope for you and me.

**GROUP B**

>    uno de promesa y amor.

>    *A Día de los Muertos reunion, when the veil between the living and*
>    *the dead is the thinnest, when love conquers death. SHAKESPEARE*
>    *gives RIFKE the pen and ink to finish the play. TITANIA delivers an*
>    *epilogue.*

**TITANIA**

>    Si esta ilusión ha ofendido,
>    Pensad, para corregirlo,
>    Que dormíais mientras salían
>    Todas estas fantasías.
>    If we shadows have offended,
>    Think but this, and all is mended,
>    That you have but slumbered here
>    While these visions did appear.
>    And this weak and idle theme,
>    No more yielding but a dream.[62]

**SHAKESPEARE**

>    El mundo es un gran teatro,
>    Y los hombres y mujeres son actores.

>    *SHAKESPEARE blows out the candle.*

**END OF PLAY**

---

62  *A Midsummer Night's Dream*, 5.1.409–14

# Curtain Call

*All sing and dance to "Aires Vascos."*

> Viva la gente del pueblo (¡Que viva!)
> Viva la gente torera (¡Olé!)
> Viva todo aquel que diga (¡La uva!)
> Sal el sol por donde puede
>
> Beber, beber
> Beber es un gran placer
> El agua es para lavarse
> Y para las ranas que nadan bien
>
> Cada vez que te emborrachas, Manuel
> Tu vienes en busca mía, Manuel
> Ojalá te emborracharas, Manuel
> Todas las horas del día, Manuel
> Ay Manuelito, Manuel, Manuelito, Manuel
>
> Y a mi me gusta el pimpiririm pim pim
> De la botella el pan pararan pan pan
> Con el pimpiririm pim pim
> Con el pan pararan pan pan
> El que no beba vina
> Sera un animal, sera un animal
>
> Cuando yo me muera
> Tengo ya dispuesto
> En mi testamento
> Que me han de enterrar
> Que me han de enterrar
> Con una botella bien llena de vino
> Y un racimo de uvas en el paladar
> En el paladar
>
> Beber, beber
> Beber es un gran placer
> El agua es para lavarse
> Y para las ranas que nadan bien
> ¡Salud!

# Glossary

*This glossary is not intended to be comprehensive or to serve in place of a dictionary but rather as a list of keywords, key terms, and lesser-known words and phrases, some of which are specific to the Borderlands, that will aid readers of the plays in this anthology.*

| | |
|---|---|
| agüitado | sad, depressed, bummed out |
| alférez | ensign; military officer rank below lieutenant |
| altar | table used for religious rituals. During Día de los Muertos, homemade altars are decorated with pictures, mementos, and offerings to ancestors and loved ones who have passed. |
| asina | like this, like that |
| ay te watcho | I'll see you; see you around |
| baboso | idiot, fool |
| barrio | often used in the U.S. to refer to a predominantly Spanish-speaking, working-class neighborhood |
| El Borracho | an inebriated man, a figure pictured on traditional Loteria cards |
| botica | store, pharmacy, sometimes where natural medicines are dispensed. |
| cabezón | stubborn |
| cabrón | bastard, asshole |
| calavera | Día de los Muertos skull; sometimes refers to a skeleton, also called a calaca |
| carnal | friend, brother |
| cempasúchitl | marigolds, traditionally placed on Día de los Muertos altars to attract the spirits of the dead. |

| | |
|---|---|
| charro | Mexican cowboy |
| chale | used to show disagreement, hell no |
| chamaco | kid |
| chingado | fuck, fucker, fucking, fucked, depending on context |
| chisme(s) | gossip |
| chorro de luces | beam of lights, a lot of lights |
| cholo/a | originally a derogatory term referring to someone of mixed-race or low-class background, the term was reclaimed by Chicano youth in the 1960s. The cholo/a style is derived from pachuco subculture of the 1930s and 40s. |
| chulo/a | cute, pretty |
| Citlali | a Nahua creator goddess, often depicted with a skirt of stars |
| Coatlicue | the Nahua mother goddess of creation and destruction, often depicted with a skirt of serpents |
| Chief Popay | Tewa Pueblo leader who led the Pueblo Revolt of 1680; also spelled Po'Pay |
| coconut | derogatory word for someone considered "Brown on the outside and white on the inside" |
| colibrí | hummingbird; *see* huitzilin |
| consejo | advice, guidance |
| corrido | Mexican ballad |
| coyote | trafficker who brings people across the border |
| Cualli Tlanecic | "Good morning" in Nahuatl |
| Cuauhtemoc | the last Mexica ruler of Tenochtitlan, who ruled from 1520–1521 |
| curandera/o | traditional Indigenous healer in the Americas |
| Día de los Chicos | In Día de los Muertos celebrations, the first day (November 1st) is reserved specifically for remembering children who have passed. |
| Día de los Difuntos | In Día de los Muertos celebrations, the second day (November 2nd) is dedicated to honoring those who have passed and praying for their souls. |

| | |
|---|---|
| Día de Todos los Santos | Catholic celebration known in English as All Saints' Day that coincides with annual Día de los Muertos rituals |
| dreamers | undocumented Americans brought to the U.S. as children, named for the DREAM Act which provides access to in-state college tuition and a pathway to citizenship. Several versions of the bill have been proposed since 2001 but none has become law. |
| favela | slum or shantytown in or around Brazilian cities |
| gente | people, sometimes used to refer to Mexicans, Mexican Americans, or Latinxs |
| gringo | usually refers to a white, Anglo person |
| hacienda | landed estate or plantation in the colonies or former colonies of the Spanish Empire |
| huitzilin | Nahuatl for hummingbird; sacred in Nahua mythology and associated with warriors, particularly Huitzilopochtli, the god of sun and war |
| Indio | Spanish for Indian |
| Iztaccíhuatl | one of a pair of volcanos in Mexico whose formation is explained by a legend about a Tlaxcala princess, Iztac-cíhuatl, who was betrothed to a Chichimeca warrior named Popocatépetl. They are often referred to as the Mexican Romeo and Juliet because their love story has a similarly tragic ending brought about by rivalry, miscom-munication, and grief. |
| kivas | rooms used in Pueblo culture for ceremonial rites, prac-tices, and gatherings |
| La Llorona | in Mexican mythology, a ghostly woman who wails as she mourns the children she drowned |
| Lucha Libre | Mexican wrestling |
| Maestre de Campo | high-ranking officer in the Spanish army |
| malcriado | bad-mannered, rude, spoiled |
| mancha | stain, blemish, spot |
| medicine man | traditional healer in some Indigenous communities in North America |
| Mictlán | the Nahua underworld |

| | |
|---|---|
| mano | shortened version of hermano (brother) |
| mija/o | contraction of mi + hija/o, used as a term of endearment or address |
| El Movimiento | used to refer to the Chicano Movement for civil and labor rights, beginning in the 1960s. |
| ofrenda | offering placed on the altar to the dead during Día de los Muertos |
| órale | an affirmation in Mexican Spanish slang |
| pan de muerto | pastry served as part of Día de los Muertos ceremonies |
| papeles | papers, often used to refer to immigration documentation |
| pelado | person of low social class; literally meaning "bald," the term is derived from the practices of shaving the heads of incarcerated people |
| pelón | bald, poor, and/or stupid; similar to "pelado" |
| peleonero | someone who is aggressive or hotheaded |
| pendejo | idiot, stupid |
| peregrino | pilgrim |
| pietà | a work of art that depicts the Virgin Mary holding the dead body of Christ |
| pinche | fucking |
| pingo | rascal |
| plaza | an open public space in a city or town, often a square with a cathedral and administrative buildings |
| pocho/a | derogatory term used to describe someone of Mexican heritage who has assimilated or become Americanized; sometimes reclaimed as a term of pride |
| PrEP | HIV prevention medication |
| primo/a | cousin, often used colloquially to refer to family members or close friends |
| que chivo | how cool |
| que espanto | how scary |
| querida | dear, beloved |
| rebozo | shawl |

| | |
|---|---|
| repartimiento | Spanish colonial labor system imposed on Indigenous Peoples |
| ruca | girl or hot girl |
| sangrón | disagreeable, annoying |
| simón | yes, hell yeah; used to respond affirmatively |
| sinvergüenza | shameless; someone without shame |
| sugar skulls | decorative skulls made out of sugar to represent a departed soul and placed on altars during Día de los Muertos |
| Tejano | a Mexican American inhabitant of Texas |
| teniente | a rank in the Kingdom of Spain's military equivalent to a lieutenant |
| Tenochtitlán | the center of the Mexica, or Aztec, Empire; now the center of Mexico City |
| Tezcatlipoca | a central deity for the Nahua whose name means Smoking Mirror and whose animal disguise was a jaguar |
| thirteen heavens | the afterlife, believed by many Mesoamerican peoples to be divided into thirteen levels |
| TJ | nickname for Tijuana |
| Tonatiuh | Nahua sun deity who was responsible for fertility but also demanded sacrifice |
| travieso | mischievous, naughty |
| vato | Mexican/Chicano slang for "dude" or "man," sometimes used to mean "cholo" |
| vendido | sellout |
| veneno | poison |
| La Virgen de Guadalupe | the patron saint of Mexico who represents the nation's hybrid Catholic and Indigenous spiritual heritage |
| wetback | derogatory term for an undocumented person, reflecting the fact that many cross the Rio Grande in the process of migrating |
| xiuhuitzolli | a turquoise diadem or crown that was worn by several Nahua deities as a symbol of power |
| Xochiquetzal | a Nahua goddess of beauty, love, and household arts; often associated with flowers |
| yoloxochitl | magnolia (Nahuatl) |

# Bibliography

## Bibliography of Works Cited

Anzaldúa, Gloria E. *Borderlands/La Frontera: The New Mestiza*. 5th ed. San Francisco: Aunt Lute Press, 2022.

———. "Preface: (Un)natural Bridges, (Un)safe Spaces." In *This Bridge We Call Home: Radical Visions for Transformation*, edited by Gloria E. Anzaldúa and AnaLouise Keating, 1–5. New York: Routledge, 2002.

Biggers, Jeff. "Who's afraid of 'The Tempest'?" *Salon*, January 13, 2012. https://www.salon.com/2012/01/13/whos_afraid_of_the_tempest/.

Boffone, Trevor. "Queering Machismo from Michoacán to Montrose: *Purple Eyes* by Josh Inocéncio." *HowlRound*, July 14, 2016. https://howlround.com/queering-machismo-michoacan-montrose.

Boffone, Trevor, and Carla Della Gatta, eds. *Shakespeare and Latinidad*. Edinburgh: Edinburgh University Press, 2021.

Césaire, Aimé. *A Tempest*. Translated by Philip Crispin. London: Oberon Books, 2015.

———. *Une Tempête*. Paris: Éditions du Seuil, 1969.

Chapman, Matthieu. "Chicano Signifyin': Appropriating Space and Culture in *El Henry*." *Theatre Topics* 27, no. 1 (2017): 61–69. https://doi.org/10.1353/tt.2017.0003.

Darby, Jaye T., Courtney Elkin Mohler, and Christy Stanlake, eds. *Critical Companion to Native American and First Nations Theatre and Performance: Indigenous Spaces*. London: Bloomsbury, 2020.

Delgadillo, Theresa. *Spiritual Mestizaje: Religion, Gender, Race, and Nation in Contemporary Chicana Narrative*. Durham, NC: Duke University Press, 2011.

Della Gatta, Carla. "From *West Side Story* to *Hamlet, Prince of Cuba*: Shakespeare and Latinidad in the United States." *Shakespeare Studies* 44 (2016): 151–56.

de Onís, Catalina (Kathleen) M. "What's in an 'x'?: An Exchange about the Politics of 'Latinx.'" *Chiricú Journal: Latina/o Literatures, Arts, and Cultures* 1, no. 2 (2017): 78–91.

Desmet, Christy, and Sujata Iyengar. "Adaptation, Appropriation, or What You Will." *Shakespeare* 11, no. 1 (2015): 10–19. https://doi.org/10.1080/17450918.2015.1012550.

Espinosa, Ruben. "Beyond *The Tempest*: Language, Legitimacy, and *La Frontera*." In *The Shakespeare User: Critical and Creative Appropriations in a Networked Culture*, edited by Valerie M. Fazel and Louise Geddes, 41–61. New York: Palgrave, 2017. https://doi.org/10.1007/978-3-319-61015-3_3.

———. "'Don't it Make My Brown Eyes Blue': Uneasy Assimilation and the Shakespeare-Latinx Divide." In *The Routledge Handbook of Shakespeare and Global Appropriation*, edited by Christy Desmet, Sujata Iyengar, and Miriam Jacobson, 48–58. New York: Routledge, 2019. https://doi.org/10.4324/97813 15168968.

———. "Stranger Shakespeare." *Shakespeare Quarterly* 67, no. 1 (2016): 51–67. https://doi.org/10.1353/shq.2016.0012.

———. "Traversing the Temporal Borderlands of Shakespeare." *New Literary History* 52, nos. 3/4 (2021): 605–23. https://doi.org/10.1353/nlh.2021.0028.

Favate, Sam. "Shakespeare's 'The Tempest' Barred from Arizona Public Schools." *The Wall Street Journal*, January 17, 2012. https://www.wsj.com/articles/BL-LB-41723.

Fernández Retamar, Roberto. *Calibán. Apuntes sobre la cultura en nuestra América*. México: Diogenes, 1971.

———. "Caliban: Notes Toward a Discussion of Culture in Our America." Translated by Lynn Garafola, David Arthur McMurray, and Roberto Márquez. *The Massachusetts Review* 15, nos. 1/2 (1974): 7–72.

Fielder, Brigitte. "Blackface Desdemona: Theorizing Race on the Nineteenth-Century American Stage." *Theatre Annual* 70 (2017): 39–59. http://dx.doi.org/10.17613/M6K284.

González, José Cruz, and David Lozano. "Diálogo: On Making Shakespeare Relevant to Latinx Communities." In *Shakespeare and Latinidad*, edited by Trevor Boffone and Carla Della Gatta, 154–59. Edinburgh: Edinburgh University Press, 2021. https://doi.org/10.3366/edinburgh/9781474488488.003.0014.

Greenberg, Marissa. "Critically Regional Shakespeare." *Shakespeare Bulletin* 37, no. 3 (2019): 341–63. https://doi.org/10.1353/shb.2019.0039.

Grier, Miles P. "Staging the Cherokee *Othello*: An Imperial Economy of Indian Watching." *The William and Mary Quarterly* 73, no. 1 (2016): 73–106.

Gumbs, Alexis Pauline. "Daily Bread: Nourishing Sustainable Practices for Community Accountable Scholars." *Brilliance Remastered*, July 31, 2012. https://brokenbeautiful.wordpress.com/2012/07/.

Gutiérrez-Jones, Carl. "Humor, Literacy and Trauma in Chicano Culture." *Comparative Literature Studies* 40, no. 2 (2003): 112–26. https://doi.org/10.1353/cls.2003.0014.

Herrera-Sobek, María. "Gloria Anzaldúa, Place, Race, Language, and Sexuality in the Magic Valley." *PMLA* 121, no. 1 (2006): 266–71. https://doi.org/10.1632/003081206X129800.

———. "The Border Patrol and Their Migra Corridos: Propaganda, Genre Adaptation, and Mexican Immigration." *American Studies Journal* 57 (2012). https://doi.org/10.18422/57-06.

Huerta, Jorge A. *Chicano Drama: Performance, Society and Myth*. Cambridge, UK: Cambridge University Press, 2000.

———. "Feathers, Flutes, and Drums: Images of the Indigenous Americans in Chicano Drama." In *Native American Performance and Representation*, edited by S. E. Wilmer, 182–92. Tucson: University of Arizona Press, 2009.

Inocéncio, Josh. "Mixing the Culture Pot: Growing Up Gay and Austro-Mexican in Houston." *OutSmart Magazine*, September 1, 2016. https://www.outsmartmagazine.com/2016/09/mixing-the-culture-pot-growing-up-gay-and-austro-mexican-in-houston/.

Klein, Elizabeth, and Michael Shapiro. "Shylock as Crypto-Jew: A New Mexican Adaptation of *The Merchant of Venice*." In *World-Wide Shakespeares: Local Appropriations in Film and Performance*, edited by Sonia Massai, 31–39. New York: Routledge, 2005. https://doi.org/10.4324/9780203356944.

Kliman, Bernice W., and Rick J. Santos. "*Mestizo* Shakespeares: A Study of Cultural Exchange." In *Latin American Shakespeares*, edited by Bernice W. Kliman and Rick J. Santos, 11–20. Madison, NJ: Fairleigh Dickinson University Press, 2005.

Little, Arthur L., Jr. "Re-Historicizing Race, White Melancholia, and the Shakespearean Property." *Shakespeare Quarterly* 67, no. 1 (2016): 84–103. https://doi.org/10.1353/shq.2016.0018.

Mason, Susan. "Romeo and Juliet in East L.A." *Theater* 23, no. 2 (1992): 88–92. https://doi.org/10.1215/01610775-23-2-88.

Merla-Watson, Cathryn Josefina. "(Trans)Mission Possible: The Coloniality of Gender, Speculative Rasquachismo and Altermundos in Luis Valderas's Chican@futurist Visual Art." In *Altermundos: Latin@ Speculative Literature, Film, and Popular Culture*, edited by Cathryn Josefina Merla-Watson and B. V. Olguín, 352–70. Los Angeles: UCLA Chicano Studies Research Center, 2017.

Merla-Watson, Cathryn Josefina, and B. V. Olguín, "Altermundos: Reassessing the Past, Present, and Future of the Chican@ and Latin@ Speculative Arts." In *Altermundos: Latin@ Speculative Literature, Film, and Popular Culture*, edited by Cathryn Josefina Merla-Watson and B. V. Olguín, 1–36. Los Angeles: UCLA Chicano Studies Research Center, 2017.

Mignolo, Walter. *The Darker Side of the Renaissance: Literacy, Territoriality, and Colonization*. 2nd ed. Ann Arbor: University of Michigan Press, 2003.

Modenessi, Alfredo Michel. "'A double tongue within your mask': Translating Shakespeare in/to Spanish-Speaking Latin America." In *Shakespeare and the Language of Translation*, edited by Ton Hoenselaars, 240–54. London: Arden Shakespeare, 2004. http://dx.doi.org/10.5040/9781408179734.ch-013.

———. "'Meaning by Shakespeare' South of the Border." In *World-Wide Shakespeares: Local Appropriations in Film and Performance*, edited by Sonia Massai, 104–11. New York: Routledge, 2007.

Montaño, Mary Caroline. *Tradiciones Nuevomexicanas: Hispano Arts and Culture of New Mexico*. Albuquerque: University of New Mexico Press, 2001.

Paredes, Américo. *"With His Pistol in His Hand": A Border Ballad and Its Hero*. Austin: University of Texas Press, 1958.

Pérez, Emma. *The Decolonial Imaginary: Writing Chicanas into History*. Bloomington: Indiana University Press, 1999.

Peterson, Kaara L., and Deanne Williams, eds. *The Afterlife of Ophelia*. New York: Palgrave MacMillan, 2012.

Phippen, J. Weston, and National Journal. "How One Law Banning Ethnic Studies Led to Its Rise." *The Atlantic*. July 19, 2015. https://www.theatlantic.com/education/archive/2015/07/how-one-law-banning-ethnic-studies-led-to-rise/398885/.

Pinsky, Mark. "Una Noche to Remember: Hispanic Playwrights Project Takes Center Stage at SCR Beginning Tonight." *The Los Angeles Times*, August 8, 1991. https://www.latimes.com/archives/la-xpm-1991-08-08-ol-268-story.html.

Román, David. "Latino Performance and Identity." *Aztlán: A Journal of Chicano Studies* 22, no. 2 (1997): 151–67.

Rosa, Jonathan. *Looking Like a Language, Sounding Like a Race: Raciolinguistic Ideologies and the Learning of Latinidad.* Oxford: Oxford University Press, 2019.

Sanchez Saltveit, Olga. "¡O Romeo! Shakespeare on the Altar of Día de los Muertos." In *Shakespeare and Latinidad*, edited by Trevor Boffone and Carla Della Gatta, 38–44. Edinburgh: Edinburgh University Press, 2021. https://doi.org/10.1515/9781474488501-005.

Sanders, Julie. *Adaptation and Appropriation.* 2nd ed. New York: Routledge, 2016.

Sandoval, Chela, Arturo J. Aldama, and Peter J. García. "Toward a De-Colonial Performatics of the US Latina and Latino Borderlands." In *Performing the US Latina and Latino Borderlands*, edited by Arturo J. Aldama, Chela Sandoval, and Peter J. García, 1–30. Bloomington: Indiana University Press, 2012.

Santos, Adrianna M. "Surviving the Alamo, Violence Vengeance, and Women's Solidarity in Emma Pérez's *Forgetting the Alamo, Or, Blood Memory.*" *The Journal of Latina Critical Feminism* 2, no. 1 (2019): 37–49.

Sayet, Madeline. "Interrogating the Shakespeare System." *HowlRound*, August 31, 2020. https://howlround.com/interrogating-shakespeare-system.

Scott, Jean Bruce, and Randy Reinholz. "Native Voices at the Autry." In *Casting a Movement: The Welcome Table Initiative*, edited by Claire Syler and Daniel Banks, 147–58. New York: Routledge, 2019.

Shakespeare, William. *The Norton Shakespeare.* 3rd ed. Edited by Stephen Greenblatt, Walter Cohen, Suzanne Gossett, Jean E. Howard, Katharine Eisaman Maus, and Gordon McMullan. New York: Norton, 2015.

Shapiro, James. *Shakespeare in a Divided America: What His Plays Tell Us About Our Past and Future.* New York: Penguin Press, 2020.

———, ed. *Shakespeare in America: An Anthology from the Revolution to Now.* New York: The Library of America, 2014.

Stevens, Scott Manning. "Shakespeare and the Indigenous Turn." In *Histories of the Future: On Shakespeare and Thinking Ahead*, edited by Carla Mazzio. Philadelphia: University of Pennsylvania Press, forthcoming.

Szymkowicz, Adam. "I Interview Playwrights Part 931: Joshua Inocéncio," April 30, 2017. http://aszym.blogspot.com/2017/04/i-interview-playwrights-part-931-joshua.html.

Thompson, Ayanna. *Passing Strange: Shakespeare, Race, and Contemporary America.* Oxford: Oxford University Press, 2011.

*The T.R.U.T.H Project.* Telling Real Unapologetic Through Healing (T.R.U.T.H.), Inc. Project. Accessed June 16, 2022. https://truthprojecthtx.org/.

Villarreal, Edit. "Catching the Next Play: The Joys and Perils of Playwriting."
   In *Puro Teatro: A Latina Anthology*, edited by Alberto Sandoval-Sánchez
   and Nancy Saporta Sternbach, 330–33. Tucson: University of Arizona Press,
   2000.

Watts, James D., Jr. "Arts Scene: First Friday Hosts Art Market After Dark;
   Beethoven Gets Exposed." *Tulsa World*, October 28, 2018. https://tulsaworld.
   com/entertainment/arts-scene-first-friday-hosts-art-market-after-dark-
   beethoven-gets-exposed/article_aadd8f42-5488-541c-9244-ff07f1b99440.
   html.

Weaver, Jace. "Shakespeare Among the 'Salvages': The Bard in Red Atlantic Performance." *Theater Journal* 67, no. 3 (2015): 433–43. https://doi.org/10.1353/
   tj.2015.0109.

Yarbro-Bejarano, Yvonne. "The Female Subject in Chicano Theatre: Sexuality,
   'Race,' and Class." *Theatre Journal* 38, no. 4 (1986): 389–407. https://doi.org/
   10.2307/3208283.

Ybarra, Patricia A. *Latinx Theater in the Times of Neoliberalism.* Evanston, IL:
   Northwestern University Press, 2017.

Ybarra-Frausto, Tomás. "Rasquachismo: A Chicano Sensibility." In *Chicano Art:
   Resistance and Affirmation, 1965–1985,* edited by Richard Griswold del Cas-
   tillo, Teresa McKenna, and Yvonne Yarbro-Bejarano, 155–62. Los Angeles:
   Wright Art Gallery, University of California, 1991.

Yim, Laura Lehua. "Reading Hawaiian Shakespeare: Indigenous Residue Haunting Settler Colonialism." *Journal of American Studies* 54, no. 1 (2020): 36–43.
   https://doi.org/10.1017/S0021875819001993.

Younging, Gregory. *Elements of Indigenous Style: A Guide for Writing by and
   about Indigenous Peoples.* Edmonton: Brush Education, 2018.

## A Bibliography of Borderlands Shakespeare

Boffone, Trevor. "Queering Machismo from Michoacán to Montrose: *Purple
   Eyes* by Josh Inocéncio." *HowlRound*, July 14, 2016. https://howlround.com/
   queering-machismo-michoacan-montrose.

Boffone, Trevor, and Carla Della Gatta, eds. *Shakespeare and Latinidad.* Edinburgh: Edinburgh University Press, 2021.

Chapman, Matthieu. "Chicano Signifyin': Appropriating Space and Culture in
   *El Henry.*" *Theatre Topics* 27, no. 1 (2017): 61–69. https://doi.org/10.1353/
   tt.2017.0003.

Della Gatta, Carla. "From *West Side Story* to *Hamlet, Prince of Cuba*: Shakespeare and Latinidad in the United States." *Shakespeare Studies* 44 (2016): 151–56.

———. "Shakespeare and American Bilingualism: Borderlands Productions of *Romeo and Julieta*." In *Renaissance Shakespeare: Shakespeare Renaissances; Proceedings of the Ninth World Shakespeare Congress*, edited by Martin Pro-cházka, Michael Dobson, Andreas Höfele, and Hanna Scolnicov, 286–95. Newark: University of Delaware Press, 2014.

Espinosa, Ruben. "A Darker Shade of Shakespeare." *Shakespeare's Globe* (blog). August 23, 2020. https://www.shakespearesglobe.com/discover/blogs-and-features/2020/08/23/a-darker-shade-of-shakespeare/.

———. "Beyond *The Tempest*: Language, Legitimacy, and *La Frontera*." In *The Shakespeare User: Critical and Creative Appropriations in a Networked Culture*, edited by Valerie M. Fazel and Louise Geddes, 41–61. New York: Palgrave, 2017. https://doi.org/10.1007/978-3-319-61015-3_3.

———. "Chicano Shakespeare: The Bard, the Border, and the Peripheries of Performance." In *Teaching Social Justice Through Shakespeare: Why Renaissance Literature Matters Now*, edited by Hillary Eklund and Wendy Beth Hyman, 76–84. Edinburgh: Edinburgh University Press, 2019. https://www.jstor.org/stable/10.3366/j.ctvrs912p.11.

———. "'Don't it Make My Brown Eyes Blue': Uneasy Assimilation and the Shakespeare-Latinx Divide." In *The Routledge Handbook of Shakespeare and Global Appropriation*, edited by Christy Desmet, Sujata Iyengar, and Miriam Jacobson, 48–58. New York: Routledge, 2019. https://doi.org/10.4324/9781315168968.

———. "Postcolonial Studies." In *The Arden Handbook of Contemporary Shakespeare Criticism*, edited by Evelyn Gajowski, 159–72. London: Bloomsbury Arden, 2020.

———. "Shakespeare and Your Mountainish Inhumanity." *The Sundial*. August 16, 2019. https://medium.com/the-sundial-acmrs/shakespeare-and-your-mountainish-inhumanity-d255474027de.

———. "Stranger Shakespeare," *Shakespeare Quarterly* 67, no. 1 (2016): 51–67. https://doi.org/10.1353/shq.2016.0012.

———. "Traversing the Temporal Borderlands of Shakespeare." *New Literary History* 52, nos. 3/4 (2021): 605–23. https://doi.org/10.1353/nlh.2021.0028.

Gillen, Katherine. "Language, Race, and Shakespeare Appropriation on San Antonio's Southside: A Qualities of Mercy Dispatch." *The Sundial*, August 19, 2020. https://medium.com/the-sundial-acmrs/language-race-and-shake

speare-appropriation-on-san-antonios-southside-a-qualities-of-mercy-9ba
ed8e93599.

———. "Shakespearean Appropriation and Queer Latinx Empowerment in Josh
Inocéncio's *Ofélio*." In *The Routledge Handbook of Shakespeare and Global
Appropriation*, edited by Christy Desmet, Sujata Iyengar, and Miriam Jacob-
son, 90–101. London: Routledge, 2019.

Gillen, Katherine, and Adrianna M. Santos. "Borderlands Shakespeare: The
Decolonial Visions of James Lujan's *Kino and Teresa* and Seres Jaime Magaña's *The Tragic Corrido of Romeo and Lupe*." *Shakespeare Bulletin* 38, no. 4
(2020): 1–23. https://doi.org/10.1353/shb.2020.0066.

———. "The Power of Borderlands Shakespeare: Seres Jaime Magaña's *The Tragic
Corrido of Romeo and Lupe*." In *Shakespeare and Latinidad*, edited by Trevor
Boffone and Carla Della Gatta, 57–74. Edinburgh: Edinburgh University
Press, 2021. https://doi.org/10.3366/edinburgh/9781474488488.003.0005.

Greenberg, Marissa. "Critically Regional Shakespeare." *Shakespeare Bulletin* 37,
no. 3 (2019): 341–63. https://doi.org/10.1353/shb.2019.0039.

———. "Rethinking Local Shakespeare: The Case of *The Merchant of Santa Fe*."
*Journal of the Wooden O* 12, no. 1 (2012): 15–24.

———. "Shakespeare's Ghosts: Staging Colonial Histories in New Mexico."
In *Shakespeare and Latinidad*, edited by Trevor Boffone and Carla Della
Gatta, 97–111. Edinburgh: Edinburgh University Press, 2021. https://doi.
org/10.3366/edinburgh/9781474488488.003.0009.

Klein, Elizabeth, and Michael Shapiro. "Shylock as a Crypto-Jew: A New Mexican
Adaptation of *The Merchant of Venice*." In *World-Wide Shakespeares: Local
Appropriations in Film and Performance*, edited by Sonia Massai, 31–39. New
York: Routledge, 2005. https://doi.org/10.4324/9780203356944.

Sanchez Saltveit, Olga. "¡O Romeo! Shakespeare on the Altar of Día de los Muertos." In *Shakespeare and Latinidad*, edited by Trevor Boffone and Carla Della
Gatta, 38–44. Edinburgh: Edinburgh University Press, 2021. https://doi.
org/10.1515/9781474488501-005.

Santos, Kathryn Vomero. "Seeing Shakespeare: Narco Narratives and Neocolo-
nial Appropriations of *Macbeth* in the U.S.–Mexico Borderlands." *Literature
Compass* (2021). https://doi.org/10.1111/lic3.12636.

———. "¿Shakespeare para todos?" *Shakespeare Quarterly* 73, nos. 1–2 (2022):
49–75. https://doi.org/10.1093/sq/quac044.

Zingle, Laura. "*El Henry*: Herbert Siguenza's Epic Chicano Version of Shakespeare's *1 Henry IV*." *TheatreForum* 46 (2014): 56–61.